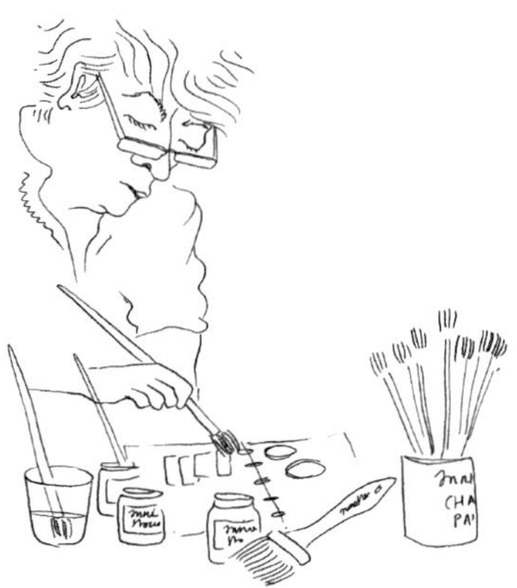

"It all boils down to sharing my passion for style and colour. I want to inspire everyone to get creative!"

Annie Sloan

Annie Sloan is all about inspiring people to get creative. From the best paints in the world to the highest quality waxes and brushes, our products are all designed by Annie to give you the tools to go and create!

THE COLOURIST Annie Sloan®

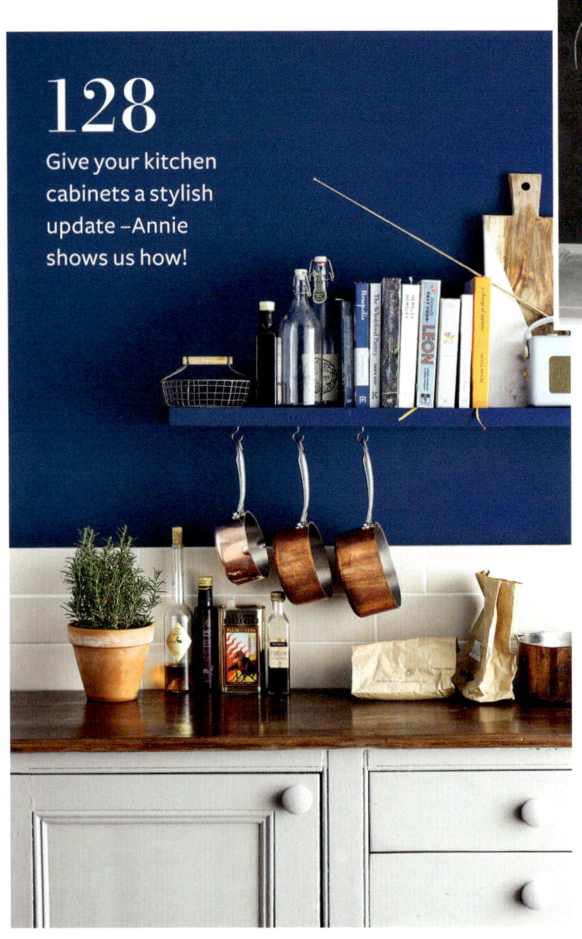

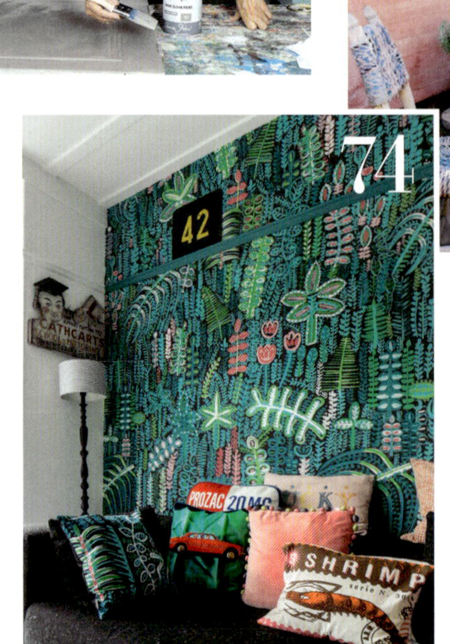

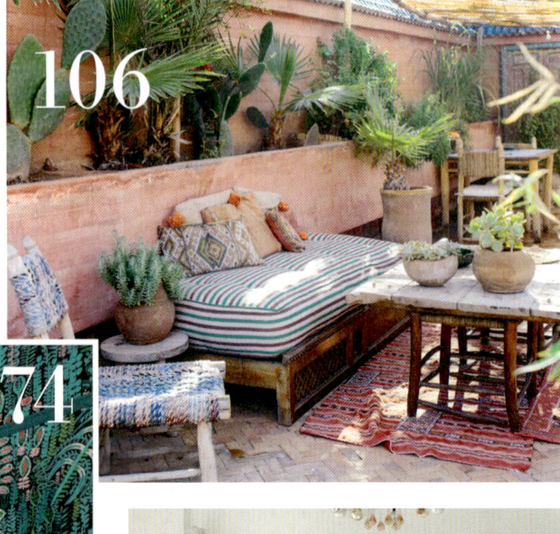

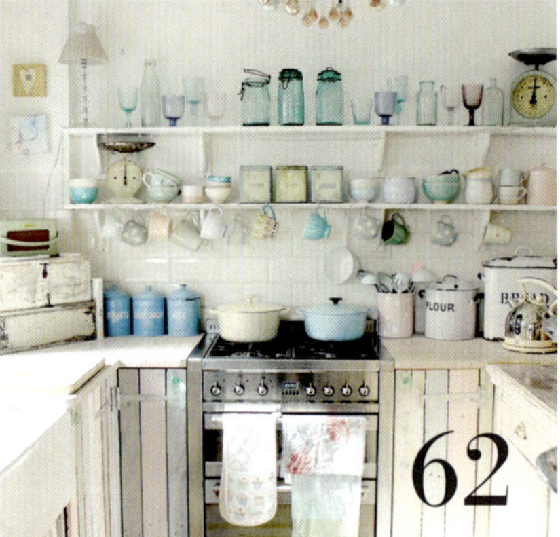

THE COLOUR HUNTER

INSPIRATION

THE HOMES COLLECTION

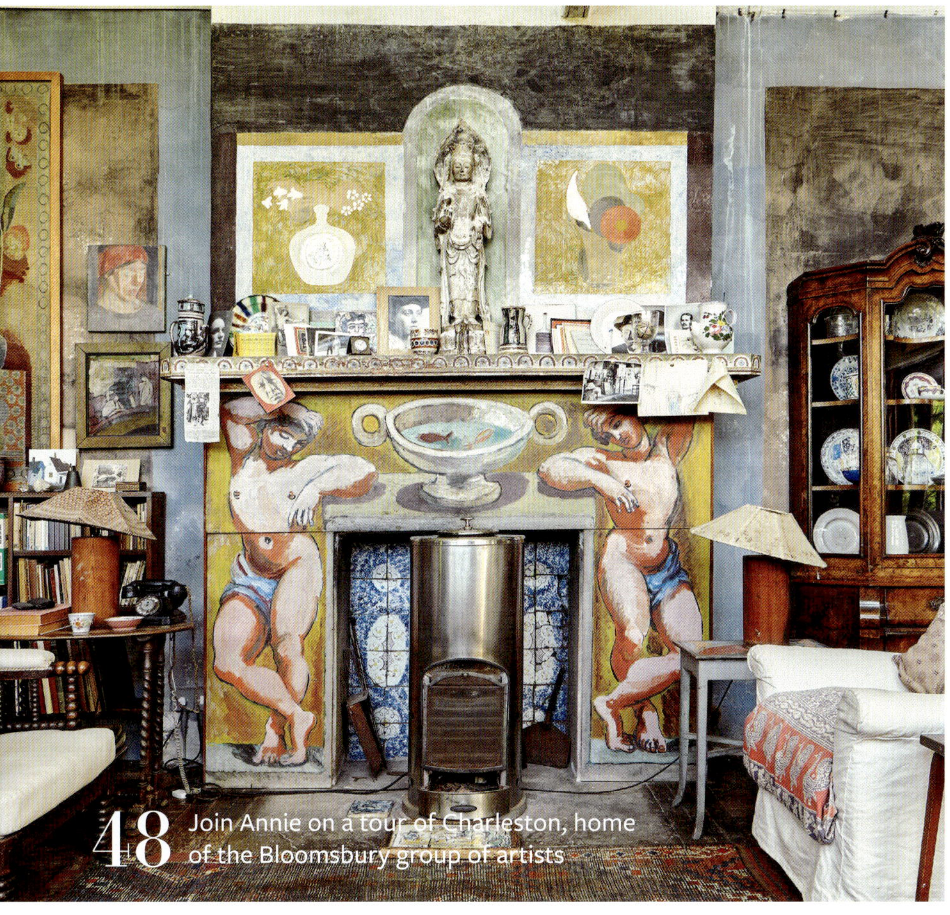

48 Join Annie on a tour of Charleston, home of the Bloomsbury group of artists

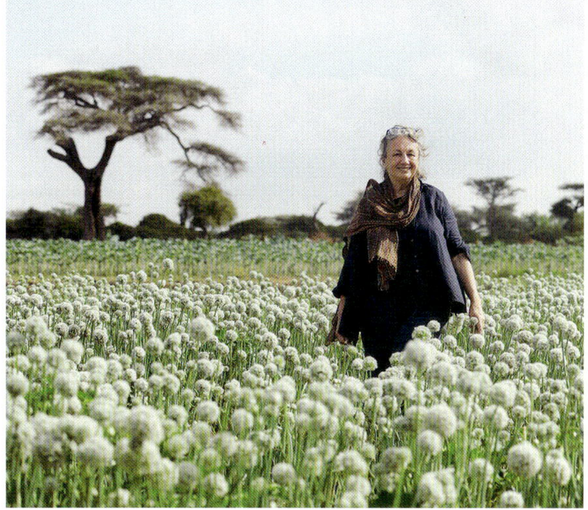

90 Read all about Annie's inspirational trip to the allium fields of Ethiopia with Oxfam

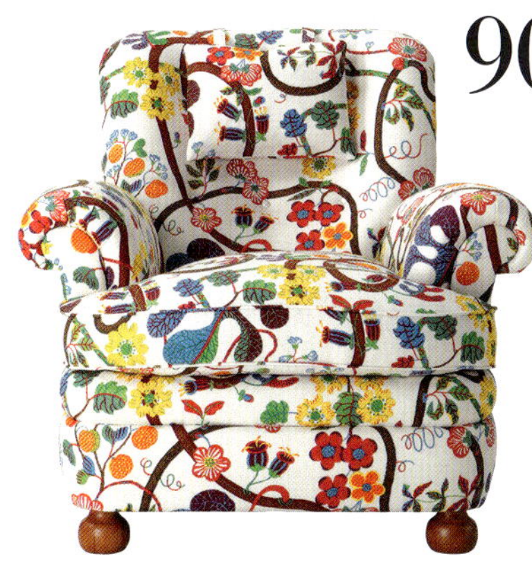

35 Josef Frank – the story behind the founder of Swedish Modern style

THE CURIOUS TRAVELLER

THE OUTDOOR LIFE

THE HOW-TOS

YOUR FREE STENCIL Exclusive tile stencil designed by Annie Sloan inserted into the pages of this bookazine. Please see your retailer if your stencil is missing

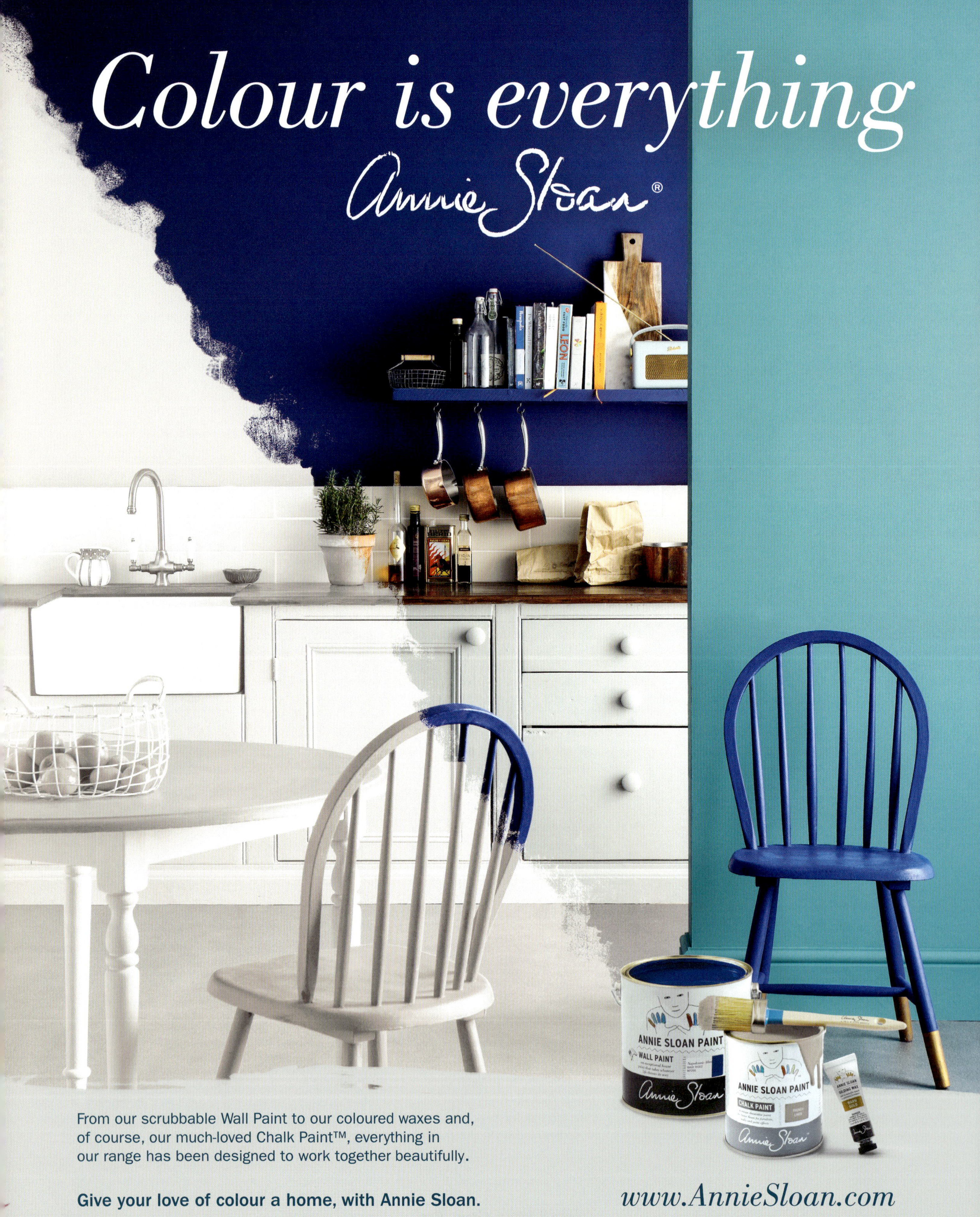

Colour is everything
Annie Sloan®
ANNIE SLOAN PAINT
WALL PAINT
Annie Sloan
ANNIE SLOAN PAINT
CHALK PAINT
Annie Sloan
From our scrubbable Wall Paint to our coloured waxes and, of course, our much-loved Chalk Paint™, everything in our range has been designed to work together beautifully.
Give your love of colour a home, with Annie Sloan.
www.AnnieSloan.com

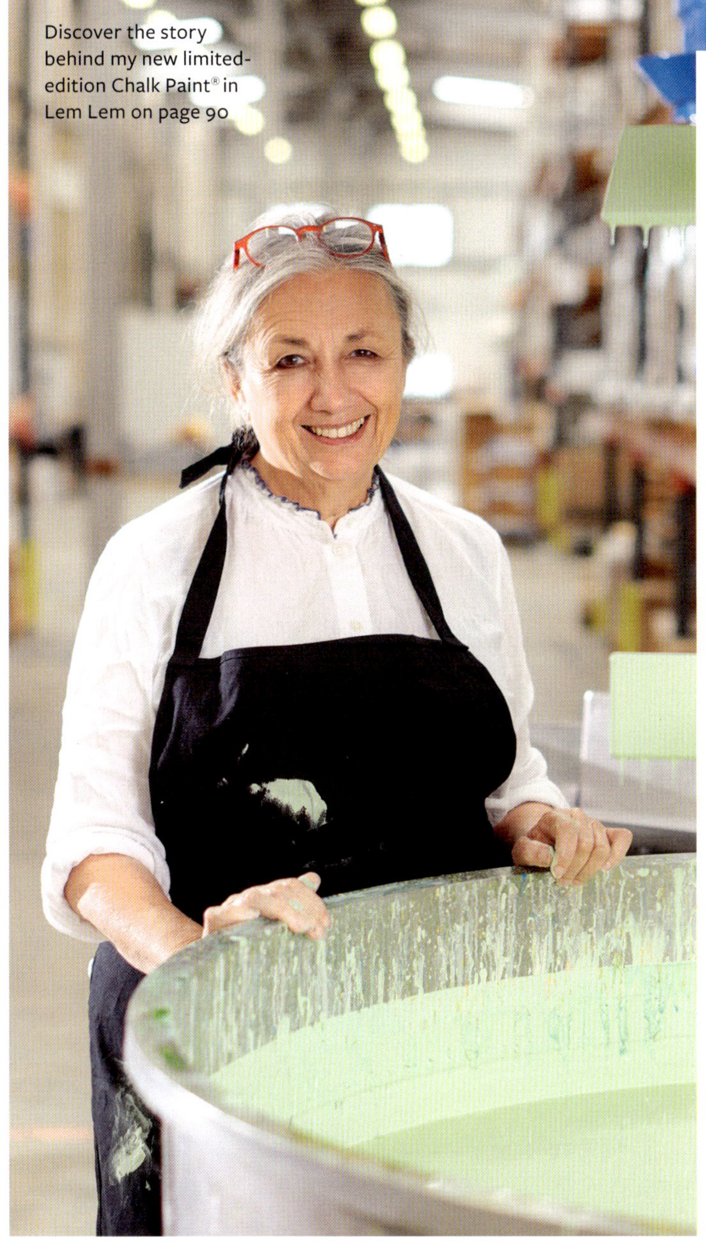

PHOTOGRAPH: TINA HILLIER

Celebrate the joy of colour with me!

Welcome to The Colourist! Bringing you buckets of colour-filled inspiration and stimulation for your home and painted furniture. In fact, for everything and everywhere in your life because colour is what ignites and unites pattern and shape.

I love all aspects of colour – everything from quiet and subtle whites and neutrals, to brilliant shout-outs of bold and bright. As an artist, I constantly want to challenge myself and what's expected of me.

I'm thrilled to announce a dream come true for me – a collaboration with Charleston, the home of the Bloomsbury group. It includes three new Chalk Paint® colours and the Annie Sloan with Charleston Decorative Paint Sets and Paint-Your-Own Keepsake Boxes.

Another highlight is stylist Tamsyn Morgans' home, where you'll see dreamy whites and soft-veiled pastels. And in complete contrast, designer Lucy Tiffney's knockout bold colours in her home, with explosive chock-a-block combinations in myriad hues.

Come with me to America, Canada, Portugal, Ethiopia, The Netherlands, South Africa, England, France and Sweden, where we'll meet artists and designers who use colour, pattern and paint in their own unique and special way. We'll see abstract colour-blocking, overlaid bohemian patterns, and classical, understated design.

Putting together these pages has been a treat. I hope you enjoy them as much as I do.

Annie

PS Need a room revamp? Turn to page 21 – we're giving away a host of Annie Sloan® products!

For each issue of The Colourist I choose a colour palette from the Chalk Paint® range to set the mood. This issue I've chosen one of my favourite colour combinations. 1 **Antibes Green** 2 **Scandinavian Pink** and 3 **Antoinette**

THIS SEASON I WILL BE **LISTENING TO (MUSIC)** Iggy Pop's radio show, Iggy Confidential. He plays loads of interesting music from Brian Eno to Miles Davis. **LISTENING TO (WORDS)** podcasts – I relax to these when I paint, fly, go walking or unwind in hotels. Favourites are the Radiolab, Malcolm Gladwell's Revisionist History, Freakonomics and This American Life. **TRAVELLING TO** Helsinki, Finland for the first time to see my distributor and stockists in September; to Australia in November for the Painters and Makers Market in Melbourne; and São Paulo, Brazil where my eldest son Henry now lives, for a family Christmas! **WEARING** Humphries and Begg, a fabulous clothing brand based in England that use bold prints made in India. **LOOKING AT** art from the 1930s.

CONTRIBUTORS

Meet some of the creative people who helped bring you this issue

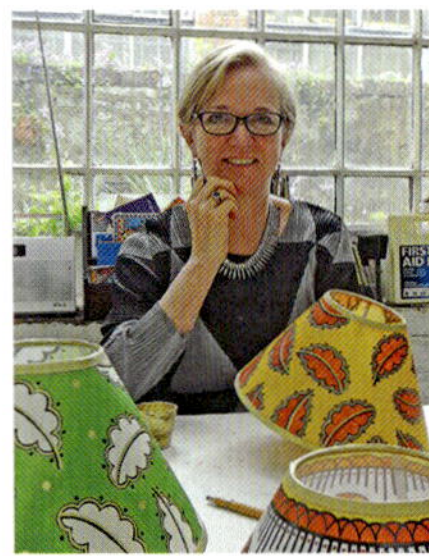

Cressida Bell

Cressida is an English artist and designer, specialising in textiles, interior design, cake decoration and illustration. Although influenced by her Bloomsbury forebears, she has forged her own uncompromisingly decorative style over the past 25 years.

www.cressidabell.co.uk

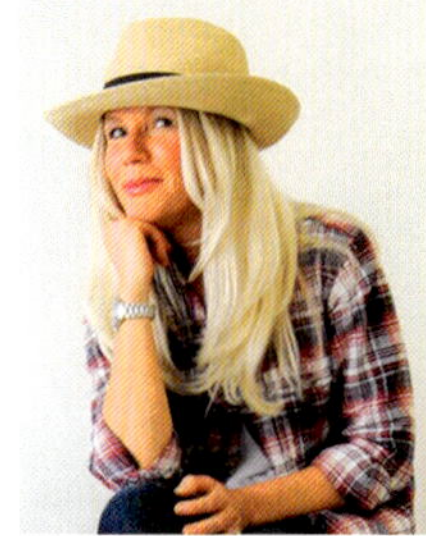

Ildiko Horvath

Based in Ontario, Canada, Ildiko has been creating some wonderful work over the past couple of years with Chalk Paint® by Annie Sloan and products. She's a master of the ombré technique, where you gradually blend colours from one to the other.

www.restored4u.com

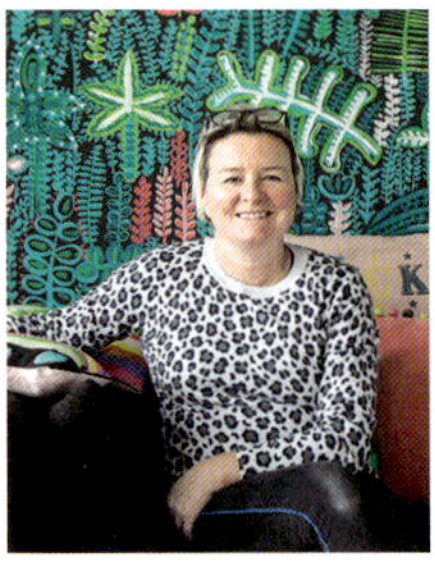

Lucy Tiffney

Lucy Tiffney's award-winning design studio was established in 2016, and her original, large scale, bold murals and beautiful wallpapers showcase her signature painterly style and unique interpretation of the natural world.

www.lucytiffneyshop.com

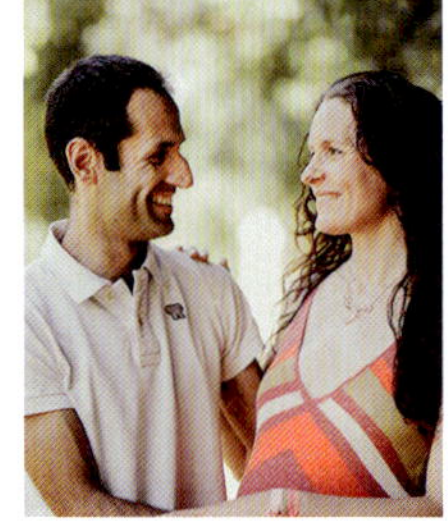

Ruth and Sérgio Faria Costa

Ruth and Sérgio opened their shop Atelier Autêntico in São Bento, Lisbon, after moving to Portugal in 2013. The Annie Sloan Stockists sell retro and industrial home décor, restore vintage furniture, and run Chalk Paint® workshops.

www.atelierautentico.pt

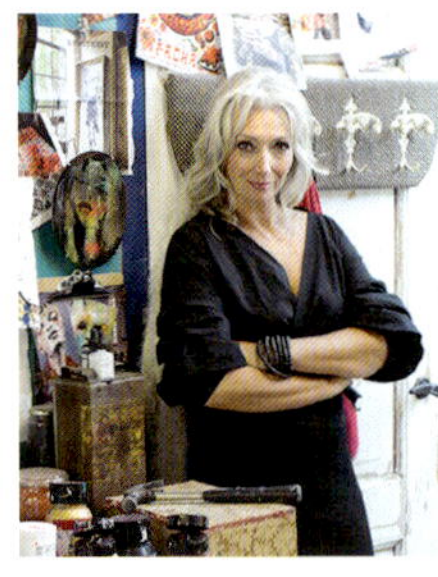

Yvon van Bergen

As well as being an Annie Sloan Stockist in Gennep, Holland, Yvon Van Bergen also creates beautiful large-scale portraits. Her studio is just as romantic and intoxicating as you'd expect from her work – a seductive space full of paint supplies and promise!

www.yvonvanbergen.nl

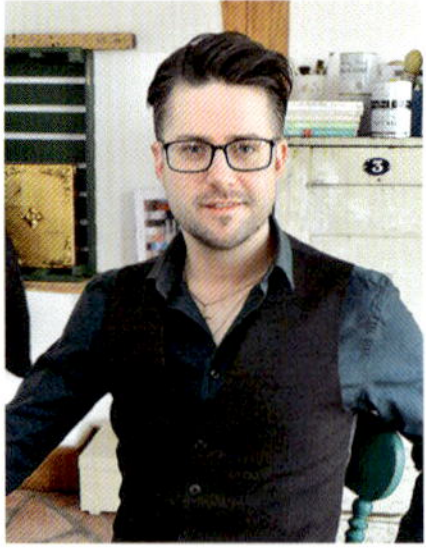

Jonathon Marc Mendes

Based in Lincolnshire, UK, Jonathon was made Annie's Painter in Residence in 2017. He's a talented painter, whose work spans many different styles. Projects bring together gorgeous colour combinations, intricate techniques and bold typography.

www.jonathonmarcmendes.com

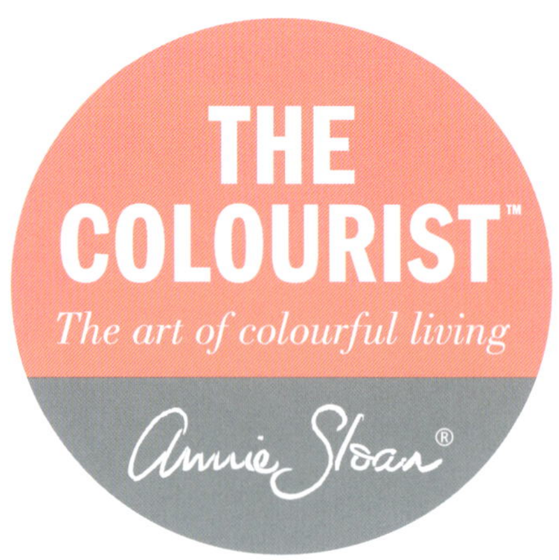

Editor-in-chief
Annie Sloan

EDITORIAL

Managing Editor/Art Director Jane Toft
Picture Editor Rosemary Watts
Production Editor Elizabeth Raderecht

PUBLISHING

Publishing Consultant Katherine Raderecht

FOR ANNIE SLOAN

CREATIVE DIRECTOR **FELIX SLOAN**
CONTRIBUTING EDITORS
ALISON CHEVERALLS, AMY HONOUR
COPY AND CONTENT
ANN TUTT, AISHI COPLEY, FIONA HOLLIDAY, JOANNA LLOYD

PRINTING

PRINTED IN ENGLAND BY PRIORITY MAILING & DIGITAL PRINT, NO 5 DOWNTON BUSINESS CENTRE, BATTEN ROAD, DOWNTON, SALISBURY SP5 3HU

WITH SPECIAL THANKS TO

ABIGAIL AND RYAN BELL, PENELOPE FEWSTER, BRETT AND DENNAE HILL, TINA HILLIER, JANICE ISSITT, AVERY MICHAELS, TAMSYN MORGANS, FIONA MURRAY, CARLEY PAGE SUMMERS, ELLIE TENNANT, JO TORRIJOS, LARA WATSON

CONTACT US

PHONE: +44 (0) 1865 803 168
EMAIL: THECOLOURIST@ANNIESLOAN.COM

WWW.ANNIESLOAN.COM

ANNIE SLOAN INTERIORS LTD IS A UK COMPANY BASED IN OXFORD. YOU CAN FIND US AT 33 COWLEY ROAD, OXFORD OX4 1HP
VAT NUMBER: 993927358

The COLOUR hunter

Our pick of designers and makers who embrace the art of colourful living

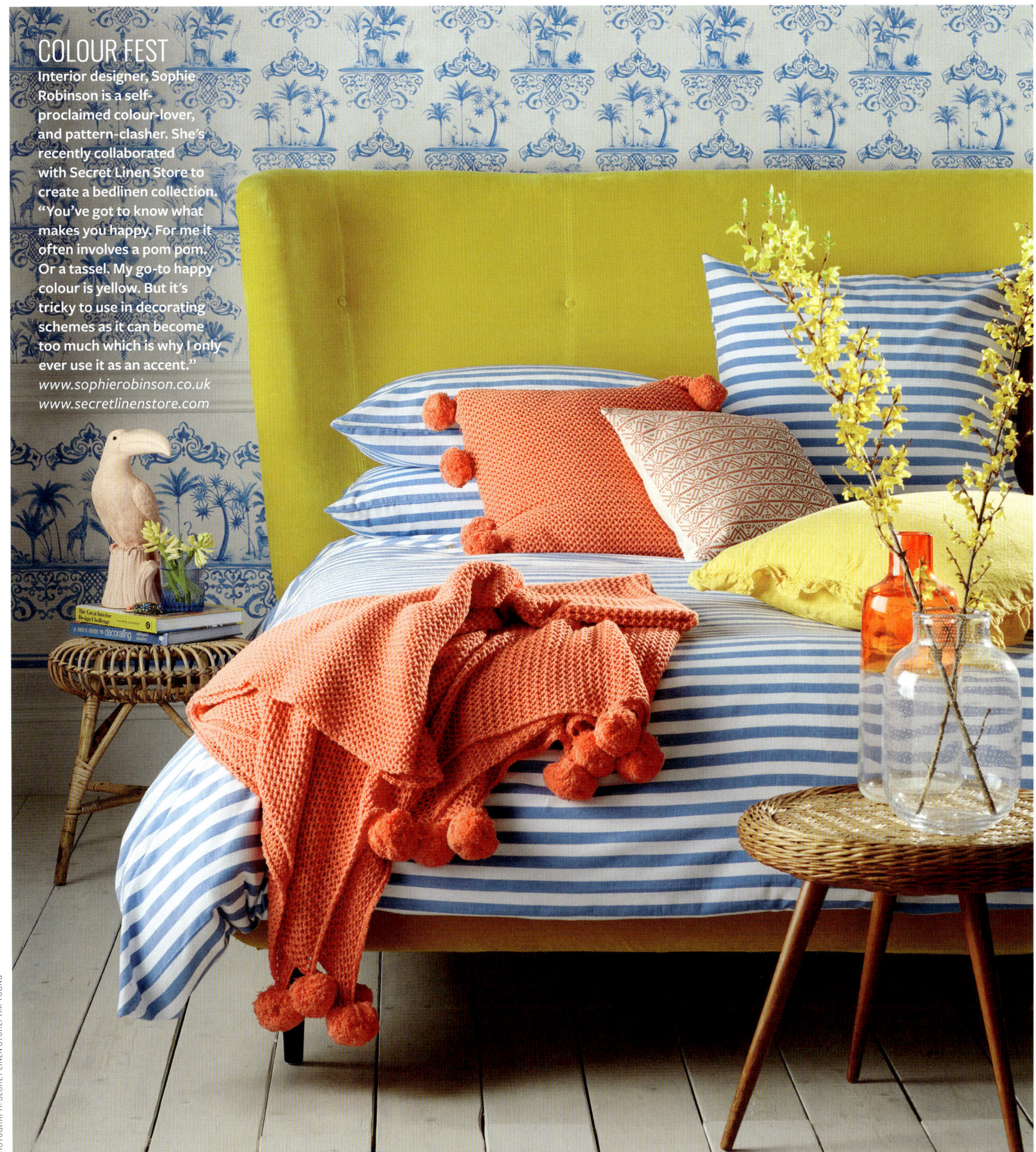

COLOUR FEST

Interior designer, Sophie Robinson is a self-proclaimed colour-lover, and pattern-clasher. She's recently collaborated with Secret Linen Store to create a bedlinen collection. "You've got to know what makes you happy. For me it often involves a pom pom. Or a tassel. My go-to happy colour is yellow. But it's tricky to use in decorating schemes as it can become too much which is why I only ever use it as an accent."
www.sophierobinson.co.uk
www.secretlinenstore.com

PHOTOGRAPH: SECRET LINEN STORE/TIM YOUNG

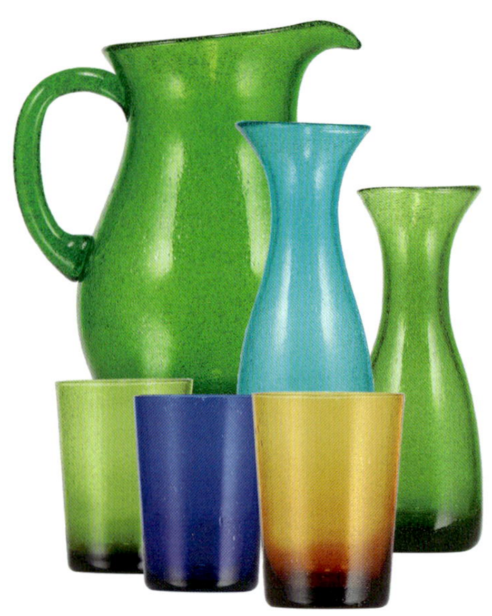

SETTING THE STANDARD

The British Colour Standard was a wonderful old colour system created in the 1930's to match products across the British Commonwealth – everything from uniforms to Battleships.
It fell out of use after World War II, but in 2015 the name was revived by Victoria Whitbread and Jackie Piper for 'modern vintage' homeware brand, British Colour Standard – the creators of the iconic Pantone mug. We love this range of mouth-blown, recycled bubble glass jugs, carafes and tumblers. BCS' aim is to make all their products either recyclable, made from recycled materials or fair trade.
www.britishcolourstandard.com
@britishcolourstandard

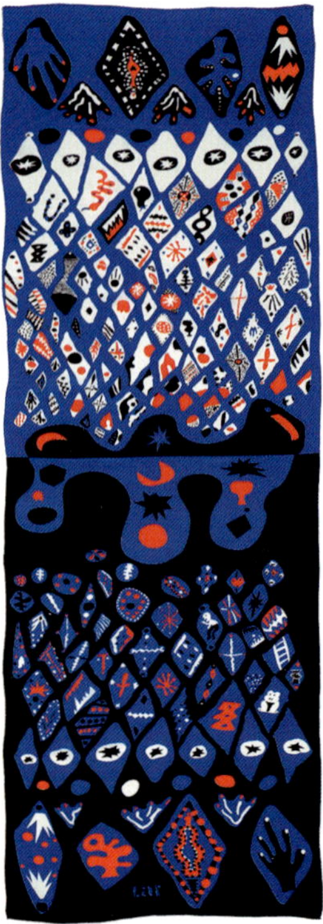

Jadis Blue 60x180cm matte silk scarf

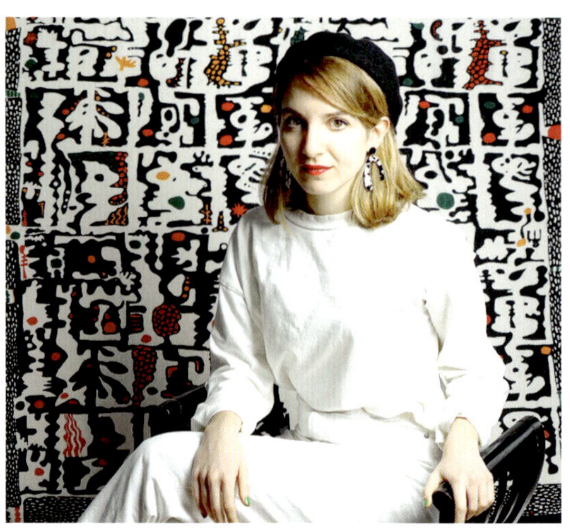

MODERNIST LOVE

Laris Alara Kilimci's first collection for her label LAR Studio was inspired by her grandmother's hand painted modernist scarves. Born in New York, Laris studied at Central Saint Martins, London but now lives and works in her native Istanbul. The designs are hand illustrated by Laris, transferred digitally then ethically produced in small amounts in Turkey.
www.lar.studio *@larofficial*

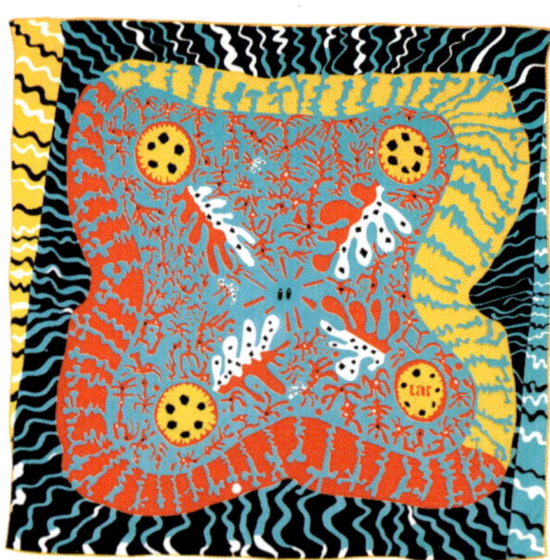

Limited Editon Harlequin Primary 90x90cm silk scarf

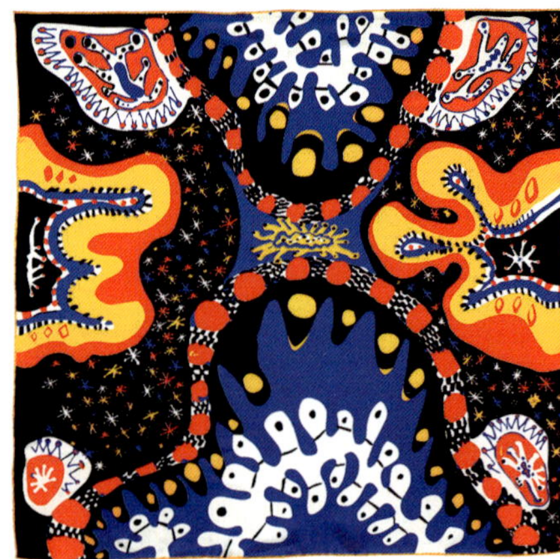

Midnight Voodoo 70x70cm satin silk scarf

INSTA-STYLE FOR YOUR LIVING SPACE

Inventive ideas and quick fixes to create a stylish home

Author and stylist Joanna Thornhill offers inspirational and practical solutions to renovating a rented home. With a growing number of people struggling to get on the property ladder, insta-STYLE proves that you can create a beautiful home that's also 'landlord-friendly'. It's packed with styling, craft and DIY tips to inspire both renters and renovators. Full step-by-step projects feature at the end of each chapter. This fantastic new edition of the previously titled Home For Now is published by CICO Books in October 2018.
rylandpeters.com *@rylandpetersandsmall*

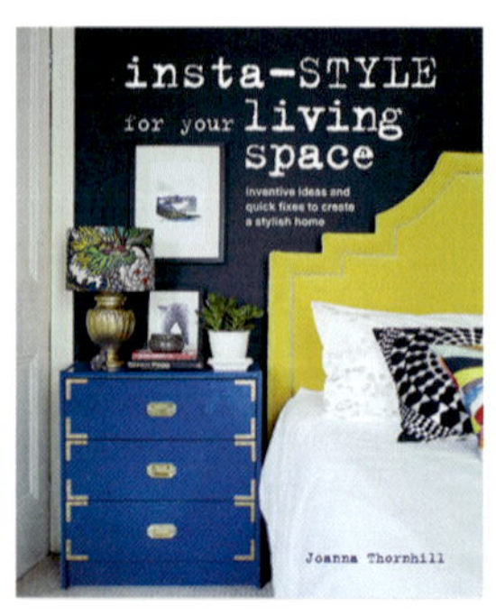

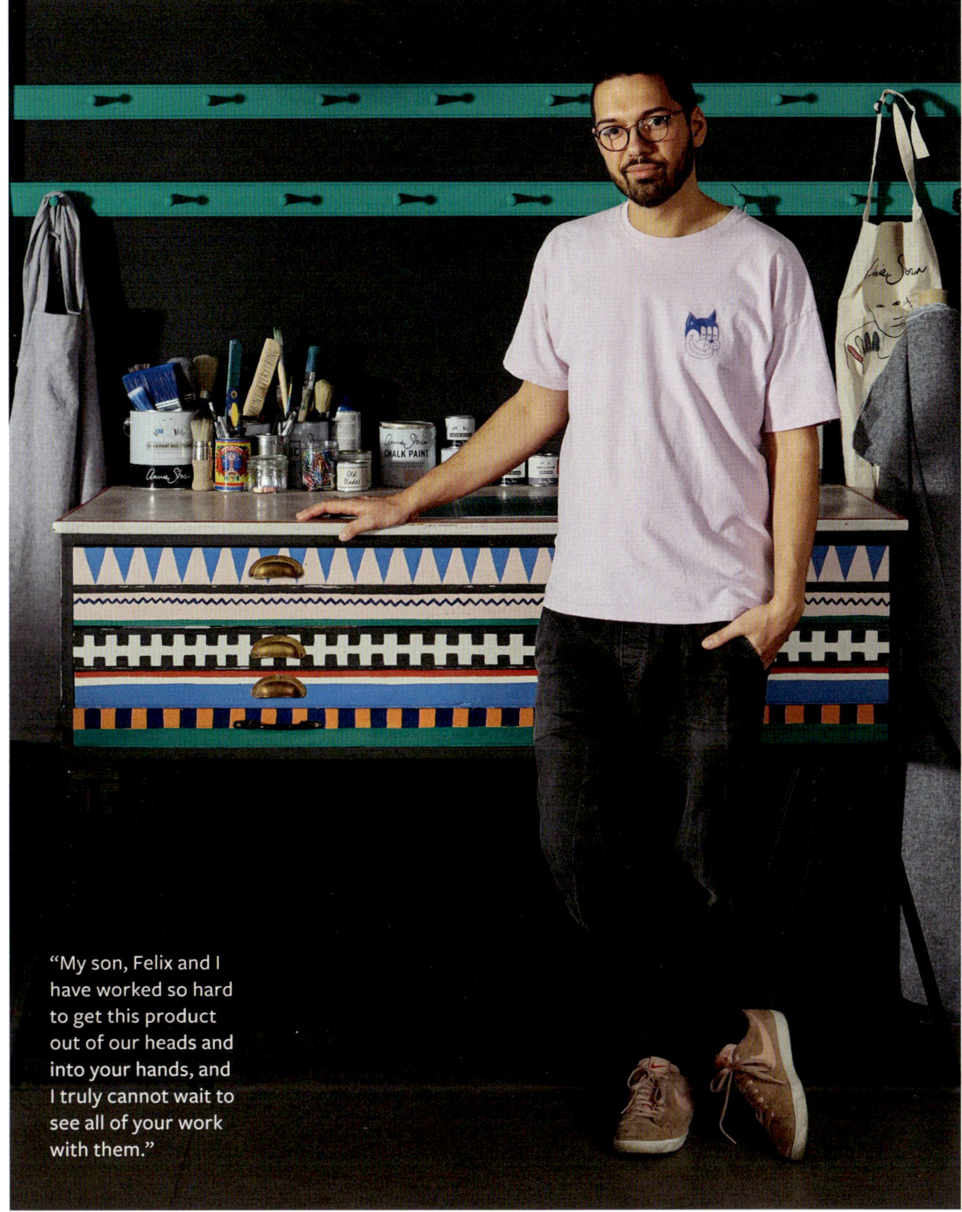

"My son, Felix and I have worked so hard to get this product out of our heads and into your hands, and I truly cannot wait to see all of your work with them."

PHOTOGRAPH: TINA HILLIER. OPPOSITE: CHRISTOPHER DRAKE

The beautiful organic forms created by Annie made a striking choice as The Colourist's cover!

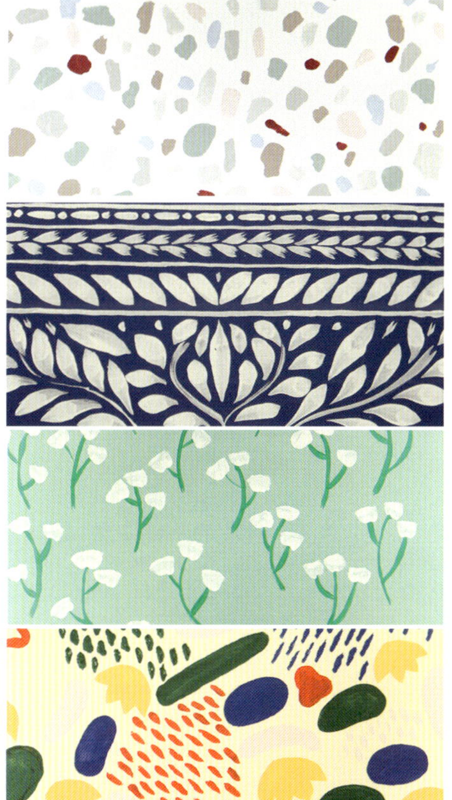

FROM THE TOP, Terrazzo painted using the Large Flat and Small Flat Detail brushes. **Bone inlay effect** with the Large Round Detail brush. **Blossoms** were made using Small Round and Small Flat Detail brushes. A **Matisse-inspired pattern** was created using Large Round Detail brush for the big shapes and larger dashes; Small Round Detail brush for the small dashes

WHAT'S NEW DETAIL BRUSHES

"You only need two shapes of brush for decorative details – one that's pointed and one that's flat"

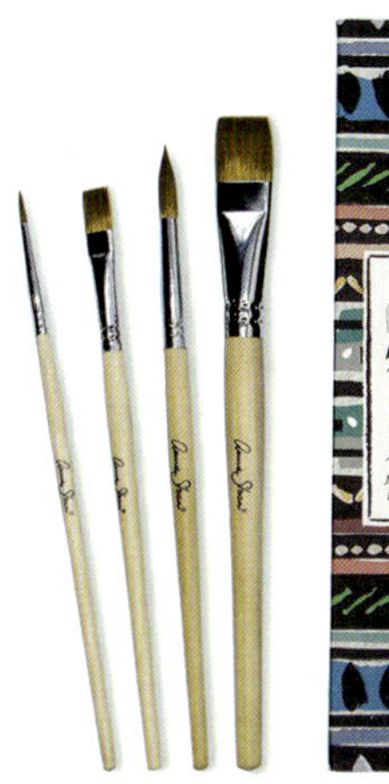

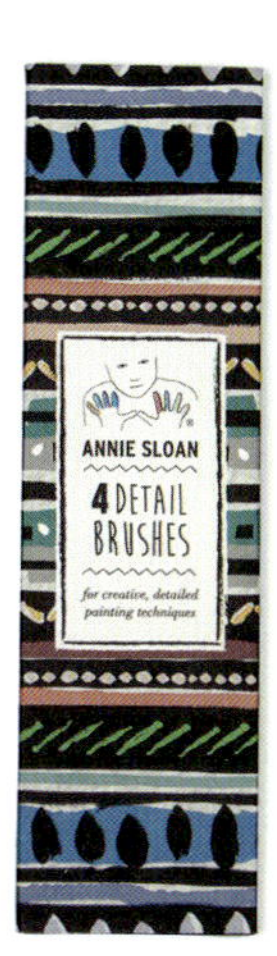

Our new Annie Sloan Detail Brush set is designed to bring a no-fuss approach to mark-making and decorative paint effects. Ideal for painting fine details and dynamic shapes using Chalk Paint®and Gilding Waxes, the four brushes give great control, amazing precision and ensure that you create an even spread of colour thanks to their soft, durable bristles. One set comes with brushes: Small Round, Small Flat, Large Round and Large Flat.

"If you're looking to create thin lines and small dots, the Small Round brush will do the job as it holds less paint, making it easy to apply details precisely. For thicker lines and dots, or for when you want to alternate between light and heavy marks, the Large Round brush should be your tool of choice, while two Flat brushes are ideal for both thin and thick lined details." explains Felix.

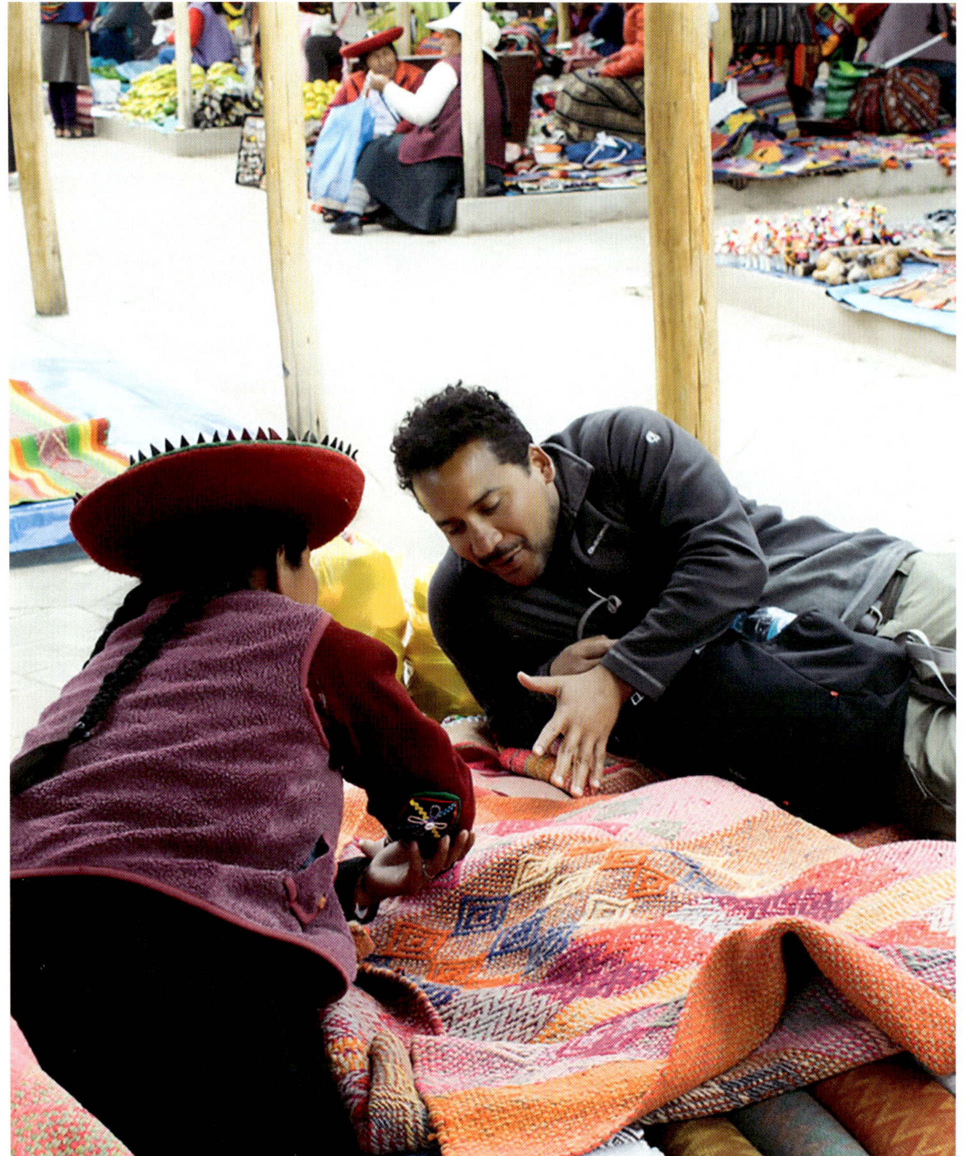

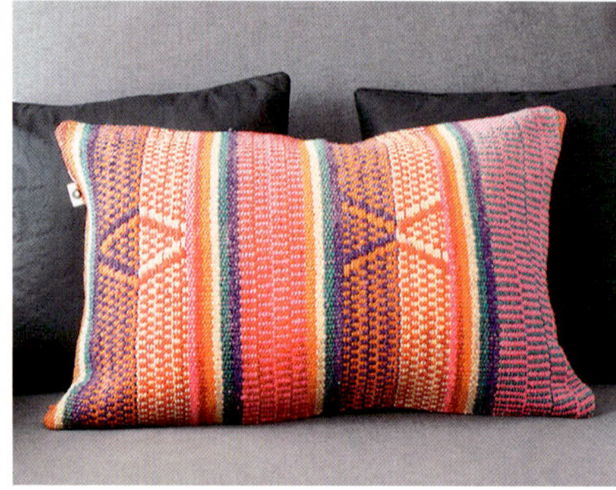

ABOVE Made entirely by hand from sheep or llama wool, the textiles are coloured using natural dyes native to the region, including cochineal, Peruvian purple corn, muña and Pacific sea salt

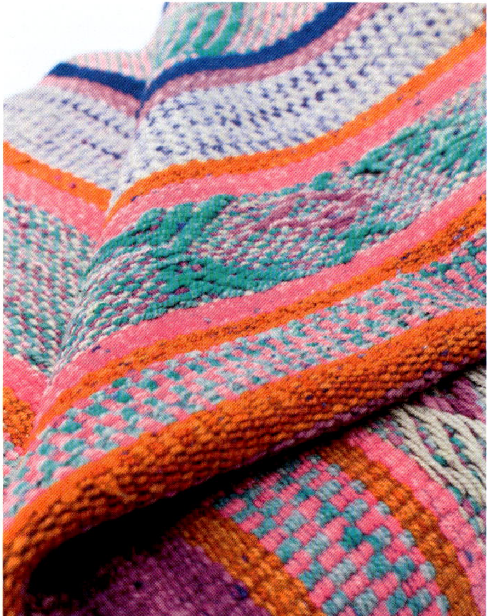

ANNIE'S PICK INKA FABRIC

"When I spotted these fabulously vibrant textiles I snapped up several rugs and cushions for my home"

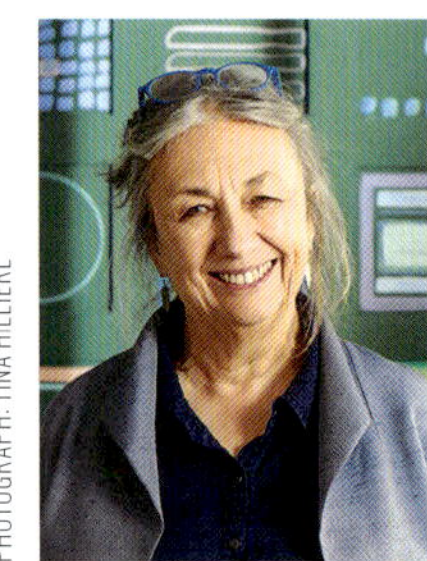

PHOTOGRAPH: TINA HILLIERL

Undoubtedly it was the amazing colours that first drew me to Inka Fabrics stall, but after chatting to owners Liz and Adolfo, their passion to preserve a part of Peruvian heritage was infectious. Married to Brit Liz, Adolfo is Peruvian: "We travel to Peru to form bonds with craftsmen and women and understand the story behind each piece of work. We work directly with the artisans from the Sacred Valley of the Incas to the High Altitudes of Puno." he explained. "The process of weaving a rug, or frazada, can be a highly spiritual and personal journey, in which a weaver will draw from the natural world, their history and memory. They use the same techniques as their Incan ancestors, making every frazada unique." Sadly the art of making frazadas is declining, but thanks to couples like Liz and Adolfo help is at hand.
www.inkafabric.co.uk *@inkafabric*

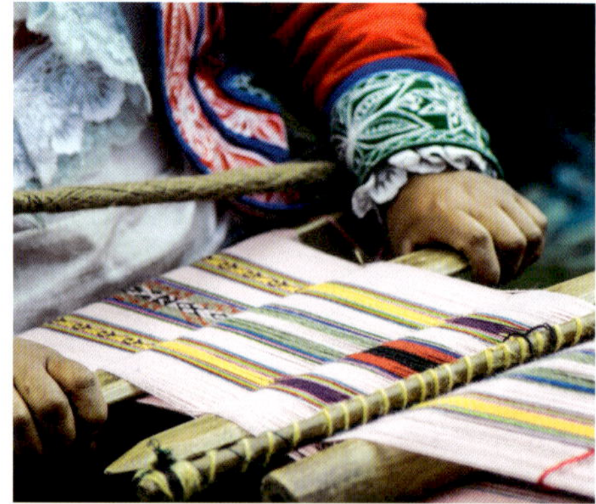

ABOVE LEFT Adolfo frequently travels to remote parts of Peru to work directly with the artisans. They use Fairtrade principles to try to keep local businesses thriving

ABOVE The process of weaving a frazada (rug/blanket) can take up to one month (approximately six hours a day), or more depending on the difficulty of design

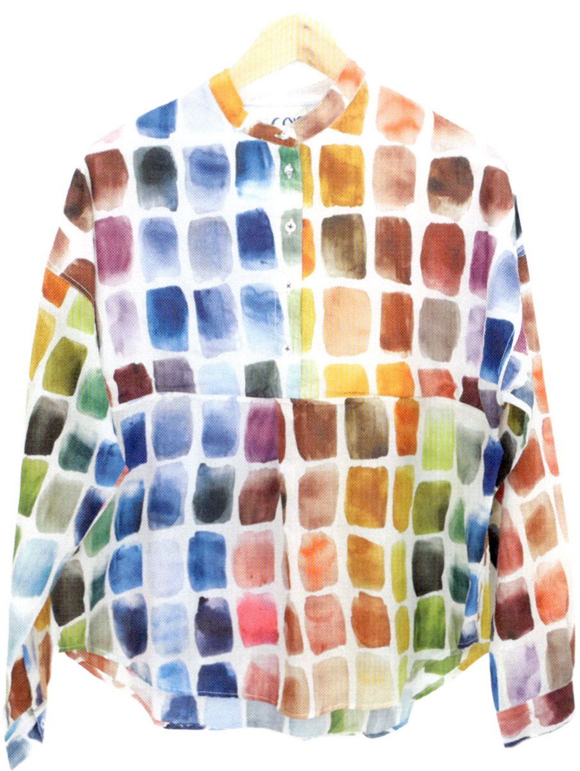

COR VALUES

Cor means colour in Portugeuse and is the perfect name for Jaz Hunt's clothing label. Artist Jaz grew up near the ocean in both Portugal and Australia. She digitally prints her original paintings onto fabric.

The Kahlo Smock Shirt (pictured left), is inspired by the classic painter's shirt. Cor is committed to using sustainable materials and production methods. "I source organic fabrics and work directly with my partners in India. Through regular visits I endeavour to foster strong and ongoing relationships with the people that make the clothing for Cor."

www.corclothes.com *@corclothes*

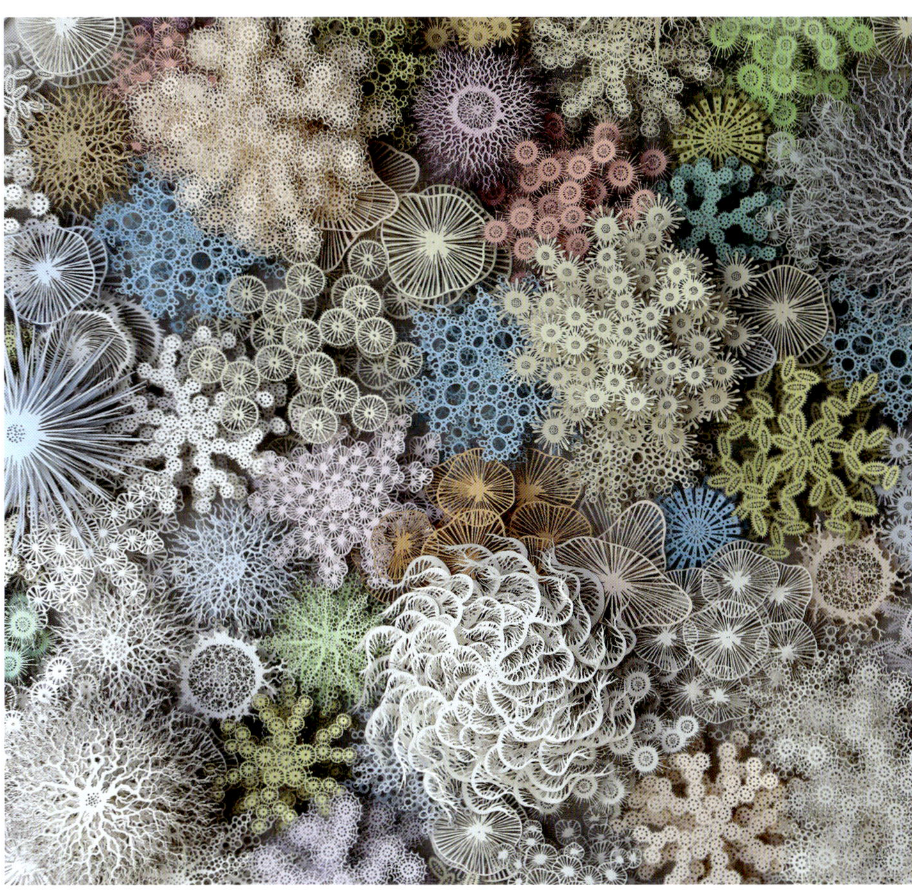

THE WOW FACTOR *In his series Magical Circle Variations, artist Rogan Brown has created amazing hand-cut paper sculptures that aim to draw a parallel between the human microbiome and coral reefs.*

www.roganbrown.com *@rogan_brown_*

TRENDING...

We're loving the vogue for leaving some areas naked!

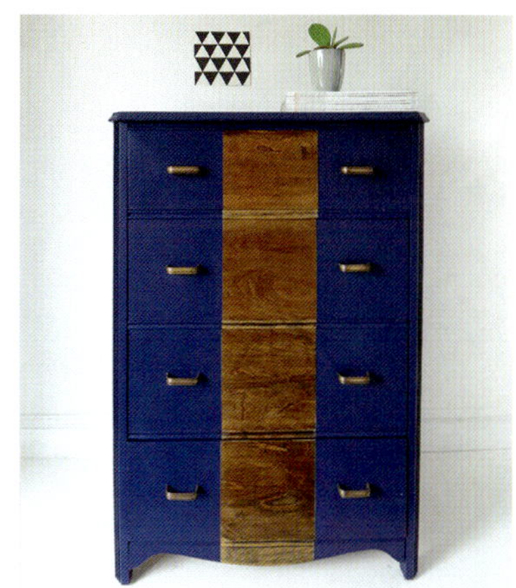

1 This handsome blue boy is the work of Chloe Kempster @maisieshouse

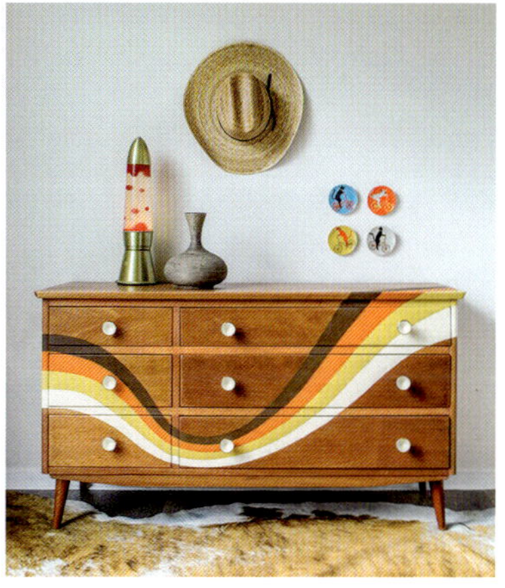

2 A definite 1970s vibe with new Painter in Residence Jeanie Simpson's stripes!

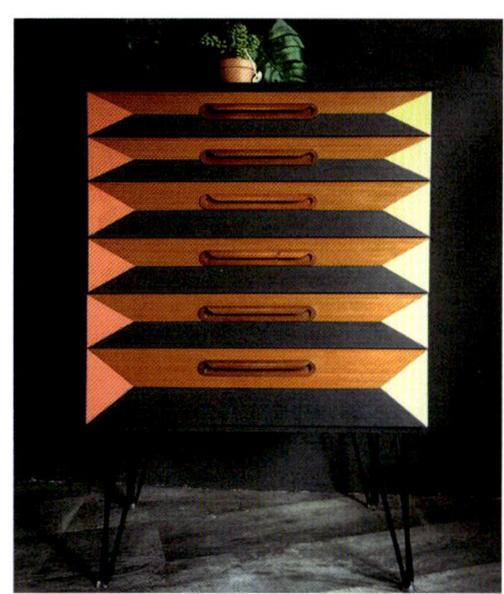

3 We're loving this 3D effect by Stockist Claire Atwood @bellemaisonvintage

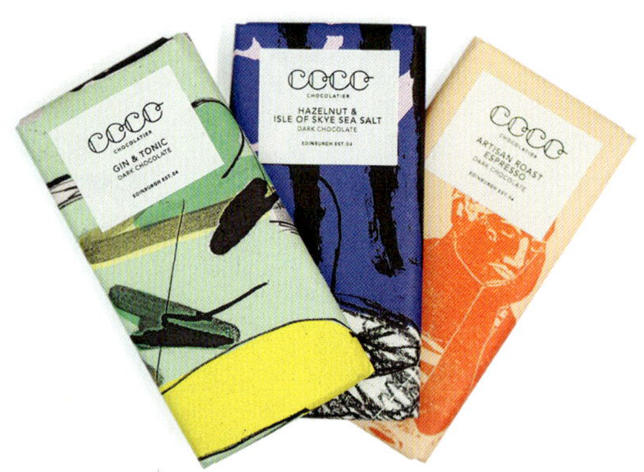

Edinburgh-based Coco Chocolatier wrap their premium chocolate bars in original designs by independent artists. The latest collection features work by Palefroi, Stephen Smith and Rachael Hood. Artilicious!
www.cocochocolatier.com *@cocochocolatier*

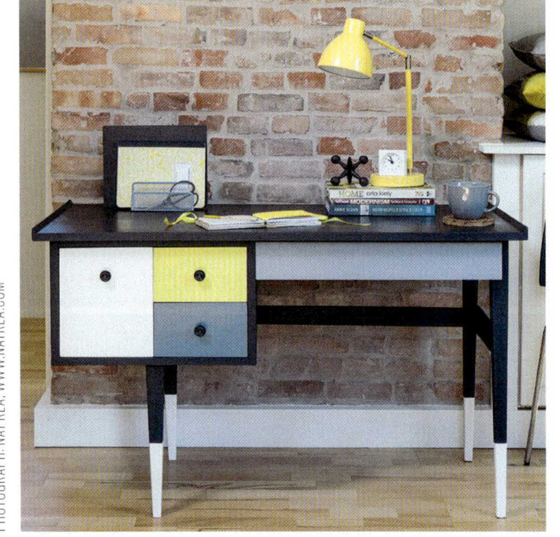
PHOTOGRAPH: NAT REA. WWW.NATREA.COM

Nancy Chace, Annie's Stockist in Bristol, Rhode Island, USA, brought new life to a 1960s desk, using Chalk Paint® by Annie Sloan in English Yellow, Graphite and Pure with two custom grey colours for the drawers. We love that yellow!
www.searosecottage.com *@searosecottage*

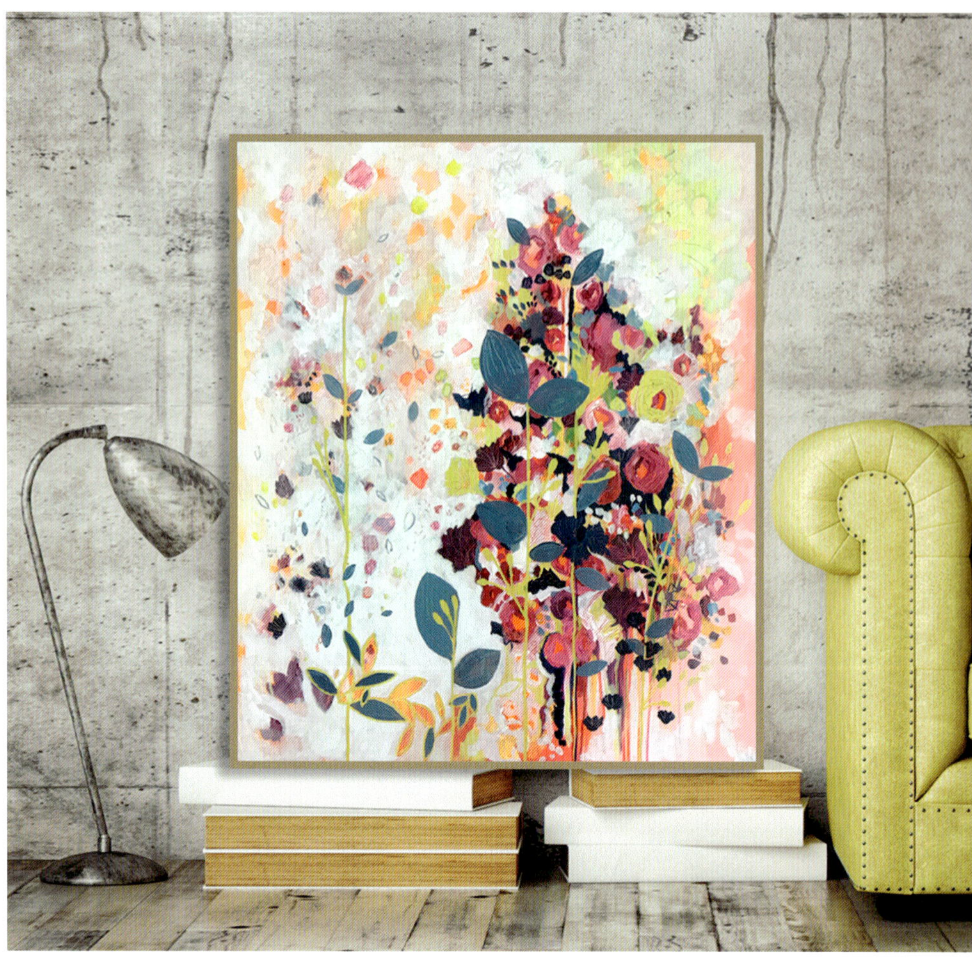

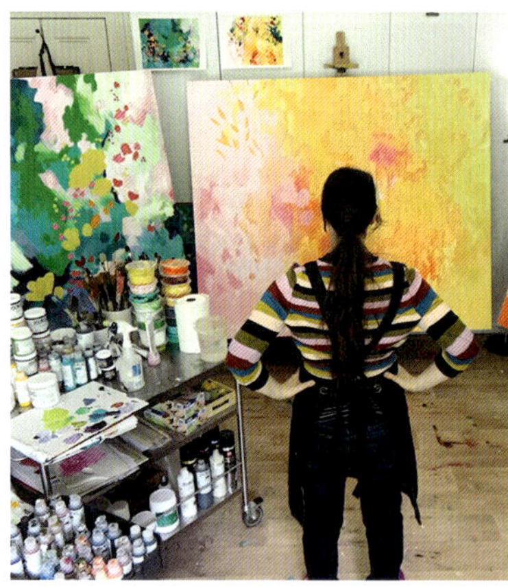

FLOWER POWER

Artist Susan Nethercote works from her home studio in Ballarat, Victoria, Australia. She has spent most of her professional life as the owner of clothing label Manque Design, but since having her first child in 2011, Susan has increasingly devoted her time to painting. Her bright, botanical abstracts are inspired by the effects of light, atmospheric qualities and the colours of nature, "To me, making art is a walk with the soul of nature."
www.susannethercote.com *@susan.nethercote*

DOOR J'ADORE

A celebration of the world's most beautiful doors

It was while travelling through Buenos Aires, Argentina, that Nick Rowell first developed an interest in photographing doors. He set up his instagram account @door_jadore to document his finds from Norway to the Netherlands, to the Faroe Islands and French Polynesia. The book reflects Nick's passion for portals. Every door tells its own intriguing story. Whether it's the particular shade of paint, the texture of the finish, an extravagant knocker, or an elegantly turned handle, each door reveals the secret of its past, and the person who lives behind it now.
rylandpeters.com *@door_jadore*

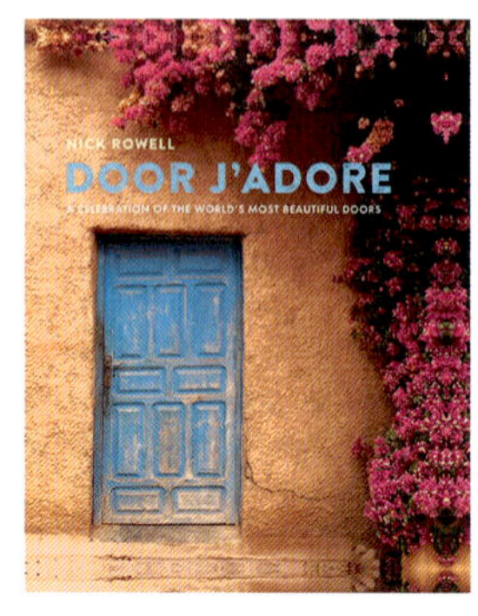

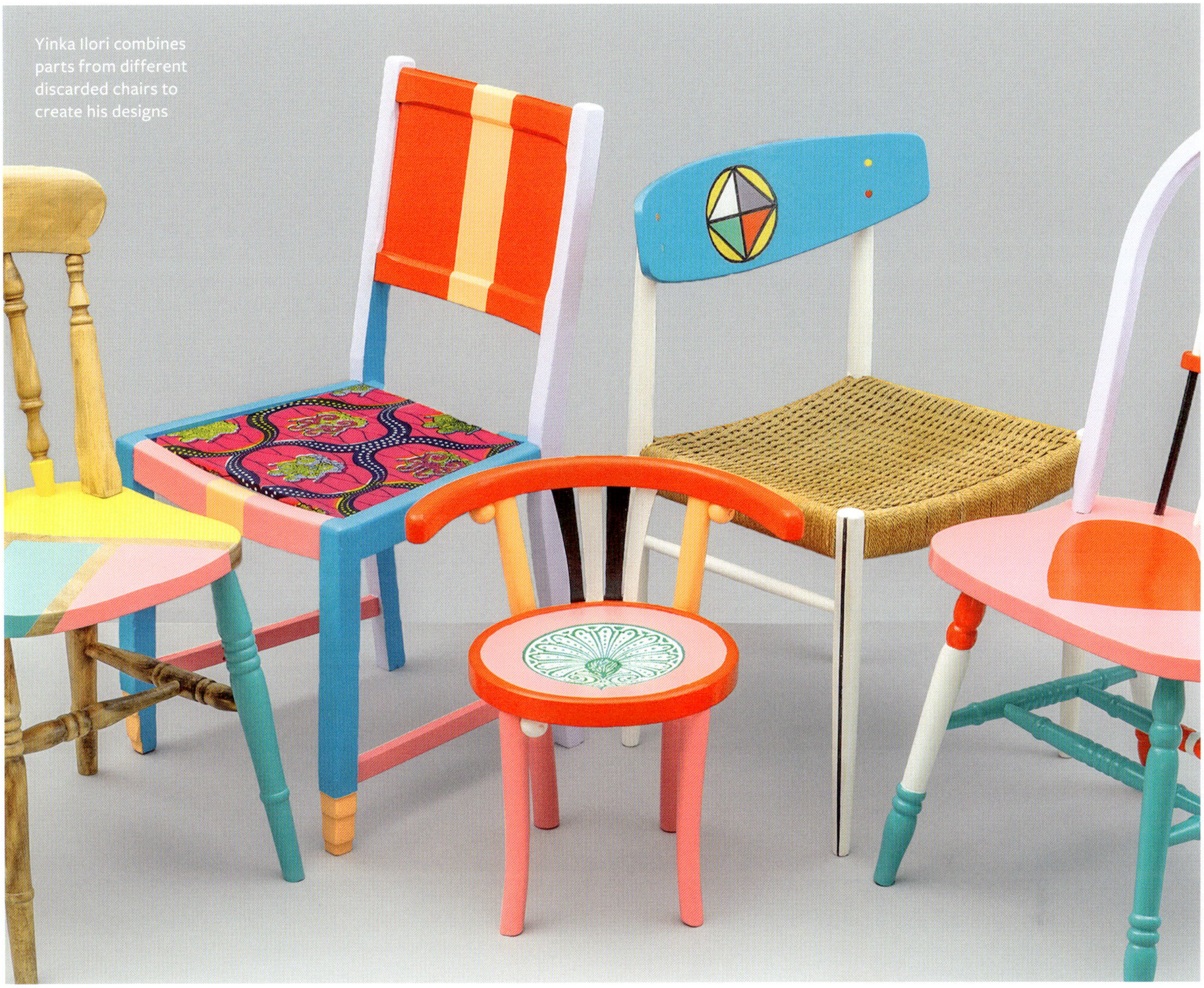

Yinka Ilori combines parts from different discarded chairs to create his designs

PHOTOGRAPHS: BELOW, VEERLE EVENS; RIGHT, DAN WEILL

DESIGNER FOCUS YINKA ILORI

"Vibrant, humorous, provocative and fun, but each piece of furniture I create has a story to tell"

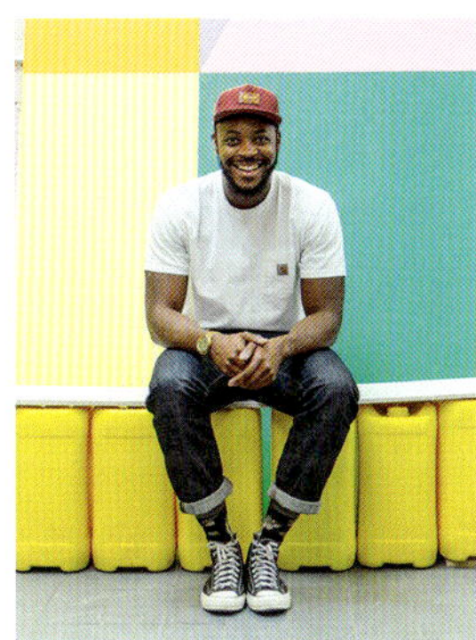

Born in Islington, London, to Nigerian parents, Yinka Ilori brings his cultural heritage to each piece of upcycled furniture he creates. The Yoruba language and Nigerians love of brightly coloured fabrics and jewellery have all influenced his work.

Each piece of furniture tells a story. He weaves the Nigerian parables of his parents into his work, touching on themes as varied as hope, sexuality and social class.

Since leaving London Metropolitan University in 2009, Yinka Ilori's success has grown. He has collaborated with eBay, producing pieces for their Fill Your Cart with Colour campaign. His most recent commission was to illustrate the cover of Jason Reynolds' new book, For Every One.
yinkailori.com *@yinka_ilori*

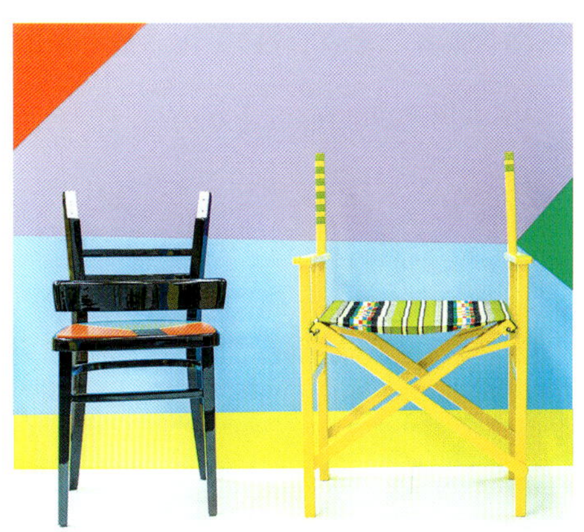

Above Each piece of recycled furniture that Yinka Ilori designs has a fun, vibrant, playful feel, but beneath the surface he has a narrative that draws on his Nigerian heritage to tell stories of modern urban life

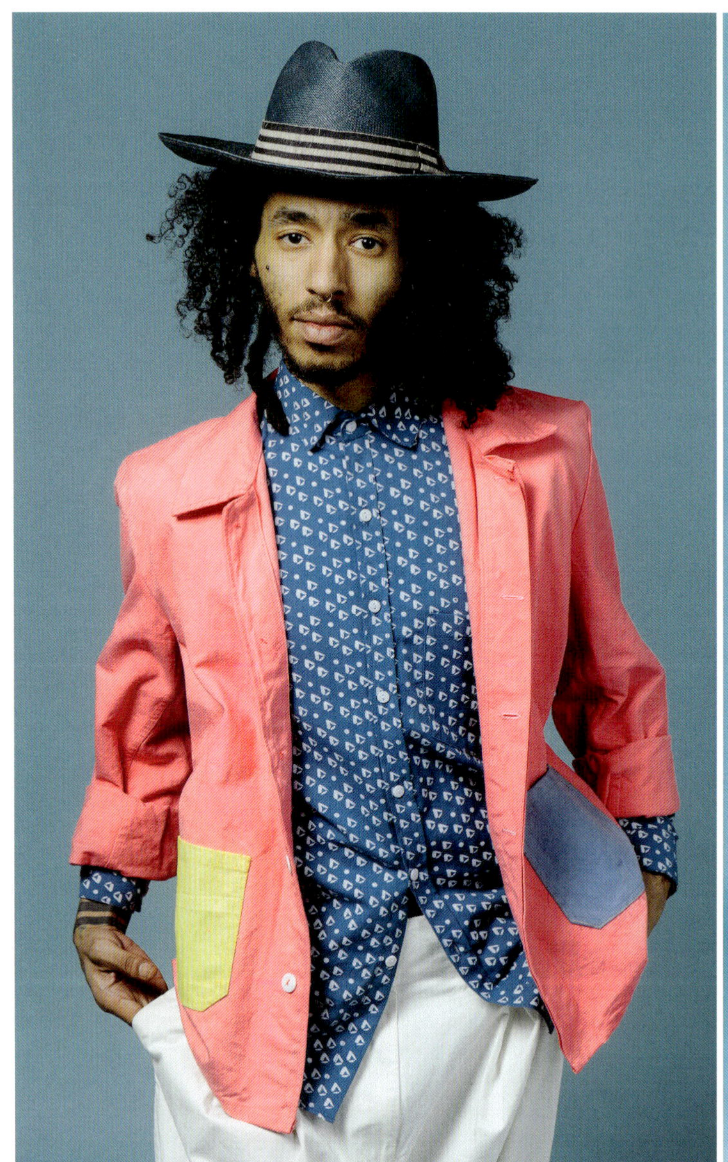

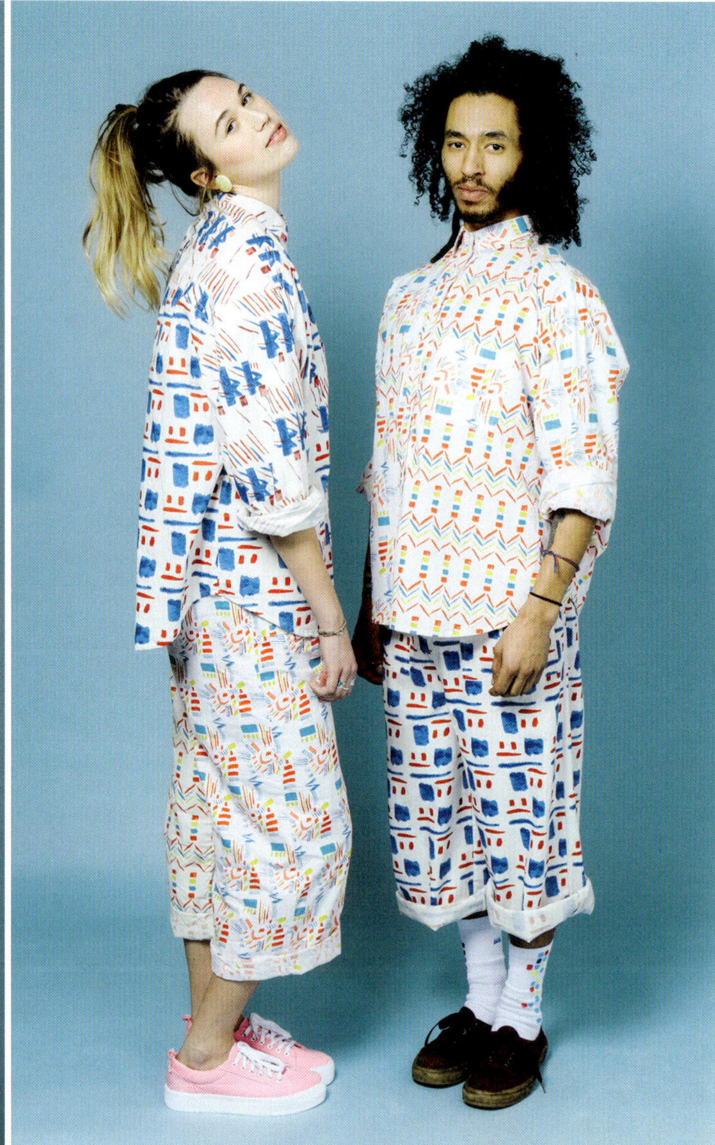

ETHICAL FASHION HUMPHRIES AND BEGG

"We're always looking for colour combinations, whether they're in a sign, a painting or piece of fabric"

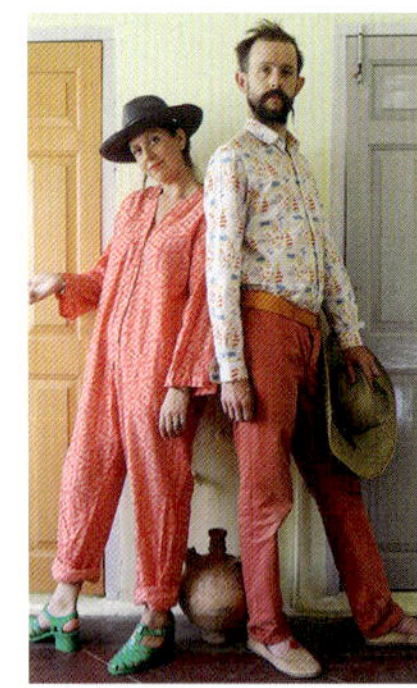

Passionate about print, British husband and wife duo Alice Begg and Robbie Humphries design boldly printed clothing for the everyday. Annie Sloan is a big fan of their ethical fashion brand. "I love the confident colour clashes and block printed patterns. The relaxed shapes mean they're so comfortable to wear too!" says Annie. In fact, turn to page 19 to see Annie wearing her own Humphries and Begg dress in Red Chili Print.

Alice designs all the prints in a playful, naive style. They are then screen printed onto 100% natural fabrics by a small team in Jaipur, India. The method means that there are always minor imperfections, giving the clothes a unique, hand-crafted, organic feel. Ensuring that their garments are made in a safe environment and that the workers are paid fairly is very important to the couple. *www.humphriesandbegg.co.uk* *@humphriesandbegg*

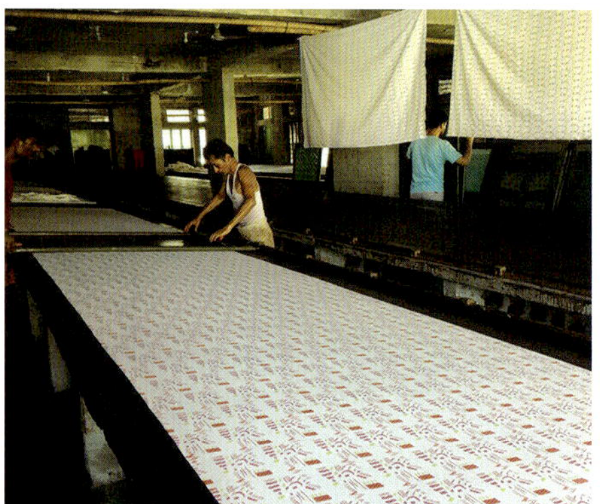

Above The fabric is printed in Jaipur by a family firm that Humphries and Begg have been working with for five years. The history of block-printing in Jaipur goes back thousands of years. The heat in the city ensures the colours dry quickly, making for a speedy production process

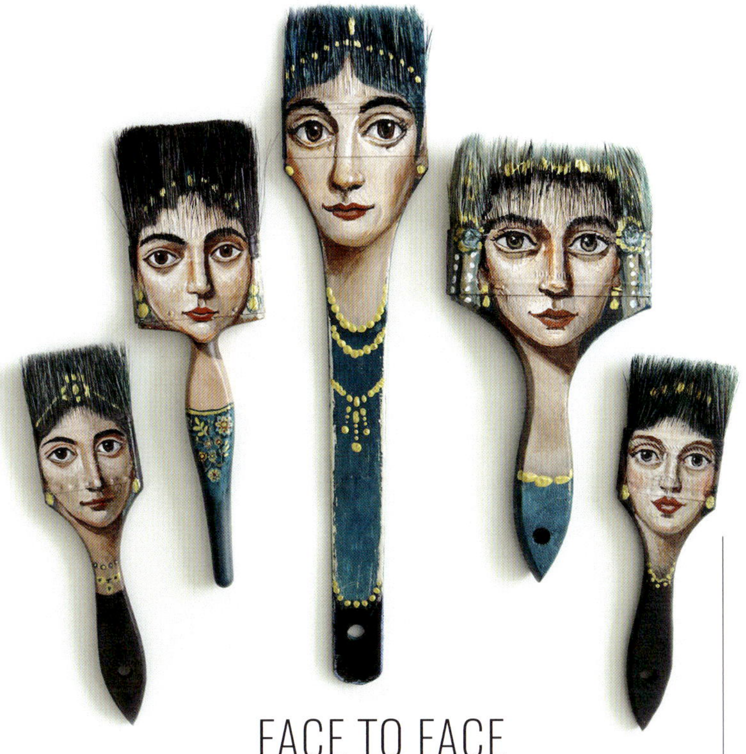

FACE TO FACE

Los Angeles-based surrealist artist Alexandra Dillon paints on found objects. Rather than start with a fixed idea for her imaginary people, she just begins to paint. "They show up and tell me who they are," she says.
www.alexandradillon.com *@alexandradillonartist*

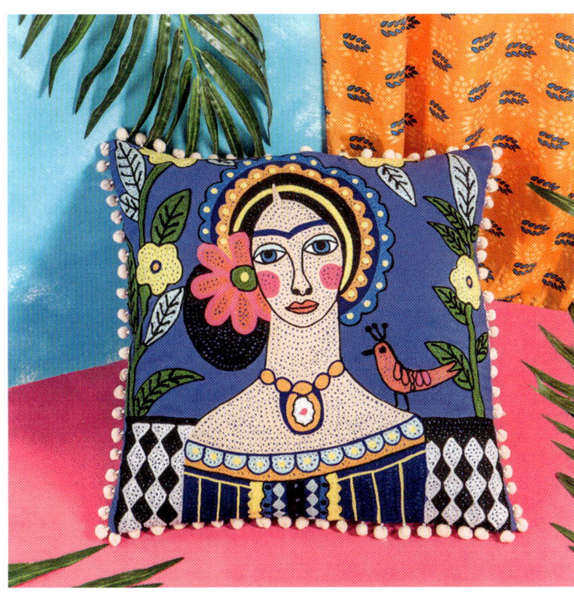

THE BOHEMIAN LIFE

Handmade, Fairtrade, bohemian. The three words that sum up Ian Snow's decorative homewares business. As a teenager Ian travelled to India and fell in love with the country and its people. This stunning crewel embroidery cushion is part of The Frida Kahlo Collection. It is handmade by a small company based in Moradabad, India that employs 35, mainly female, skilled embroiderers.
www.iansnow.com *@iansnowltd*

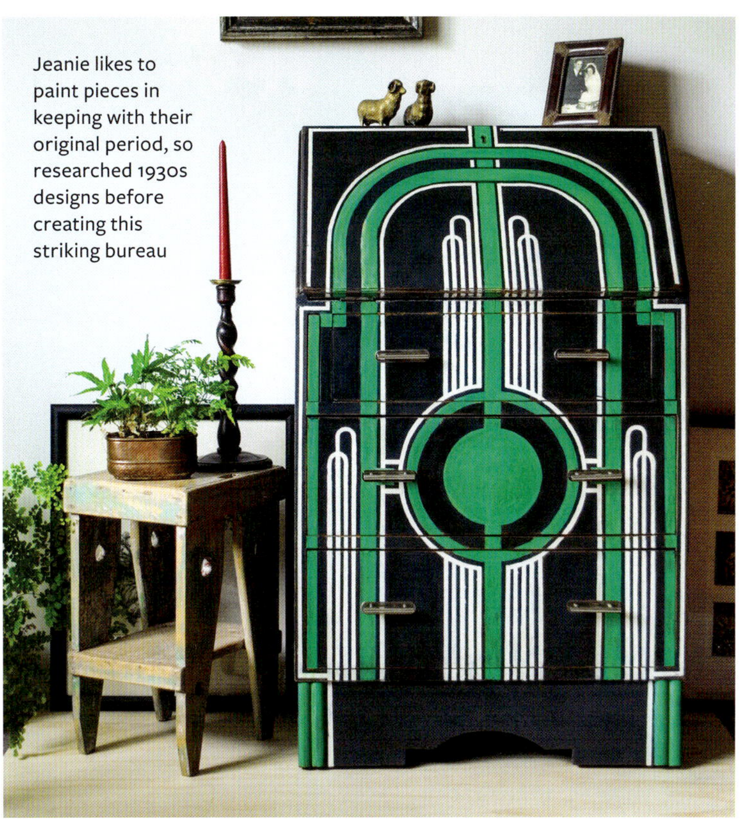

Jeanie likes to paint pieces in keeping with their original period, so researched 1930s designs before creating this striking bureau

INTRODUCING... JEANIE SIMPSON

Meet the first New Zealander to be awarded the coveted Annie Sloan Painter In Residence title

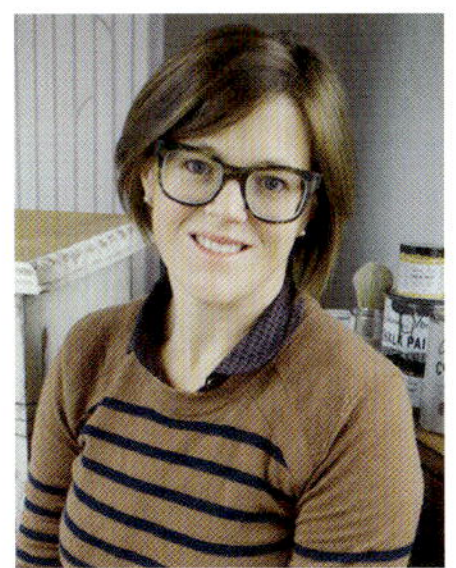

Annie discovered the work of Jeanie Simpson one evening whilst browsing the #AnnieSloan #ChalkPaint hashtags on Instagram. "Just goes to show the value of publicising your creations!" smiles Annie.

With two small children and a little extra spare time, Jeanie picked up a paintbrush and began up-cycling furniture and homeware. She's always had a strong interest in art and design - something that she draws on heavily for inspiration in her pieces. "All the work I've seen from her has been meticulously researched, which the history of art and design nerd in me absolutely loves," says Annie.

Jeanie Simpson's first project as Annie Sloan Painter in Residence is this stylish Art Deco inspired bureau (above). Jeanie painted the desk first using Chalk Paint® in Graphite to act as a dark, blank canvas and drew her dramatic design on top with pencil. Using Annie Sloan Detail Brushes and painter's tape, Jeannie painted the design using Chalk Paint® in Old White and Florence, mixed with a dash of English Yellow. Over the Art Deco design, Jeanie used a diluted wash of Olive, English Yellow and Old White to give an oxidised-copper look. Once it was dry, she took sandpaper to the piece to distress it slightly. The piece was finished in all colours of Chalk Paint Wax® by Annie Sloan; first a coat of Clear Wax was used, then Dark Wax on the green sections of the bureau, followed by a mix of White and Black Wax on the darker grey sections. The whole piece was the finished again in Clear Wax to protect it.
www.jeaniusreloved.com *@jeanius_reloved*

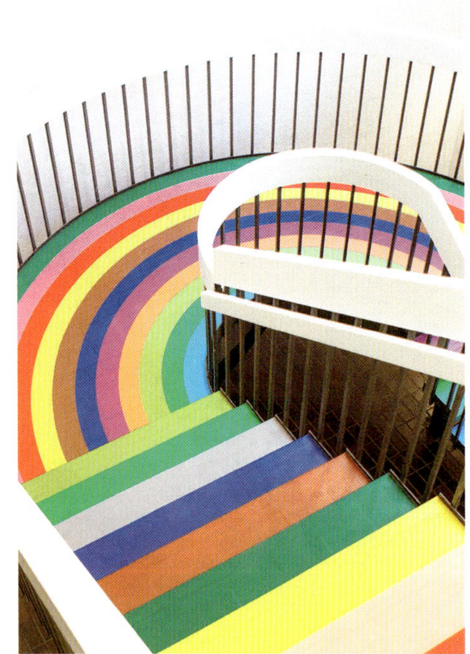

WALK THIS WAY

The Color Factory describes itself as, "a collaborative experiential exhibit designed to awaken audiences to the everyday yet brilliant presence of colour." The launch pop-up installation in San Francisco, USA, has now closed but this summer, a new 20,000-square-foot Color Factory pop-up museum is coming to 251 Spring Street, in New York's SoHo neighbourhood. You can experince a taster right now at the Manhattan Color Walk based at the Cooper Hewitt Smithsonian Design Museum New York.
www.colorfactory.co *@colorfactoryco*

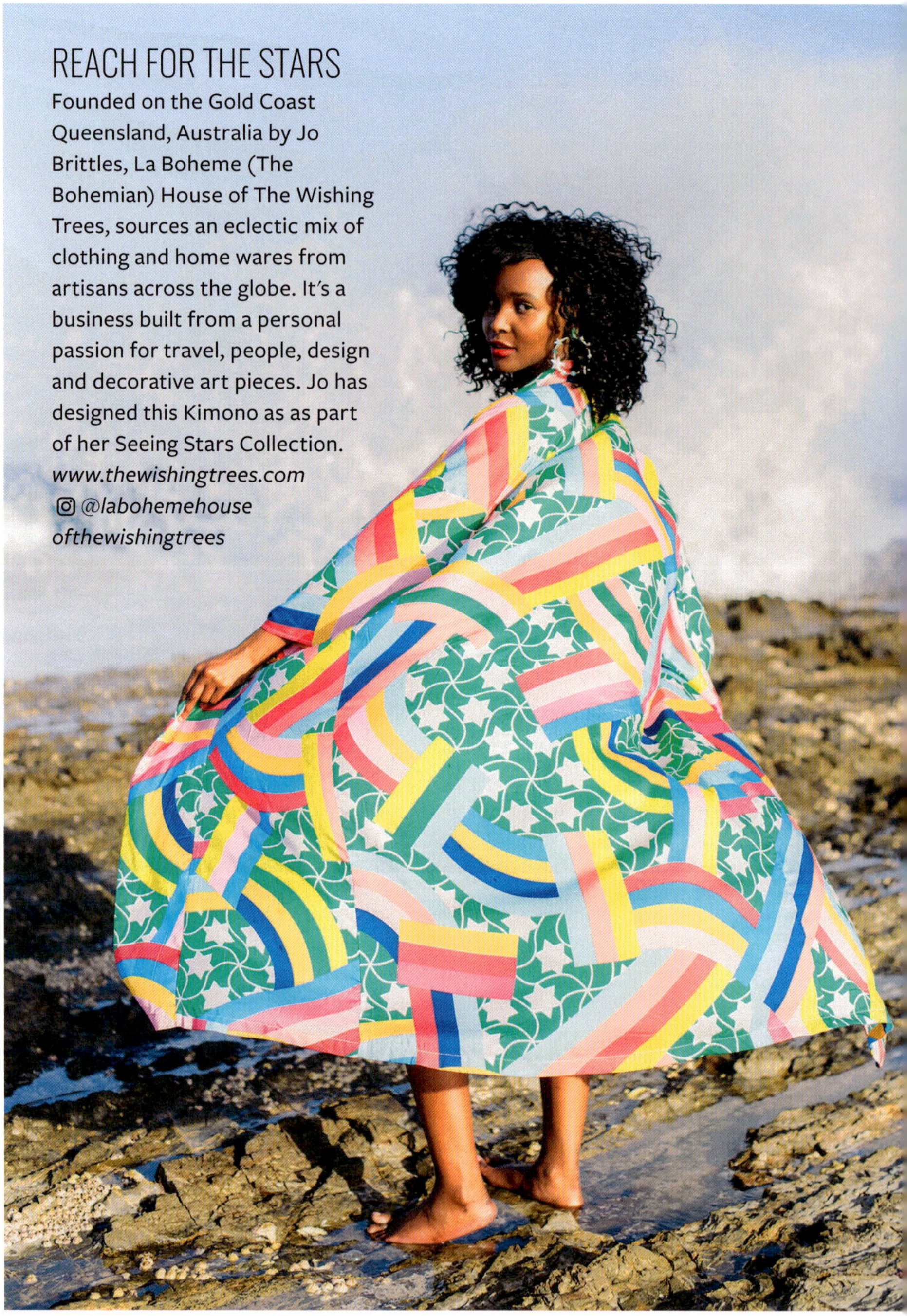

REACH FOR THE STARS

Founded on the Gold Coast Queensland, Australia by Jo Brittles, La Boheme (The Bohemian) House of The Wishing Trees, sources an eclectic mix of clothing and home wares from artisans across the globe. It's a business built from a personal passion for travel, people, design and decorative art pieces. Jo has designed this Kimono as as part of her Seeing Stars Collection.
www.thewishingtrees.com
@labohemehouse ofthewishingtrees

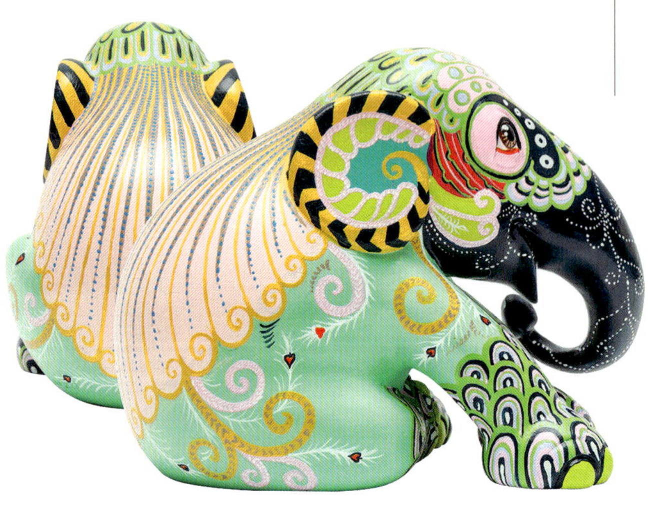

THE ART OF CONSERVATION

Elephant Parade is a social enterprise and runs the world's largest art exhibition of decorated elephant statues. Created by well-known artists and celebrities, each Elephant Parade statue is a unique art piece. The life-size, baby elephant statues are exhibited in cities around the world to raise awareness for the need for elephant conservation. Limited edition, handcrafted replicas and a select range of products are created from the exhibition elephants. 20% of Elephant Parade net profits are donated to elephant welfare and conservation projects.
www.elephantparade.com
@elephantparadefan

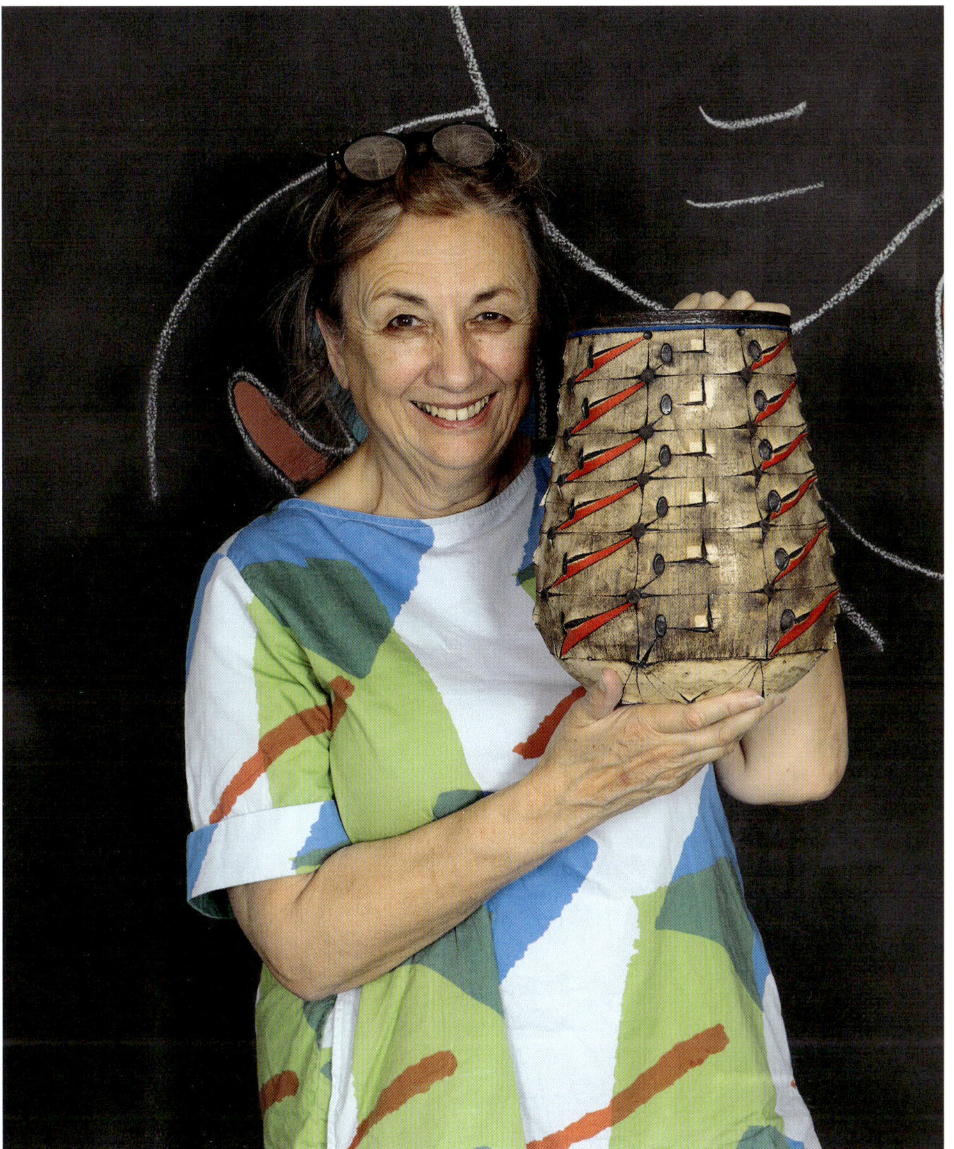

PHOTOGRAPHS: PORTRAIT OF ANNIE, FIONA MURRAY

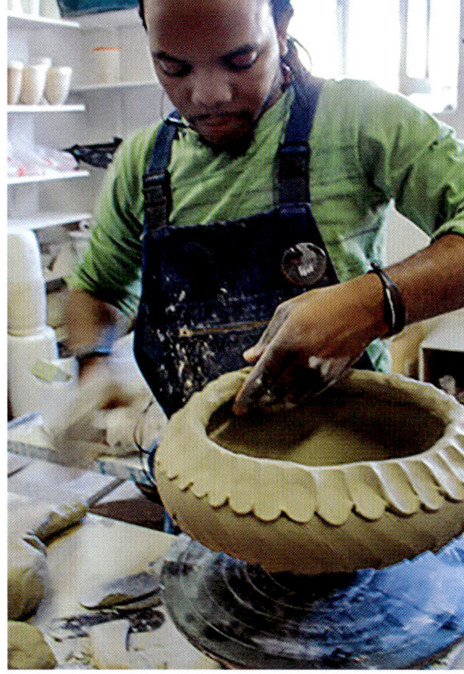

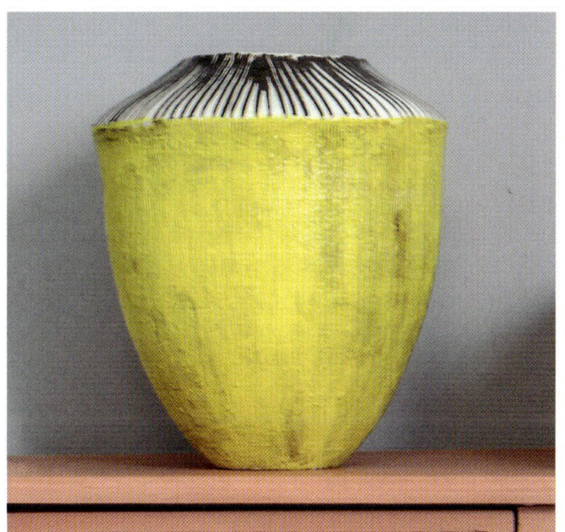

MY TREASURED OBJECTS IMISO CERAMICS

"I was knocked out by the unique surface decoration that's inspired by African tradition but feels so fresh"

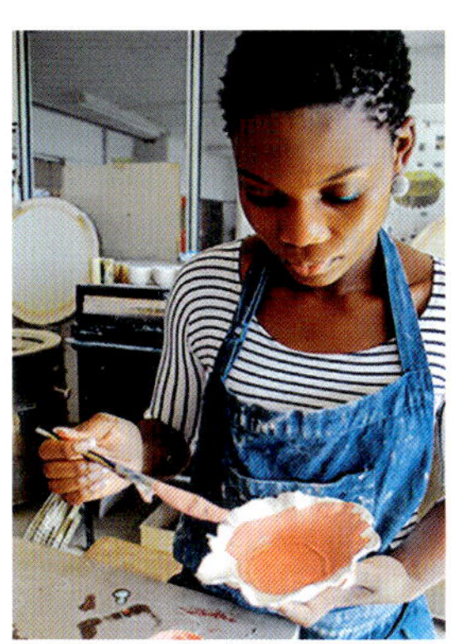

It was two years ago whilst on a visit to the creative hub at the Old Biscuit Mill in Cape Town, South Africa, that I first discovered Imiso Ceramics. I was instantly knocked out by the creativity and skill that founders, Andile Dyalvane and Zizipho Poswa pour into each piece. I'm holding a pot I bought made by Andile. He grew up in rural Transkei before studying ceramic design in Cape Town.

My pot bears the distinctive marks that are inspired by his Xhosa ancestor's face-cutting tradition of scarification. Though no longer practised, he uses it as an aesthetic motif in his Scarified Collection. My vase almost looks as if it's made of wood with its signature marks and bold red highlights. Definitely one of my treasured objects! AS

www.imisoceramics.co.za *@imisoceramics*

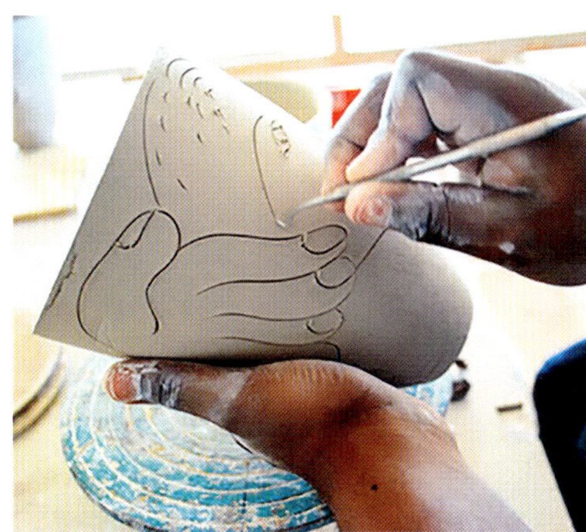

Top Andile Dyalvane at work in the Imiso Ceramics studio, pinching a hand-decorated bowl before glazing and firing

Middle Annie also couldn't resist buying this stunning yellow and black pot by Imiso Ceramics' co-founder Zizipho Poswa (left)

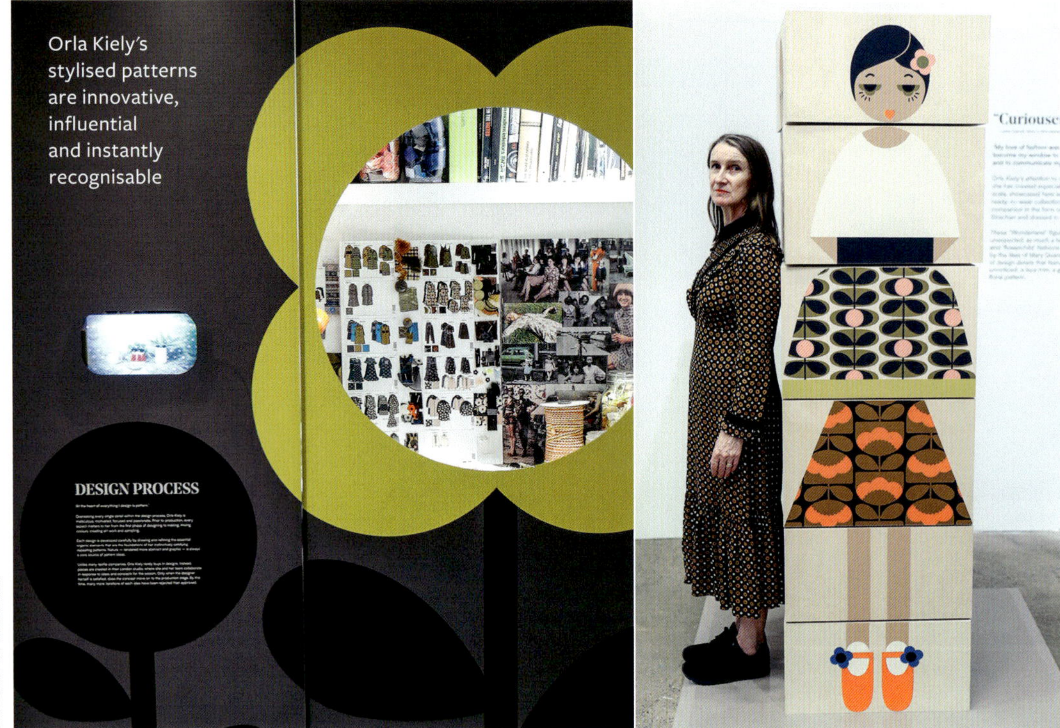

PHOTOGRAPHS: MAX CISOTTI

PLACES TO GO, THINGS TO SEE...

Our fantastic Annie Sloan Stockists around the world have given us the heads-up on the events they recommend for creative inspiration

UK

Orla Kiely: A Life in Pattern

Fashion and Textile Museum, London

UNTIL 23RD SEPTEMBER 2018

With her stylised graphic designs featured on everything from mugs and notebooks to dresses and cars, Orla Kiely is one of the UK and Ireland's most successful designers with a global reach.

www.ftmlondon.org

USA

Country Living Fairs

Columbus, Ohio

14TH – 16TH SEPTEMBER 2018

Atlanta, Georgia

26TH – 28TH OCTOBER 2018

Discover the most talented craftspeople and artisans. Great shopping, seminars, demonstrations and delicious food.

www.countryliving.com

Renegade

Detroit

15TH – 16TH SEPTEMBER 2018

The world's largest curated showcase of independent craft and design. Featuring hundreds of makers, interactive elements, inspired locales, artisanal food and great music in an al fresco street market.

www.renegadecraft.com

AUSTRALIA

Polly Borland

NGV Melbourne

28TH SEPTEMBER 2018 – 3RD FEBRUARY 2019

New and recent works by celebrated Australian artist Polly Borland, known for her photographs of noted figures including Queen Elizabeth II, Nick Cave and Gwendolyn Christie.

www.ngv.vic.gov.au

Masters of modern art from the Hermitage

Art Gallery of NSW, Sydney

13TH OCTOBER 2018 – 3RD MARCH 2019

Drawn from The State Hermitage Museum in St Petersburg, this exhibition features paintings by many of the towering figures of modern art, including Cézanne, Matisse, Picasso, Gauguin and Kandinsky.

www.artgallery.nsw.gov.au/exhibitions/hermitage

Between Two Worlds | Escher x Nendo

NGV Melbourne

2ND DECEMBER 2018 – 7TH APRIL 2019

Blockbuster Australian exhibition featuring the work of Dutch artist M.C. Escher in dialogue with the work of acclaimed Japanese design studio nendo. This exhibition creates an immersive show that seamlessly presents the worlds of both artists.

www.ngv.vic.gov.au

GERMANY

Festival of Light and Colour Berlin

Berlin

5TH – 14TH OCTOBER 2018

Every year Berlin turns into a city full of light art . International artists create installations and light displays on the famous landmarks, monuments, buildings and places.

www.festival-of-lights.de/en

FRANCE

Cubism

Pompidou Centre

17TH OCTOBER 2018 – 25TH FEBRUARY 2019

The Pompidou Centre explores the experimental and collective nature of the movement and brings together over 300 works by Cubist artists such as Picasso, Braque, Derain, Delaunay, Léger and Duchamp.

www.centrepompidou.fr/en

Maison et Object

Paris

7TH – 11TH SEPTEMBER 2018

18TH – 22ND JANUARY 2019

Professional trade fair dedicated to lifestyle, decoration and design.

www.maison-objet.com

Grayson Perry

The Monnaie de Paris

19TH OCTOBER 2018 - 3RD FEBRUARY 2019

British artist Grayson Perry works in traditional materials such as ceramics, bronze, cast iron, printmaking and tapestry, offering a darkly humorous look at identity, gender, class, religion and sexuality.

www.monnaiedeparis.fr

POLAND

Warsaw Home

Ptak Expo, Warsaw

4TH - 7TH OCTOBER 2018

Warsaw Home showcases the latest international interior and furniture designs, alongside decorative and accessories trends. With five halls and 800 exhibitors, it's the biggest interiors expo in Central Europe.

www.warsawhome.eu/en

Hand Made Days

Lodz, Poland

30TH NOVEMBER – 2ND DECEMBER 2018

A new show for lovers of interior design handicrafts, DIY and upcycling. Meet the experts, shop and take part in painting, decoupage, upholstery, restoration, sewing, cooking and carpentry workshops.

www.handmadedays.pl

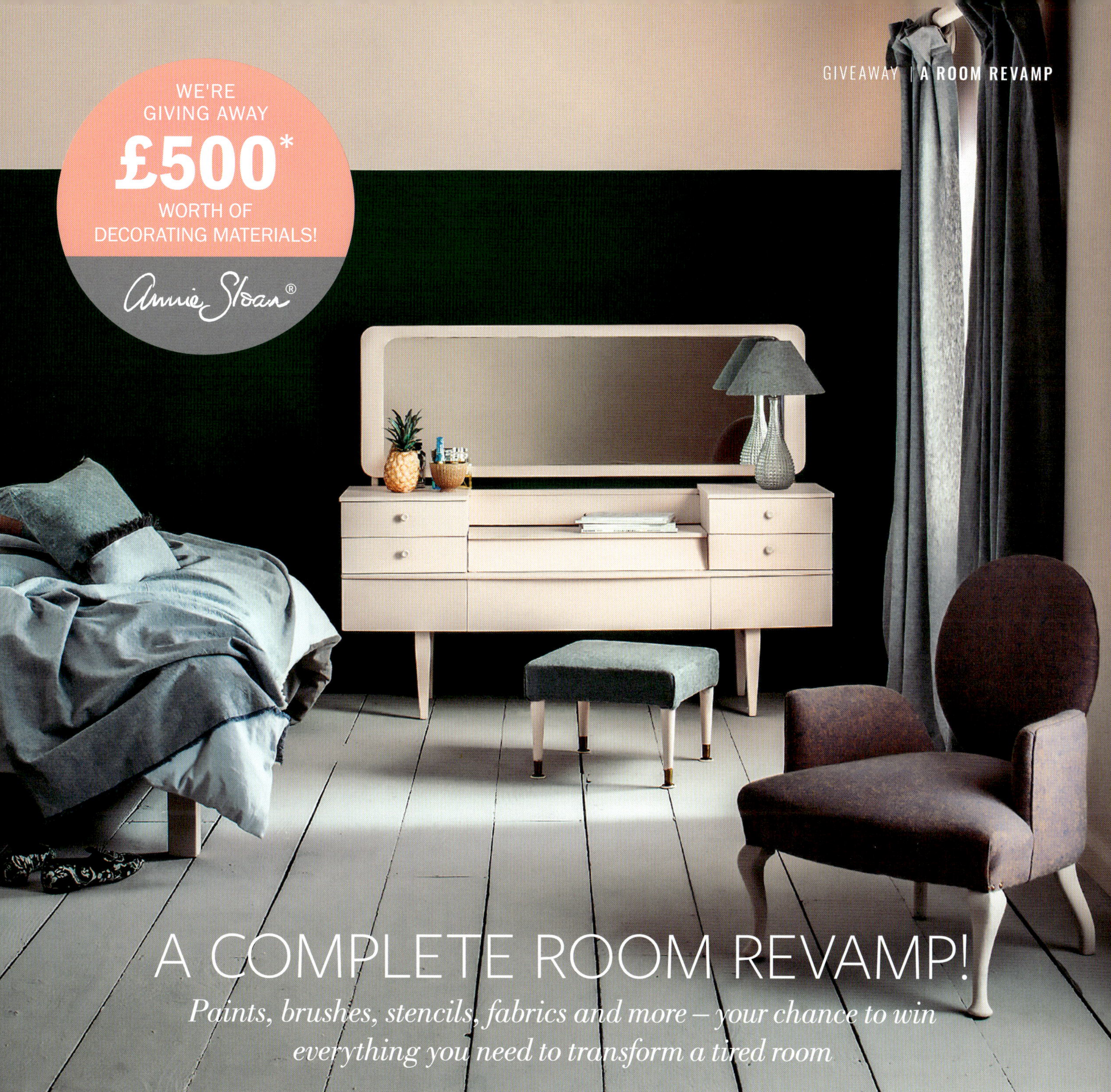

A COMPLETE ROOM REVAMP!

Paints, brushes, stencils, fabrics and more – your chance to win everything you need to transform a tired room

We're giving away everything you need to give your home an update! One lucky reader will receive everything they need to get creative with their interior, from the paints and brushes to fabrics and finishing touches.

They can choose from the Annie Sloan range of Wall Paints®, which leave walls with a luxurious semi-matt finish. For furniture, Chalk Paint®, available in 37 shades, is perfect and needs no prior sanding or priming. And for your soft furnishings, you can choose from Prints, Tickings and Linen Unions, each available in a range of colours to match the paints.

The lucky recipient will also receive a host of tools and accessories to help complete their transformation, including brushes, Clear and Dark Chalk Paint® Wax for different paint finishes and a choice of stencils. AS

HOW TO ENTER

Enter online at *www.anniesloan.com/thecolouristcompetition* Competition closes at midnight on December 31st 2018. The giveaway recipient will be chosen at random after this date and time. For full competition terms and conditions, please visit *www.anniesloan.com*

*or equivalent value in your country where supply will determine products available.

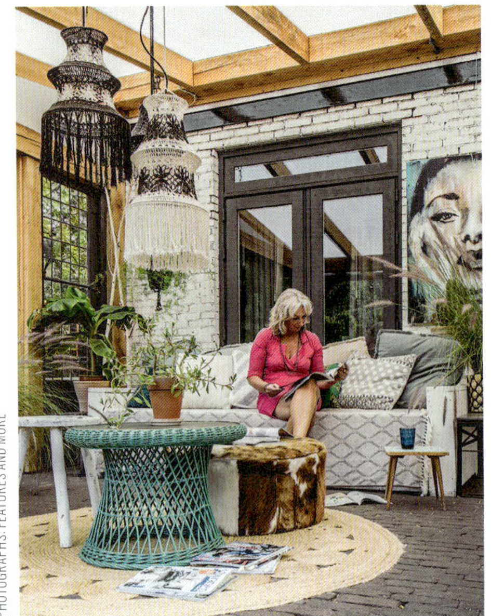

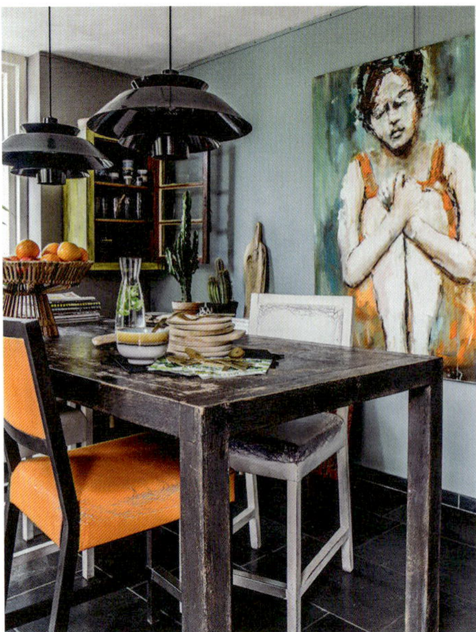

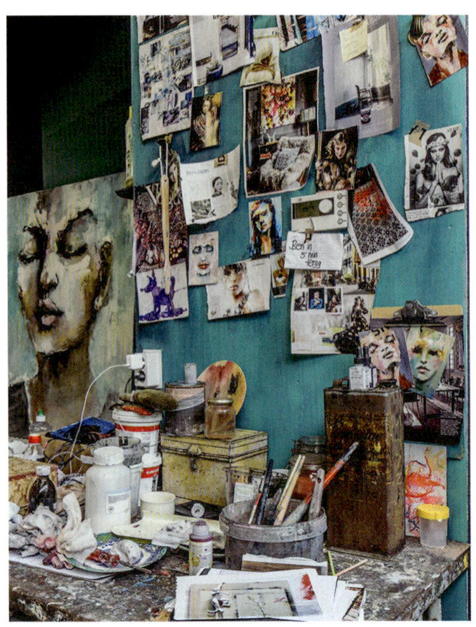

PHOTOGRAPHS: FEATURES AND MORE

Yvon van Bergen

LIVING IN COLOUR

Annie Sloan Stockist and artist, Yvon van Bergen, shares her passion for vibrant colour in her portraits, workshops and life

Tell us a little about where you live
I live in a detached house from 1900 in the town of Gennep in the upper southeastern Netherlands. The town lies at the confluence of the rivers Niers and Meuse, and is known for its old town hall, which dates from around 1620. In the year 2000 a pair of storks settled on one of the chimneys of the town hall, and they return to Gennep each summer to rear their young. I share my house with my husband Bart. We have three children: sons Rik van, 26 and Buck van, 24; and daughter René van, 21.

What is your daily routine?
I'm an early bird. I love to be up before everyone else. There's a lot of nature and greenery in the area. The peace, the silence, a wonderful walk with my two dachshunds all provide space in my head. Every day is different. I'm someone who needs something new, so I'm constantly looking for fresh initiatives.

What inspires you to be creative ?
Creativity is in my DNA. I'm very busy with all the things around me, and painting brings everything into equilibrium. That balance between the hectic and restful works well for me. Inspiration can come to me from anywhere and anything: from museums, galleries, my family, the environment, a meeting with women with ambition, attending a fashion show. But also simply sitting on a terrace can give me an idea for new work.

Describe your Annie Sloan store to us
My shop is my 'inspiration house'. I'm constantly changing the interior, so that there's something new for people to see each time they visit me. I replace the colours, furniture and accessories a number of times a year, which is challenging but so much fun to achieve! It's wonderful if the total picture is right and your house is completely in line with you.

Why is it important to decorate a home with colour?
Colour has always had a place in my life – everywhere lies the beauty of shapes and colour for the taking; you just have to look at it with a certain eye. Everybody deserves colour! Without a doubt, colour affects your mood – it always brightens me up.

As a professional colour specialist, I give advice to my clients. Most of them take photographs of their houses and furnishings so that I get a picture of their style; sometimes I visit people in their homes. I also work with companies – »

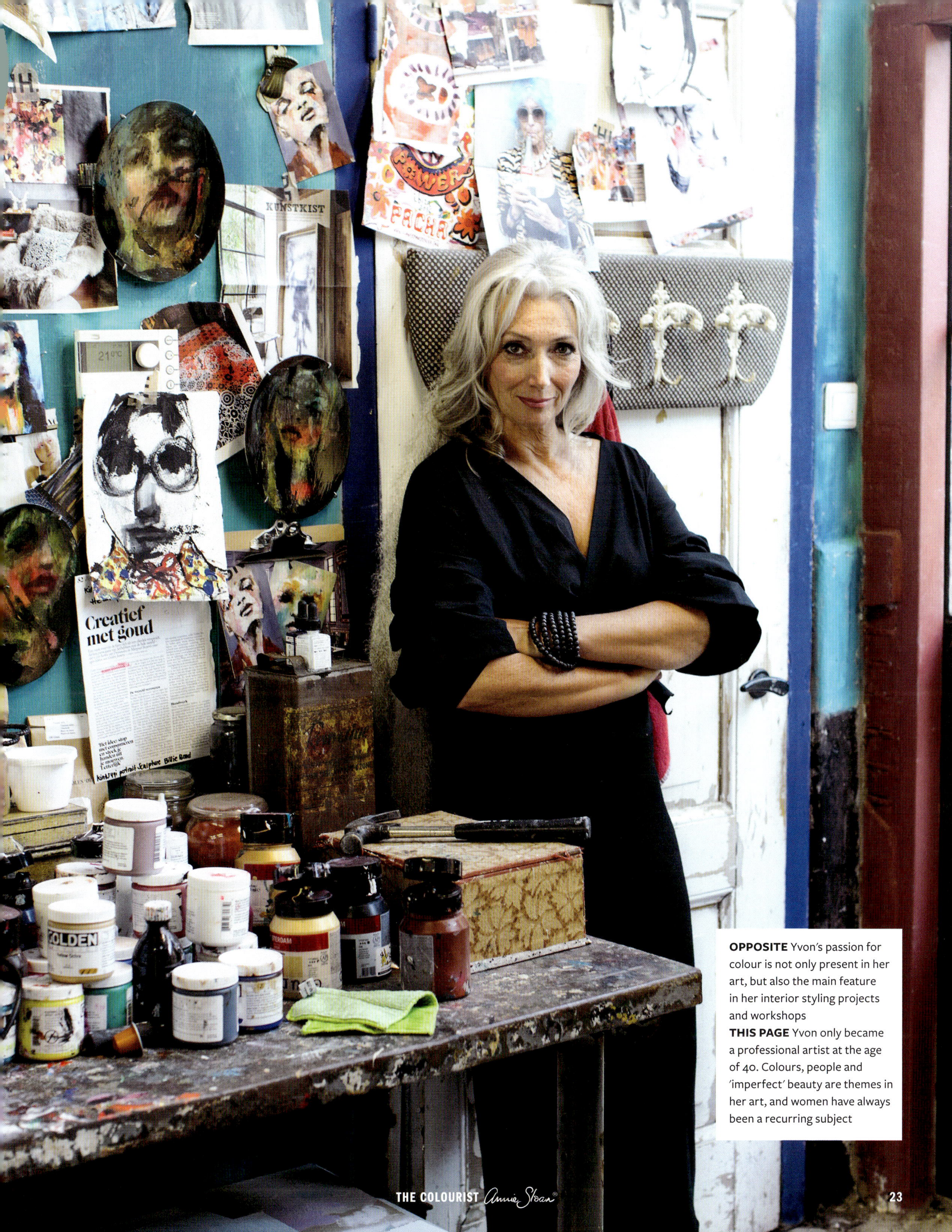

OPPOSITE Yvon's passion for colour is not only present in her art, but also the main feature in her interior styling projects and workshops
THIS PAGE Yvon only became a professional artist at the age of 40. Colours, people and 'imperfect' beauty are themes in her art, and women have always been a recurring subject

for instance, I've just finished a fun project creating a colour scheme for a women-only gym.

Tell us about your Annie Sloan workshop and the tour of your studio and home that's included
During the tours of my house I often get the remark, "You have so many different colours in your house" and, yes, it's true. I choose colours very consciously. After all, it's nice when paint can improve your furniture or colour can transform your space. It's such a powerful tool. And by playing with colour in your home, you can make spaces more personal.

What is your process when painting a portrait?
I usually go to my studio in Nijmegen. When I start painting a portrait, I listen to music – the kind of music doesn't matter to me, as long as I can express myself through dance or singing while I paint. I let the brushes dance across the canvas. My strength lies in the speed of painting, a few strokes and then I stop.

Most of my work is portraits of women, and I use layers in my art through collage, combined with realism and abstraction. I use a palette knife, and the sharp lines of the knife sometimes tear the paper and create cracks. These represent torn personalities and fragmentation. The subject is profound, but at the same time the work has a playful feel through the different techniques, colour and forms that I use.

For my mixed-media art, I first paint a portrait on canvas, photograph the painting, paint the print and then customise it with collage to create the final artwork. Recently I've also produced a series of limited-edition fine art prints made from original artworks.

Yvon's living room is painted using Chalk Paint® in Primer Red. "A beautiful colour. Almost velvety and a nice contrast to the green of the plants."

PHOTOGRAPHS: FEATURES AND MORE

What is the inspiration behind your latest paintings?
Each series of paintings has a theme, which originates from things that I experience unconsciously or see in daily life. In my series, 'Girls with a Yellow & Red Circle', which hangs in Stockholm and Amsterdam, I wanted to create something totally different, but stay true to myself. Each portrait has a yellow or red circle on it. The inspiration for this motif was Iris Apfel, the American interior designer and fashion icon, who's famous for her oversized round glasses and colourful jewellery.

How do you create space in your busy life?
Entrepreneurship is really my thing, but I have to make sure that I'm not busy working day and night. That's why I have other outlets. At the moment I'm working hard on my mind, body and soul by taking a more enthusiastic approach to sports. I do Pilates, yoga and occasionally I stand by a friend on the vibrating plate exerciser to shake everything! I get a lot of inspiration during a brisk walk early in the morning. That works very well for me. I also love cooking and eating, good wines and going on holiday to special places.

Tell us about your new online portrait class
Over the years I've been asked to teach people art but I've always said no because I paint so intuitively, and I felt that it was too hard to explain to students. Yet the idea remained at the back of my mind and after meeting life coach, Caroline van de Kamp, I finally decided to hatch a plan for a painting course. My brain is now activated, and the time is right! I've created a one-on-one online course called Intuitive Portrait Painting. I already have an enthusiastic group of people who follow the course, and we all have a playful approach to our art. This playful side of us absolutely needs space to grow and I know the perfect way to realise it! AS

Exhibitions AAF Stockholm 11th - 14th October 2018
AAF Amsterdam 31st October - 4th November 2018
www.yvonvanbergen.nl @yvonvanbergen

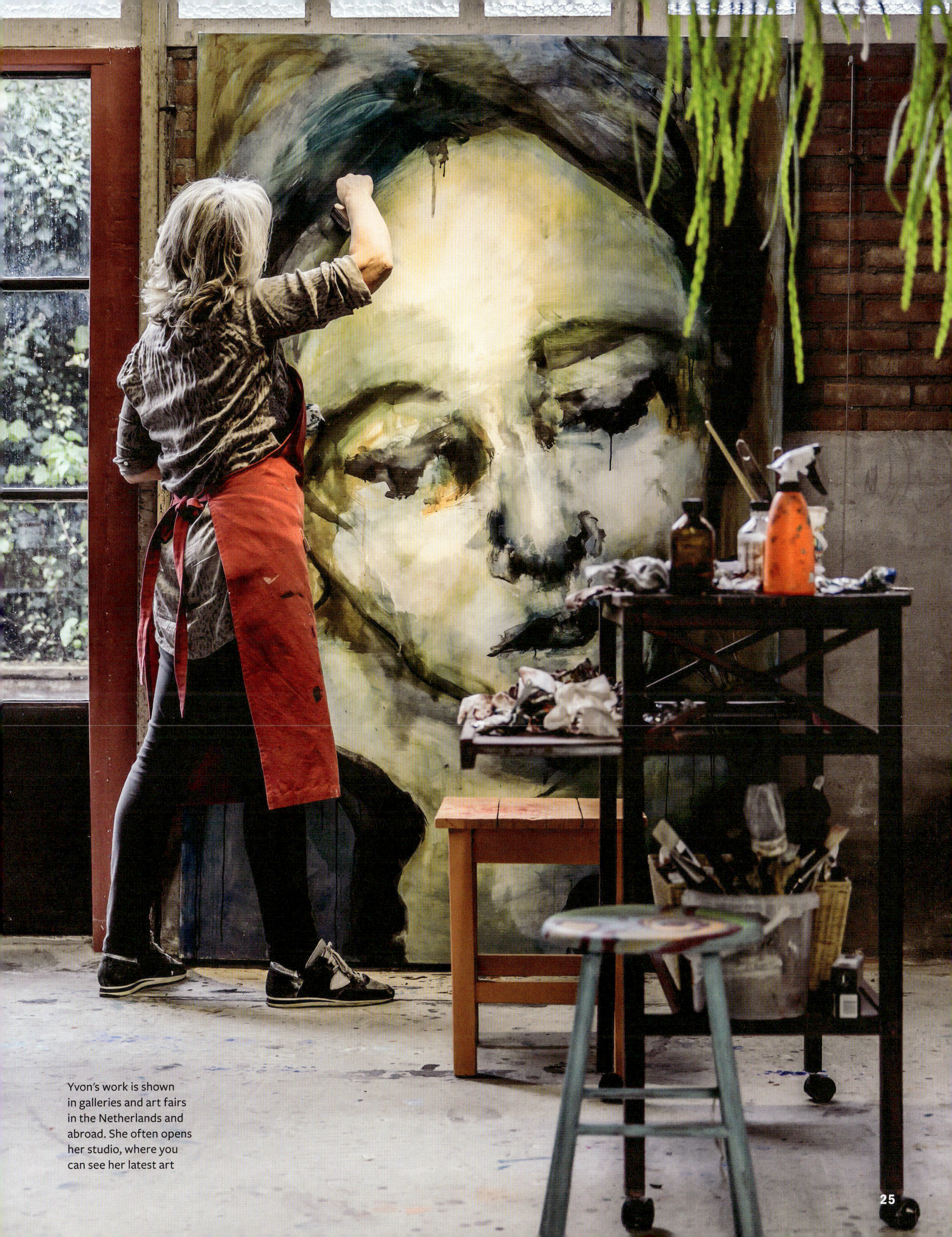

Yvon's work is shown in galleries and art fairs in the Netherlands and abroad. She often opens her studio, where you can see her latest art

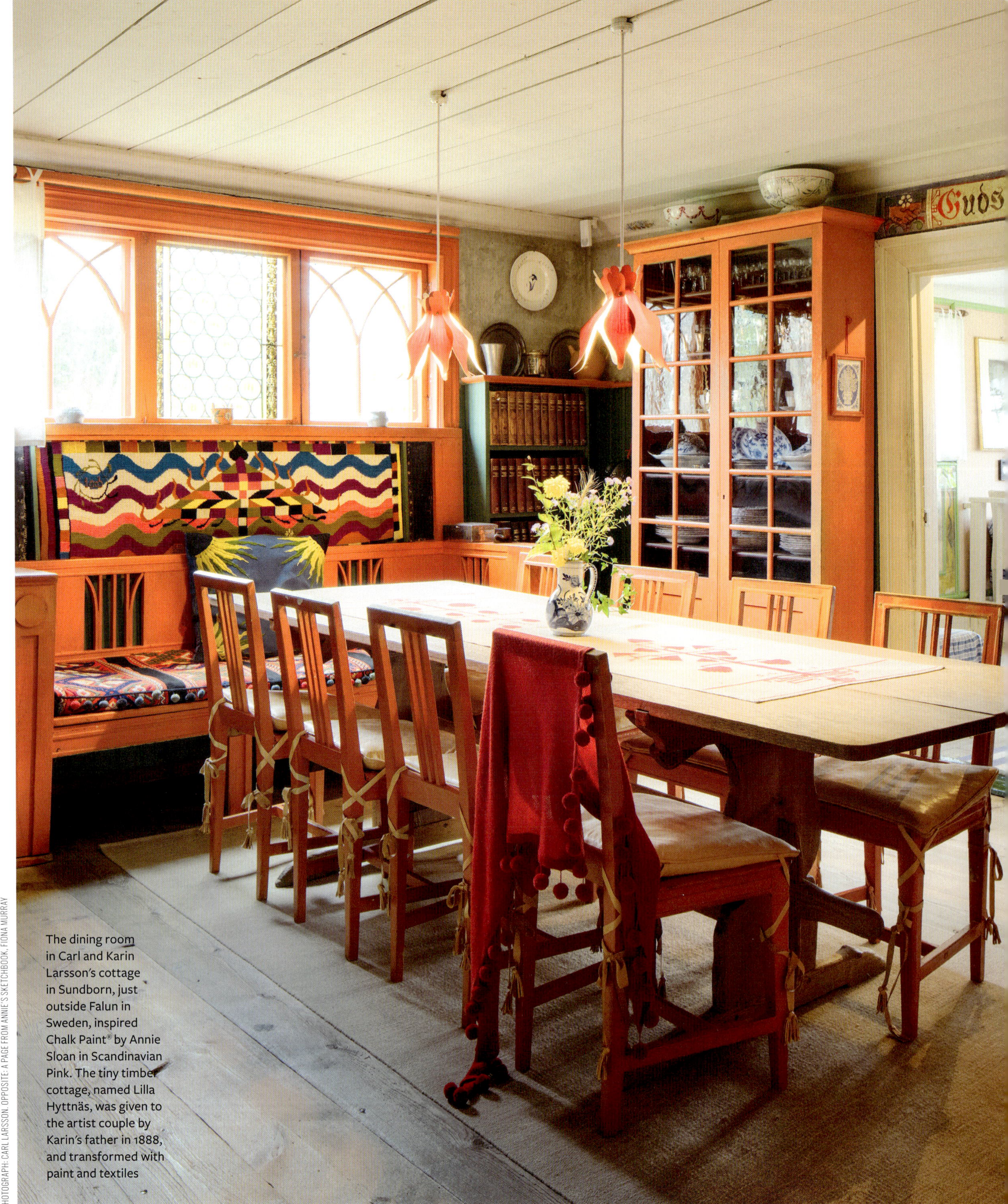

The dining room in Carl and Karin Larsson's cottage in Sundborn, just outside Falun in Sweden, inspired Chalk Paint® by Annie Sloan in Scandinavian Pink. The tiny timber cottage, named Lilla Hyttnäs, was given to the artist couple by Karin's father in 1888, and transformed with paint and textiles

PHOTOGRAPH: CARL LARSSON. OPPOSITE: A PAGE FROM ANNIE'S SKETCHBOOK. FIONA MURRAY

Scandinavian Pink

COLOUR STORY

Annie explains the fascinating history behind one of the most versatile paint shades

Mix Scandinavian Pink and Henrietta.

Chalk Paint® by Annie Sloan in Scandinavian Pink was inspired by the colour found in much traditional Swedish furniture. I was first introduced to the colour through the work of Carl Larsson, the 19th century Swedish painter. He looked to traditional Swedish decoration and folk art for his inspiration, often using a colour made from a local pigment called Falun red, a potent red brown ochre/iron oxide earth mixed with copper from the local mines. He would add various quantities of white to make it softer and used it extensively in his house. Swedish houses continue to be painted in this colour, made according to the traditional recipe, using the local pigment mixed with rye flour and linseed oil.

Chalk Paint® in Primer Red – perfect underneath gilding – is similar to Falun. Add white to Primer Red and you have the origins of Chalk Paint® in Scandinavian Pink.

I love it because it is pink but not pink. It is earthy and dusky, yet the colour of a delicate sunset. It is warm, natural and mellow, but can look sophisticated.

I use it underneath pale neutrals like Paloma or Old White; sanding it back slightly around the edges to reveal just a hint of pink. It also works beautifully as a contrasting colour for the interior of cupboards and drawers paired with Aubusson Blue or Paris Grey. Mix with Henrietta to create a cooler shade and vibrant Barcelona Orange if you're looking for a shot of hot coral! AS

Paloma and White

Chalk Paint® in Primer Red is inspired by the original Swedish pigment of Falun red (also called Falu red)

Scandinavian Pink

IN YOUR HOME

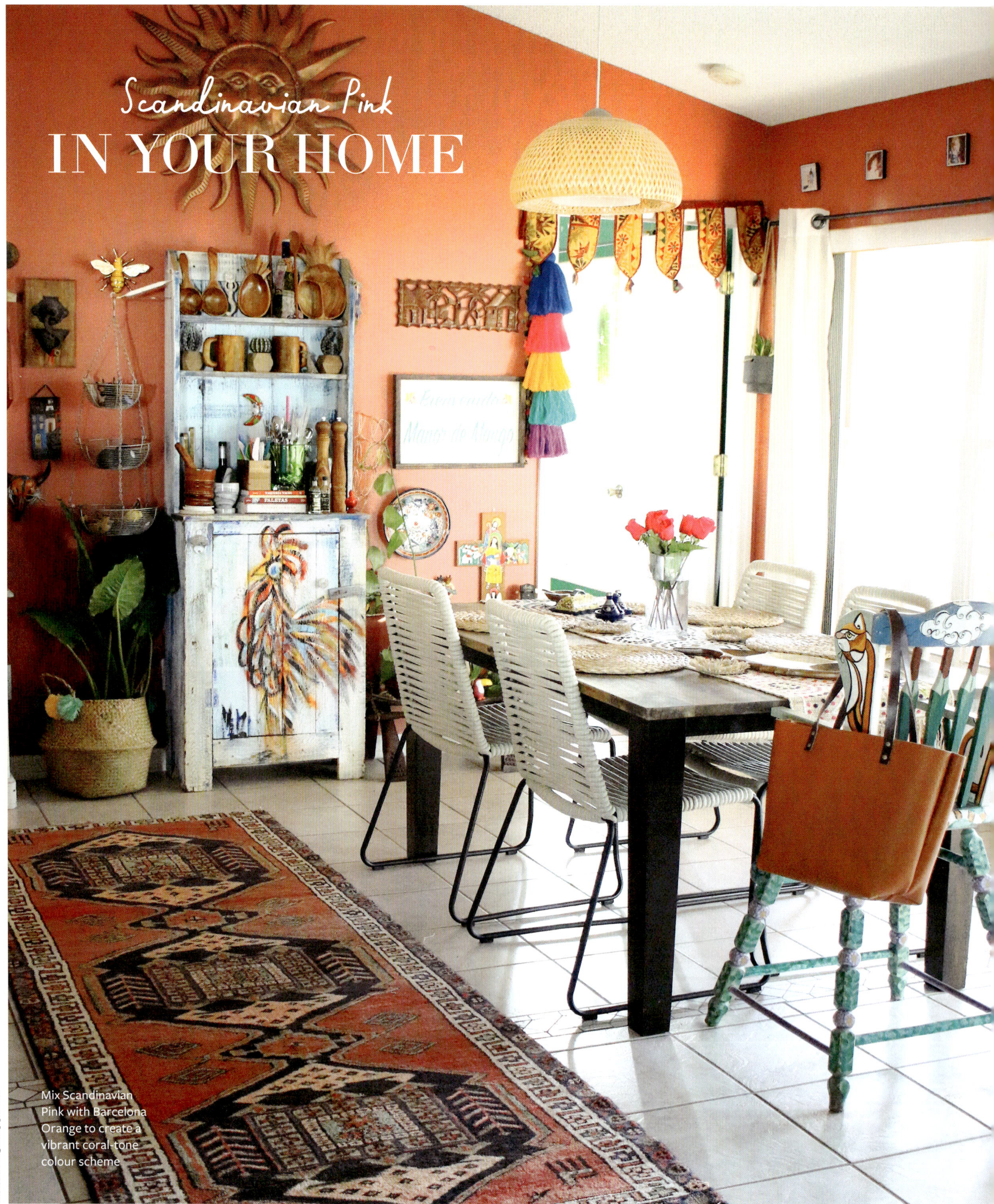

Mix Scandinavian Pink with Barcelona Orange to create a vibrant coral-tone colour scheme

PHOTOGRAPH: @KELLI_E_COLLINS

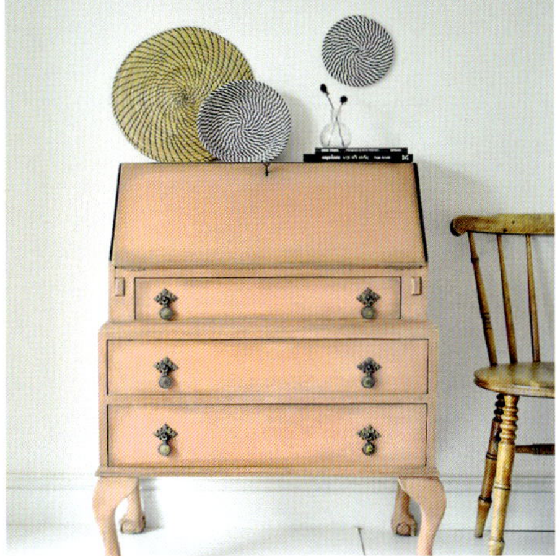

ABOVE This 1930s oak bureau was painted in Scandinavian Pink with hints of Graphite and a touch of Bright Gold Gilding Wax on the handles. It was then distressed and finished with a mix of Clear and Dark Wax to add depth

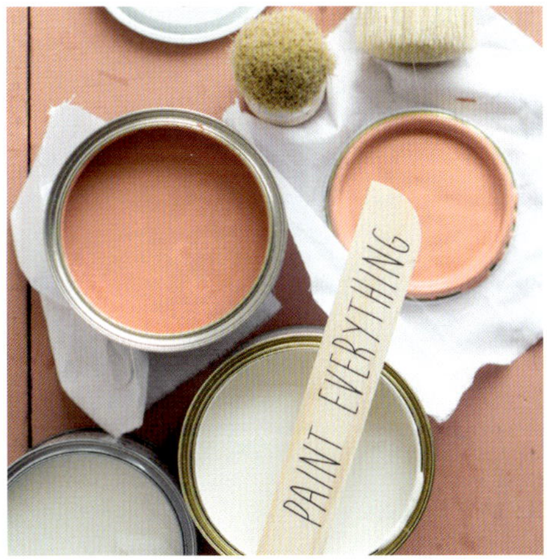

ABOVE "Both my Chalk Paint® and Waxes are completely toy and cot safe, which means you can use them freely to create wonderful, distinctive pieces to reflect all those wonderful, distinctive children in your life!"

For a seriously sophisticated look, try plaster-effect matt walls. Here Scandinavian Pink is mixed with Paloma to give a gorgeous, rough-luxe finish

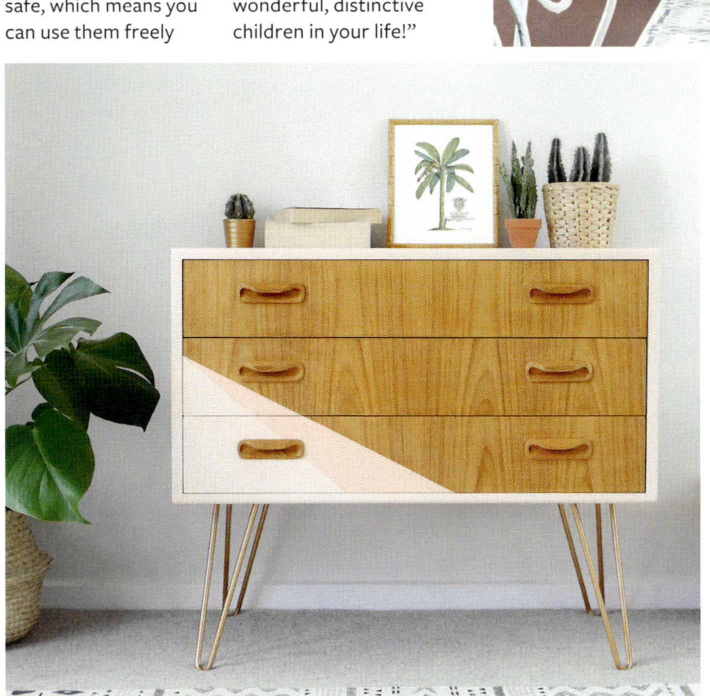

PHOTOGRAPH: ELIZABETHDOTDESIGN

LEFT Elizabeth of ElizabethDotDesign made her own colour by mixing Scandinavian Pink, Old White and English Yellow. She then waxed the bare wood with Clear Chalk Paint® Wax and added copper hairpin legs

Snap a photo and share your Scandinavian Pink projects using #AnnieSloan #ChalkPaint hashtags to share with your fellow Chalk Paint® fans, and for the chance to be featured on Annie Sloan's social media channels! @anniesloanhome

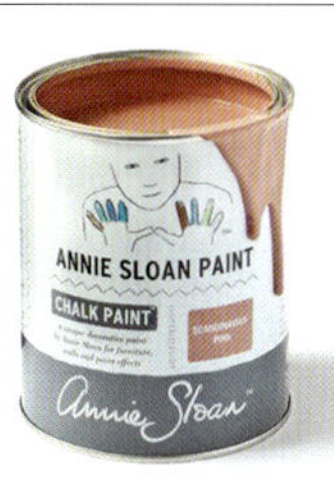

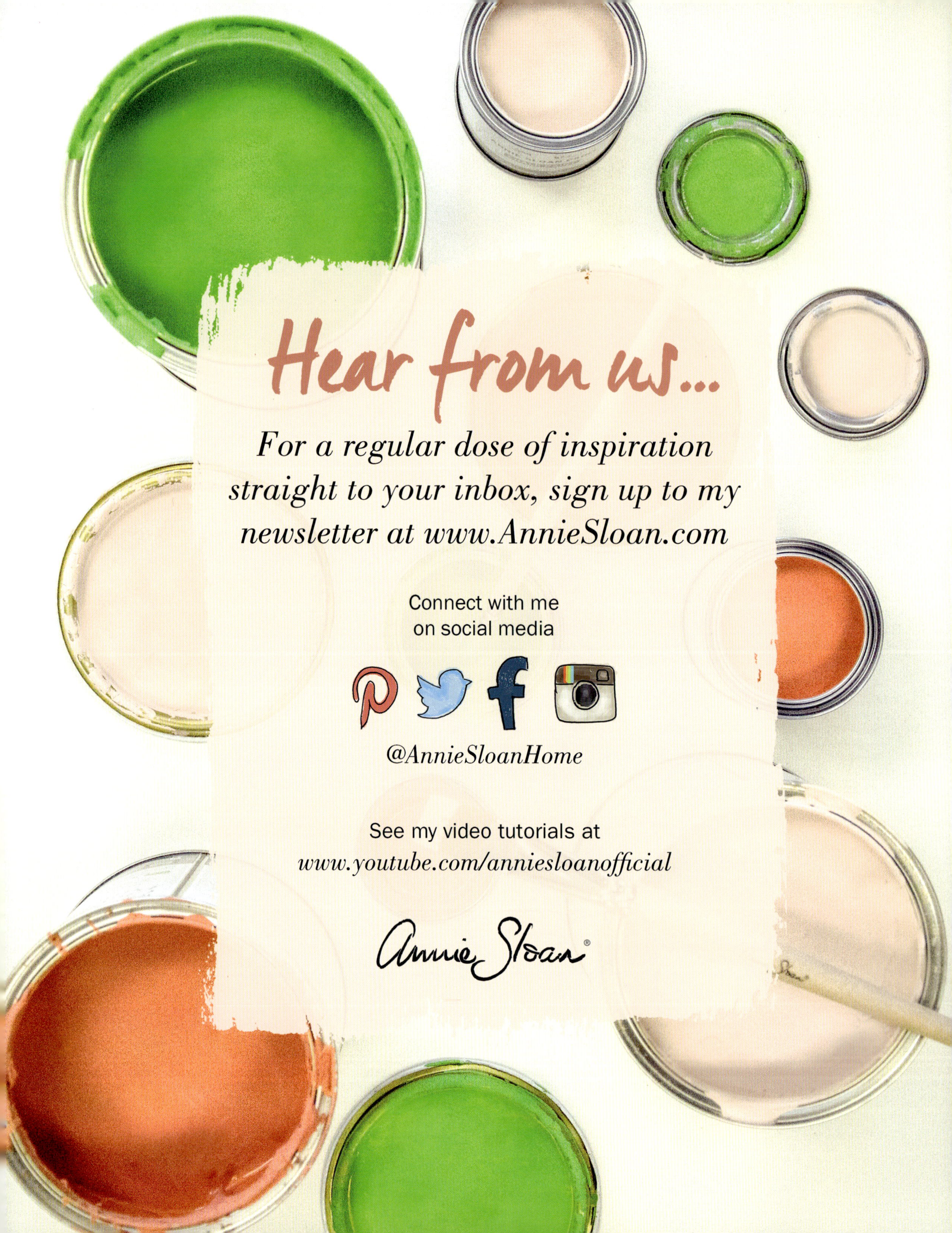
Hear from us...
For a regular dose of inspiration straight to your inbox, sign up to my newsletter at www.AnnieSloan.com
Connect with me on social media
@AnnieSloanHome
See my video tutorials at
www.youtube.com/anniesloanofficial
Annie Sloan®

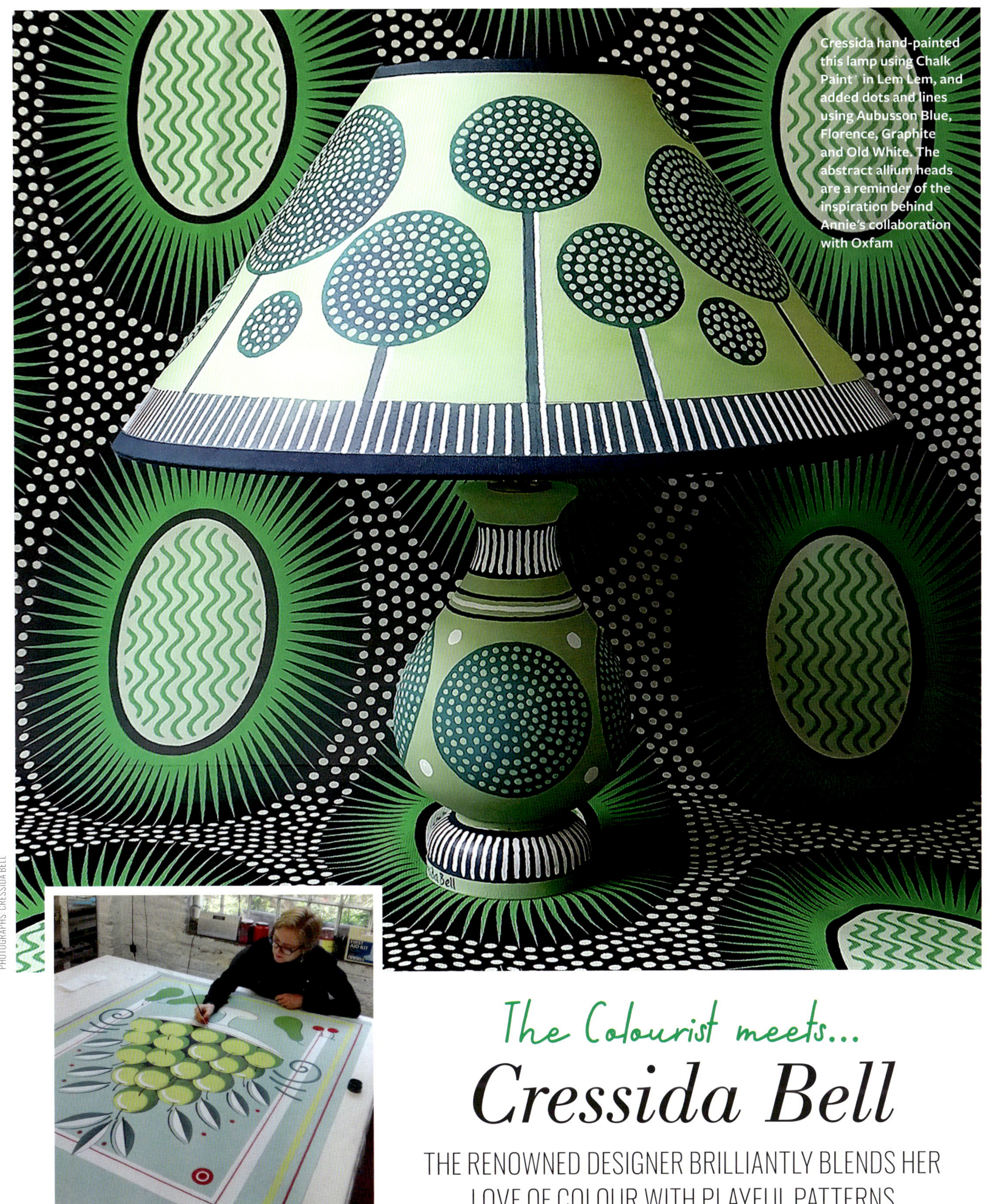

Cressida hand-painted this lamp using Chalk Paint® in Lem Lem, and added dots and lines using Aubusson Blue, Florence, Graphite and Old White. The abstract allium heads are a reminder of the inspiration behind Annie's collaboration with Oxfam

PHOTOGRAPHS: CRESSIDA BELL

The Colourist meets...

Cressida Bell

THE RENOWNED DESIGNER BRILLIANTLY BLENDS HER LOVE OF COLOUR WITH PLAYFUL PATTERNS

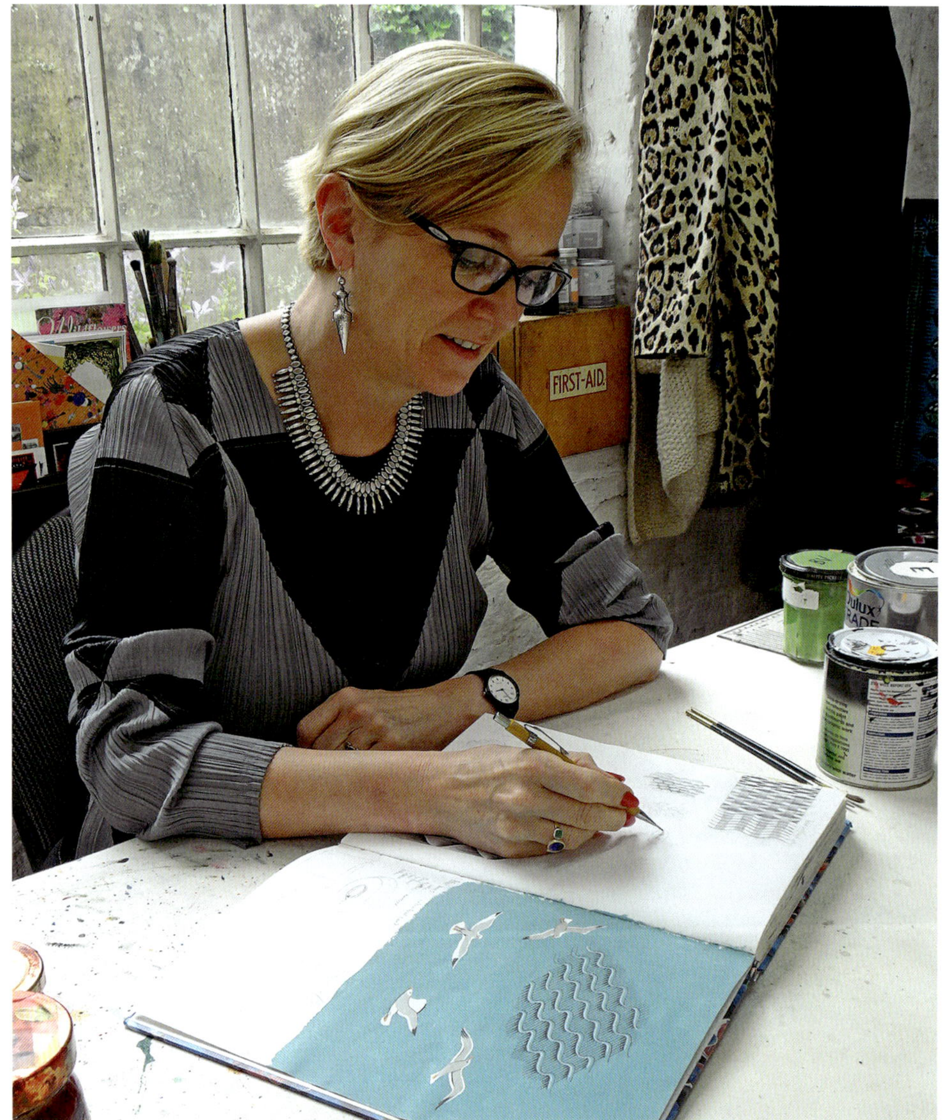

PHOTOGRAPHS: CRESSIDA BELL, I360

Artist and designer Cressida Bell has an impressive artistic family heritage. She's the daughter of critic and artist Quentin Bell, granddaughter of artist Vanessa Bell and great-niece of writer Virginia Woolf. Join us on a tour around her grandmother's home, Charleston, in England, UK, on page 48. The remote farmhouse became a hub for the Bloomsbury group of bohemian artists and writers.

Cressida studied fashion at St Martin's College, London and followed this with a master's degree, specialising in textiles, at the Royal College of Art. She went on to set up her own design studio in East London, UK, aged just 24.

She chatted to us about her design process and the role that colour plays in her life.

Does it irritate you to be referenced as Vanessa Bell's granddaughter?
It does happen often, but not enough to actually irritate me. I always hope that people will differentiate between my work and hers – we have very different strengths, but I would admit to having a colour sensibility which is informed by my heritage.

Describe your own design aesthetic
The most important aspect of my work is that it's about pattern, pure and simple. Even my illustrative work – such as my Christmas cards – is decorative and I try to bring an element of pattern whenever possible.

What are your design influences?
My influences are many and varied. I collect pottery and love the decorative motifs that can be found on ceramics. Turkish textiles and tiles are some of my favourites. The famous Chintamani design is so simple and yet so perfect. It's a hard thing to achieve – and something I aim for in my own work.

Tell us about your favourite books
I'm currently reading the blockbuster Sapiens by Yuval Noah Harari – fascinating. I think my favourite art book is a beautiful tome called Ipek by Nurhan Atasoy about

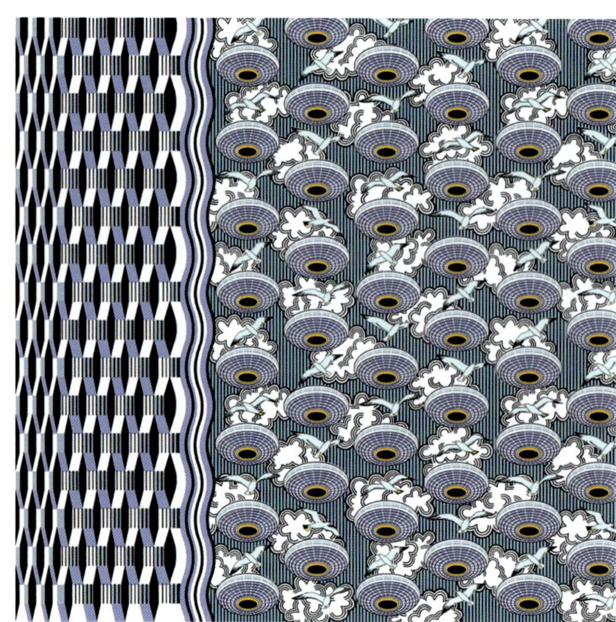

ABOVE Each project begins with doodles in her sketchbook: "I take a line for a walk, and gradually the design will take shape as it hits the sweet spot."

RIGHT The design for the British Airways i360 project in Brighton was inspired by the observation tower and the beautiful views that can be seen from the top of its glass viewing pod

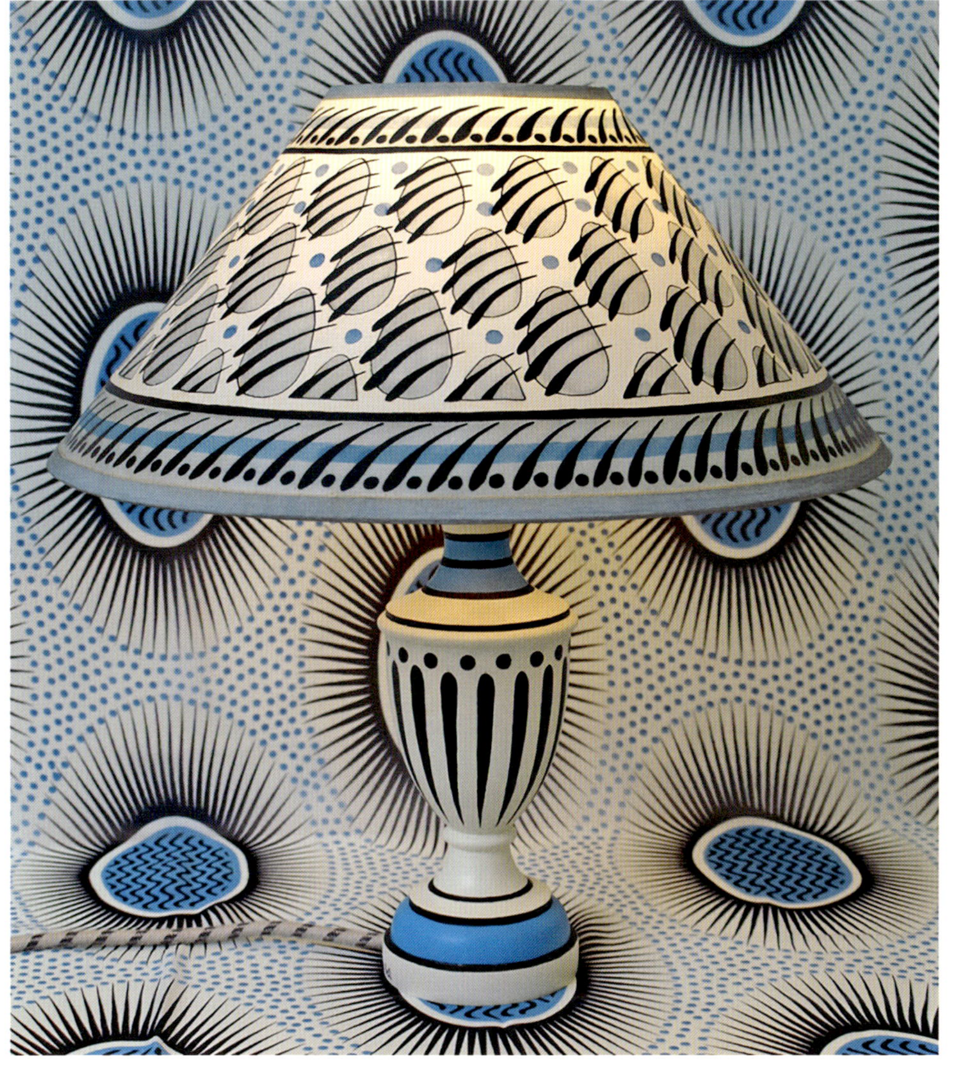

PHOTOGRAPHS: CRESSIDA BELL

LEFT "My Paw Print lamp and shade in cream and blue is one of my favourite designs. It looks pretty cool with the Eclipse print shawl in the background."

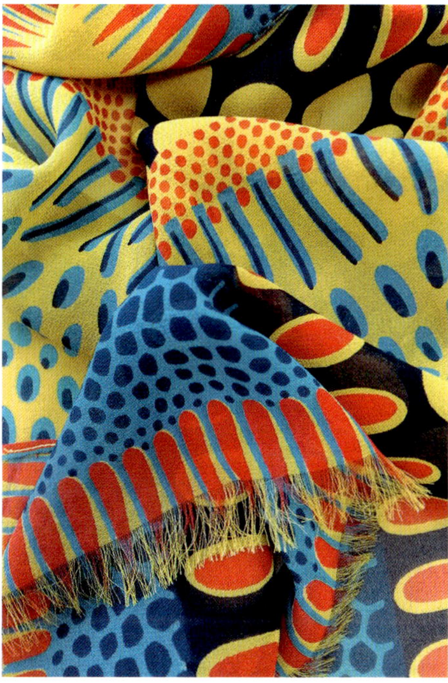

"Turkish textiles and tiles are some of my favourites. The famous Chintamani design is so simple and yet so perfect"

Ottoman textiles – with fabulous full-page illustrations of the Sultan's kaftans.

How are your printed textiles created?
My scarves and other textiles are screen-printed by hand. This means starting with white fabric, which is dyed and then pinned out onto our 10-metre print table. Each colour has a separate screen, which is printed by two people passing the dye through the screen with a squeegee. The colour needs to dry between each layer before the next colour is applied. Some colours 'discharge' the background colour, so you can print purple, red and green onto a black background. The fabric has to be steamed once the print is dry, which develops the colour. It's then cut up and washed to remove the binder and surplus dye. After ironing, the scarves are trimmed, fringed and then hemmed. A long process!

How do you approach a new commission, such as your bespoke design for British Airways i360 in Brighton?
I was approached by Julia Barfield, the architect of the i360, as she wanted some products to sell in the gift shop, and was keen on my Sussex connections (as well as my designs!). The brief was to produce a multilayered design that could be applied to a large variety of products. Initially I visited the i360 and took photos, then it was back to my studio and my sketchbook. I was asked to incorporate both the 'pod' itself and also seagulls into the design. I added clouds and a border representing the metallic mesh of the tower. All the ideas start off by being hand- drawn in my sketchbook and are then scanned into the computer and manipulated to form the final full-size repeat.

It ended up as a very complex design, but it's being used in a variety of ways – lapel-pins of the pod and a cloud, the seagulls alone on a tote bag and washbags in several coordinating versions of the design.

Who are your Instagram favourites?
I follow around 900 Instagram accounts. I seem to gravitate towards rather bookish accounts like Illustration Magazine »

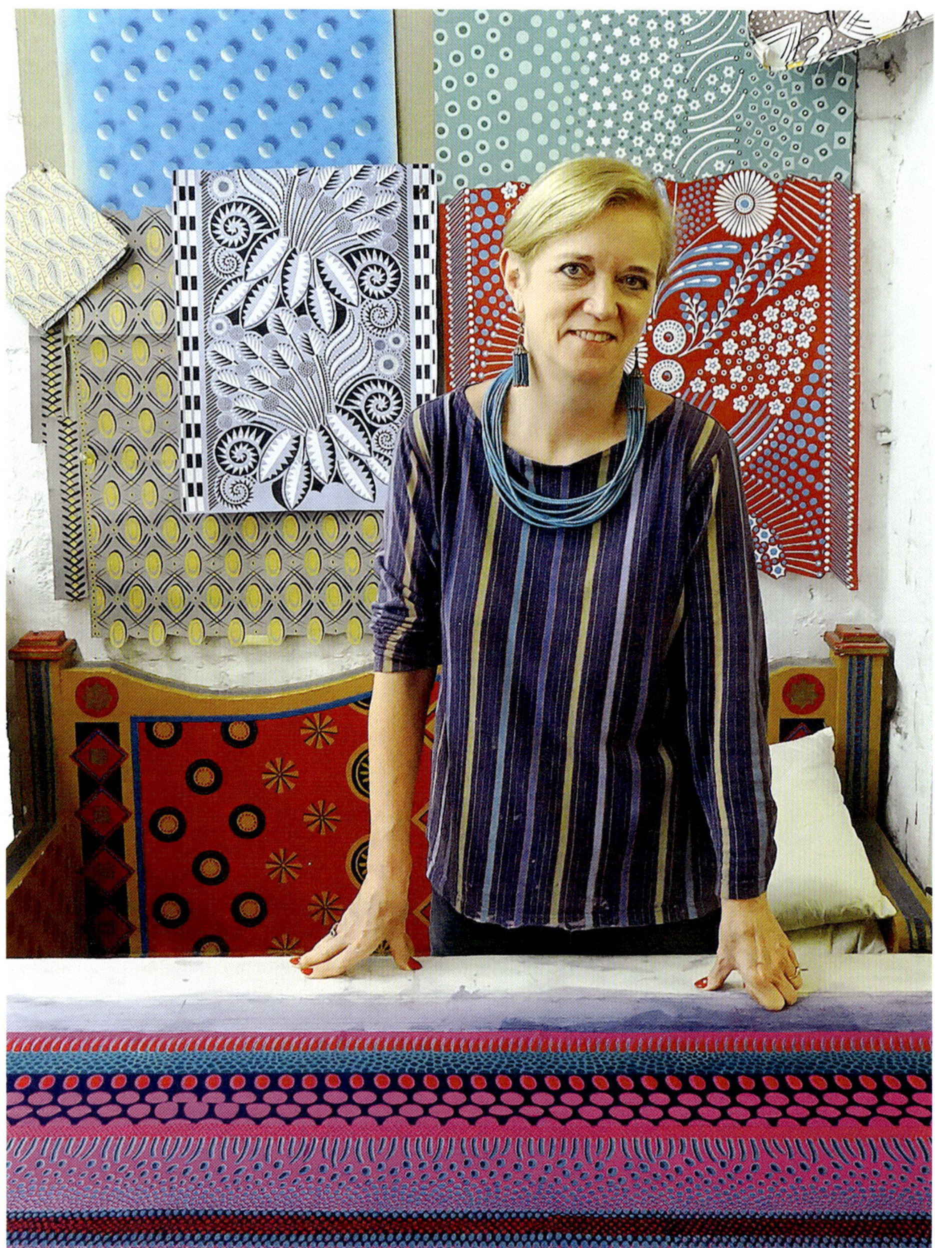

PHOTOGRAPHS: CRESSIDA BELL

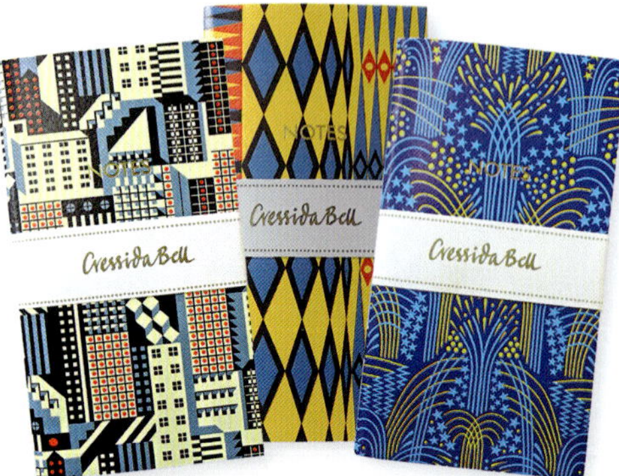

Cressida's range of stationery includes notebooks, writing sets, and cards in her signature designs

(@illustration.magazine), The Silver Locket (@the_silver_locket) and Sotheran's (@sotherans_piccadilly); printmakers like Christopher Brown Lino (@christopher brownlino), and Jane Walker (@janewalker printmaker); other textile designers, such as N&N Wares (@nandnwares), Annabel Grey (@annabel.grey) and Kiran Ravilious (@kiran_ravilious). Alex May Hughes (@alexmayhughes) is fab, as are David Herbert (@itstartedwithajug), Blackout Shop (@blackout_shop_brighton) and, of course, my sister Virginia Nicholson and brother Julian Bell.

Cressida creates around 50 silk scarves a month. "Nobody quite believes that I fringe my own scarves at home, but I find it quite therapeutic!"

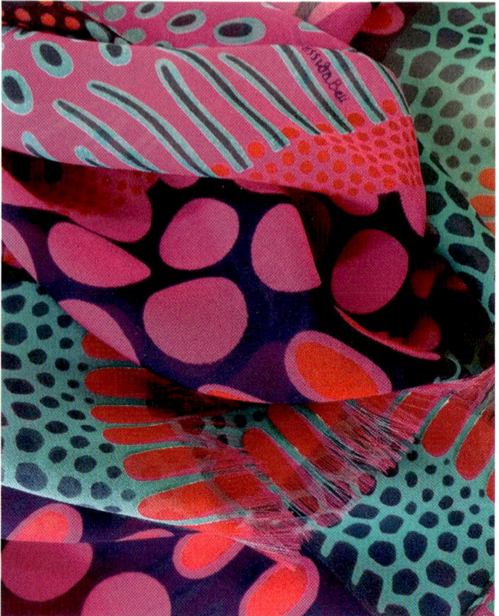

Is your home colourful?

My home is definitely colourful! From the top down: I have a spare bedroom painted pink with a red carpet; a bedroom with 6-inch stripes in apricot and grey blue; a yellow bathroom; a sitting room/study in a mauvey grey with an orange carpet; a turquoise, royal blue, cream and red kitchen; and, finally, a shocking pink front door!

Along with all these colours, there are plenty of patterned rugs, curtains, ceramics and other ornaments. My favourite colour is red but, for my living space, I tend to choose something different. The mauve and orange in my sitting room is a current favourite.

What new projects are coming up?

A new line for Burford Garden Company – trays, aprons, oven gloves and stationery. Charleston have a rug of mine for sale and I've designed another one which we hope to put into production soon. I have my ongoing relationship with Museums & Galleries who will be producing a new range of my Christmas cards and gift wrap this autumn. I also have a couple of courses coming up – a lampshade-painting masterclass at my Hackney studio in September and a cake-decorating class at Charleston before Christmas 2018. AS

www.cressidabell.co.uk *@Cressidabell*

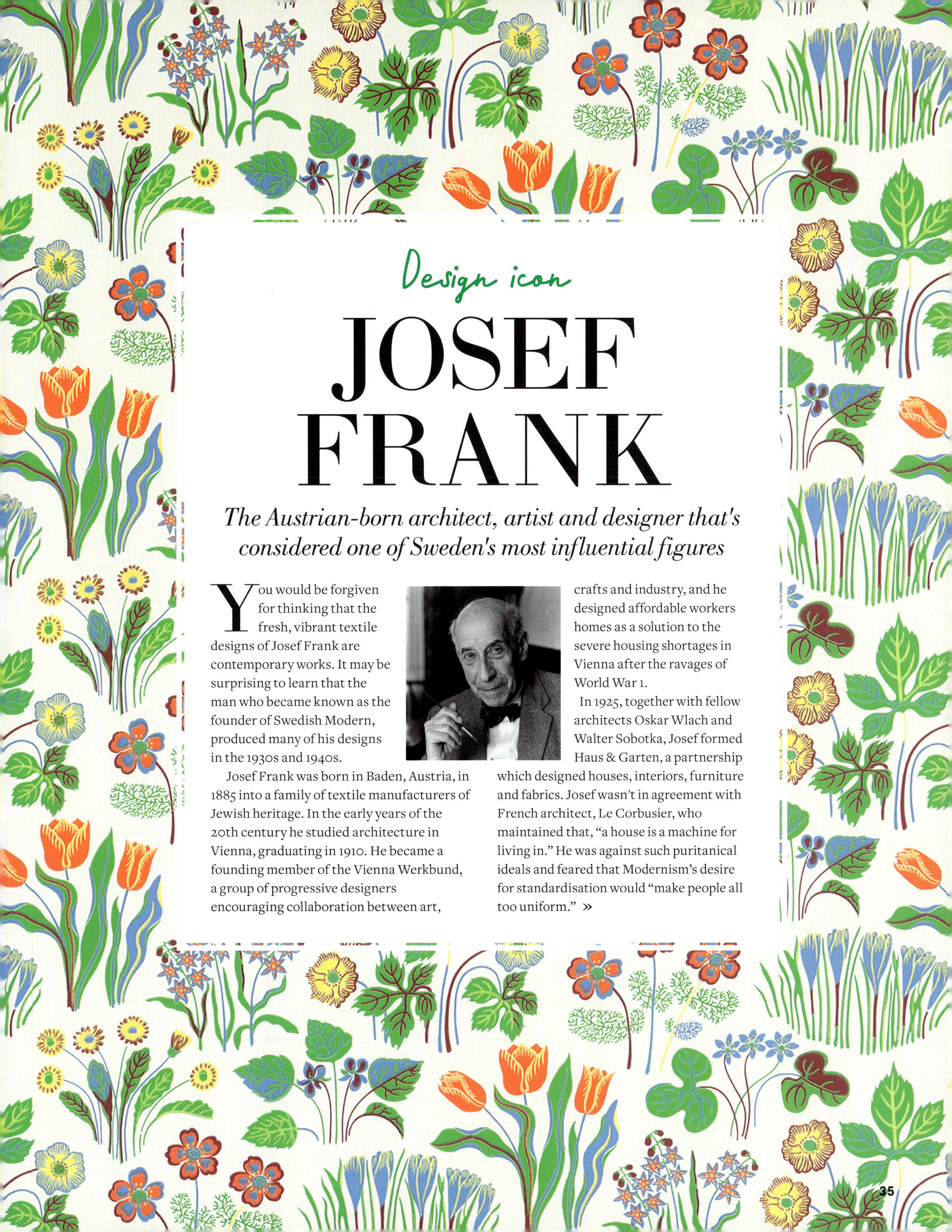

Design icon

JOSEF FRANK

The Austrian-born architect, artist and designer that's considered one of Sweden's most influential figures

You would be forgiven for thinking that the fresh, vibrant textile designs of Josef Frank are contemporary works. It may be surprising to learn that the man who became known as the founder of Swedish Modern, produced many of his designs in the 1930s and 1940s.

Josef Frank was born in Baden, Austria, in 1885 into a family of textile manufacturers of Jewish heritage. In the early years of the 20th century he studied architecture in Vienna, graduating in 1910. He became a founding member of the Vienna Werkbund, a group of progressive designers encouraging collaboration between art, crafts and industry, and he designed affordable workers homes as a solution to the severe housing shortages in Vienna after the ravages of World War 1.

In 1925, together with fellow architects Oskar Wlach and Walter Sobotka, Josef formed Haus & Garten, a partnership which designed houses, interiors, furniture and fabrics. Josef wasn't in agreement with French architect, Le Corbusier, who maintained that, "a house is a machine for living in." He was against such puritanical ideals and feared that Modernism's desire for standardisation would "make people all too uniform." »

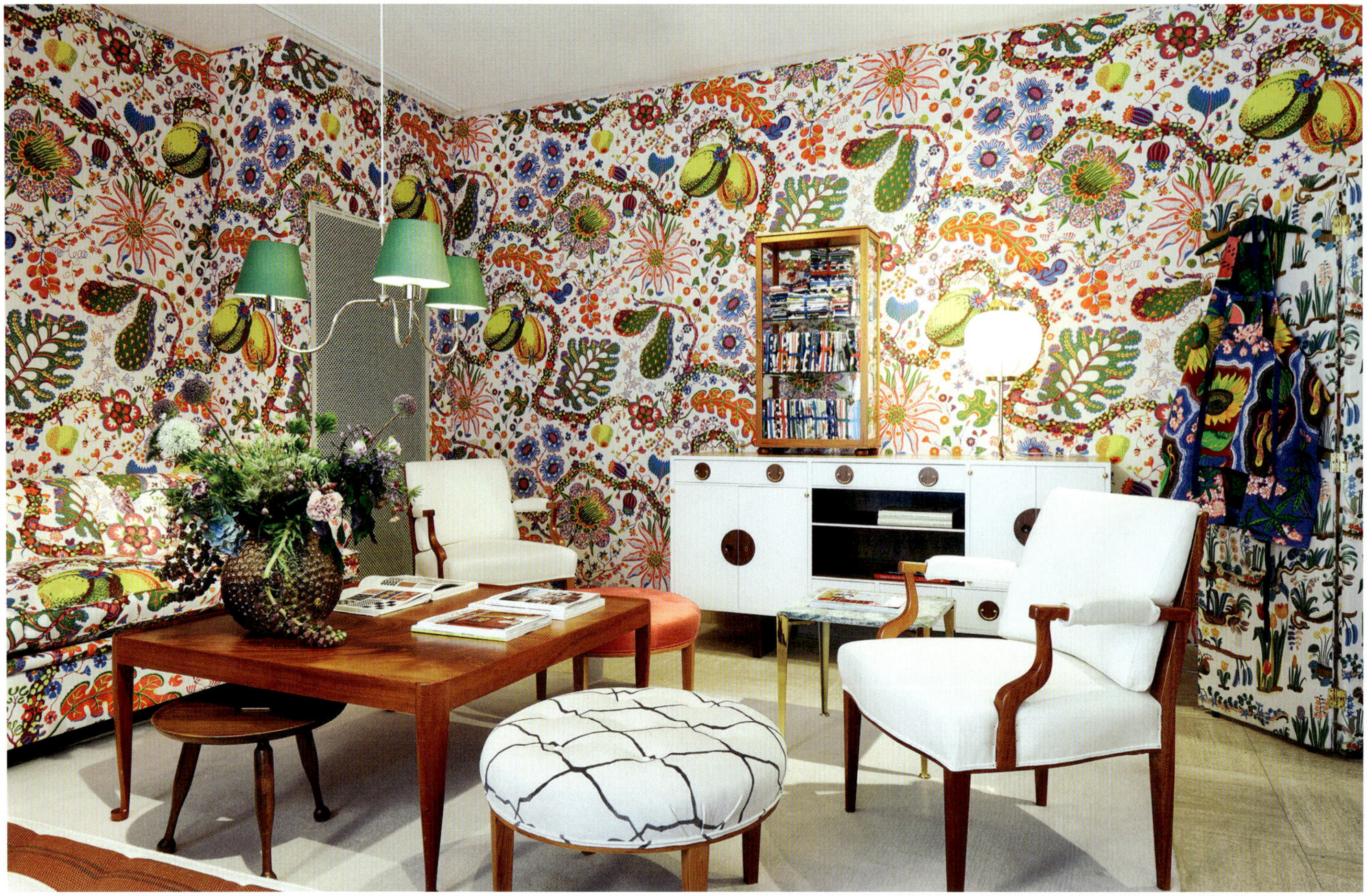

ABOVE A display at Svenskt Tenn's store on Strandvägen 5, Stockholm. When Annie first visited the store, she couldn't believe how modern Josef Frank's designs appeared

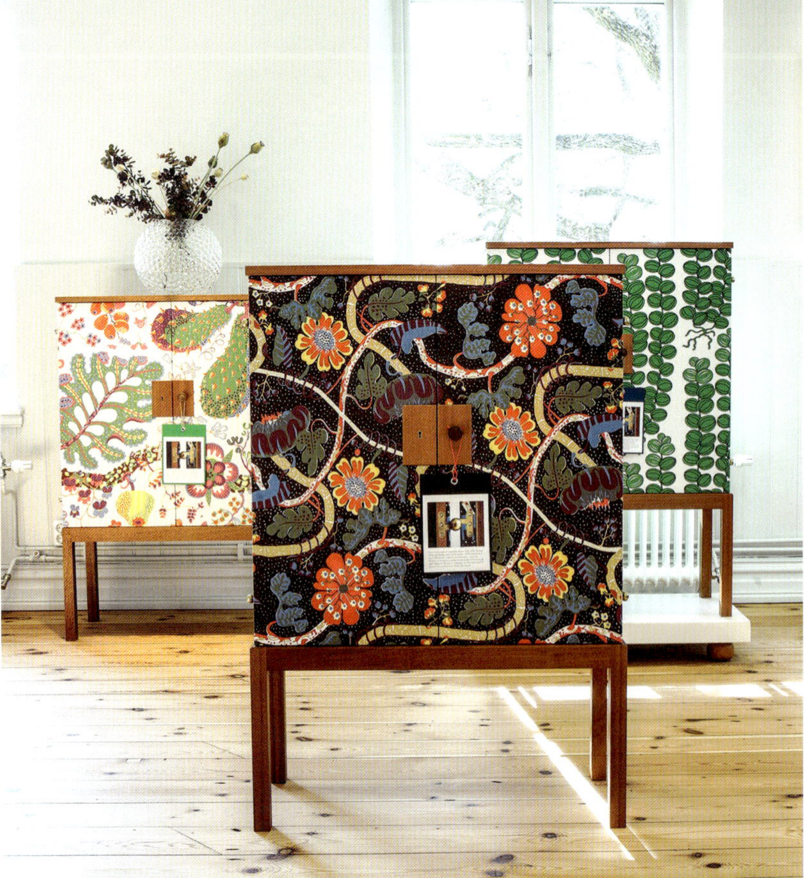

LEFT In 2013 an exhibition was held in Estrid Ericson's former school in Hjo. Cabinet 522 designed in 1934-1935 is made of mahogany and clad with Celotocaulis Green, Mirakel Brown and Brazil fabric

BELOW Armchair 336 was designed in 1934. It epitomises Frank's belief that comfort was an essential part of design – achieved through double springs and padding

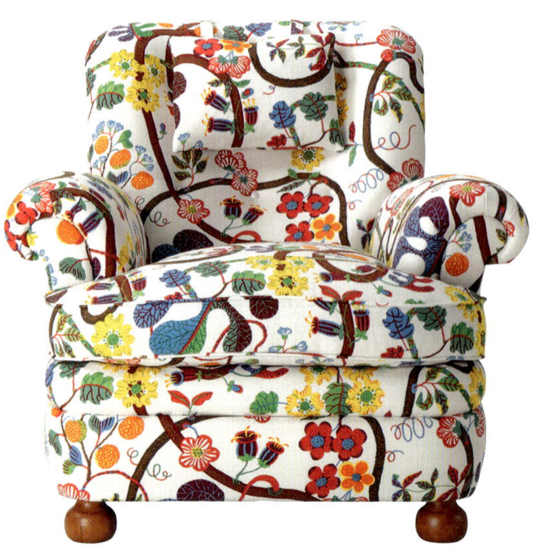

PHOTOGRAPHS: SVENSKT TENN

Josef's take on Modernism was much freer and more artistic, based on values such as comfort – his pieces used soft, well upholstered cushions, and rounded edges – pattern and colour. He believed that a piece of furniture should not only be fit for its purpose, but also bring pleasure to the user.

MOVE TO STOCKHOLM

It was while working at Haus & Garden in Vienna, that Josef first came to the attention of Estrid Ericson. Estrid trained as an art teacher and, after receiving an inheritance, founded the Swedish Svenskt Tenn brand (the name translates as 'Swedish Pewter') in 1924. When the store opened in Stockholm there were 300 pewter objects designed by craftsman Nils Fougstedt and Estrid herself. However, by the early 1930s her interest in interior design and furniture had increased and Svenskt Tenn developed into a creative centre, with Estrid skilled at spotting promising design talent.

In 1933 Josef and his Swedish wife Anna moved to Stockholm to escape the rise of Nazism in his native Vienna. Having been forced to begin a new chapter in his career at the age of 48, Estrid asked him to come and work for her at Svenskt Tenn.

THE EVOLUTION OF A STYLE

In 1934, Josef represented Svenskt Tenn in an exhibition at Liljevalchs art gallery in Stockholm. Swedish taste at the time was influenced by German and Dutch functionalism – practical furniture, free from any ornamentation and embellishment. In total contrast, Josef and Estrid exhibited a 'Hollywood-style' room set complete with a 2.5-metre curved sofa upholstered in a floral print, a leopard skin rug and a glamorous drinks cabinet! It was a complete break with convention and naturally caused a big reaction.

A sofa was the first piece of furniture that Josef designed for Svenskt Tenn and it became known as the Liljevalchs Sofa. It had a generous seating depth of 140cm at a time when the standard depth was just 80cm. The Liljevalchs Sofa is still in production today.

Writing in the magazine Form in 1934, Josef explained his philosophy: "If one desires the room to be comfortable, its demarcations must be clearly discernible, that is, all pieces of furniture should allow for a free view of the separating line between the floor and the wall. A cabinet without legs breaks this line and thus reduces the feeling of space." He favoured white walls, but maintained that repeat patterns were calming, "A monochrome surface is tiring; the more ornamentation, the more calming is the effect, because the viewer is unconsciously affected by the slow approach »

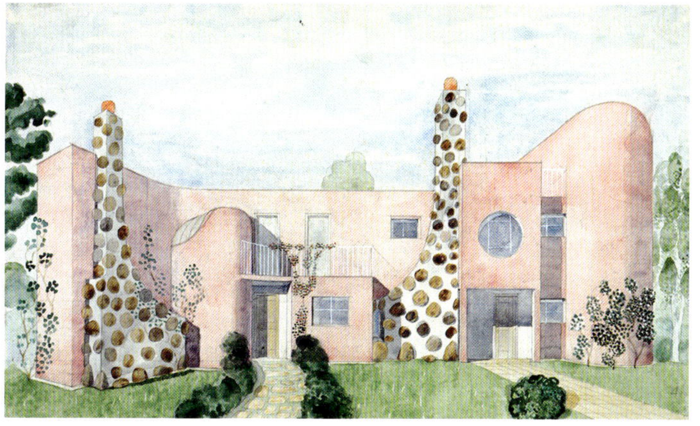

LEFT Between 22th July and 15th August 1947 in correspondence with Anna Frank's cousin Dagmar Grill, Josef Frank designed a series of 13 fantasy houses for a dream estate. These included the pink Double-D-House or Giraffe House

"It doesn't matter if you mix old and new, or different styles, colours and patterns. The things you like will always blend… into a peaceful whole"

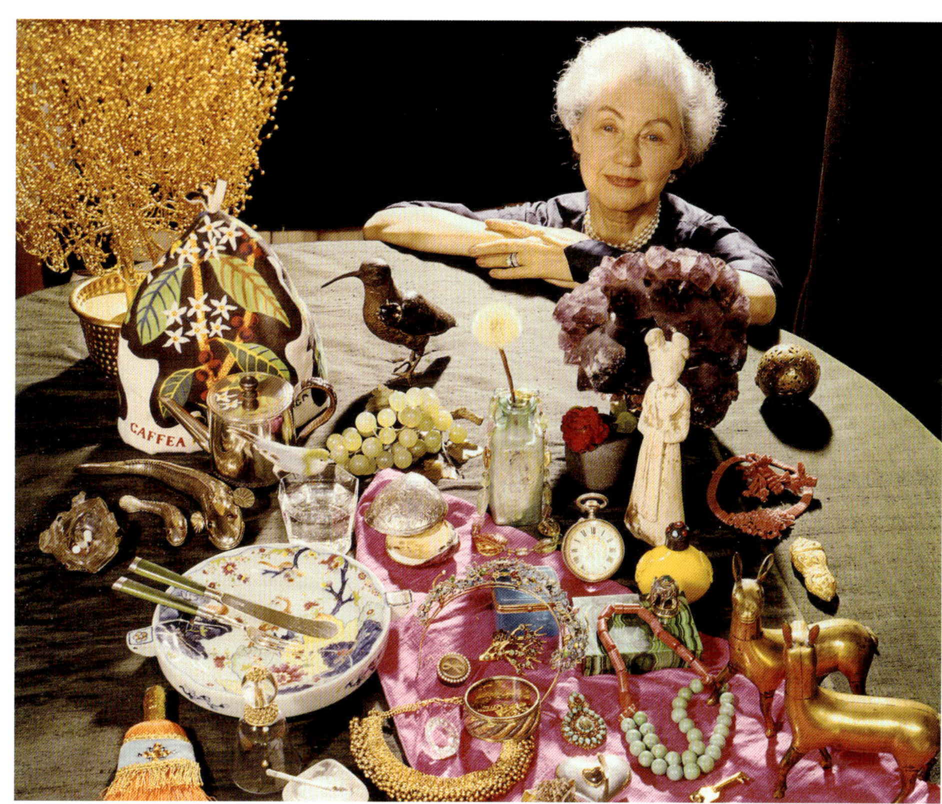

ABOVE Estrid Ericson (1894-1981) was pivotal in the career of Josef Frank. She offered him work after he fled Nazism in 1930s Austria, becoming his long-time collaborator, bringing colour and pattern to Swedish interiors. "The simplicity of the room – the richness of the details," was her take on Josef Frank's philosophy. Together they established the Swedish Modern look

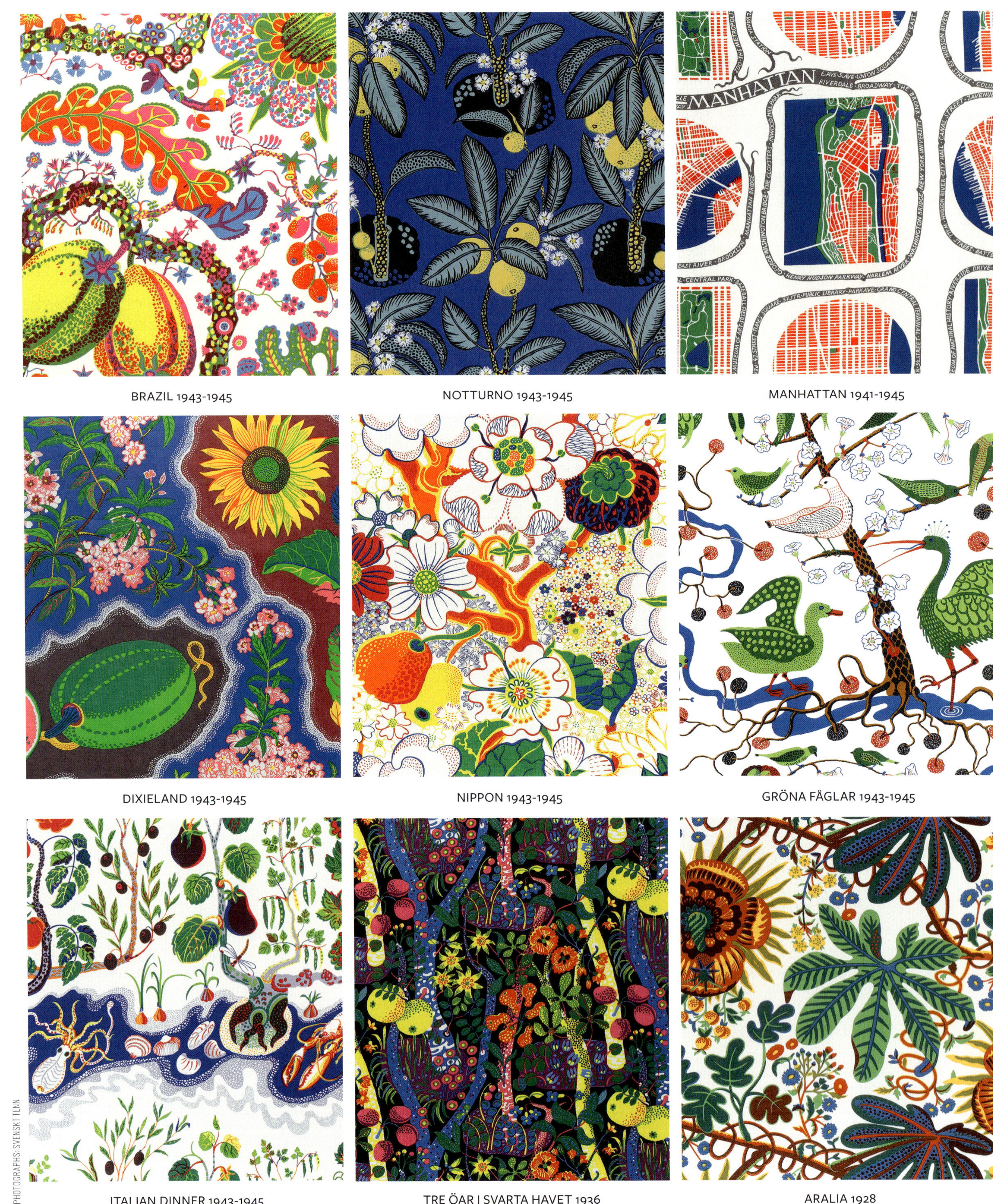

BRAZIL 1943–1945

NOTTURNO 1943–1945

MANHATTAN 1941–1945

DIXIELAND 1943–1945

NIPPON 1943–1945

GRÖNA FÅGLAR 1943–1945

ITALIAN DINNER 1943–1945

TRE ÖAR I SVARTA HAVET 1936

ARALIA 1928

PHOTOGRAPHS: SVENSKT TENN

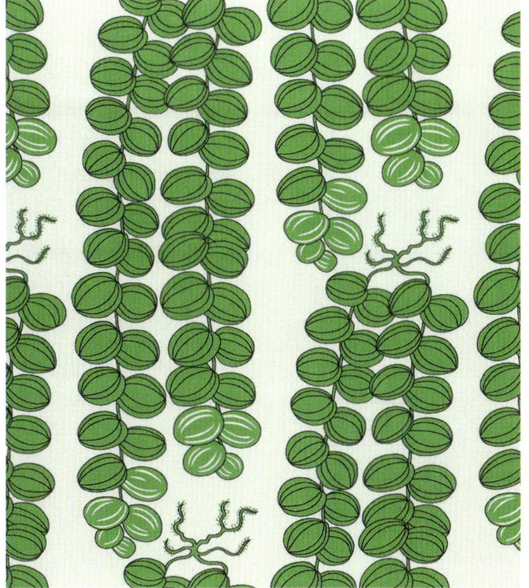

CELOTOCAULIS 1930

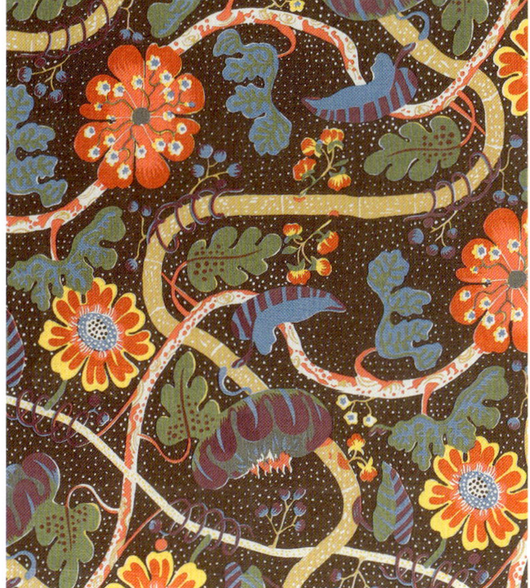

MIRAKEL 1928

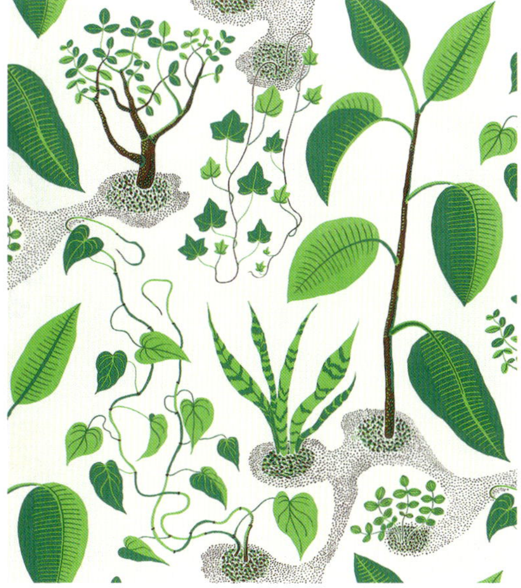

WINDOW 1941-1946

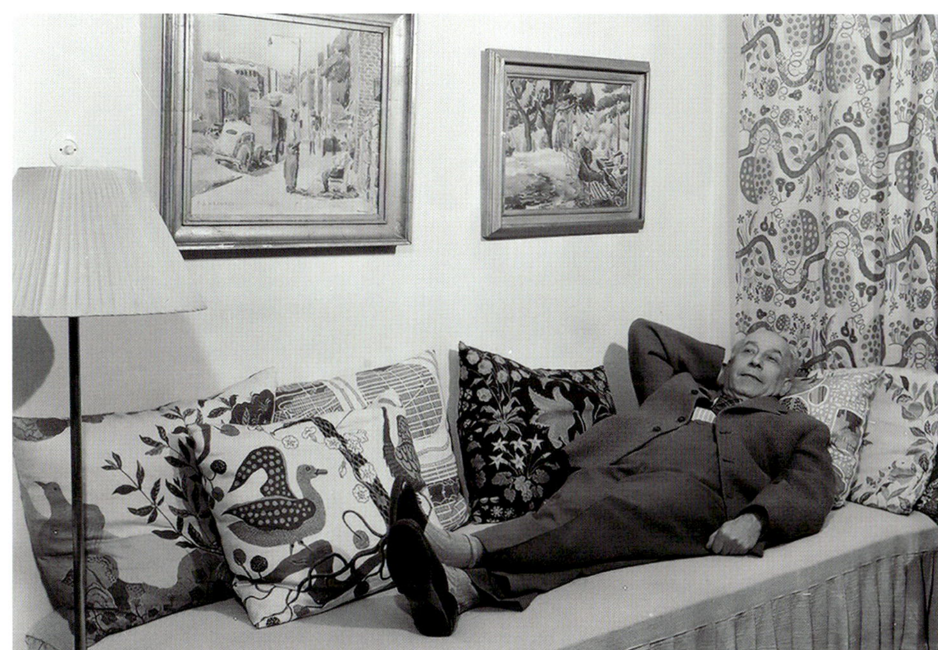

"It takes time to fathom a rich ornamentation; a monochrome surface, however, is immediately decipherable and thus no longer of interest"

that is behind it. It takes time to fathom a rich ornamentation; a monochrome surface, however, is immediately decipherable and thus no longer of interest."

INTERNATIONAL RECOGNITION

The international breakthrough for Josef and Svenkst Tenn came in 1937 when they designed an exhibition room for the World Exposition in Paris. They followed this by exhibiting in the Swedish Pavilion at the 1939 New York World's Fair. At both fairs they yet again turned their backs on the interior design trends of the time and displayed bold shapes, flamboyant patterns and contrasting colours. It was this aesthetic that became the dominant design direction in Sweden and, somewhat paradoxically, later became known as Swedish Modern.

MOVE TO MANHATTAN

In 1938 the German annexation of Austria meant Josef became stateless. After applying for Swedish citizenship he and his wife fled to Manhattan, New York in 1941. They remained for the duration of the World War II. His time in Manhattan proved to be a creative and prolific period for his textile »

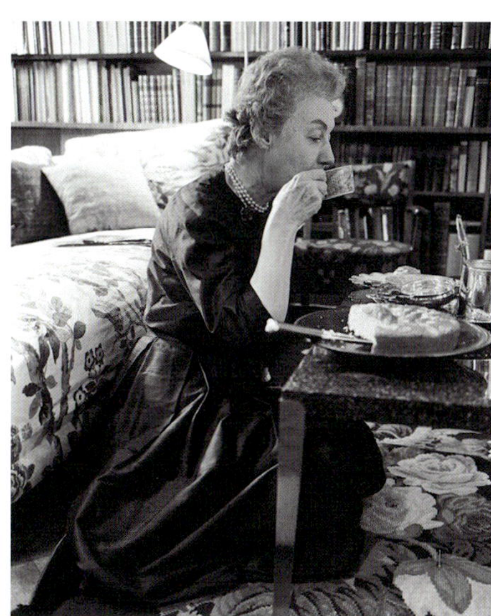

ABOVE Estrid Ericson taking tea and cake in front of the Liljevalchs Sofa in her apartment in the same building as her store on Strandvägen, Stockholm. Initially the colour scheme was muted, but was soon transformed by Josef Frank's colourful patterns and designs

PHOTOGRAPHS: SVENSKT TENN

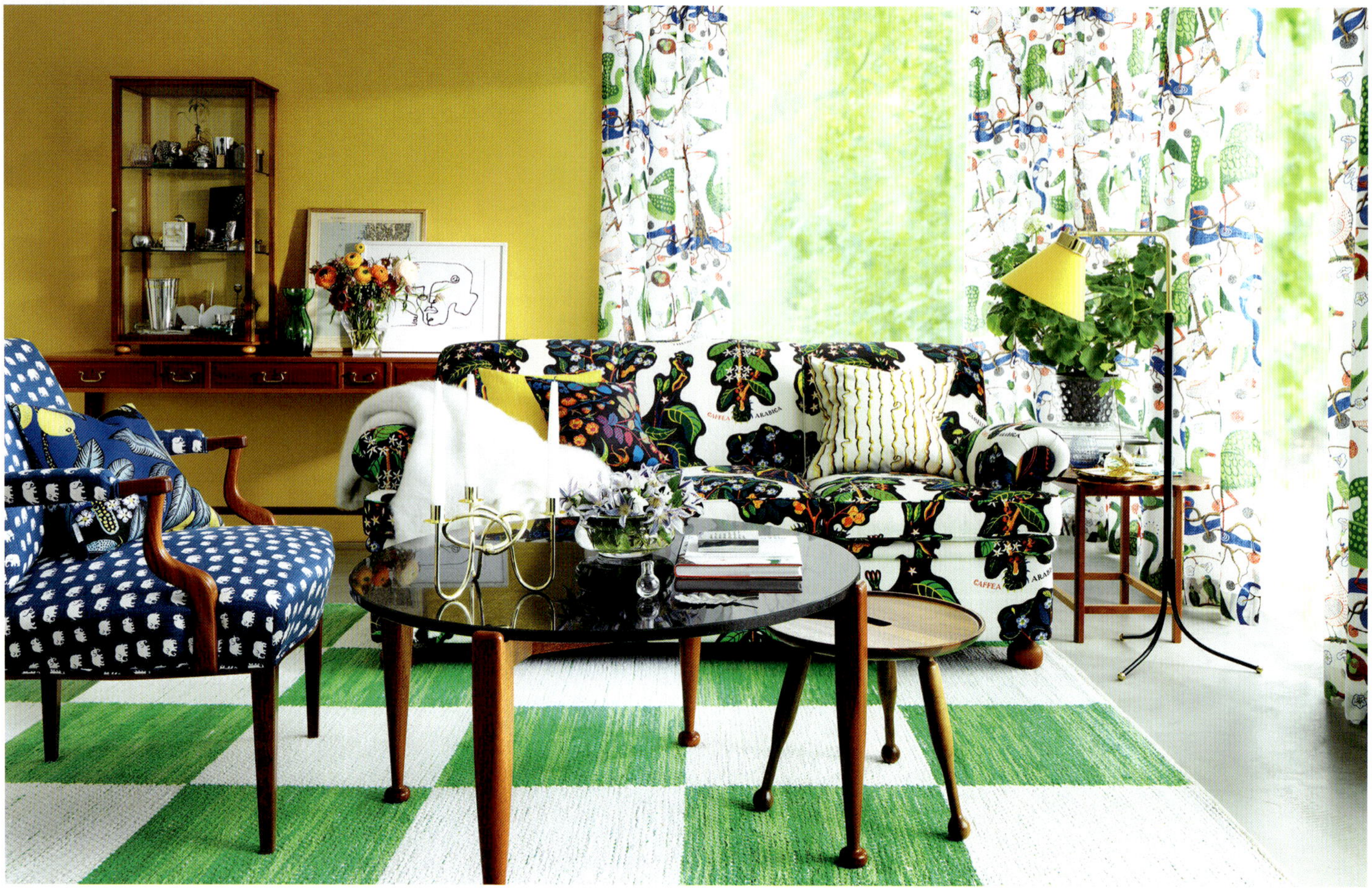

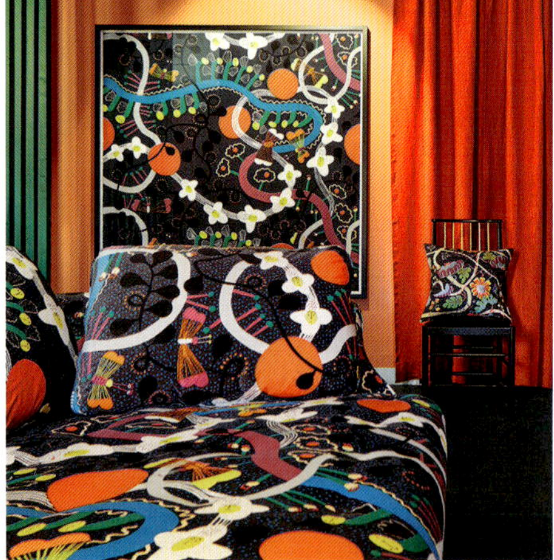

PHOTOGRAPHS: SVENSKT TENN

TOP Josef happily blended different types of materials in his furniture. Table 965, designed in 1938, is made from mahogany and finished with a polished black granite top

ABOVE Design student Kotone Utsunomiya created The Story of Flowers print in conjunction with Svenskt Tenn's Ten Textile Talents exhibition held in the spring of 2018

"All pieces of furniture should allow for a free view of the separating line between the floor and the wall"

designs in particular. Many of his most popular designs were created while living in New York, including Italian Dinner, Dixieland and Manhattan (see page 40). Included in the Manhattan print is Washington Bridge, The Cloisters and Inwood Hill Park. This was the area where Josef and Anna lived, not far from the most northern part of Broadway. While still exiled in New York, Josef sent 50 new textile designs to Estrid as a gift for her 50th birthday on 16th September 1944.

POST WORLD WAR II

In 1946, Josef and Anna Frank returned to Stockholm where he continued his close collaboration with Estrid and Svenskt Tenn, designing furniture, accessories and textiles. He created 160 textile designs during his time at Svenskt Tenn and produced thousands of designs for sofas, tables, lamps and cabinets. In the 1950s, at the age of 68, the ever-prolific Joseph Frank began to paint watercolours.

Josef died in Stockholm on 8th January 1967, aged 81. He donated all his designs to Estrid and Svenskt Tenn, where 45 of his textile designs and around 100 pieces of furniture are still in production today.

Josef is now firmly established as the one of the fathers of Swedish Modern. His colourful designs continue to be a rich source of inspiration for today's young textile designers. His influence also lives on in today's quintessentially Scandinavian brands, Ikea (www.ikea.com) and Marimekko (www.marimekko.com). AS

www.svenskttenn.se @svenskttenn

The HOMES collection

Stylish interiors full of character and fresh inspiration for your home

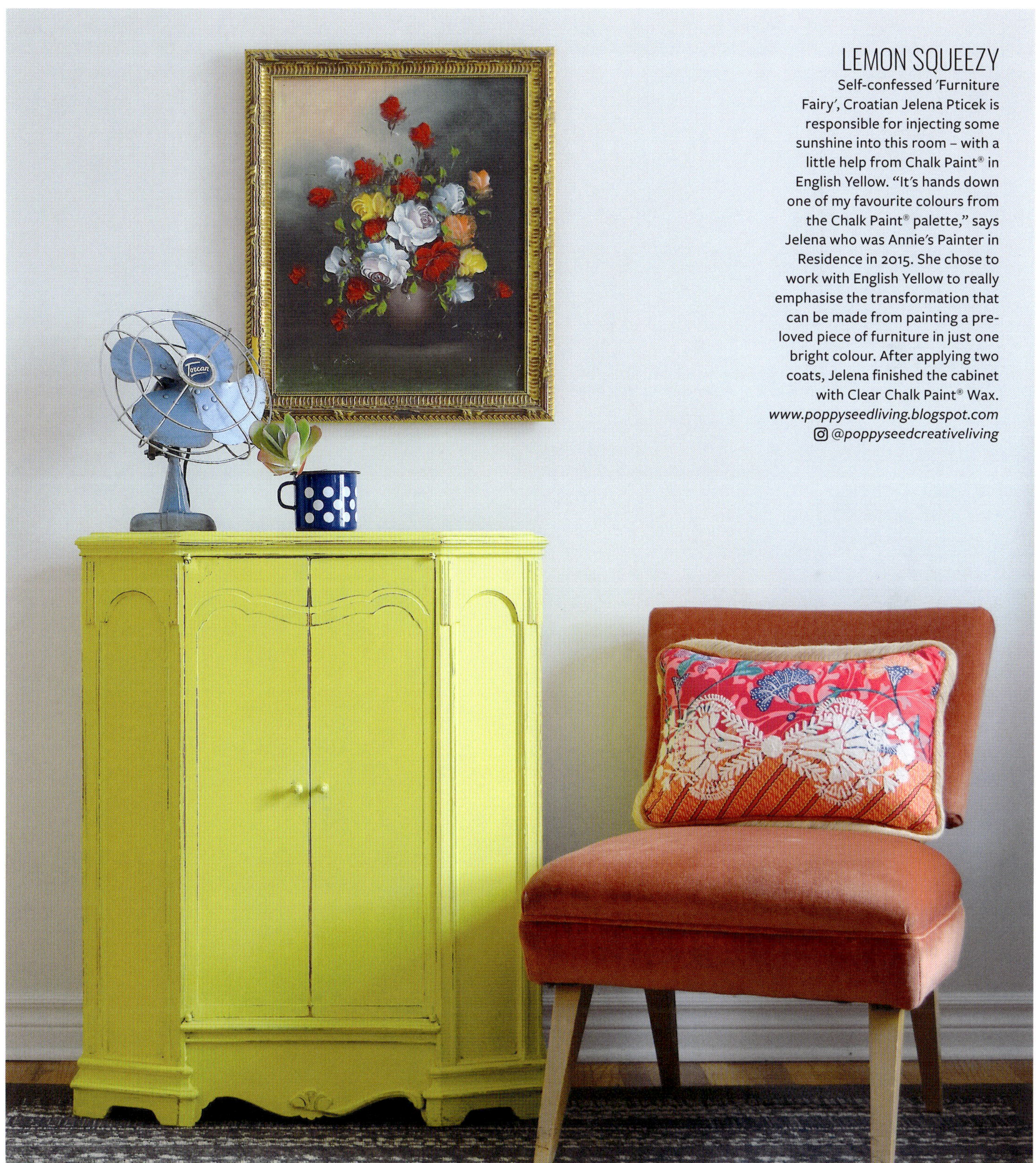

LEMON SQUEEZY

Self-confessed 'Furniture Fairy', Croatian Jelena Pticek is responsible for injecting some sunshine into this room – with a little help from Chalk Paint® in English Yellow. "It's hands down one of my favourite colours from the Chalk Paint® palette," says Jelena who was Annie's Painter in Residence in 2015. She chose to work with English Yellow to really emphasise the transformation that can be made from painting a pre-loved piece of furniture in just one bright colour. After applying two coats, Jelena finished the cabinet with Clear Chalk Paint® Wax.
www.poppyseedliving.blogspot.com
@poppyseedcreativeliving

PHOTOGRAPH: JALENA/POPPY SEED CREATIVE LIVING

BOLD BOTANICALS

FROM FEATHERY FERNS TO SHOW-STOPPING PINEAPPLES, HERE'S HOW TO BRING BOTANICAL BEAUTY TO YOUR HOME

Illustrations: **ANNIE SLOAN** Words: **ELLIE TENNANT**

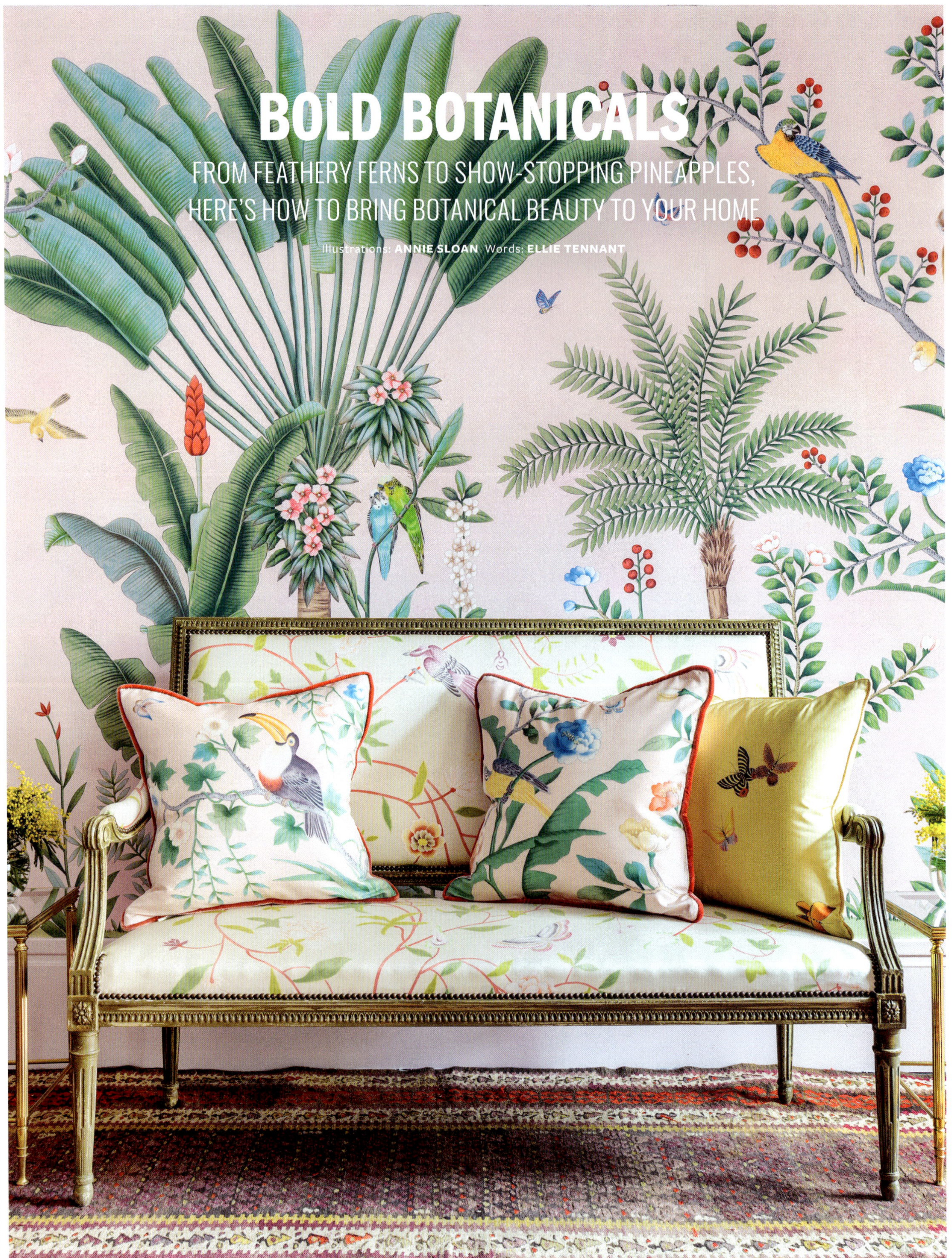

PHOTOGRAPH: MARIAM MEDVEDEVA

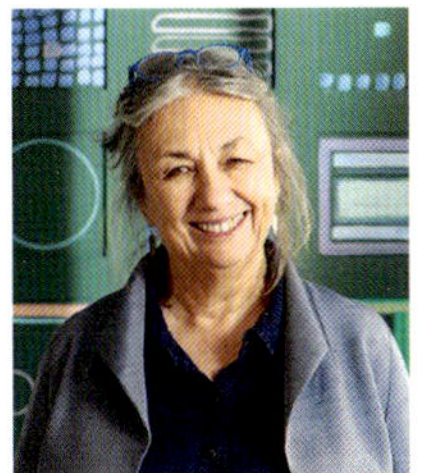

"I'm so inspired by the current trend for bold botanical prints. Follow my guide to decorating with lush green foliage and statement florals"

1 USE PINK WITH GREEN

Green botanical prints, patterns and plants always sit well in a scheme with pink colours. This is because red (and by extension, pink) and green are on opposite sides of the colour wheel, so are always 'complementary'. Choose similar depths of colour for the best results, so use a deep emerald green alongside a strong fuchsia, or a pale turquoise green with a pastel pink.

2 PLAY WITH SCALE

If you're using two or more different botanical patterns together in the same scheme, make sure you choose prints with varying scales so the patterns don't compete for attention and the room won't look too busy. For example, you might choose a wallpaper that features over-sized murals of palm fronds, then introduce cushions that are decorated with smaller-scale leaf prints.

3 GET THE BALANCE RIGHT

You can use several different botanical patterns in different colours in the same scheme, as long as there are plain elements separating them. Balance your patterns with plains – working to a roughly 50-50 approach. For example, if your sofa is plain, add interest with botanical cushions and throws. But if the walls are decorated with botanical patterns, keep the flooring plain. »

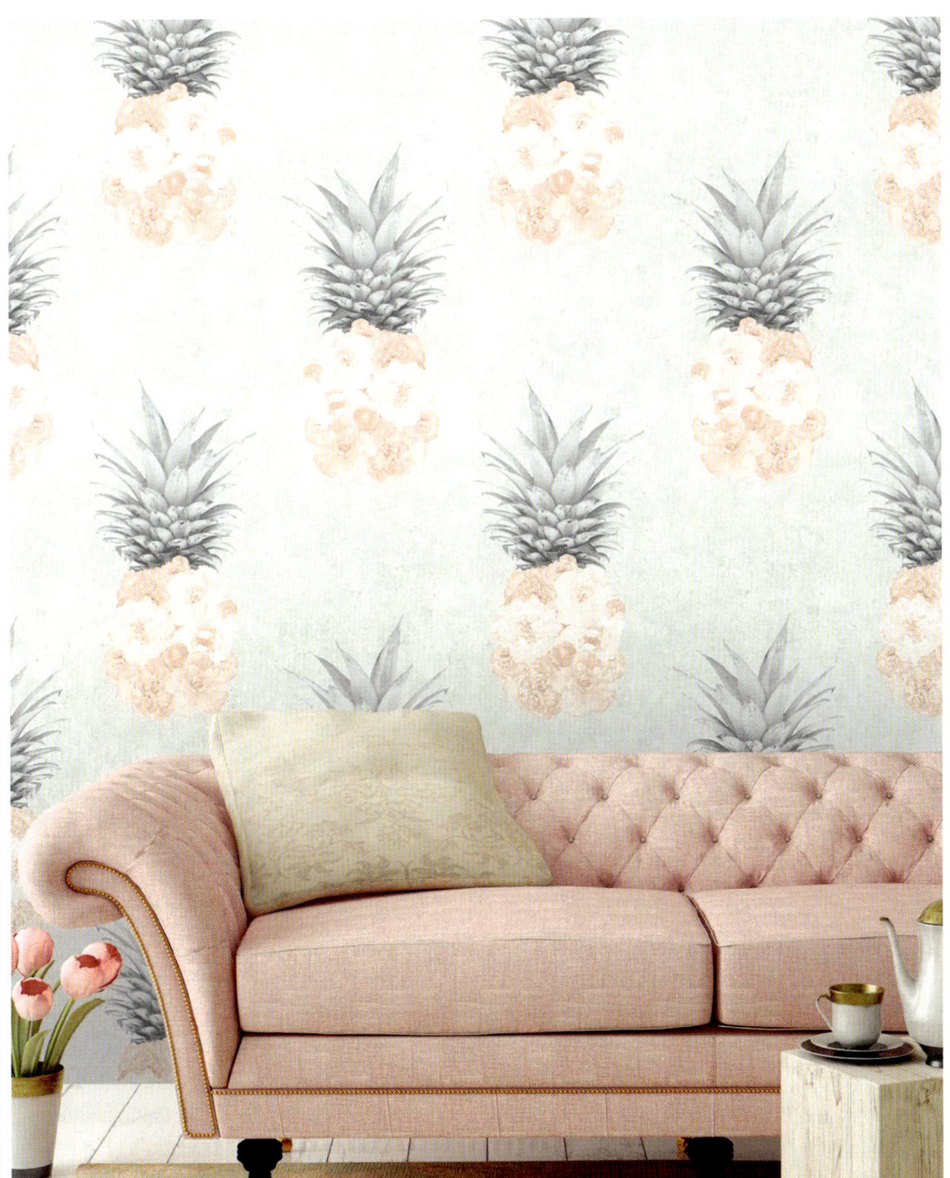

PHOTOGRAPH: MTLAPCEVIC; WOODCHIP & MAGNOLIA. PORTRAIT OF ANNIE, TINA HILLIER

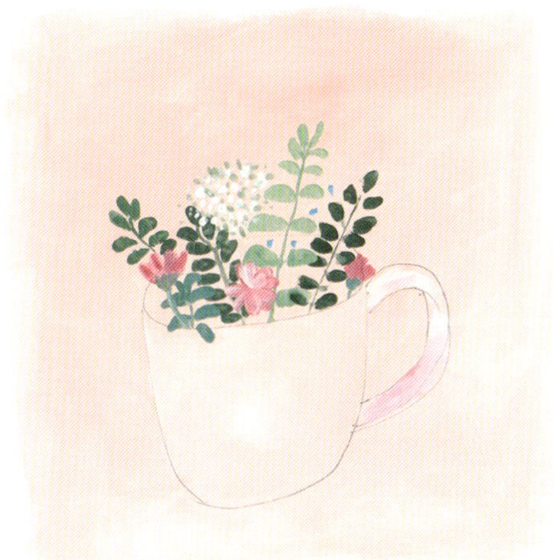

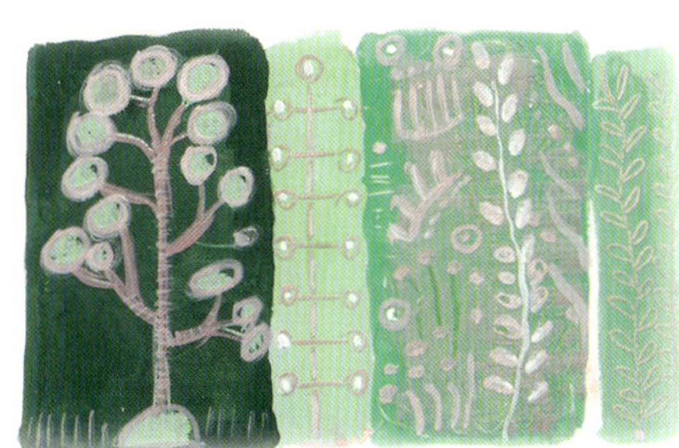

OPPOSITE Make an impact with an oversized wallpaper mural, such as this Amazonia design on custom pink Edo painted Xuan paper by de Gournay *www.degournay.com*

LEFT Shake it up with a perfect cocktail of Blush pink, peony-filled pineapples with grey foliage. Ludic by Woodchip & Magnolia, *www.woodchipandmagnolia.co.uk*

ABOVE "I always find it useful to sketch out ideas for interior decorating in my notebooks, even if it's just a quick doodle. I then water down Chalk Paint® to create a simple wash of colour."

4 MAKE A STATEMENT

Choose a bold, graphic botanical pattern with over-sized leaves for a real show-stopping focal point. For maximum impact, keep the rest of your scheme neutral, plain and simple, and introduce your chosen 'hero' pattern in one enormous dose – on a rug, for example, or a wallpapered feature wall – for a stand-out, striking look. This is a quick and easy way to liven up a lifeless room.

5 PICK UP A PLANT

For large, tropical-looking leaves with striking silhouettes, consider a Banana plant (Musa Dwarf Cavendish), with its glossy heart-shaped leaves or a Swiss Cheese plant (Monstera Deliciosa). Cacti and Aloe Vera plants are best for sculptural spikes, while Lace Fern (Asparagus Setaceus) has feathery sprays for a delicate look. Trailing vines like String of Pearls (Senecio Rowleyanus) and String of Hearts (Ceropegia Woodii) look fabulous in hanging containers because they drape beautifully.

6 GO FAUX

If keeping houseplants alive isn't your forte, invest in a few realistic faux plants for an instant hit of greenery. Thanks to advances in technology, fake plants are no longer plasticky or tacky – Abigail Ahern has a great range that look incredibly real. They're brilliantly low maintenance - just remember to wipe their leaves occasionally to remove dust and fluff.

7 BE BRAVE

If you can't quite pluck up the courage to embrace bold botanicals in a key room like a living room or bedroom, experiment first in a smaller space – for example, wallpaper your downstairs cloakroom, cover a bed headboard with botanical fabric, or put up a shelf and add a few sculptural house plants. »

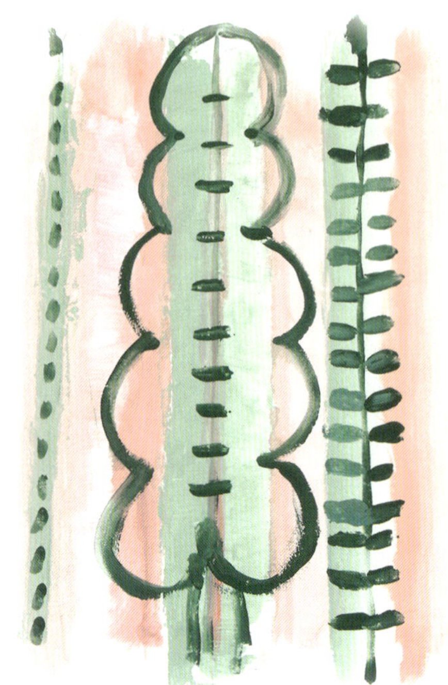

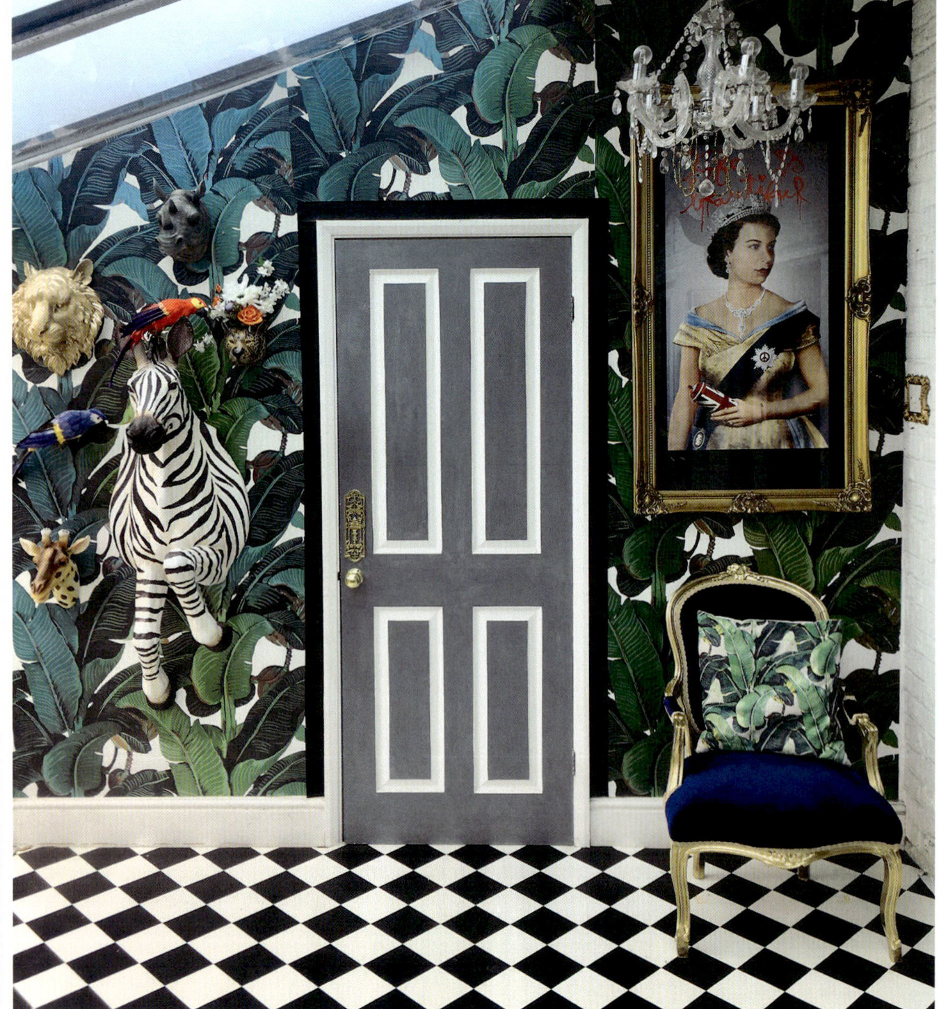

PHOTOGRAPHS: HAYLEY BROOKE/WWW.AUDENZA.COM

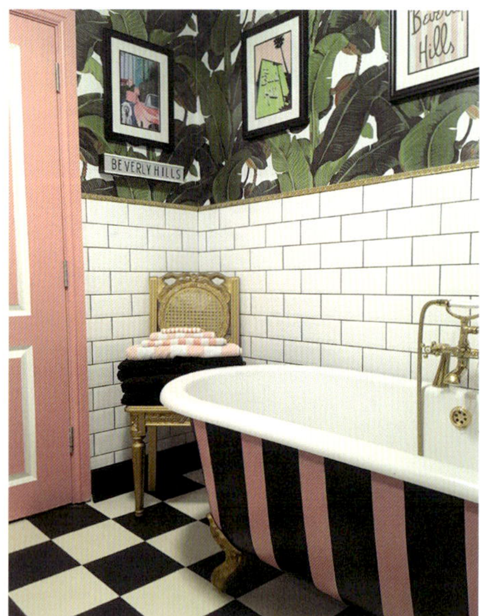

ABOVE Hayley Anne Brooke's opulent bathroom is a great example of how pink and green can work together in a scheme with fabulous results

LEFT Hayley has used leafy botanical wallpaper with eccentric accessories to create a high-end boutique-style interior. @hayleyannebrooke

RIGHT Use bold botanicals with 1950s-style bubblegum pink and touches of gold such as this glamorous, retro scheme finished with a custom Beni Ourain rug from Baba Souk *www.babasouk.ca*

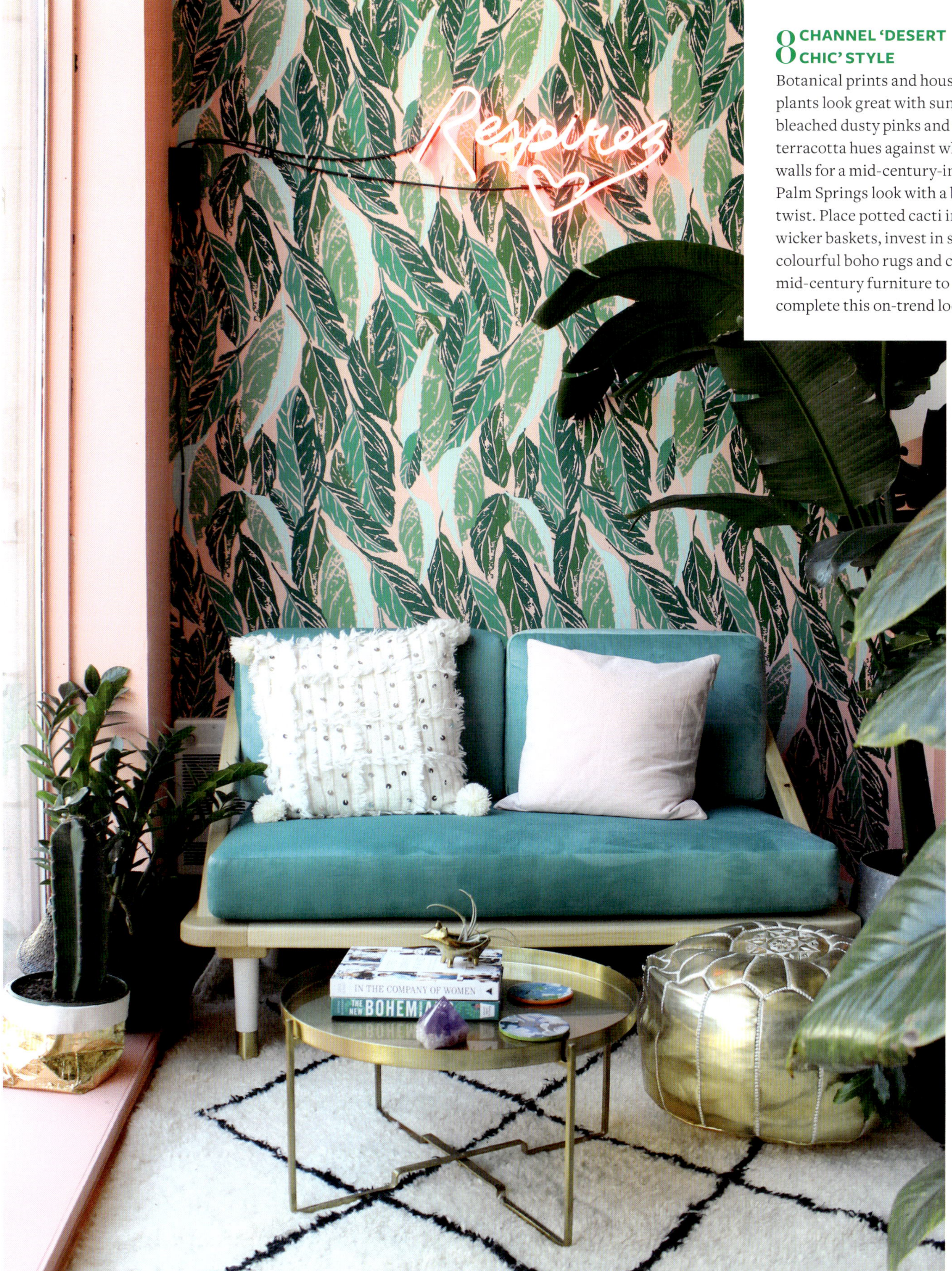

8 CHANNEL 'DESERT CHIC' STYLE

Botanical prints and house plants look great with sun-bleached dusty pinks and warm terracotta hues against white walls for a mid-century-inspired Palm Springs look with a boho twist. Place potted cacti in wicker baskets, invest in some colourful boho rugs and choose mid-century furniture to complete this on-trend look.

PHOTOGRAPH: BABA SOUK

9 ADD SOME METALLICS

Bold botanicals always look fabulous when used with touches of metallic finishes – gold and brass work well with green, and even just introducing a few elements in these finishes can give a room a glamorous feel. Annie Sloan Gilding Wax or Metal Leaf Booklets in Brass, Copper or Aluminium can be used to introduce a hit of shine to furniture or carved surfaces.

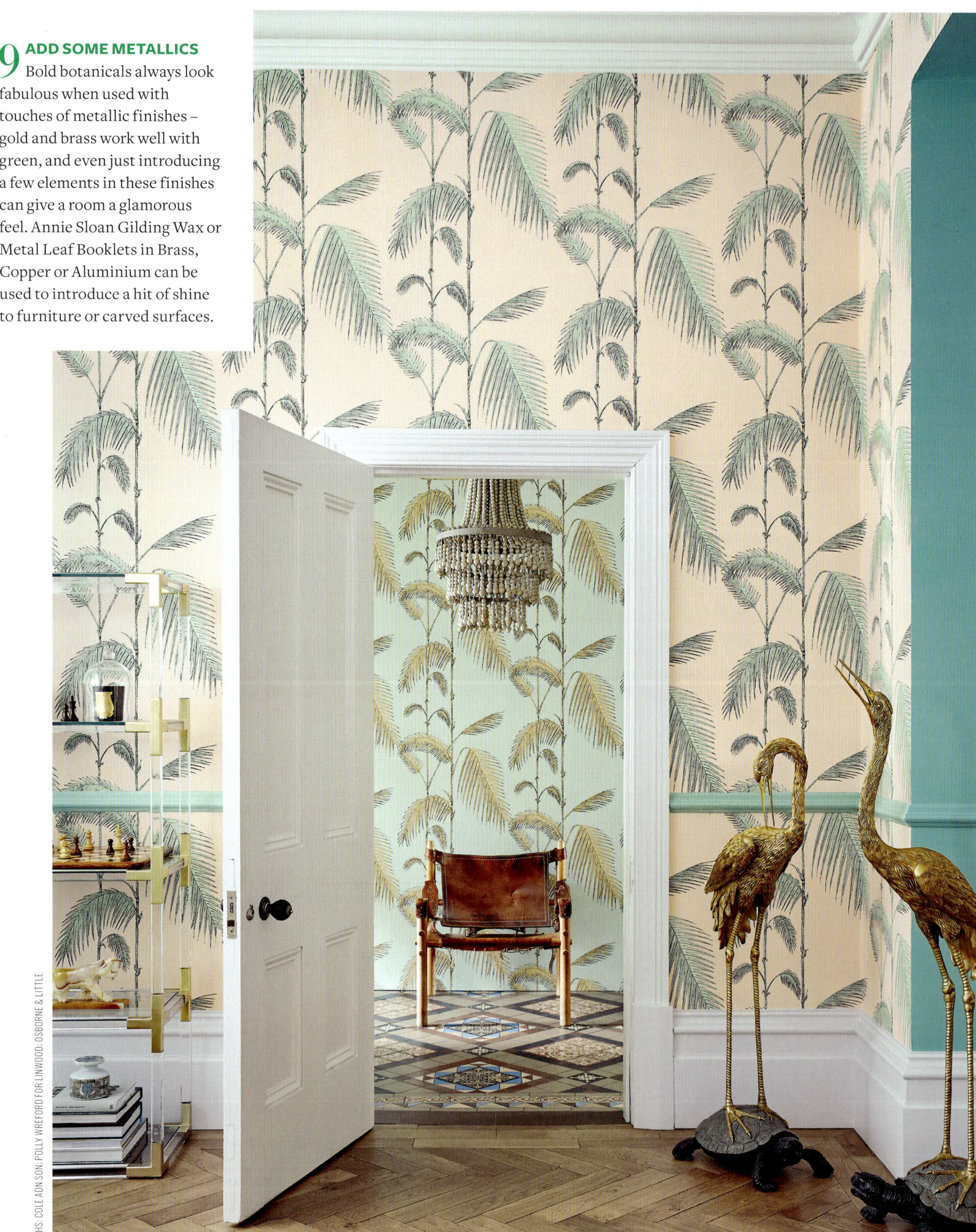

PHOTOGRAPHS: COLE ADN SON: POLLY WREFORD FOR LINWOOD: OSBORNE & LITTLE

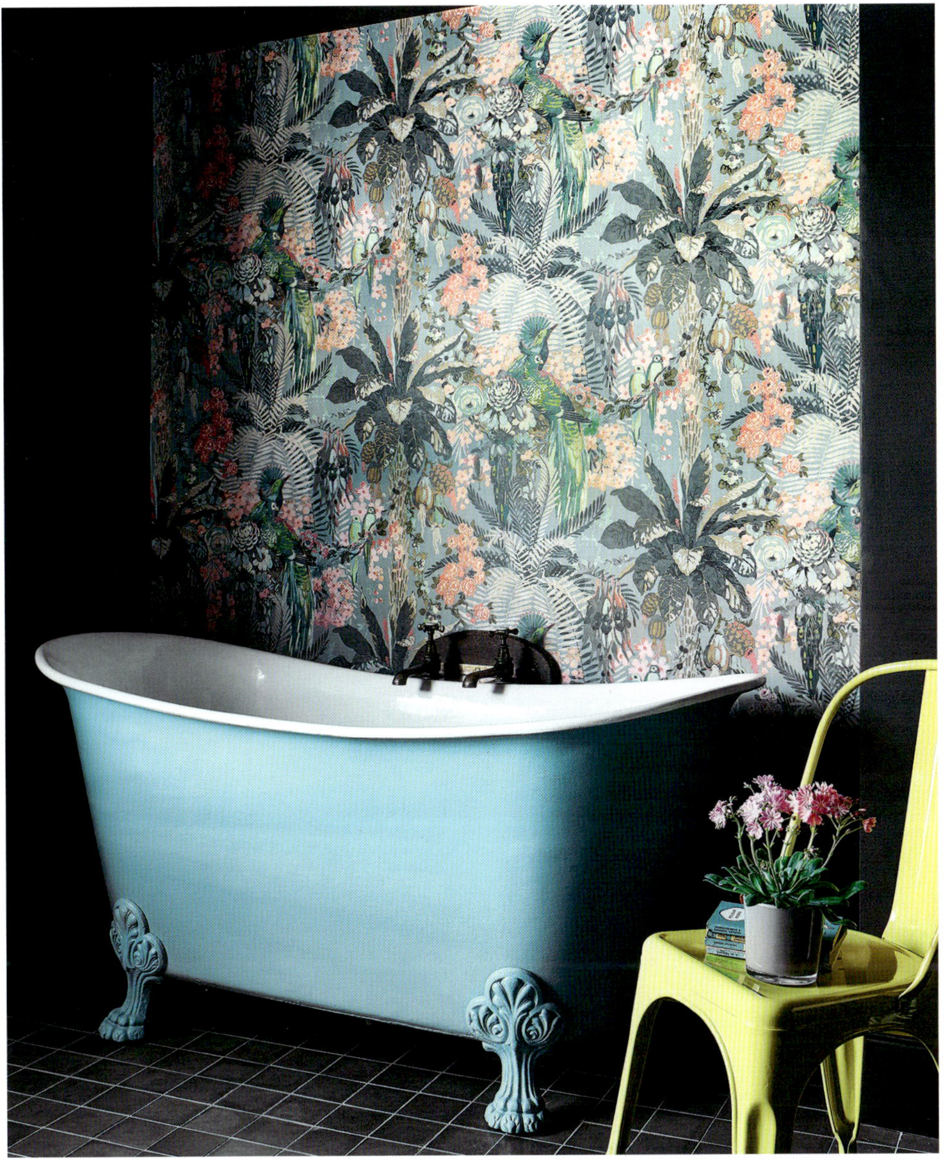

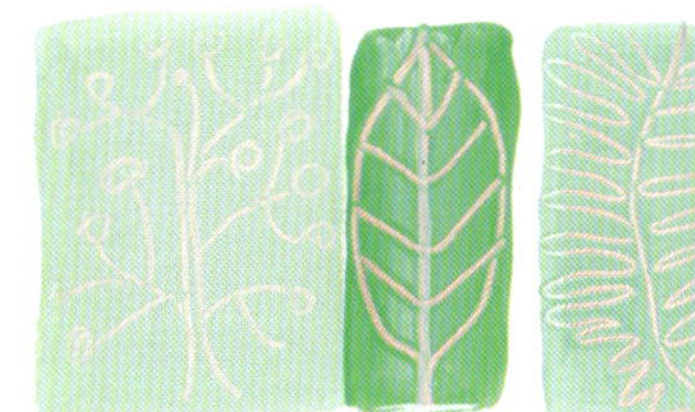

10 DO YOUR RESEARCH

Browse botanical books to give you fresh ideas for your home. Botanical (Hoxton Mini Press) has elegant botanical photography by Samuel Zeller who captures the strange beauty of exotic plants seen through the dappled glass of greenhouses. Botanical Style by Selina Lake (Ryland Peters & Small) will transform your home into a 'leafy haven', while Urban Jungle by Igor Josifovic and Judith de Graaff (Callwey) is packed with inspiring botanical images.

11 REPEAT AND REVERSE

If you plan to use the same bold botanical print in two places in a room – on a feature wall and on curtains, for example – you can avoid a dated, busy look by seeking out designs that come in reverse colourways and using two opposite colourways in the same scheme.

12 EMBRACE THE DARK SIDE

For a bold, ultra-cool look, seek out botanical fabrics, wallpapers and accessories with deliciously dark backgrounds that make the tropical leaf patterns pop. Tropicana wallpaper by Matthew Williamson at Osborne & Little (*www.osborneandlittle.com*) or Amazonia wallpaper in Dark colourway, by Witch and Watchman at Rockett St George (*www.rockettstgeorge.co.uk*) are both perfect choices if you want to go for a dark, maximalist look. AS

Hashtags to search for on Instagram:
#botanicalpickmeup #urbanjunglebloggers #planthoarder #plantpackedparadise #thesill #welcometothejungle #jungalow #interiorrewilding #plantsofinstagram #botanicalhome #botanicalstyle #botanicalwallpaper #indoorplants #crazyplantlady #houseplantclub

Three inspiring Instagram accounts to follow:
The Future Kept (@*thefuturekept*); Jungalow (@*thejungalow*); Artemis Russell (@*junkaholique*)

LEFT The same elegant palm-patterned wallpaper has been used here in adjacent rooms but in contrasting colourways, to link the spaces visually. Palm Leaves Icons 112/2005 wallpaper, (front room) and Palm Leaves Icons 112/2006 wallpaper (back room) by Cole & Son *www.cole-and-son.com*

ABOVE To transform a small bathroom into a show-stopping space, keep walls and floors deliciously dark, then add a punchy tropical feature wall. Rainforest Rabble wallpaper, in LW075/002 Powder Blue from the Tango Wallpaper collection at Linwood *www.linwoodfabric.com*

RIGHT Pattern on pattern can work if you go for the 'chameleon' effect – here, the fabric on the sofa matches the wallpaper on the wall behind for a contemporary, playful look. Tropicana W6801-01 wallpaper and Tropicana F6791-01 fabric are both by Matthew Williamson at Osborne & Little *www.osborneandlittle.com*

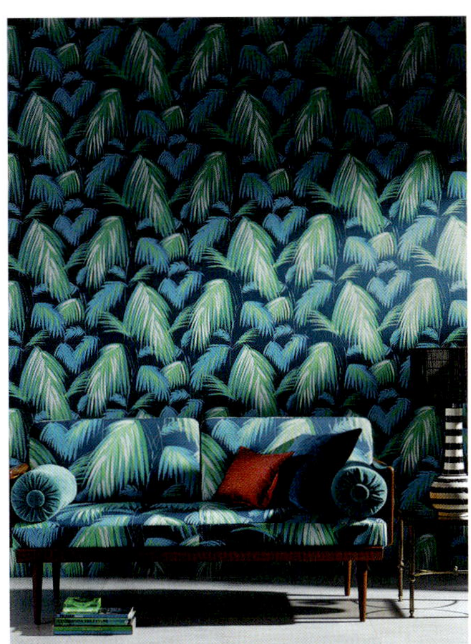

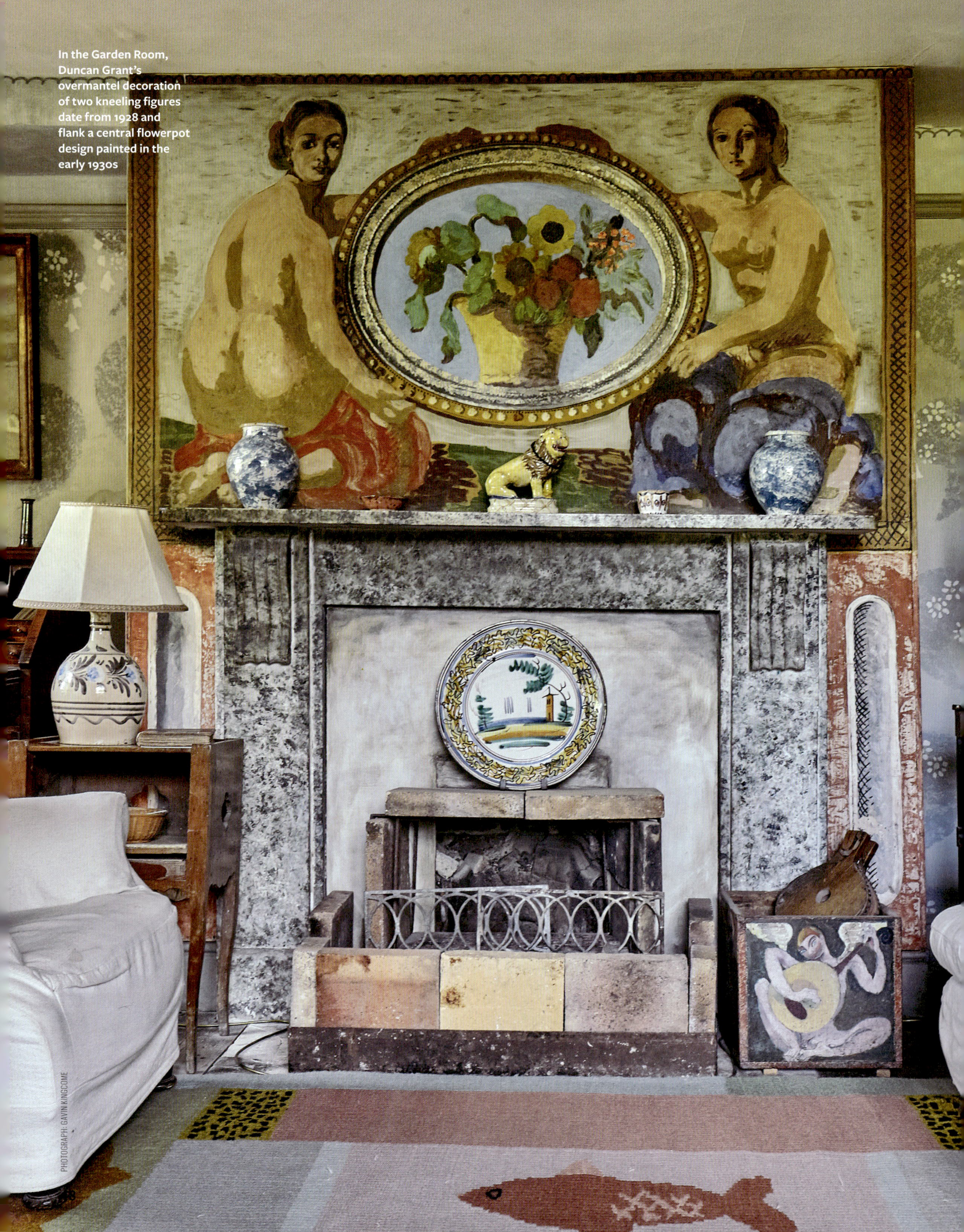

In the Garden Room, Duncan Grant's overmantel decoration of two kneeling figures date from 1928 and flank a central flowerpot design painted in the early 1930s

PHOTOGRAPH: GAVIN KINGCOME

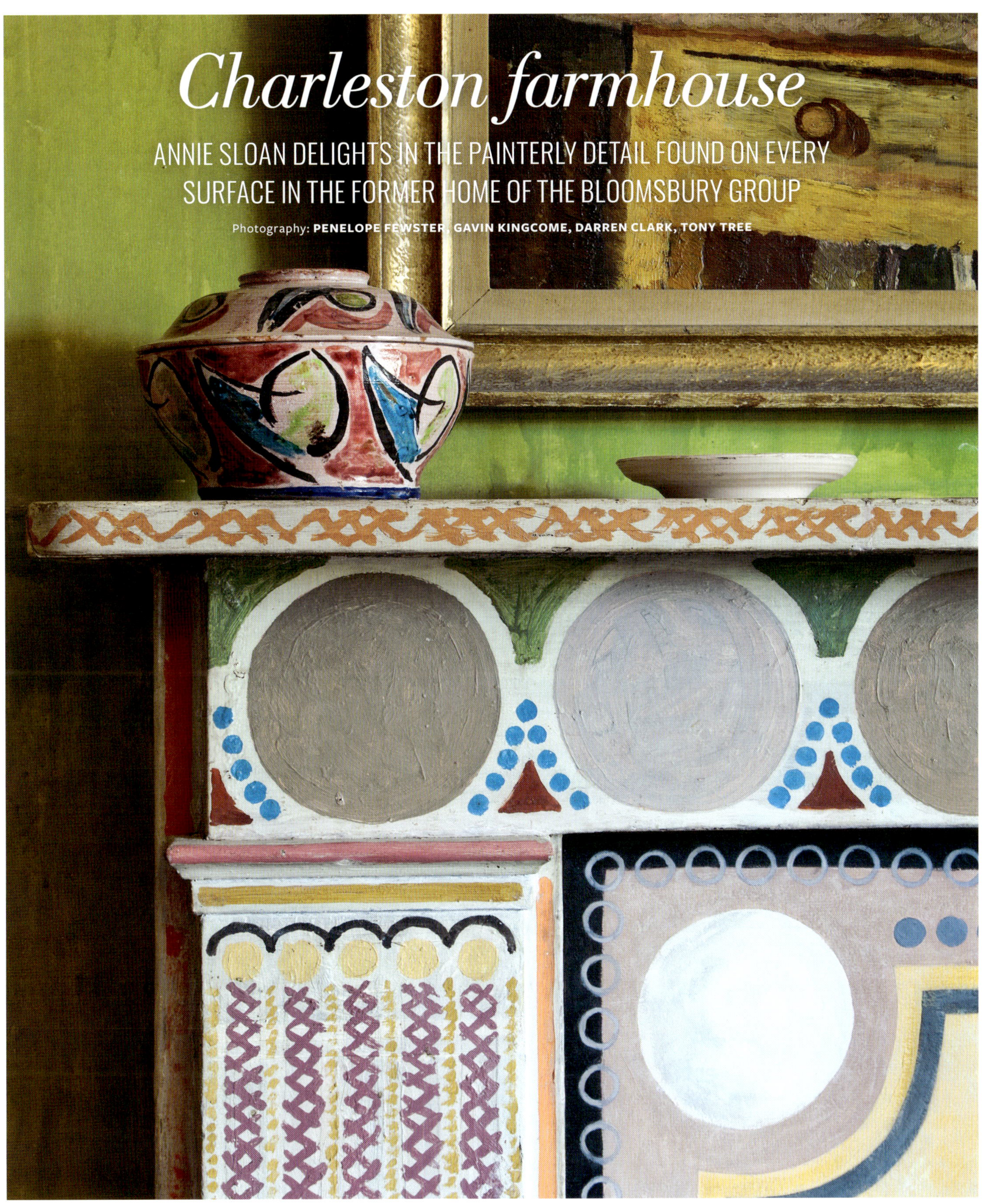

Charleston farmhouse

ANNIE SLOAN DELIGHTS IN THE PAINTERLY DETAIL FOUND ON EVERY SURFACE IN THE FORMER HOME OF THE BLOOMSBURY GROUP

Photography: **PENELOPE FEWSTER, GAVIN KINGCOME, DARREN CLARK, TONY TREE**

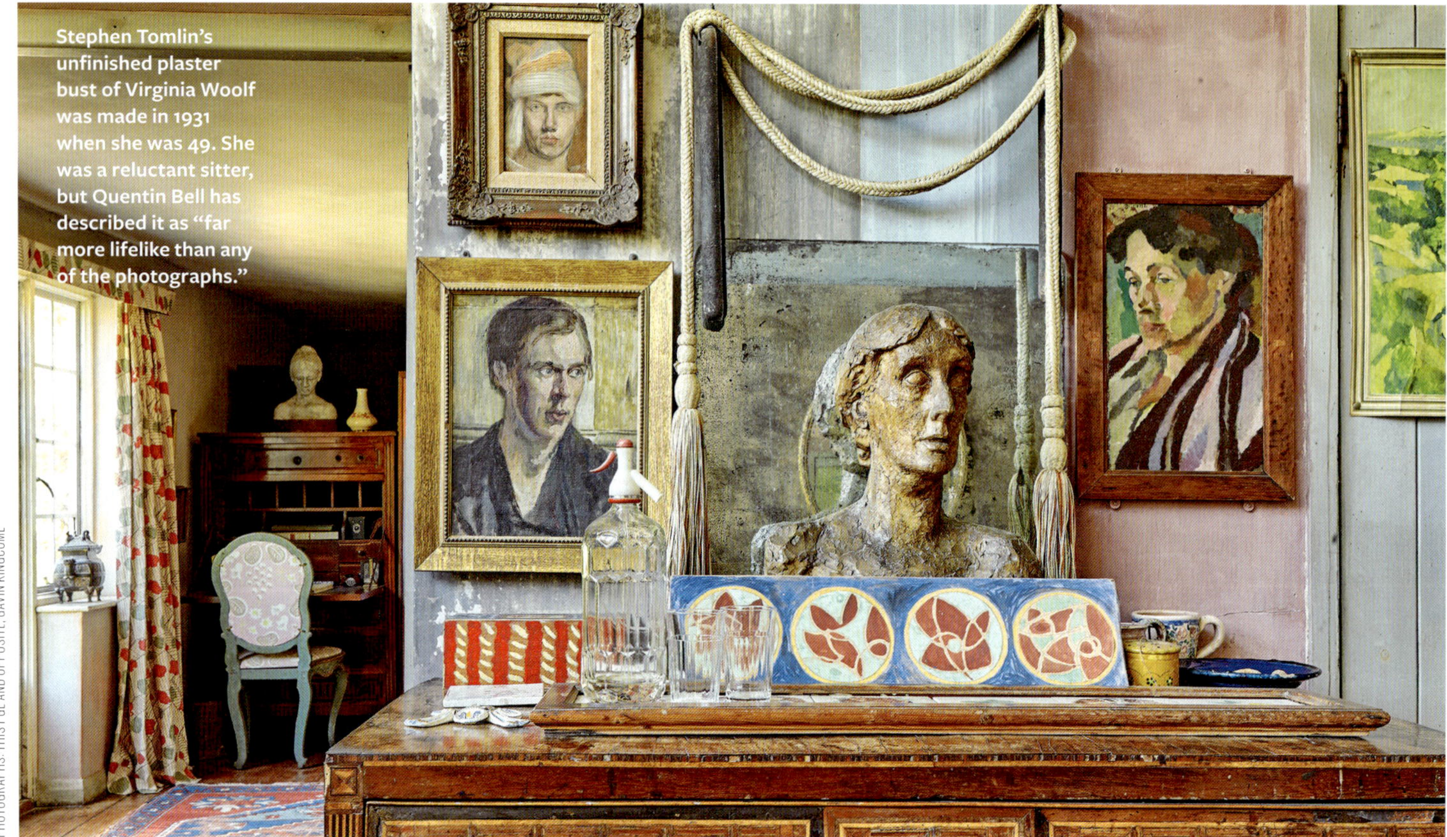

Stephen Tomlin's unfinished plaster bust of Virginia Woolf was made in 1931 when she was 49. She was a reluctant sitter, but Quentin Bell has described it as "far more lifelike than any of the photographs."

PHOTOGRAPHS: THIS PGE AND OPPOSITE, GAVIN KINGCOME

"For such a long time I felt like Charleston was my special secret. It was such a cherished find!"

I remember finding out about the Bloomsbury group when I was a student studying fine art. I had bought stacks of illustrative books which led me to discover a fascinating group of English artists and the story of their country retreat, Charleston farmhouse in East Sussex, England.

In 1916, the painters Vanessa Bell and Duncan Grant, his friend and lover David Garnett, and Vanessa and Clive Bell's two sons, Julian and Quentin, moved to Charleston. Over the next 64 years the farmhouse would be transformed by a group of like-minded artists, writers and intellectuals who became known collectively as Bloomsbury, after the district of London where they had first gathered from 1904. The seclusion of the farmhouse enabled them to continue to explore unconventional artistic lifestyles. On Christmas Day 1918 Vanessa gave birth to a daughter, Angelica, by Duncan Grant. Throughout their time at Charleston they transformed the house with decoration on every surface.

Vanessa Bell died in 1961, Clive in 1964. Duncan Grant continued to live at Charleston almost until his death in 1978. His daughter Angelica then lived there alone until 1980, when The Charleston Trust was formed. Charleston has become, as Quentin Bell wrote, 'a kind of time capsule in which the public can examine a world which has vanished'.

For such a long time I felt like Charleston was my special secret. It was such a cherished find! It felt like it was mine and no one else knew about it.

I love the artists' spontaneous and free approach to painting. It feels so punk! They pushed boundaries and took chances in an absolutely joyful way. You can tell they really loved paint and colour. The way they balanced historical and modern references from different cultures comes together seamlessly through their style.

In 1971, when I was at Reading University studying for my MFA in Fine Art, I actually wrote to Duncan Grant to invite him to our arts club. Sadly he declined!

So you can imagine, when the chance came to work on a collaboration with The Charleston Trust it was a dream come true for me – turn to page 59 for all the details. Meanwhile, let's take a tour together and I'll show you some of my favourite corners of Charleston... AS

www.charleston.org.uk *@charlestontrust* »

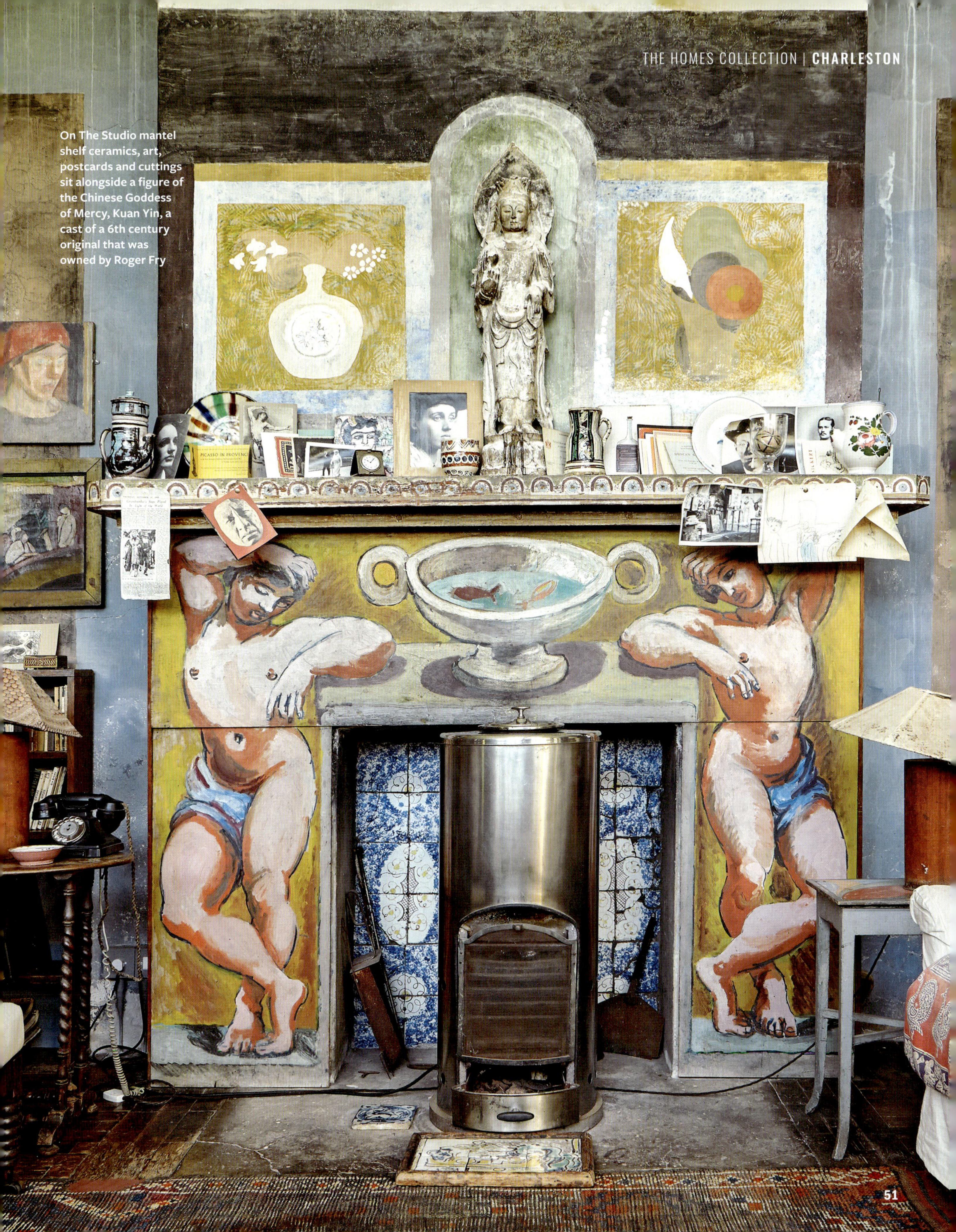

On The Studio mantel shelf ceramics, art, postcards and cuttings sit alongside a figure of the Chinese Goddess of Mercy, Kuan Yin, a cast of a 6th century original that was owned by Roger Fry

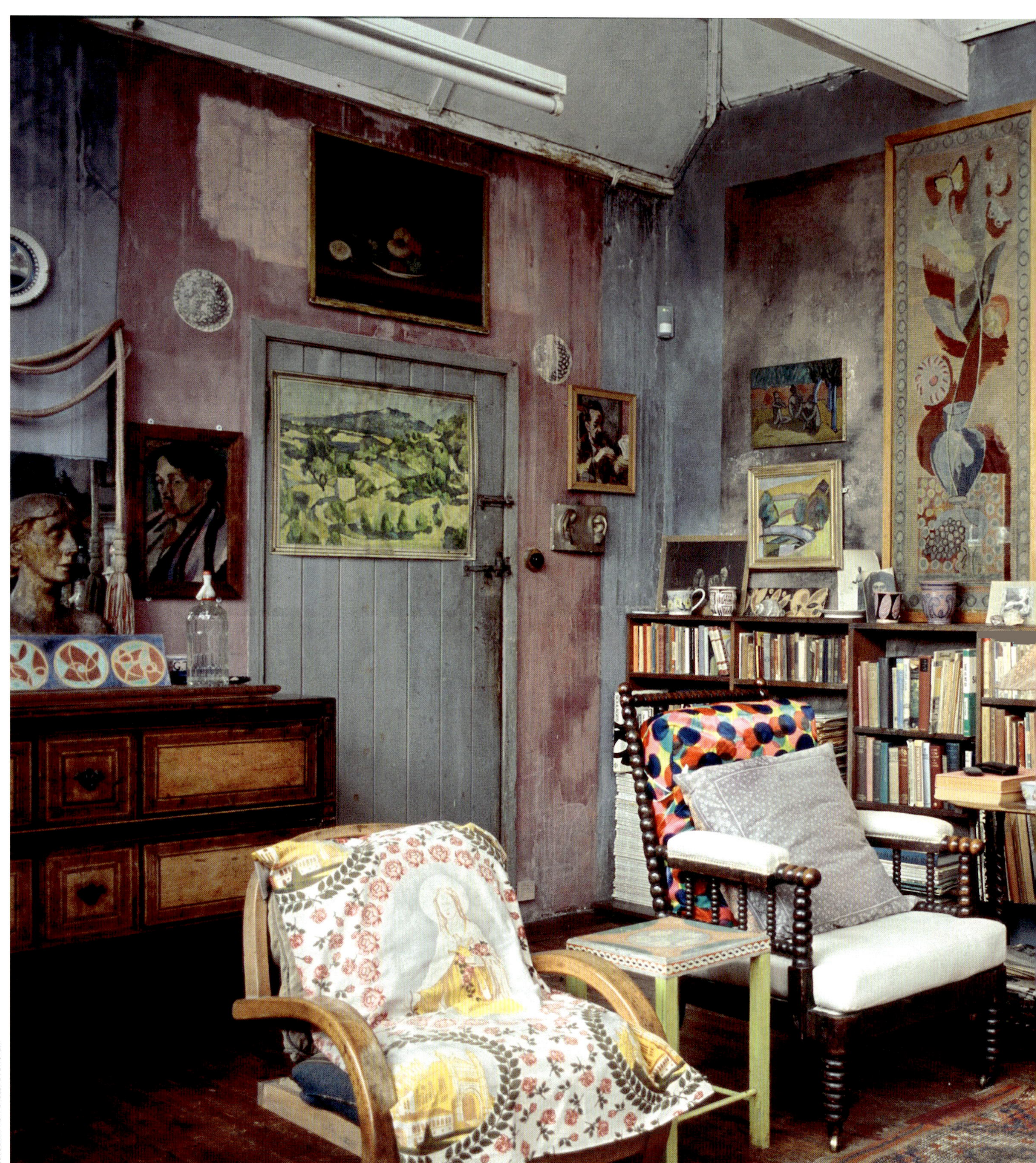

PHOTOGRAPHS: PENELOPE FEWSTER

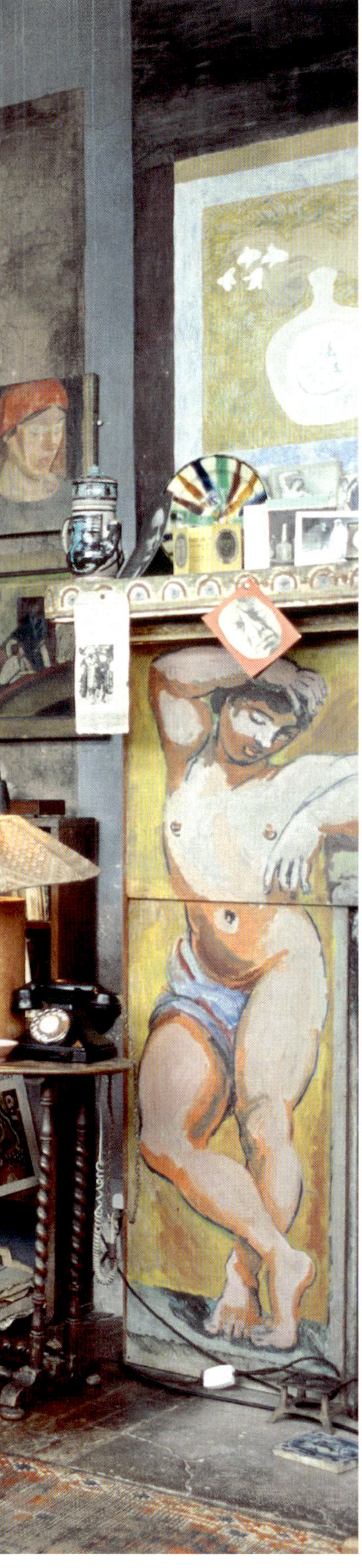

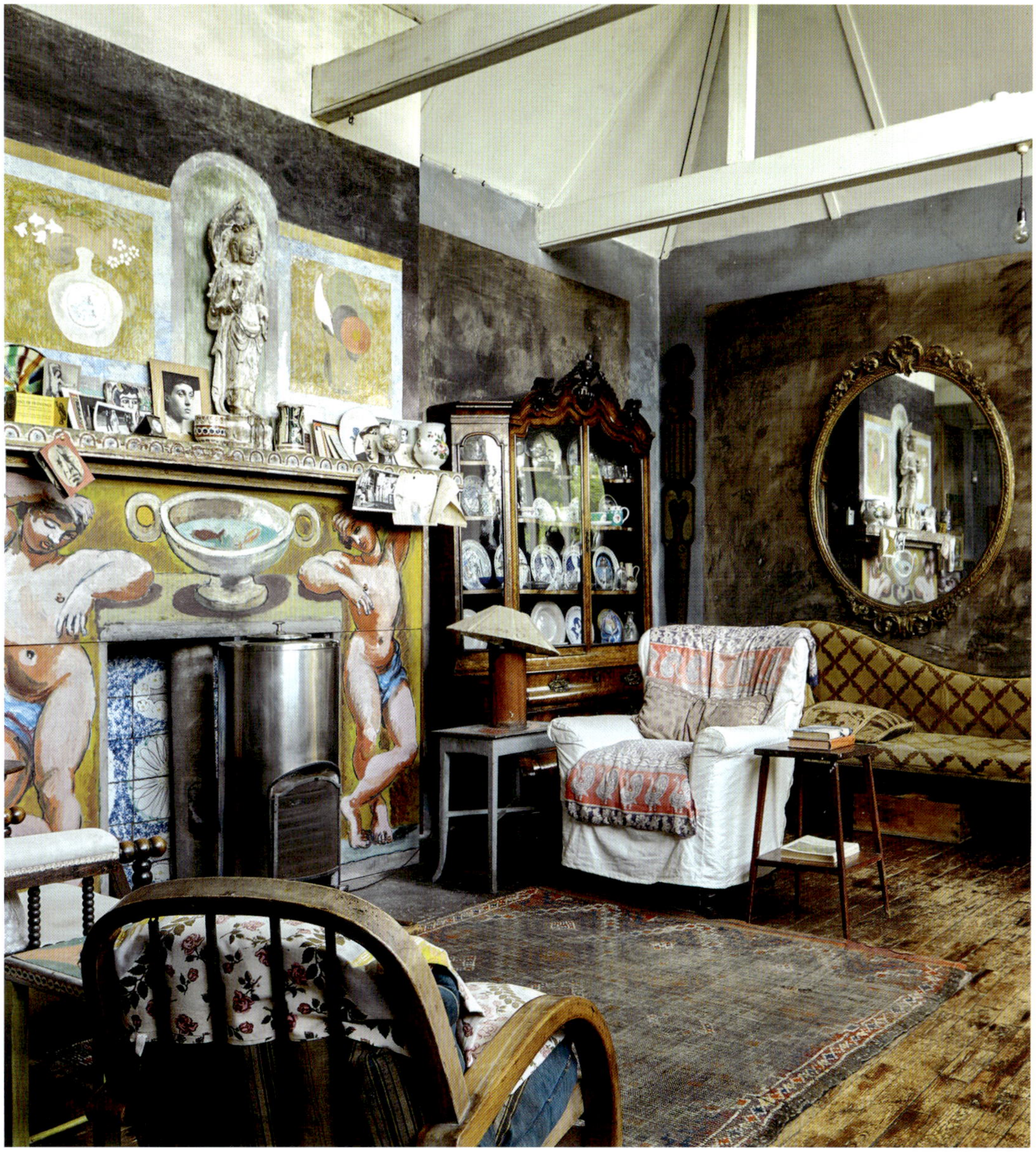

PHOTOGRAPH: GAVIN KINGCOME

Bold brushstrokes **LEFT** The Studio is one of the highlights at Charleston. Duncan Grant continued to work here almost until his death in 1978, and the room still contains many of his painting materials, equipment and the ephemera of his daily life. **ABOVE** The glass cabinet in The Studio contains a collection of glass and ceramics, some decorated by the Charleston artists, including four Famous Women plates from a service decorated for Kenneth Clark in 1932. On the west wall there are two Italian fairground figures bought from a stall in Italy by Duncan Grant in 1913.

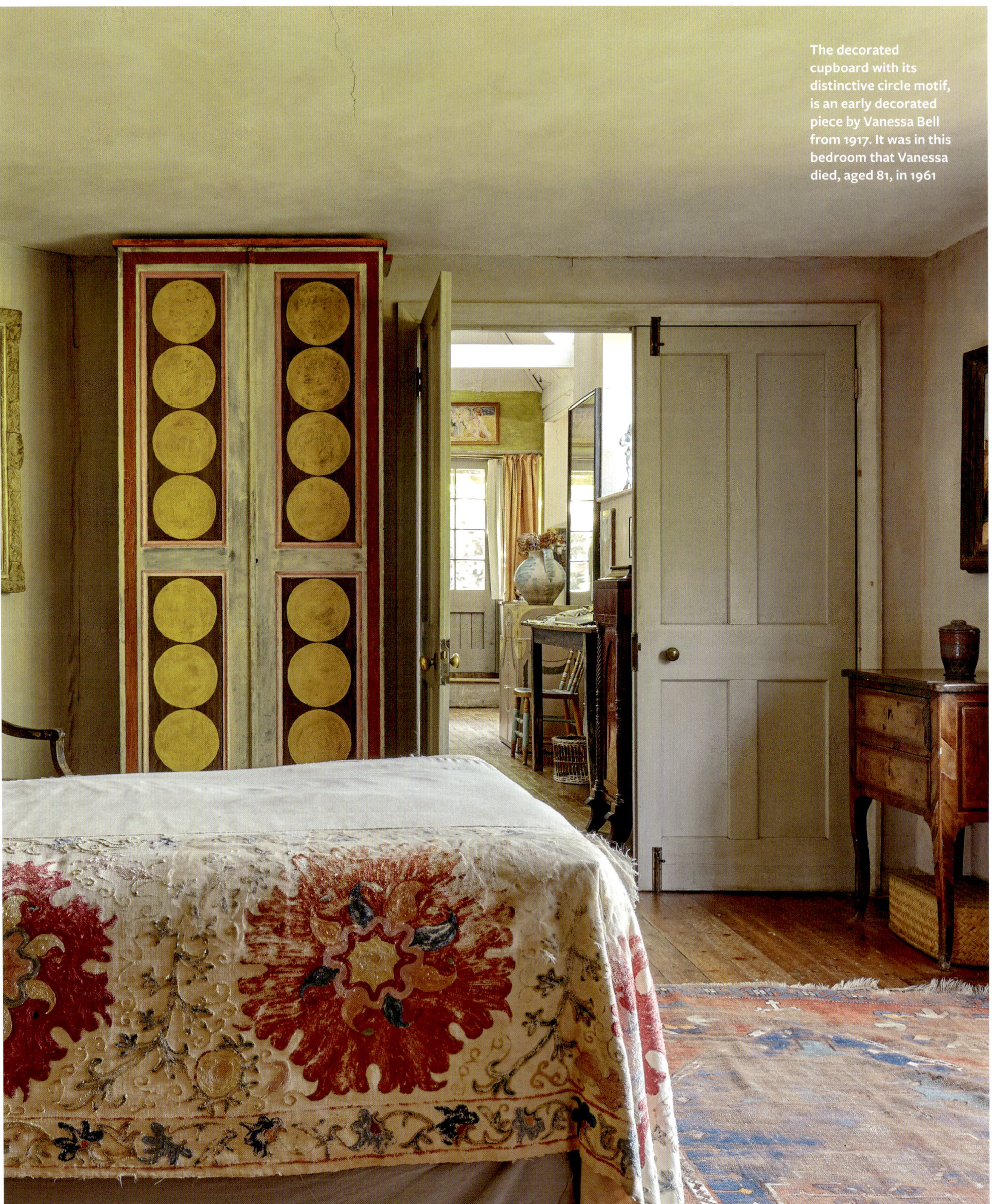

The decorated cupboard with its distinctive circle motif, is an early decorated piece by Vanessa Bell from 1917. It was in this bedroom that Vanessa died, aged 81, in 1961

PHOTOGRAPH: GAVIN KINGCOME

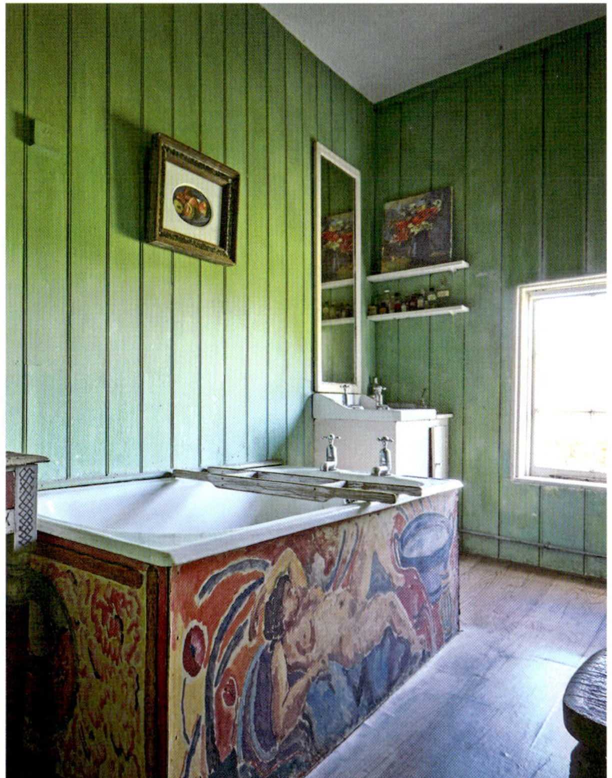

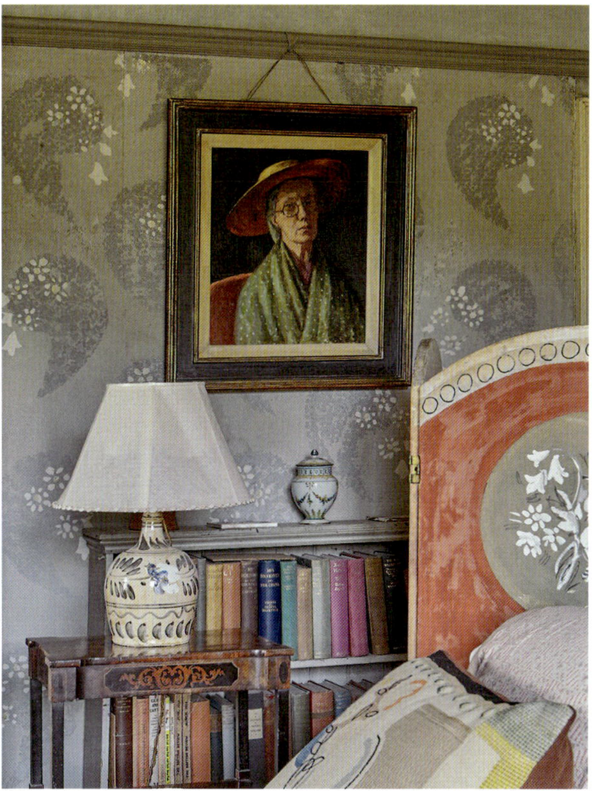

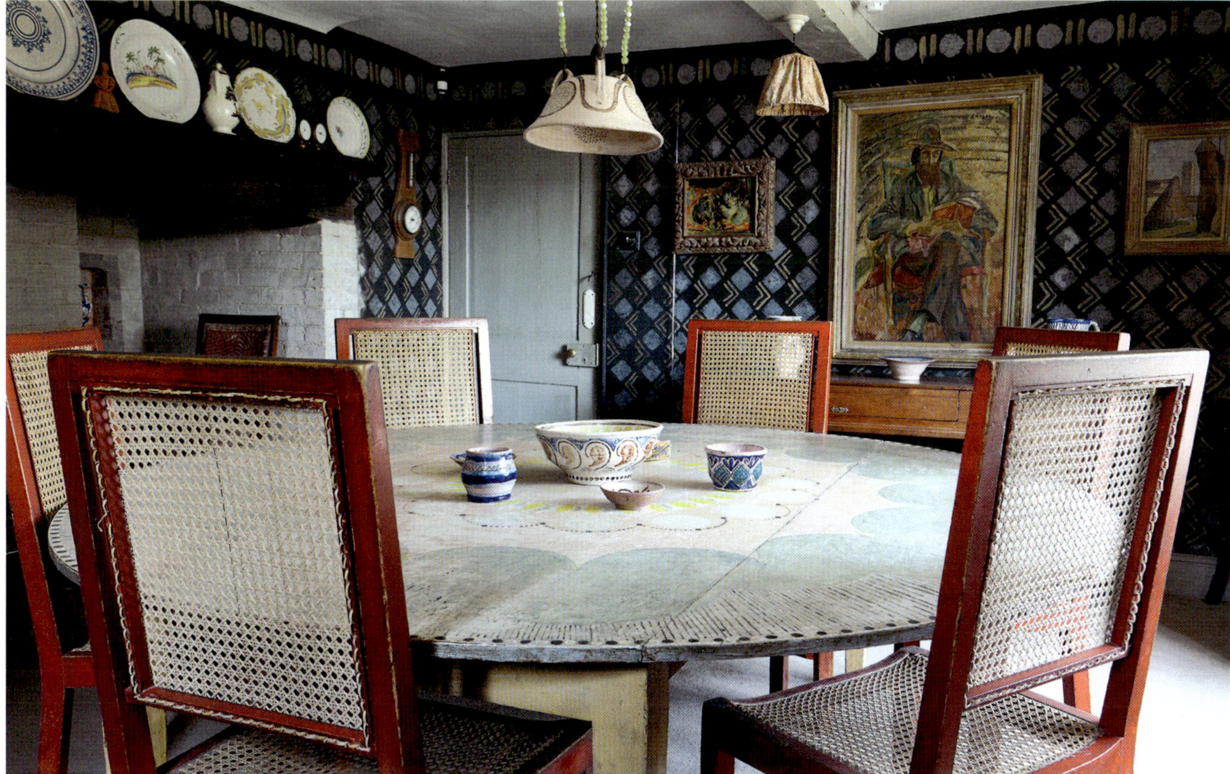

PHOTOGRAPHS: PENELOPE FEWSTER, GAVIN KINGCOME

Colour and pattern **TOP LEFT** The panels in the Green Bathroom were painted around 1969 by Duncan Grant's friend Richard Shone, who based the design on a drawing by Delacroix. **TOP RIGHT** The Garden Room's decorative scheme of grey stencilled paisley shapes, with freehand white flowers was carried out in 1945. The self-portrait by Vanessa Bell was painted in her studio age 80. **BOTTOM** The Dining Room's red lacquer and cane chairs are from the Omega Workshops, designed by Roger Fry in 1913. The geometric print on the walls was the inspiration for the packaging for my new Tilton Bloomsbury Set paint box.

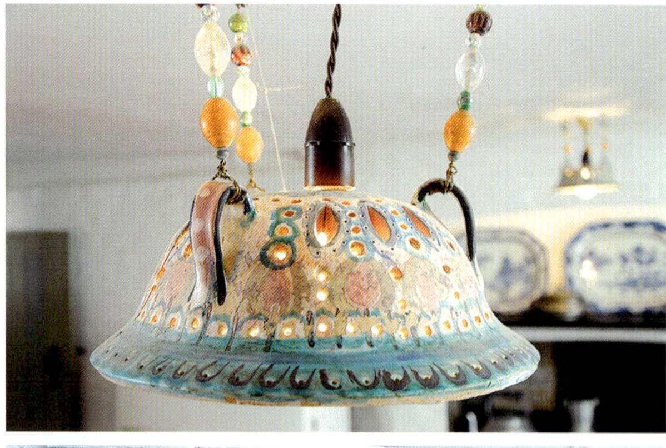

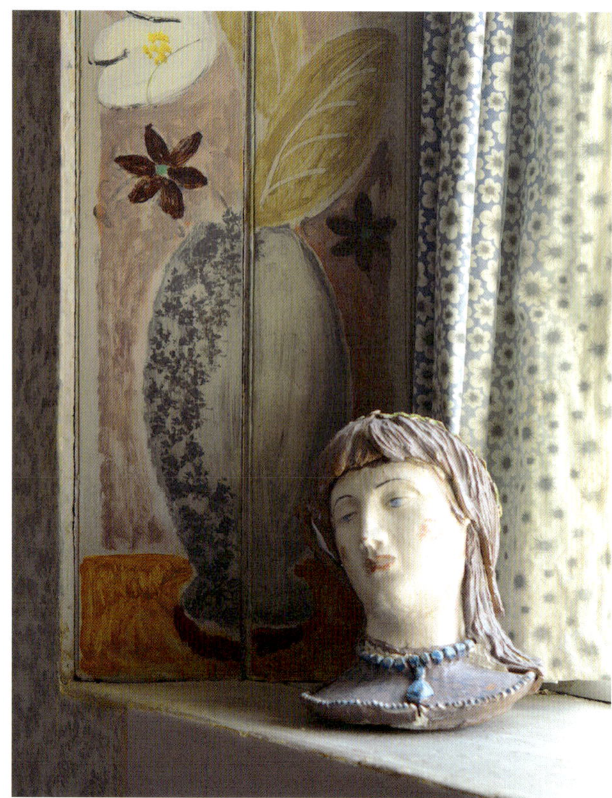

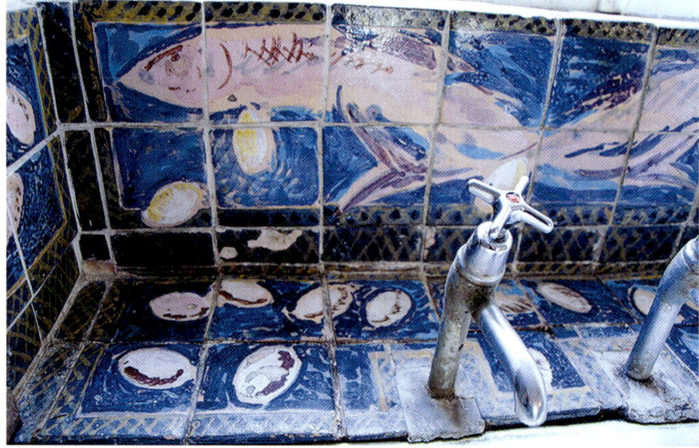

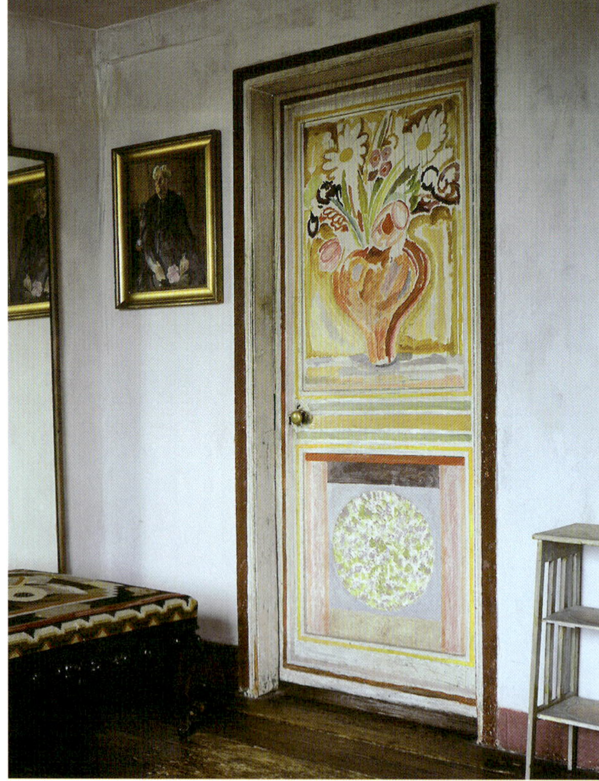

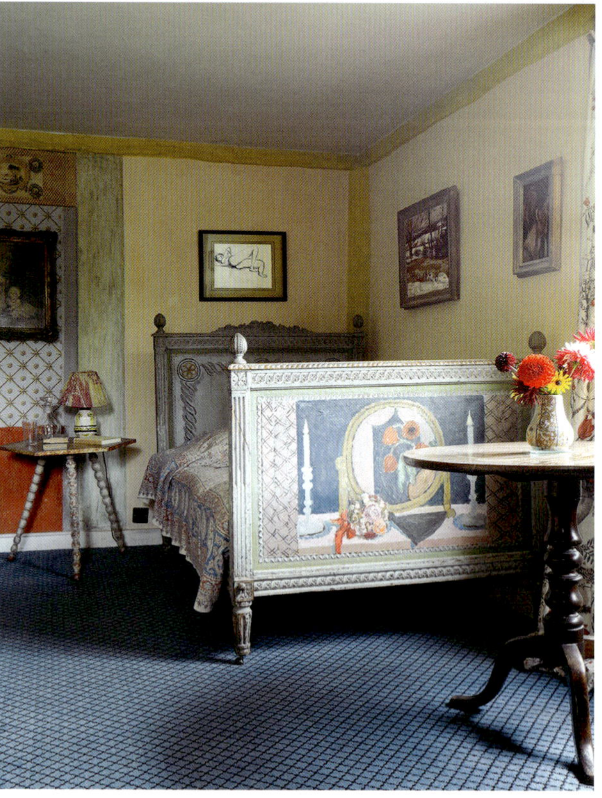

PHOTOGRAPHS: PENELOPE FEWSTER, DARREN CLARK, GAVIN KINGCOME, TONY TREE

All in the detail **TOP LEFT** Quentin Bell's pottery assistant, Victoria Walton, made this ceramic and bead lampshade for the Kitchen. **TOP RIGHT** From the moment they moved in, the artists began to transform Charleston with decoration. **MIDDLE LEFT** Throughout the house uninhibited colours and patterns adorn the walls, furniture, ceramics and tiles. **BOTTOM LEFT** The painted doors in Duncan Grant's Bedroom were decorated by Vanessa Bell in 1918. **BOTTOM RIGHT** The colour scheme in Clive Bell's Bedroom dates from around 1917, when Vanessa Bell used it as a studio. His antique French bed was decorated by Vanessa in around 1950.

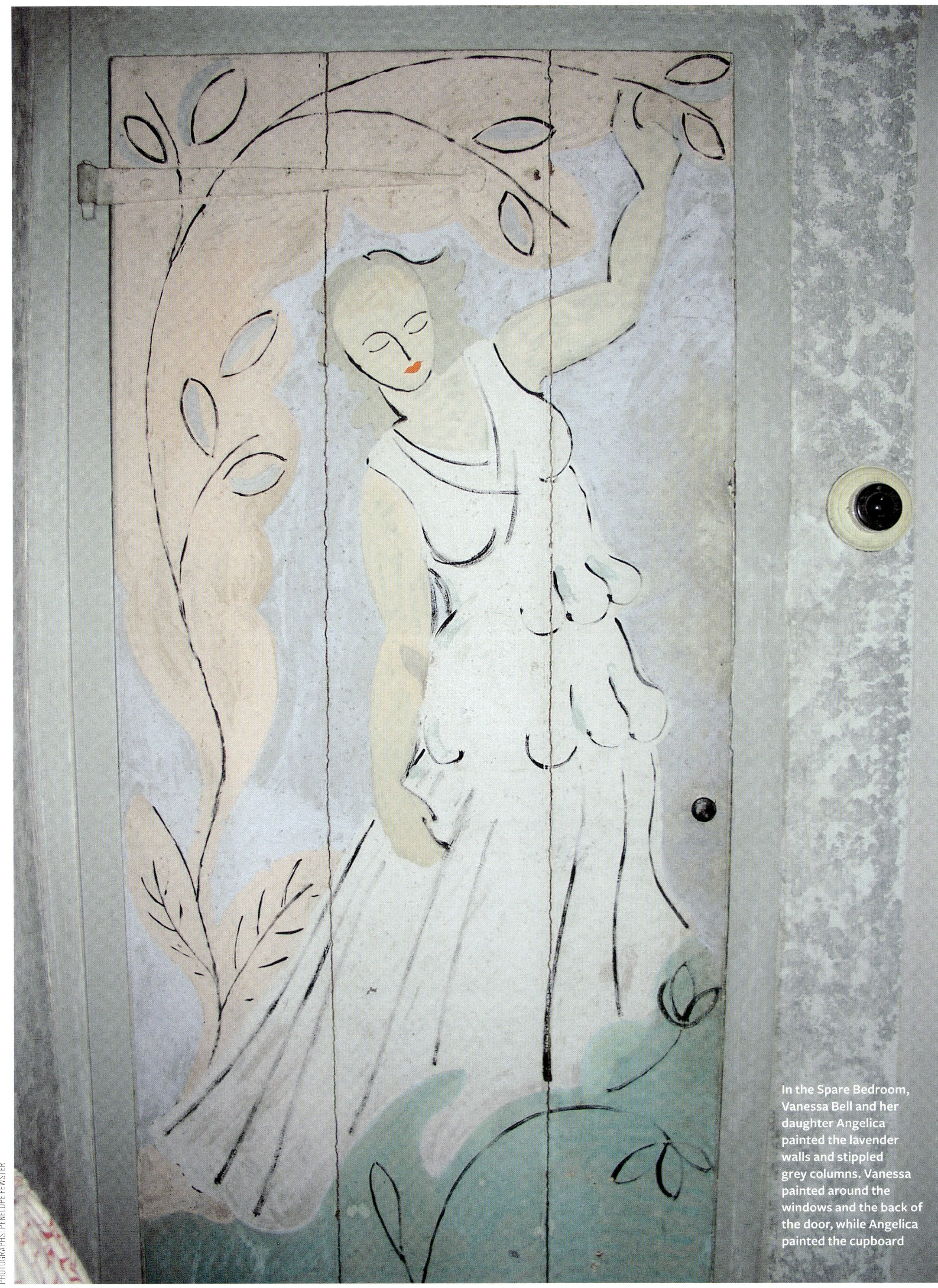

In the Spare Bedroom, Vanessa Bell and her daughter Angelica painted the lavender walls and stippled grey columns. Vanessa painted around the windows and the back of the door, while Angelica painted the cupboard

PHOTOGRAPHS: PENELOPE FEWSTER

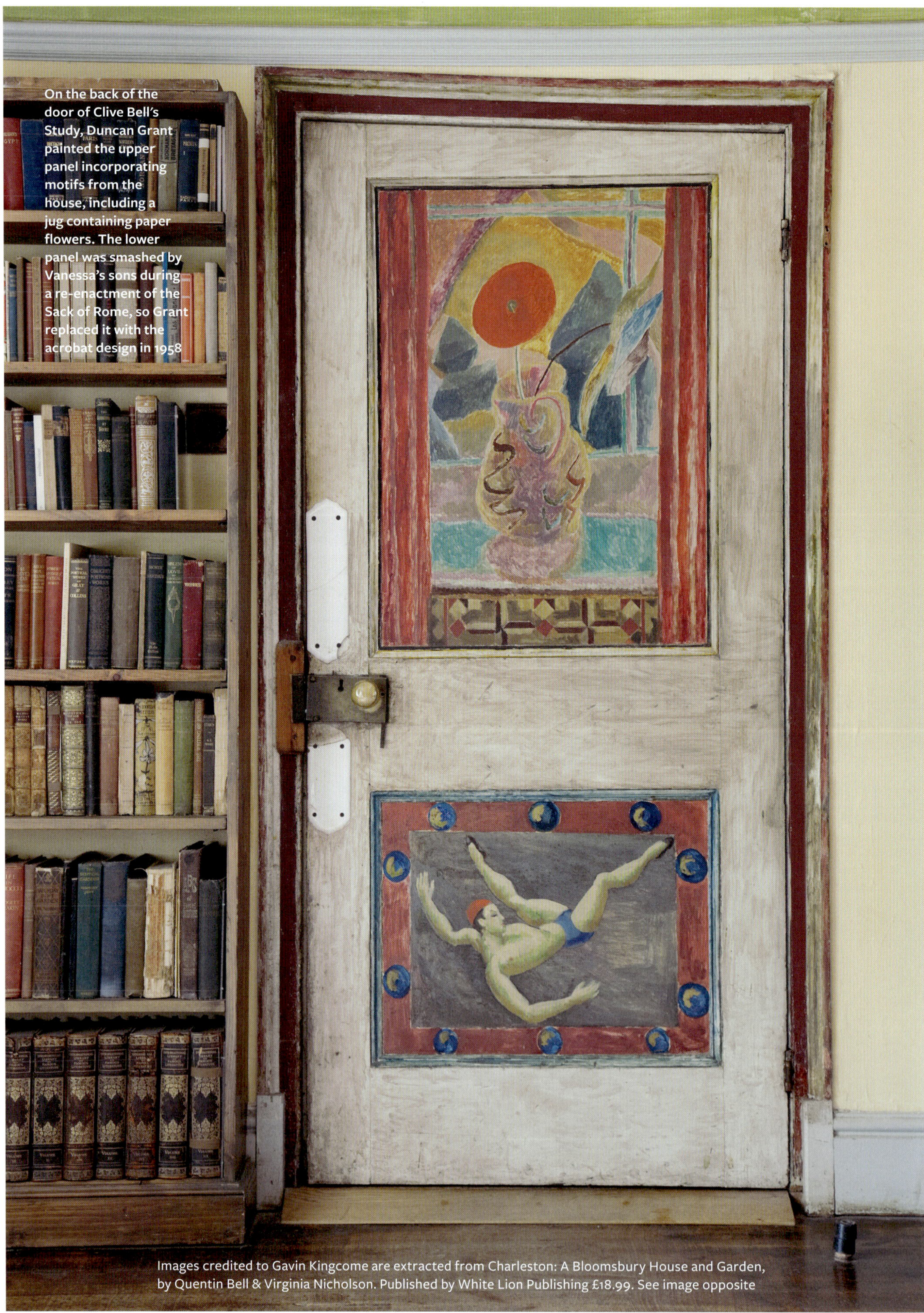

On the back of the door of Clive Bell's Study, Duncan Grant painted the upper panel incorporating motifs from the house, including a jug containing paper flowers. The lower panel was smashed by Vanessa's sons during a re-enactment of the Sack of Rome, so Grant replaced it with the acrobat design in 1958

Images credited to Gavin Kingcome are extracted from Charleston: A Bloomsbury House and Garden, by Quentin Bell & Virginia Nicholson. Published by White Lion Publishing £18.99. See image opposite

PHOTOGRAPH: PENELOPE FEWSTER

Get the look

ANNIE'S BLOOMSBURY STYLE FOR YOUR HOME

Style Secrets

I've been inspired by Charleston for many years, and it's fascinating to see how today's interior design trends such as upcycling, crafts and Jungalow style can be traced back to what the Bloomsbury group were doing there 100 years ago. If you want to create their bohemian, colourful style in your own home, the shop at Charleston is the perfect place to start: you'll find wonderful rugs, cushions, ceramics, accessories, prints and much more.
And, of course, all of these tie in perfectly with my three Charleston-inspired Decorative Paint Sets featuring three new Chalk Paint® colours – Rodmell, Tilton and Firle – and two current Chalk Paint® colours.

PHOTOGRAPH: ANNIE, HARRIET MATTHEWS, RUG, CRESSIDA BELL

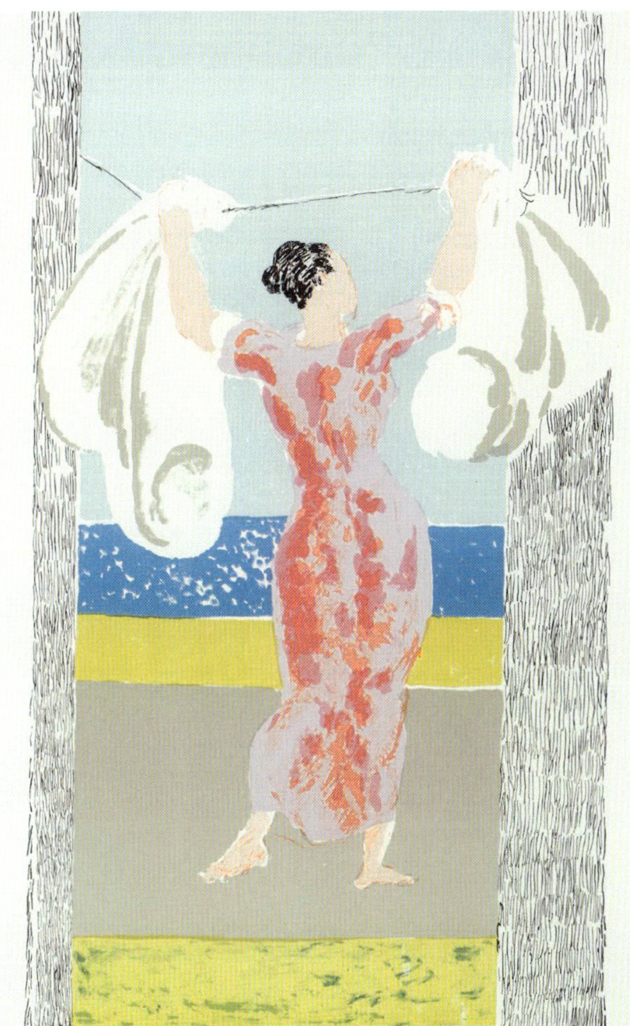

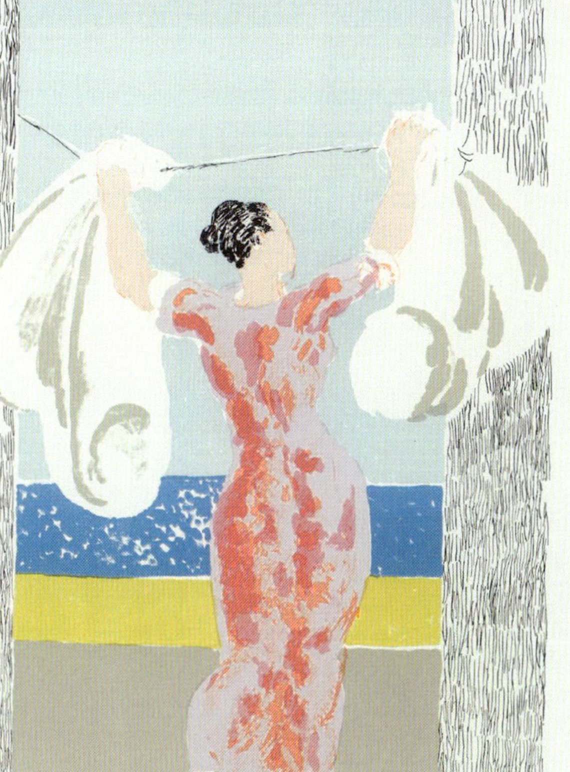

ANNIE SLOAN Annie Sloan with Charleston Paint-Your-Own Keepsake Box *www.anniesloan.com*

CHARLESTON: A Bloomsbury House and Garden, by Quentin Bell & Virginia Nicholson. Published by White Lion Publishing *www.quartoknows.com*

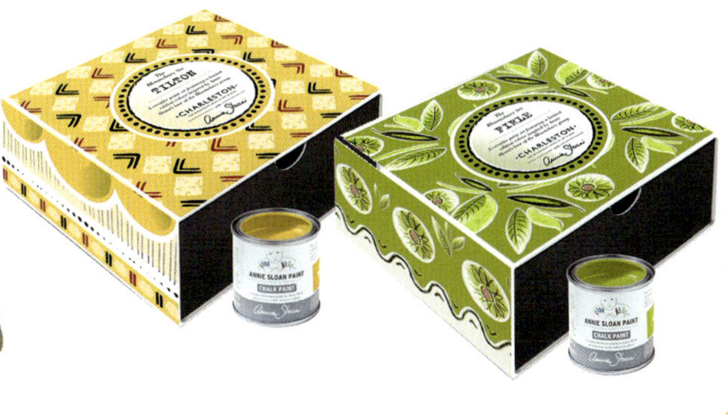

(CENTRE) DUNCAN GRANT Standing Woman Lithograph **(ABOVE) CRESSIDA BELL** Limited-edition rug **LOUISE GARDELLE** Espresso Cup **IRENA SIBRIJNS** Bowl *www.charleston.org.uk*

(ABOVE LEFT) DUNCAN GRANT Queen Mary Cushion *www.charleston.org.uk*

(ABOVE) ANNIE SLOAN Annie Sloan with Charleston Decorative Paint Set *www.anniesloan.com*

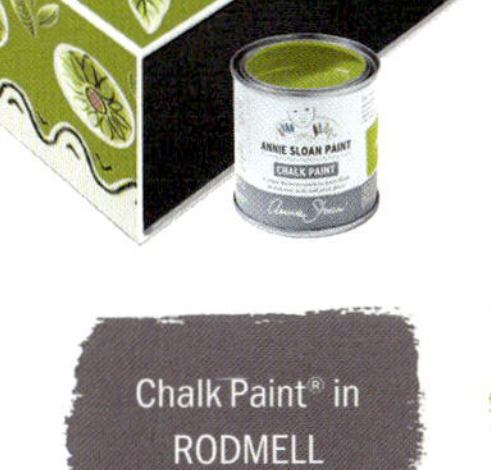

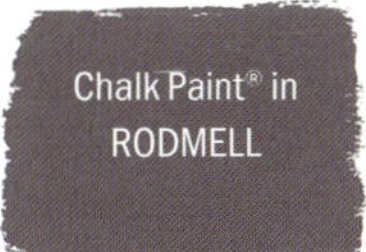

Chalk Paint® in TILTON

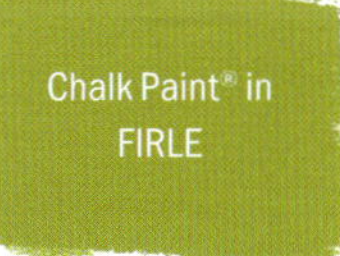

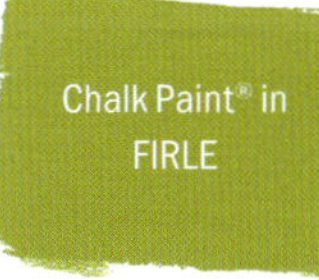

NEW CHALK PAINT® COLOURS *www.anniesloan.com*

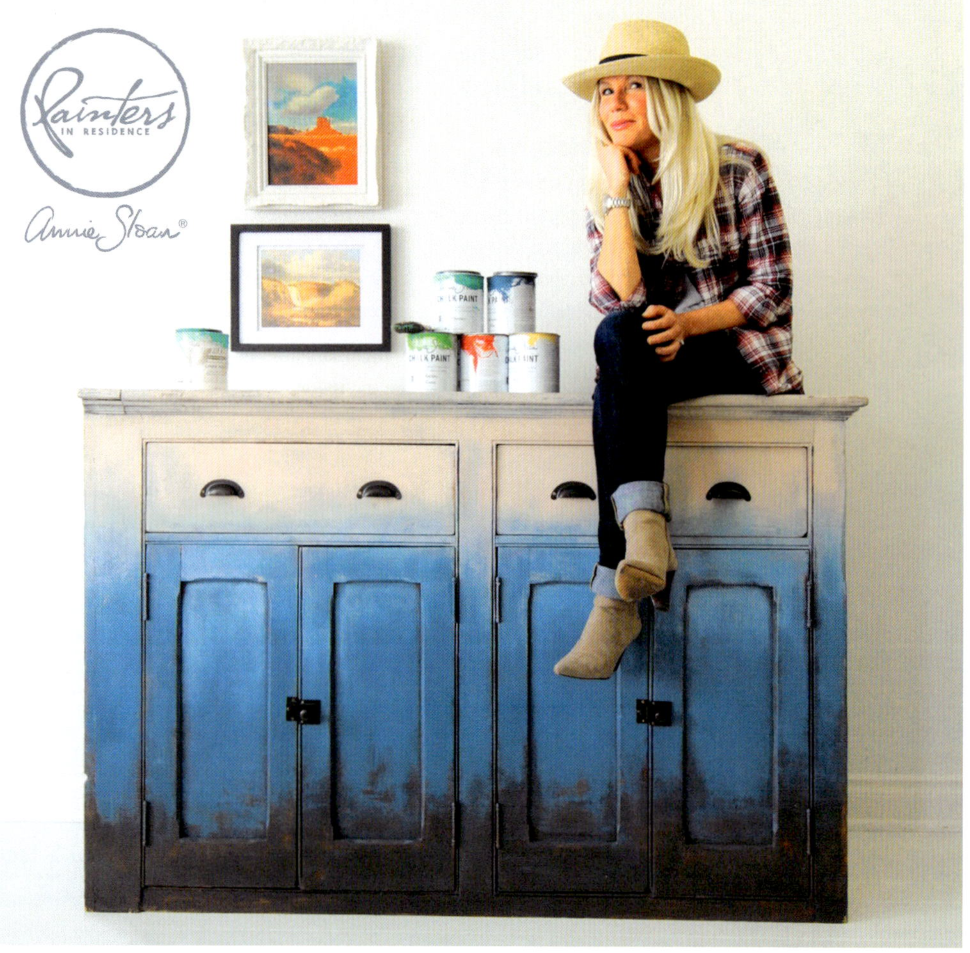

PHOTOGRAPHS: ILDIKO HORVATH

Ildiko Horvath

"I have come to see the pieces I paint as works of art and they give me pure joy"

Born in Sopron, Hungary, Ildiko left to start a new life in Ontario when she met her Canadian husband.

Whilst renovating their first house on a tight budget, Ildiko was thrilled to win a design contest in Canadian House and Home magazine. This success lead to friends asking if she could paint and restore furniture for them. Ildiko soon realised that she could turn her passion into a business, and six years ago she launched her website, Restored4U.

Her mastery of layering, shading, and her signature ombré technique, prompted Annie Sloan to invite Ildiko to become her Painter in Residence in October 2017. Unbelievably, the old farmhouse sideboard (above) was the first ombré piece Ildiko painted and is still one of her favourites.

Because Chalk Paint® dries so quickly, Ildiko can often finish a project in a day. Naturally drawn to deep but bright colours, her favourite Chalk Paint® colour is Florence. "The gorgeous teal colour looks really stunning on painted pieces and it's so easy to make it work pretty much with any colour palette and decor."

Ildiko has some sound advice to anyone starting out, "Please don't be scared – it's only paint and if you're not happy with the results, don't give up, just repaint it!" AS

www.restored4u.com *@ildikoh67*
www.etsy.com/uk/shop/VintageRefinished

Turn to page 124 to follow Ildiko's step-by-step guide to creating a stunning ombré paint effect

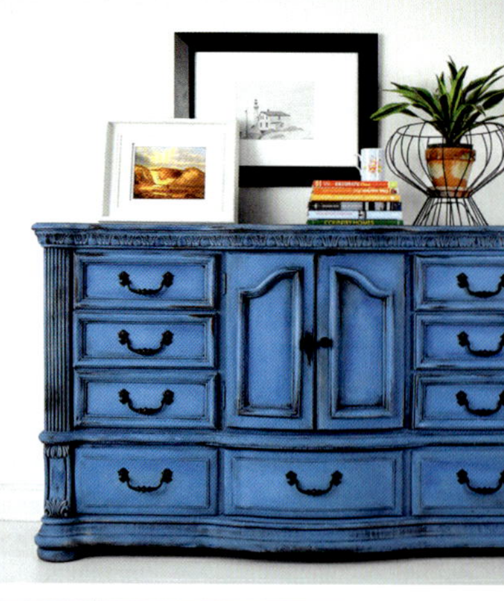

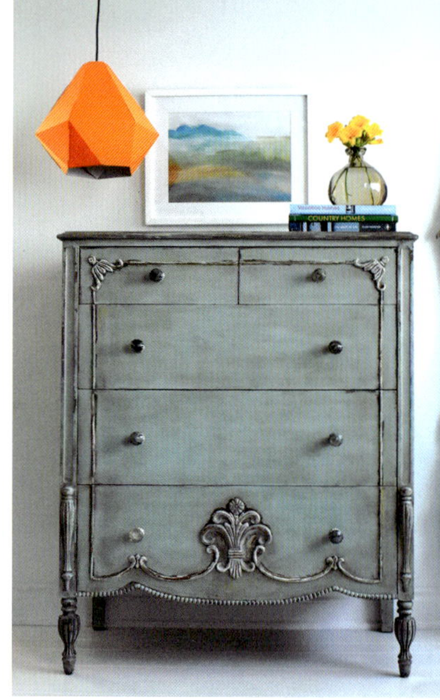

ABOVE Main colour Chalk Paint® in Duck Egg. **Accent colours** Arles, Red Primer, Old White. Clear and Dark Wax

Main colour Chalk Paint® in Florence, Aubusson Blue, Pure. **Under colour** Graphite. **Accent colours** Dry-brushed Country Grey, Olive, Coco. Clear Wax

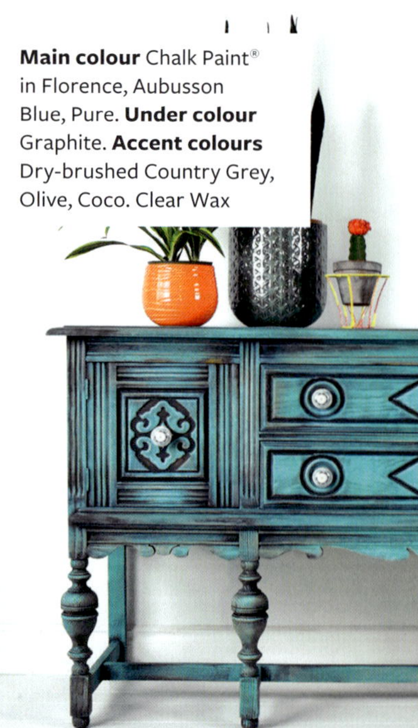

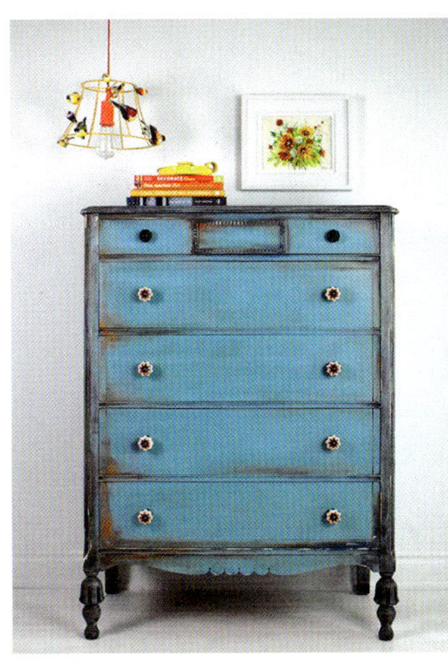

LEFT Main colour Chalk Paint® in Napoleonic Blue, Duck Egg 50/50. **Under colour** Graphite. **Accent colours** Country Grey, French Linen. Clear Wax

RIGHT Main colour Chalk Paint® in Provence. **Accent colours** Old White, Primer Red, Barcelona Orange, Napoleonic Blue. Clear Wax

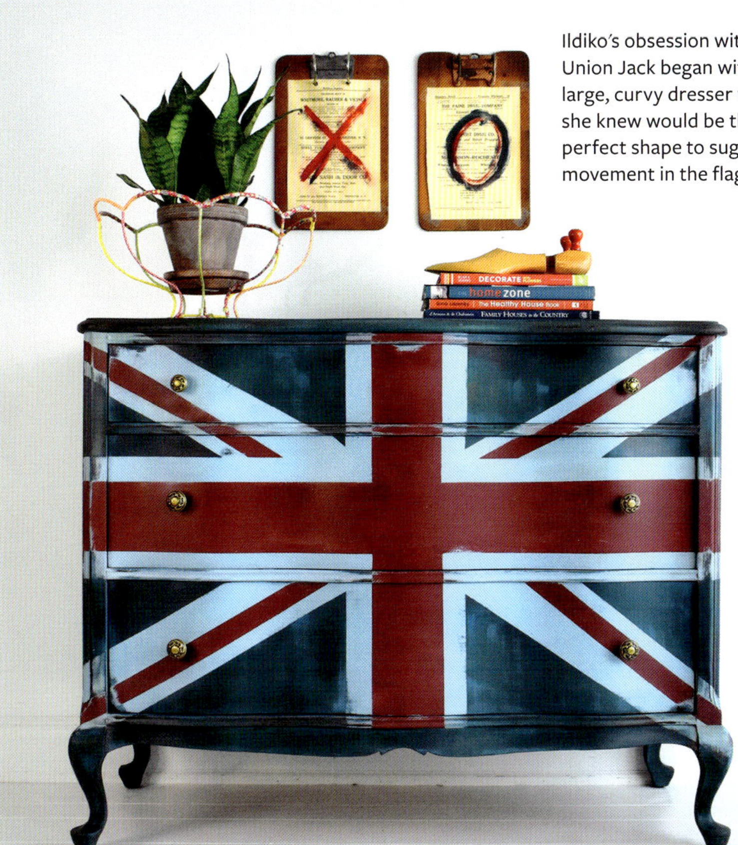

Ildiko's obsession with the Union Jack began with a large, curvy dresser which she knew would be the perfect shape to suggest movement in the flag

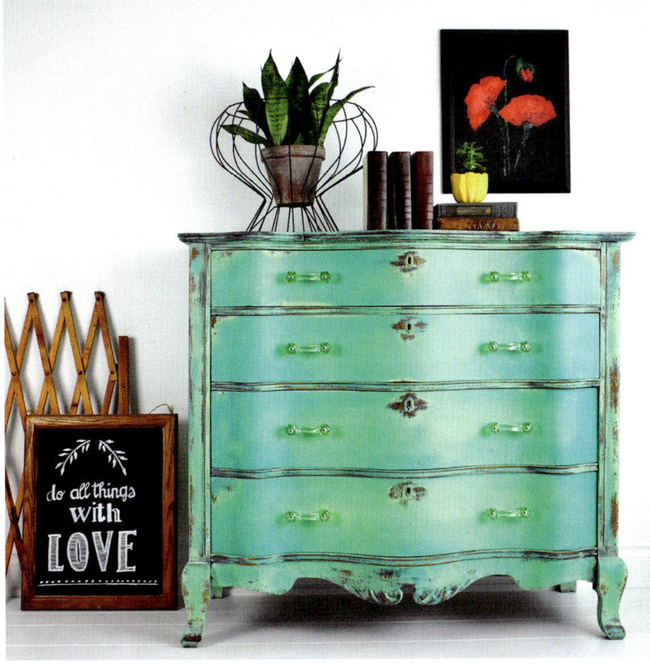

ABOVE Main colour Chalk Paint® in Lem Lem, Florence, Pure. Florence wash over main colour. Wet distressed. Clear Wax

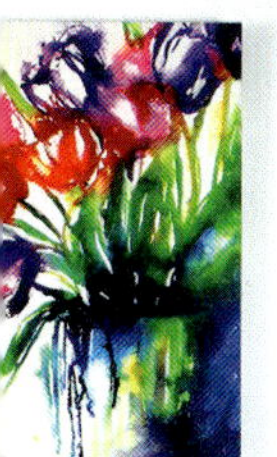

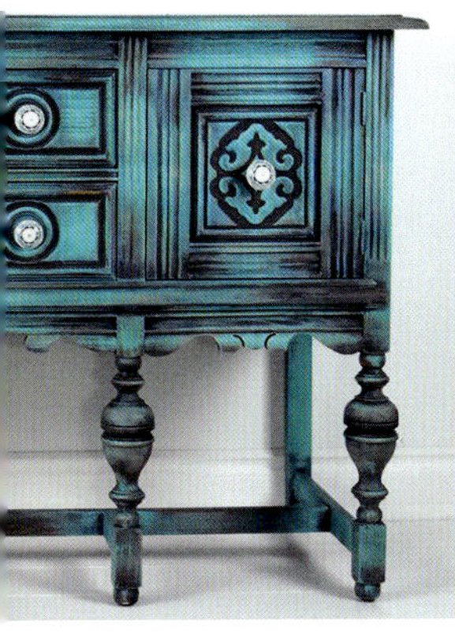

PAINTERS IN RESIDENCE

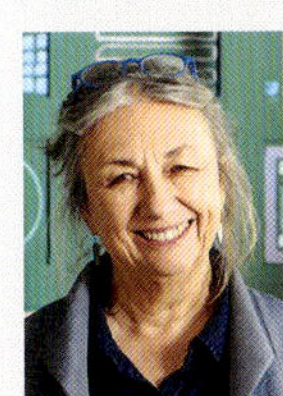

"I set up my Painters in Residence programme in 2014 to collaborate with like-minded people and showcase the high-quality, innovative, and sometimes 'leftfield' things they're doing with Chalk Paint® and my other products.

"The concept is loosely based on the way an art gallery or museum will have an 'artist in residence' as a way to get inspired to create works at the venue. Each Painter in Residence is carefully selected by me based on their style and the work they create. They explore the boundaries of decorative furniture painting and are all different in their approach, colour, tone and texture."

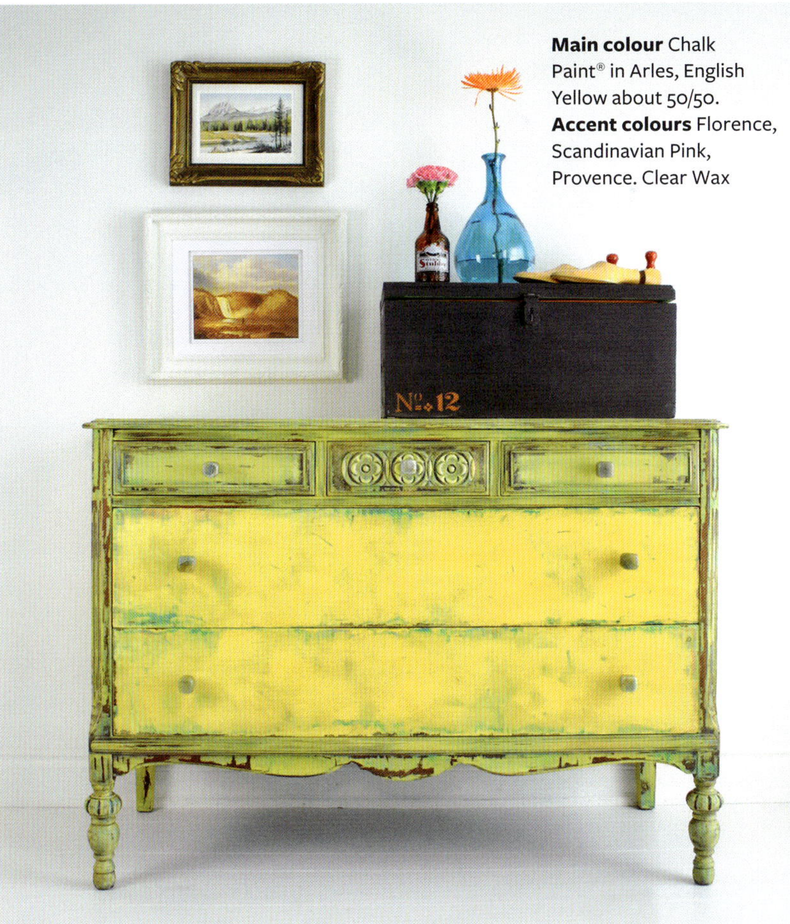

Main colour Chalk Paint® in Arles, English Yellow about 50/50. **Accent colours** Florence, Scandinavian Pink, Provence. Clear Wax

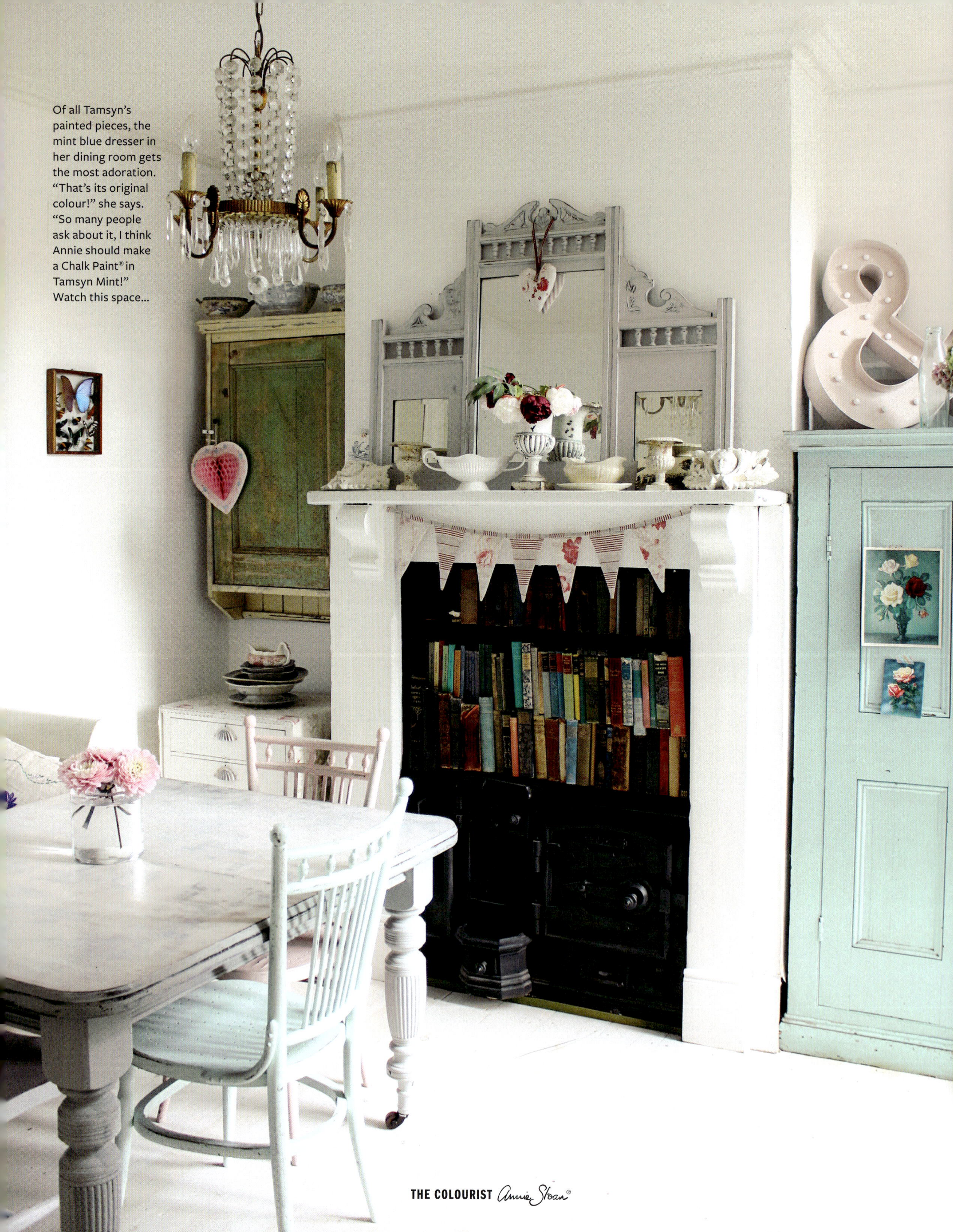

Of all Tamsyn's painted pieces, the mint blue dresser in her dining room gets the most adoration. "That's its original colour!" she says. "So many people ask about it, I think Annie should make a Chalk Paint® in Tamsyn Mint!" Watch this space...

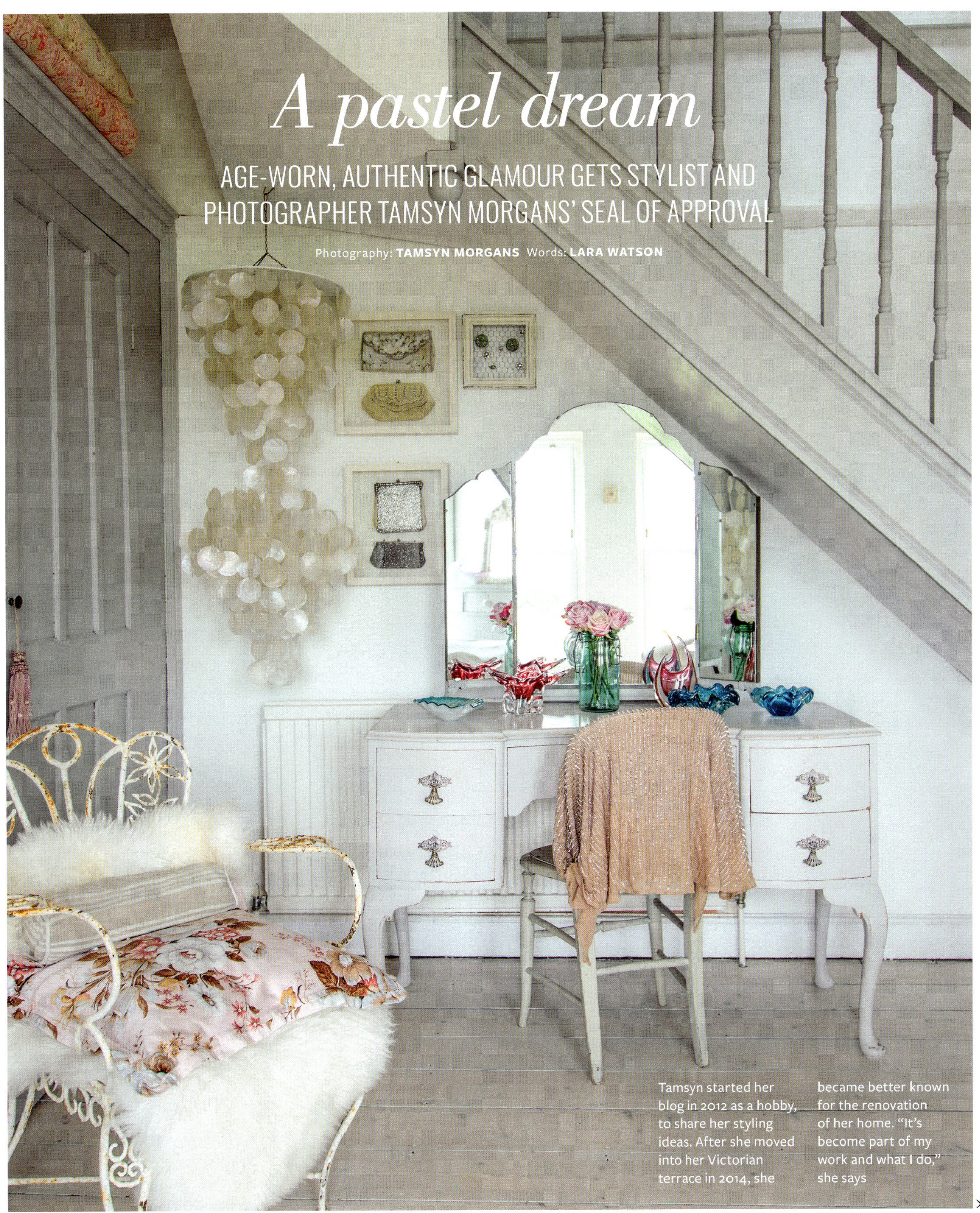

A pastel dream

AGE-WORN, AUTHENTIC GLAMOUR GETS STYLIST AND PHOTOGRAPHER TAMSYN MORGANS' SEAL OF APPROVAL

Photography: **TAMSYN MORGANS** Words: **LARA WATSON**

Tamsyn started her blog in 2012 as a hobby, to share her styling ideas. After she moved into her Victorian terrace in 2014, she became better known for the renovation of her home. "It's become part of my work and what I do," she says

»

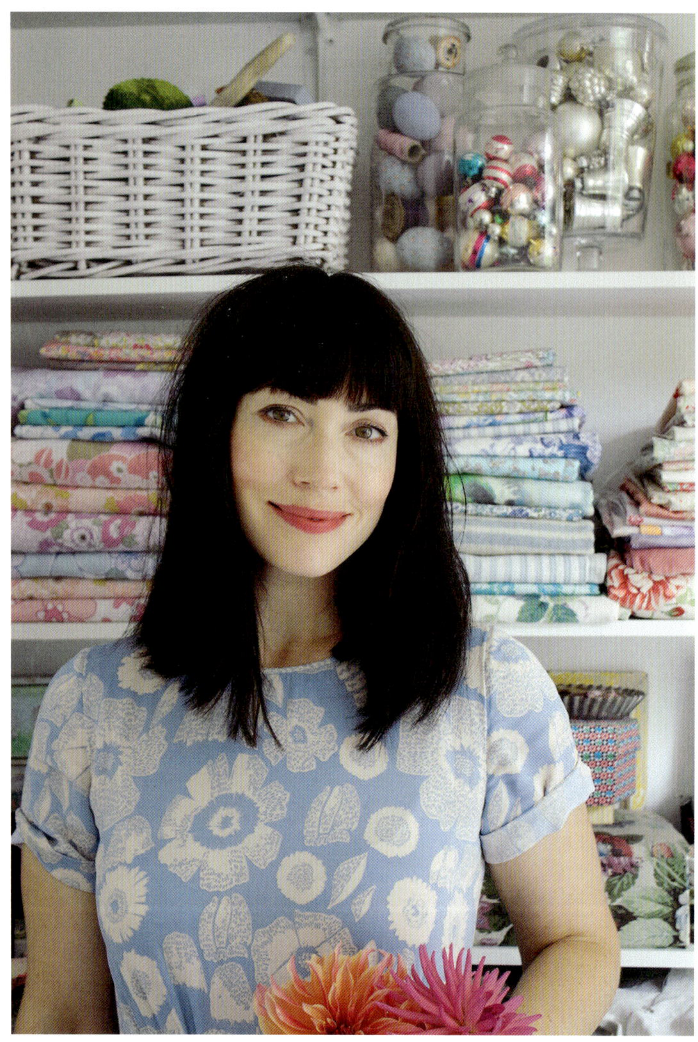

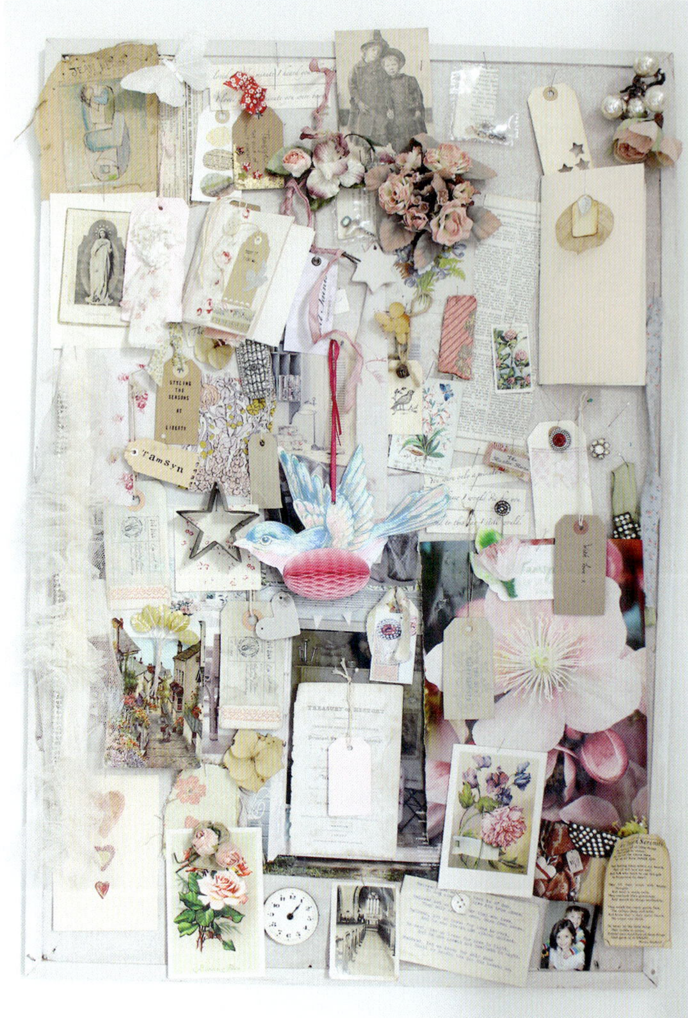

"I'm all about that time-worn look and salvaging beauty from a bygone era. I love painting over things to enhance older items and give them a new lease of life"

You'd never think it, taking in the sheer beauty of Tamsyn Morgans' Victorian terrace home in Norwich as it looks today, but it used to be less than, well... pleasant. When the blogger behind The Villa on Mount Pleasant first had a look around in 2013, it was "in a right state" as she puts it. Damp walls, horrible old carpets and rubbish stacked so high it nearly obscured the original ceiling roses may have put other renovators off, but not Tamsyn.

With a passion for transforming vintage junk into highly covetable items, this was one woman well suited to the job. Just a year later, she had a scrubbed clean, stripped back, freshly painted and decorated period home to fill with her treasured mismatched furniture and two children, Lola (13) and Finlay (10).

"Apart from some new stuff in the kitchen from places like Anthropologie, everything else in the house is from car boots, auctions and charity shops," says Tamsyn, who describes her style as "eclectic, a little bit boho, colourful and whimsical." Colour is the key holding everything together – pastel hues in particular and anything with that gorgeous patina of age. "I love faded things," says Tamsyn. "Flowers, botanical prints, bringing the outside in... I'm all about that time-worn look and salvaging beauty from a bygone era. I love painting over things to enhance older items and give them a new lease of life."

So many of Tamsyn's pieces have made a home for themselves this way. Her marble-topped bedside table has had a makeover using Chalk Paint® in Paris Grey, the old pine chest of drawers in her son's room is now »

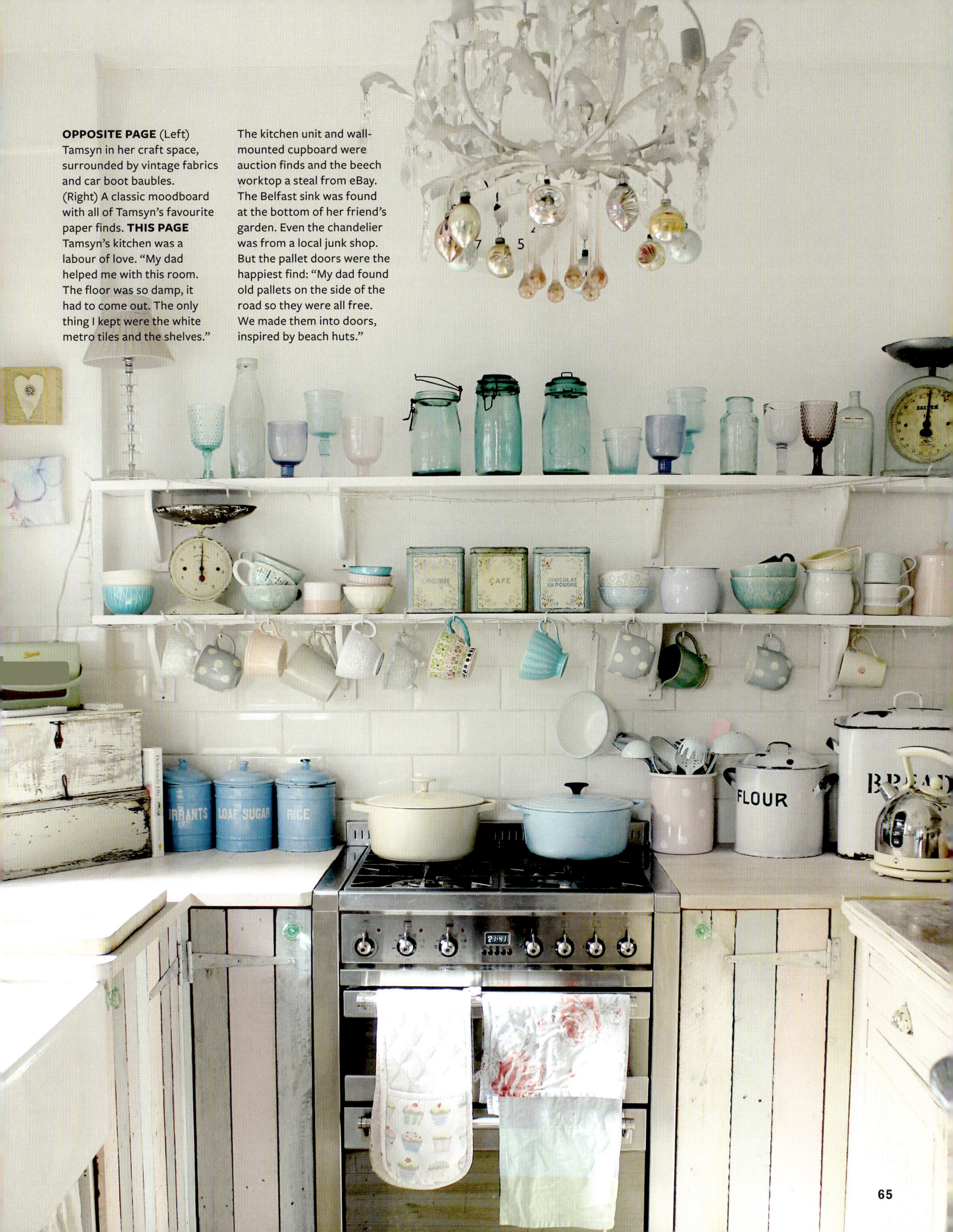

OPPOSITE PAGE (Left) Tamsyn in her craft space, surrounded by vintage fabrics and car boot baubles. (Right) A classic moodboard with all of Tamsyn's favourite paper finds. **THIS PAGE** Tamsyn's kitchen was a labour of love. "My dad helped me with this room. The floor was so damp, it had to come out. The only thing I kept were the white metro tiles and the shelves." The kitchen unit and wall-mounted cupboard were auction finds and the beech worktop a steal from eBay. The Belfast sink was found at the bottom of her friend's garden. Even the chandelier was from a local junk shop. But the pallet doors were the happiest find: "My dad found old pallets on the side of the road so they were all free. We made them into doors, inspired by beach huts."

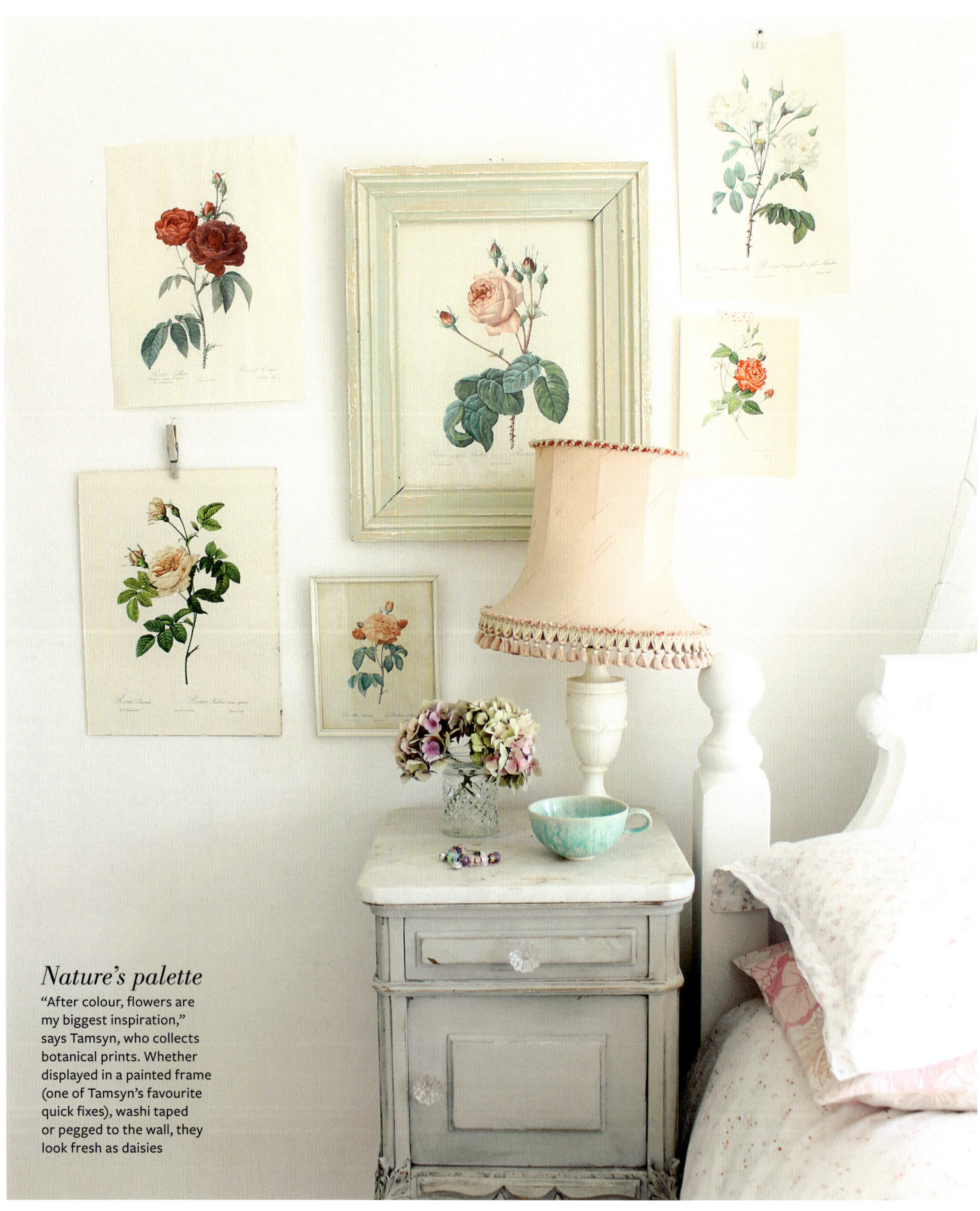

Nature's palette

"After colour, flowers are my biggest inspiration," says Tamsyn, who collects botanical prints. Whether displayed in a painted frame (one of Tamsyn's favourite quick fixes), washi taped or pegged to the wall, they look fresh as daisies

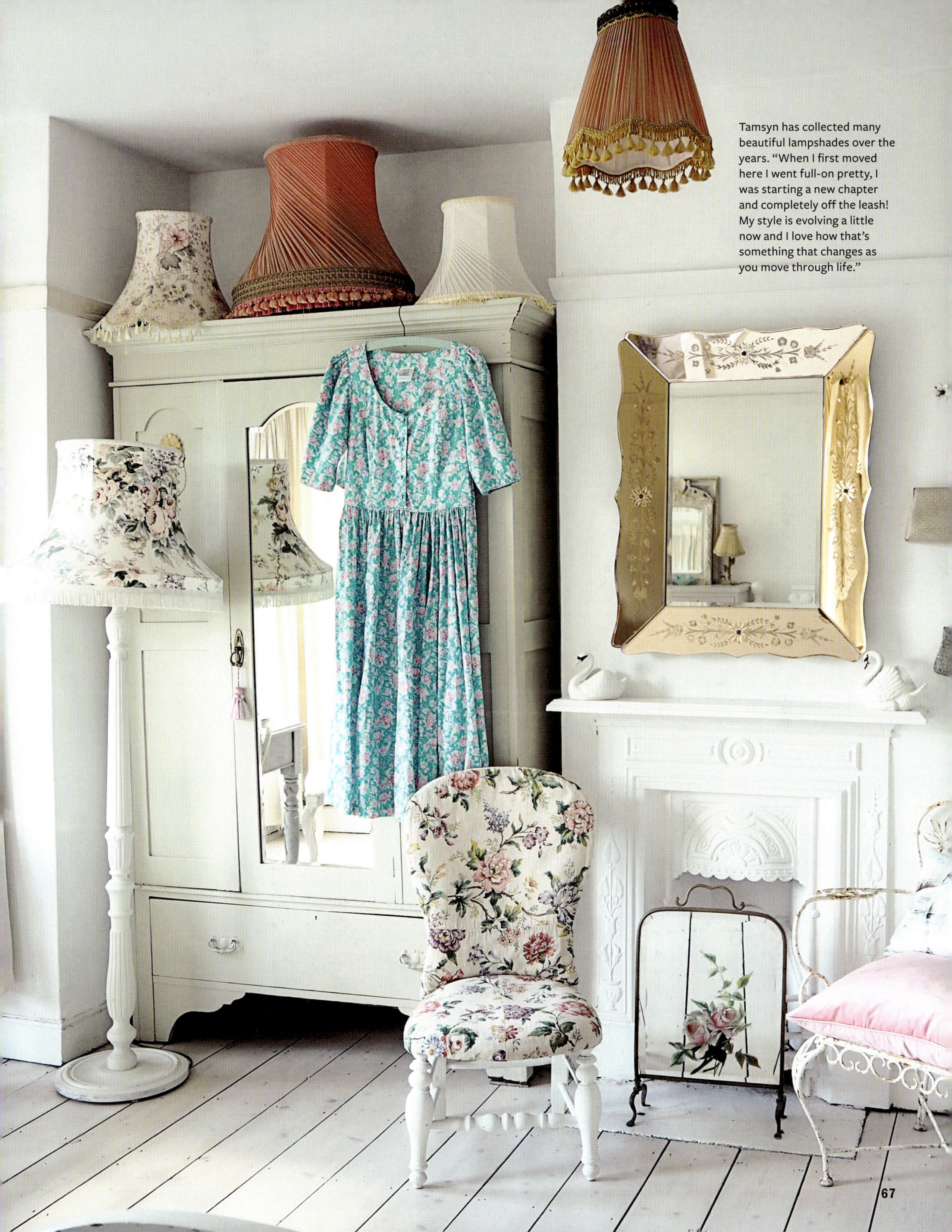

Tamsyn has collected many beautiful lampshades over the years. “When I first moved here I went full-on pretty, I was starting a new chapter and completely off the leash! My style is evolving a little now and I love how that’s something that changes as you move through life.”

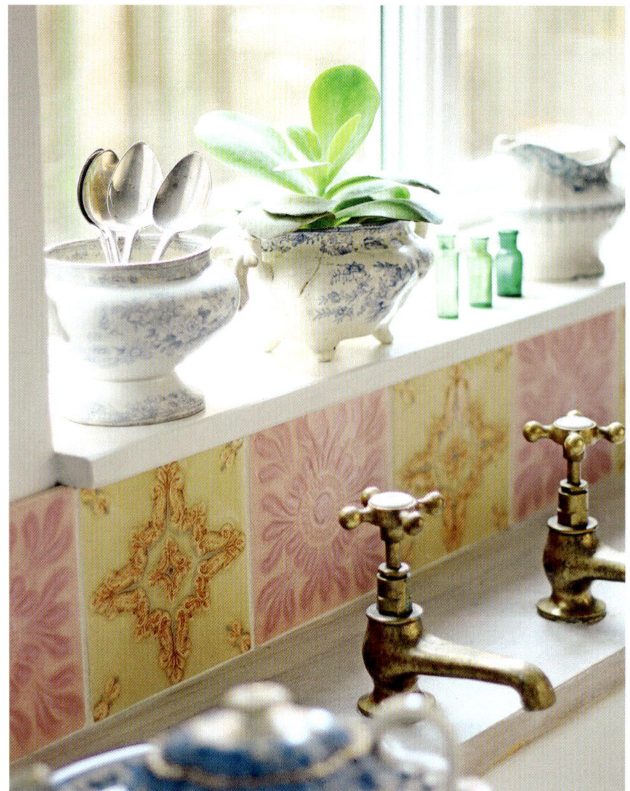

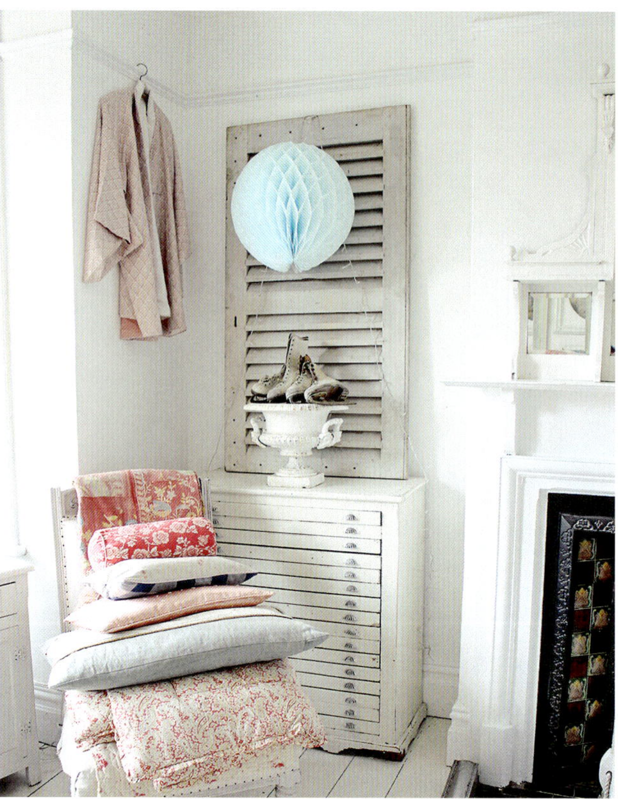

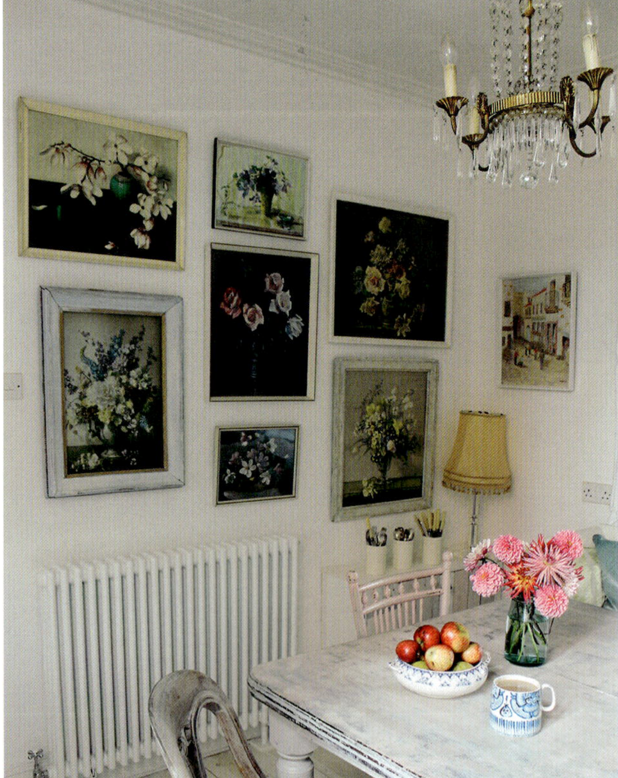

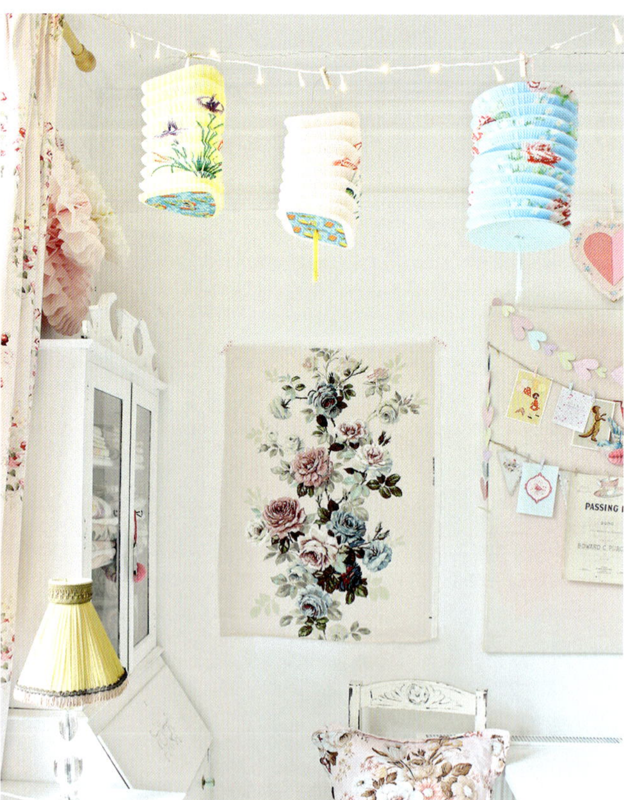

Colour crushing **TOP LEFT** Try displaying treasured like-for-like items in a row on a shelf – these pretty pots strike a balanced yet eclectic chord housing varied items such as a houseplant and antique spoons. **TOP RIGHT** Tamsyn offsets her white-painted furniture with lots of sumptuous textiles and plump pillows in perky shades. **BOTTOM LEFT** In the dining room, you can see another piece of furniture Tamsyn has rescued. "I simply sanded the top, and gave it a wash of Chalk Paint® in Old White, and then waxed it." **BOTTOM RIGHT** Add colour with accessories, like these joyous paper lanterns.

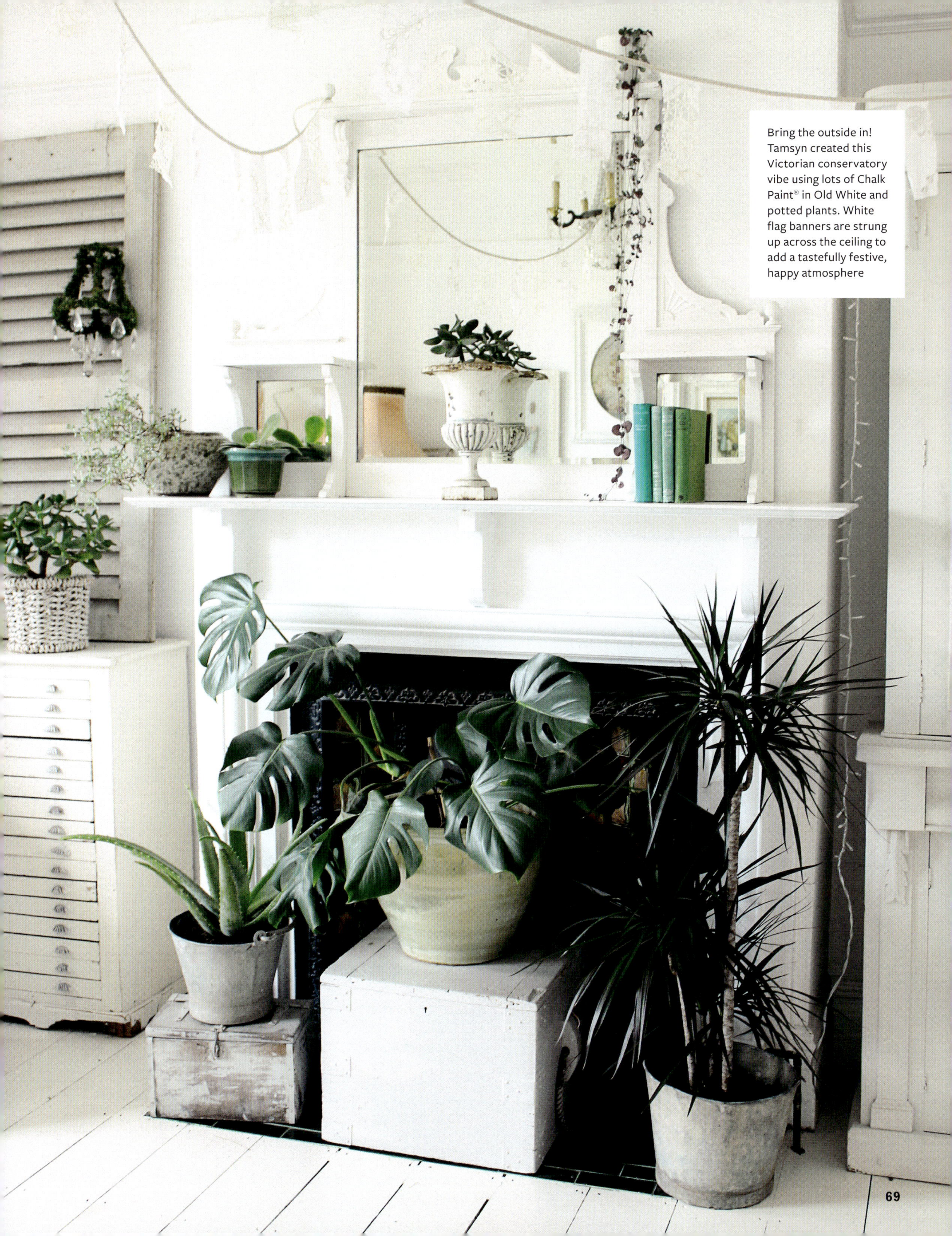

Bring the outside in! Tamsyn created this Victorian conservatory vibe using lots of Chalk Paint® in Old White and potted plants. White flag banners are strung up across the ceiling to add a tastefully festive, happy atmosphere

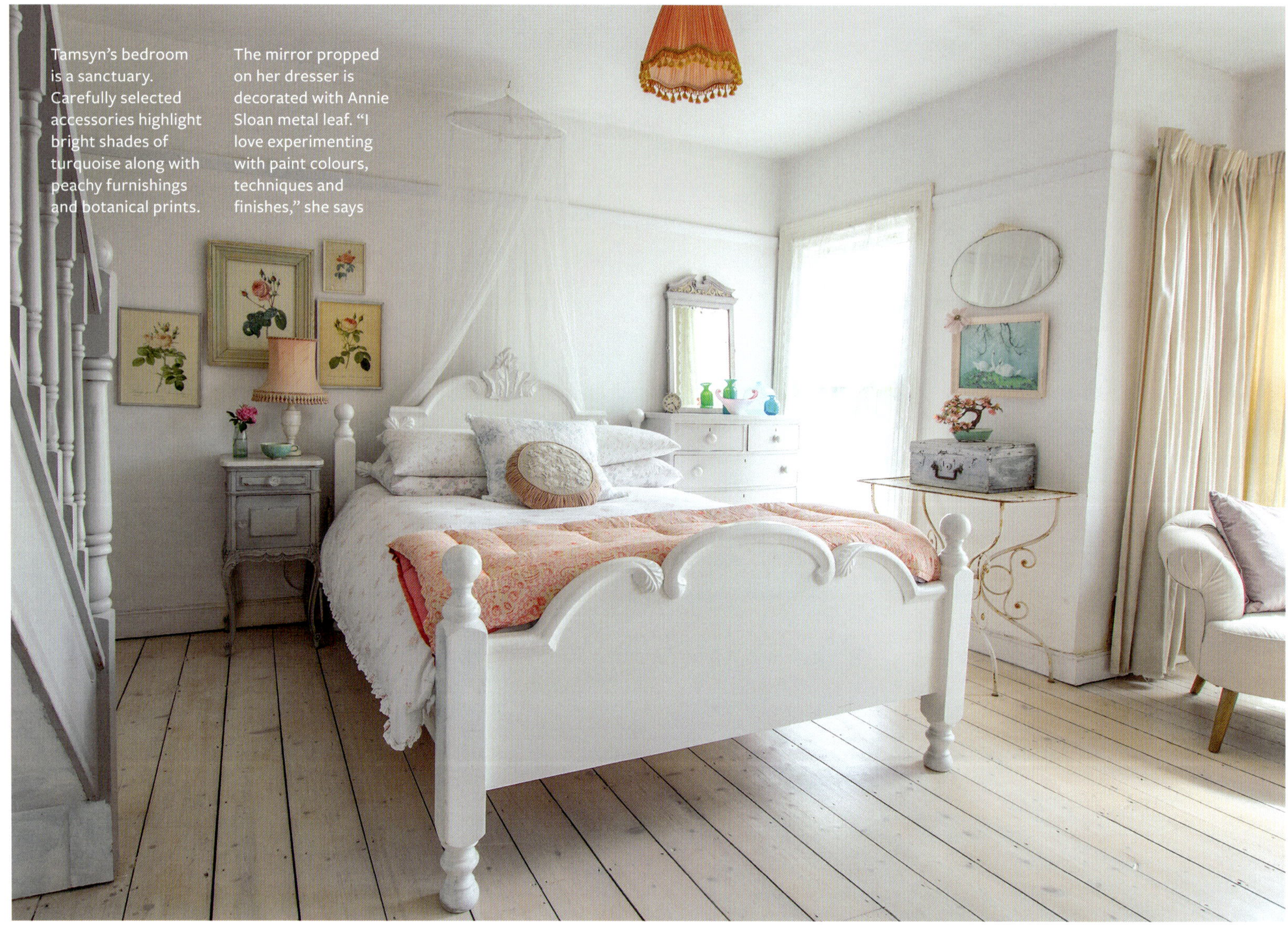

Tamsyn's bedroom is a sanctuary. Carefully selected accessories highlight bright shades of turquoise along with peachy furnishings and botanical prints.

The mirror propped on her dresser is decorated with Annie Sloan metal leaf. "I love experimenting with paint colours, techniques and finishes," she says

"For me, it's much more about creating a home with soul, rather than following trends. It's deeper than what's in the shops"

sporting a double layer of Paris Grey on top of Florence, a beautiful emerald colour, and she's just given a new, old bench a lick of Chalk Paint® in Lem Lem, too. With a style and an eye that's all her own, and despite having a huge admiration for 'shabby chic' creator, Rachel Ashwell, Tamsyn doesn't really follow any interior designers in particular. "For me, it's more about creating a home with soul, rather than following trends," she says. "It's deeper than what's in the shops, and we all buy too much stuff anyway. Your home should evolve with what you love – use what's already there, freshen it up."

Pinterest and Instagram are where Tamsyn likes to find inspiration. She recommends Dreamy Whites Lifestyle (*@dreamywhitelifestyle*), Jeska Hearne (*@lobsterandswan*), Mokkasin (*@sofiaatmokkasin*) and Blueberry Living & Co (*@blueberrylivingco*) and she always starts there when prepping for a new project. "I always have a strong idea in my head of how I want something to look," she says of her process. "My way was always to start with white walls, but lately I've been wanting to add more colour. I would add colourful art, textiles and accessories to a white backdrop. I recently redid my daughter's bedroom, though, and I started with Chalk Paint® in Paris Grey. I made a moodboard up for Lola centred on that and she really loved it."

Tamsyn's noticed that her style is gradually edging very slightly away from the ultra-feminine and more towards a pared back, industrial style – we can't wait to see what her take on merging those worlds will be. AS

www.tamsynmorgans.com *@tamsynmorgans*

Get the look

ANNIE'S PICK OF PERFECT PASTEL PARTNERS

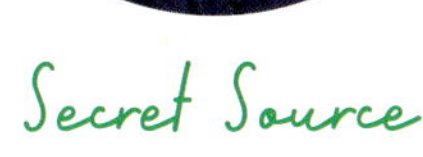

Tamsyn and I agree about the best place to source well-loved items: "Definitely car boot sales," she says. "But you have to get your hands dirty, go through all the boxes and rummage. The best stalls tend to be house clearances – that's where you get the best crockery and pretty 1930s and 1940s items with that lovely colour." I recommend getting there early, going to a lot of different venues and being almost semi-professional about it! If it's vintage furniture you're after, especially Victorian pieces with beautiful carvings and craftsmanship, I recommend auctions.

PHOTOGRAPH: ANNIE, HARRIET MATTHEWS

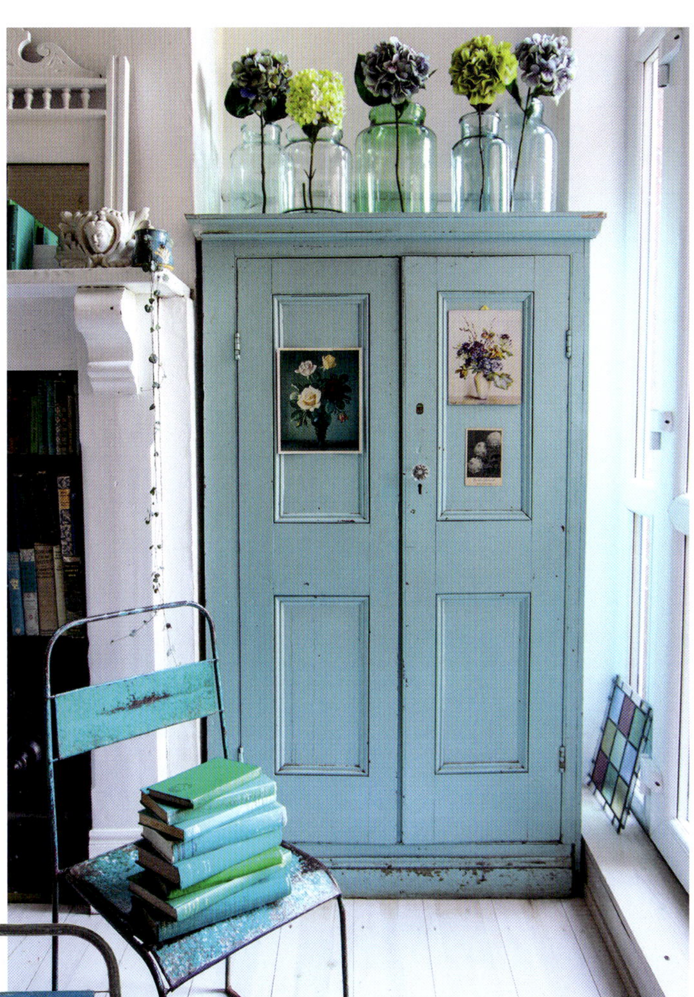

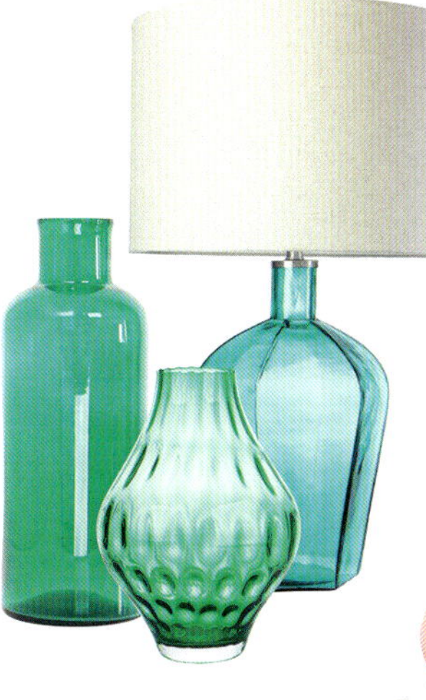

HOMESENSE
Green glass vases and lampbases
www.homesense.com

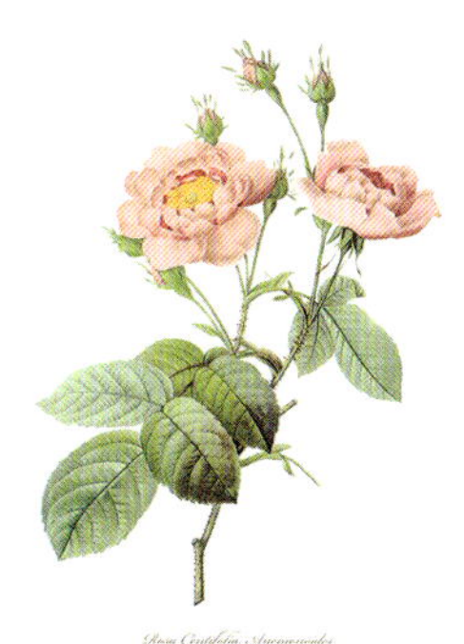

BELLE MAISON ART
Redoute floral botanical set No. 5
www.bellemaisonart.com

OHHAPPYDAY
Pink honeycomb mini paper balls
https://shop.ohhappyday.com

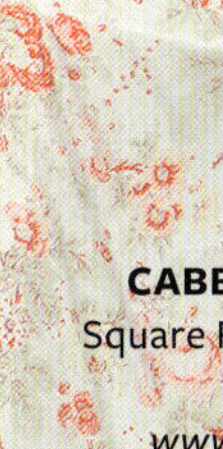

CABBAGES & ROSES
Square Francis cotton print pillowcase
www.johnlewis.com

REX LONDON
Confetti paper and string bunting
www.rexlondon.com

(TOP) IKEA FEJKA from a range of artificial potted plants *www.ikea.com*

(ABOVE) SMITHERS OF STAMFORD
Vintage stacking schoolroom chairs
www.smithersofstamford.com

Chalk Paint® in FLORENCE

Chalk Paint® in PROVENCE

Chalk Paint® in ANTOINETTE

Chalk Paint® in OLD WHITE

ANNIE'S VINTAGE PASTEL COLOUR PALETTE Chalk Paint® by Annie Sloan *www.anniesloan.com*

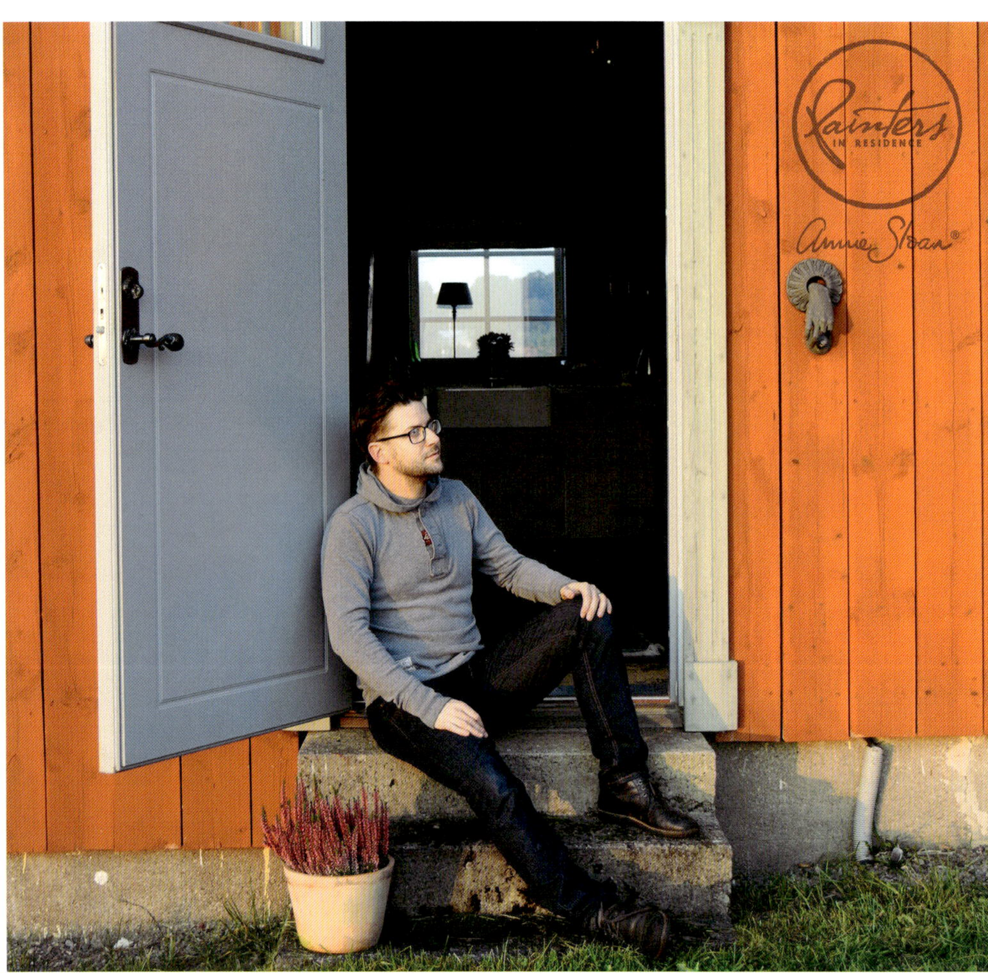

Jonathon Marc Mendes

"I get pleasure knowing I've helped my students believe in their abilities"

Since being chosen as Annie's Painter in Residence in early 2017, life has certainly changed for Jonathon Marc Mendes. He's been invited to travel the world teaching his painting. "I've met so many amazing, kind, creative people and made true friends for life," says Jonathon. "I've painted in Greece, Ireland, Sweden (pictured above), Switzerland, South Africa, Germany, and I'm going to Australia in November this year!"

"I loved working on the Homemakers Expo in Johannesburg. Although it was super hard work, I got to meet so many passionate people – and a few lions! I also adored my workshops in Greece, where the colours remind me of my husband's family home in Madeira." With ambitions to become a full-time furniture artist (and publish a book), he currently plans his workshops around his work as a hairdresser.

Born in Cleethorpes, UK, Jonathon has always been inspired by nature, "Anything from tree bark and green leaves to a rusty gatepost can influence my work." Asked about his design heroes Jonathon explains, "Rather than people, it's places and periods of time that inspire me. I love old houses, vintage signage and styles of bygone eras."

Finally, his advice for beginners is to trust your instincts "Always follow your creative passions to develop a unique style." AS

www.jonathonmarcmendes.com

Find Jonathon on Facebook, *JMMPaintedLove* and Instagram *@jonathonmarcmendes_paintedlove*

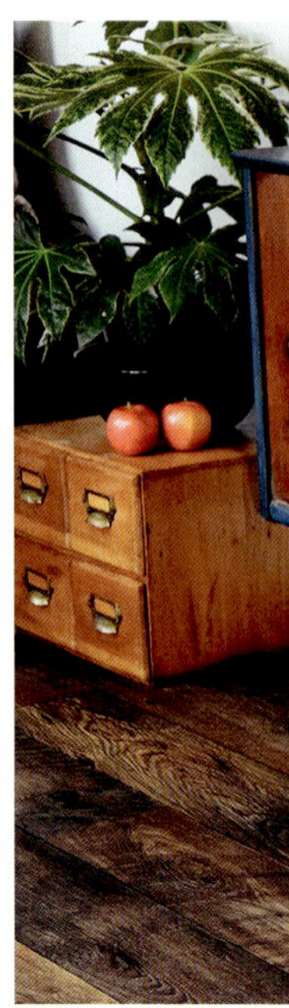

RIGHT Chalk Paint® in Aubusson Blue was used for the main body of this vintage sideboard. Jonathon expertly hand-painted all the imagery and typography himself. Brass Leaf and lashings of Dark Wax were applied to give a sense of faded grandeur to the piece

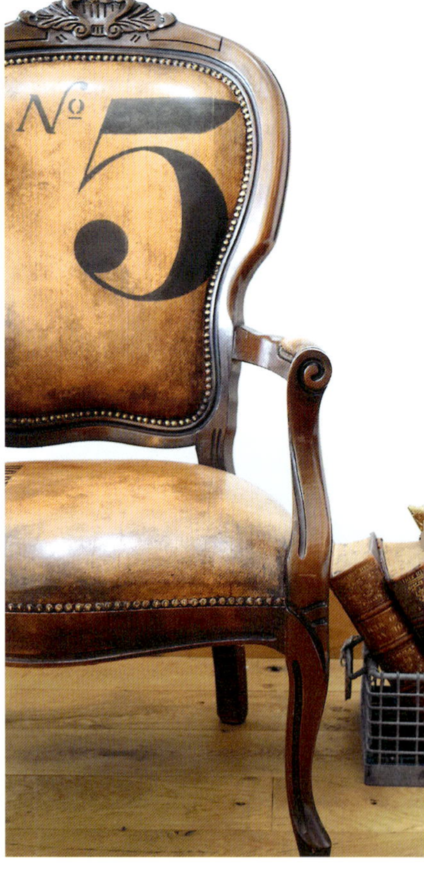

ABOVE To create an aged leather look, Jonathon added a coat of Clear Wax to this chair. He then applied Dark Wax, creating patchy darker areas. The typography was created using stencils made from card

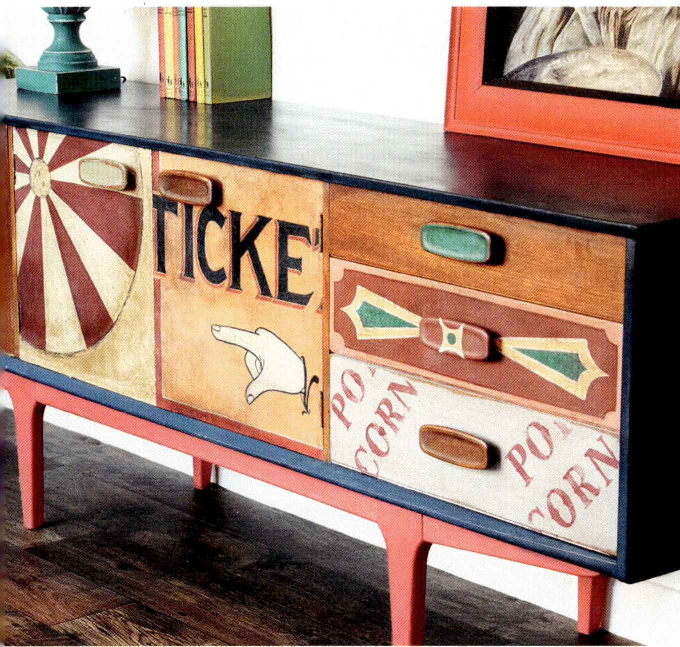

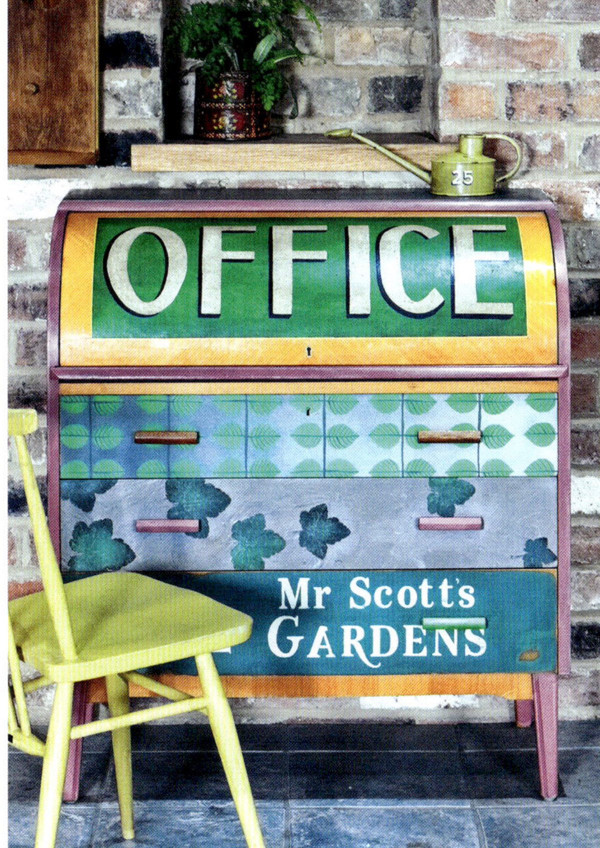

ABOVE Jonathon painted the inside of this roll-top desk with a mix of Chalk Paint® in Old Violet and French Linen. He then cracked the paint by applying direct heat from a hairdryer. The drawers and cubby holes were painted in a mix of Henrietta with a touch of Emperor's Silk. On either side of the desk there's a contemporary leaf detail, which Jonathon hand-painted using Antibes Green over a mix of Graphite and Antibes Green

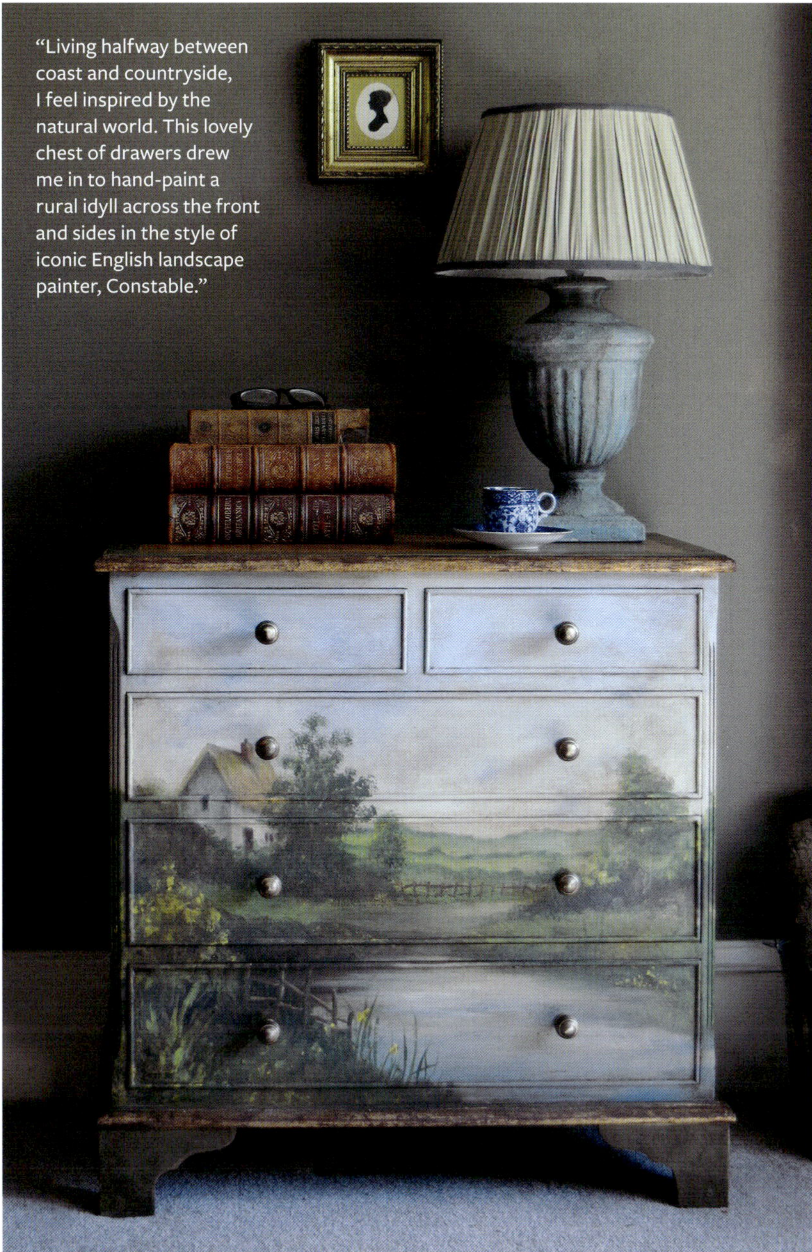

"Living halfway between coast and countryside, I feel inspired by the natural world. This lovely chest of drawers drew me in to hand-paint a rural idyll across the front and sides in the style of iconic English landscape painter, Constable."

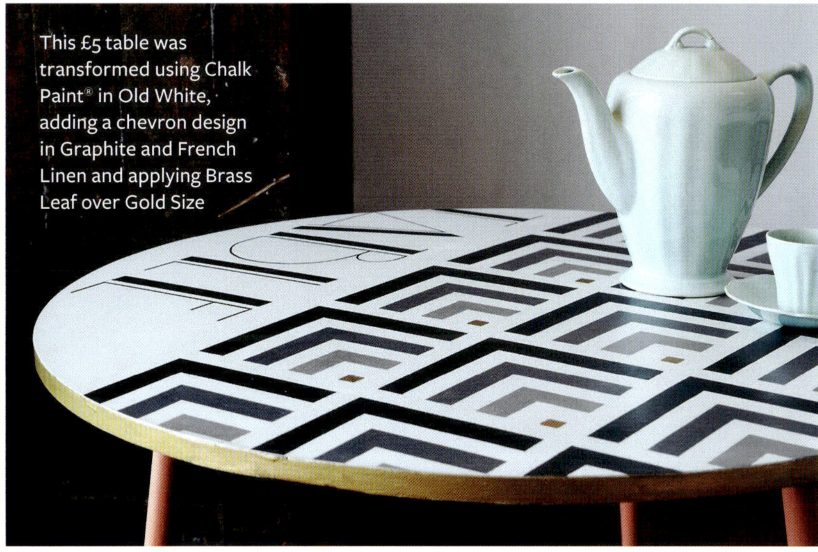

This £5 table was transformed using Chalk Paint® in Old White, adding a chevron design in Graphite and French Linen and applying Brass Leaf over Gold Size

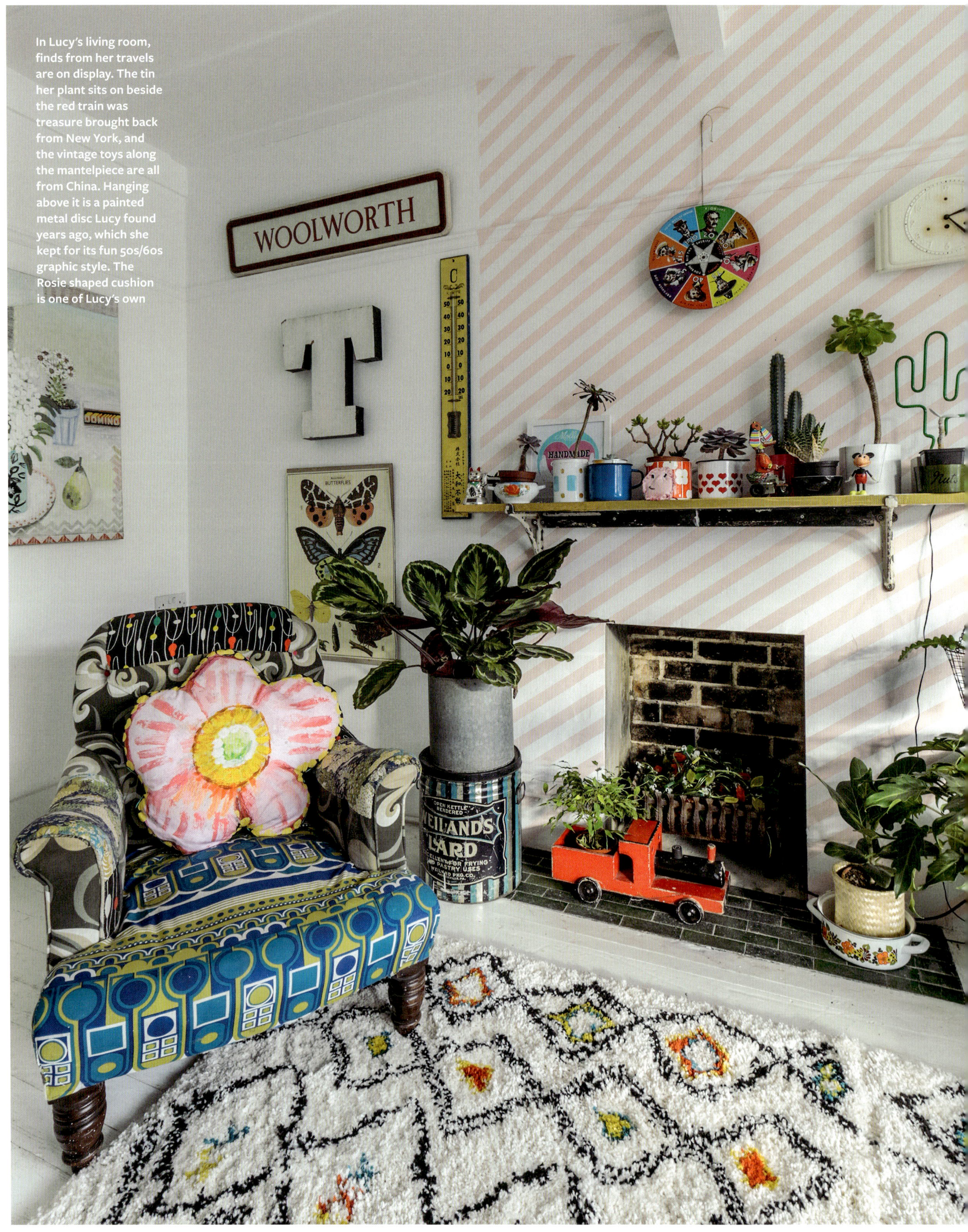

In Lucy's living room, finds from her travels are on display. The tin her plant sits on beside the red train was treasure brought back from New York, and the vintage toys along the mantelpiece are all from China. Hanging above it is a painted metal disc Lucy found years ago, which she kept for its fun 50s/60s graphic style. The Rosie shaped cushion is one of Lucy's own

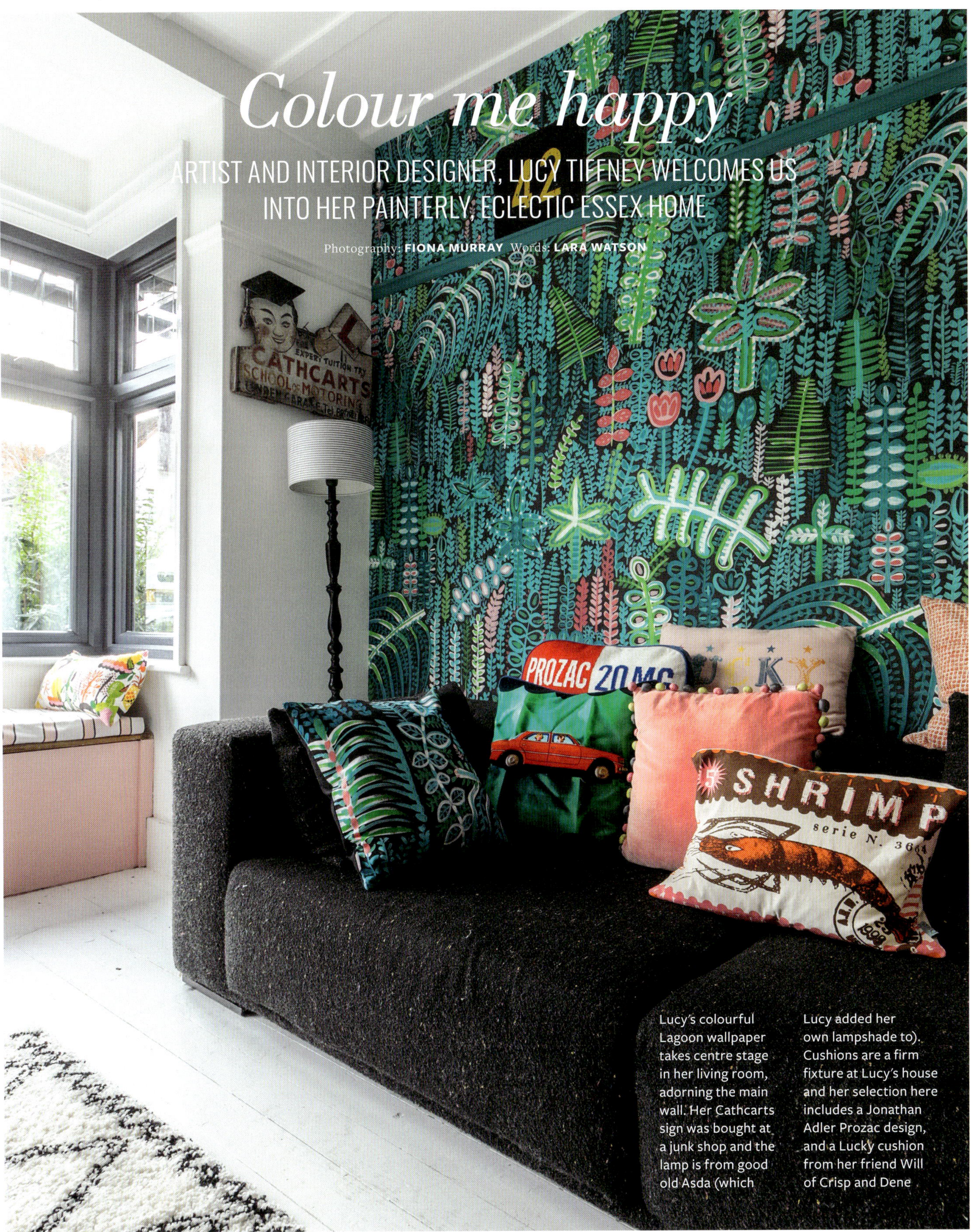

Colour me happy

ARTIST AND INTERIOR DESIGNER, LUCY TIFFNEY WELCOMES US INTO HER PAINTERLY, ECLECTIC ESSEX HOME

Photography: **FIONA MURRAY** Words: **LARA WATSON**

Lucy's colourful Lagoon wallpaper takes centre stage in her living room, adorning the main wall. Her Cathcarts sign was bought at a junk shop and the lamp is from good old Asda (which Lucy added her own lampshade to). Cushions are a firm fixture at Lucy's house and her selection here includes a Jonathan Adler Prozac design, and a Lucky cushion from her friend Will of Crisp and Dene

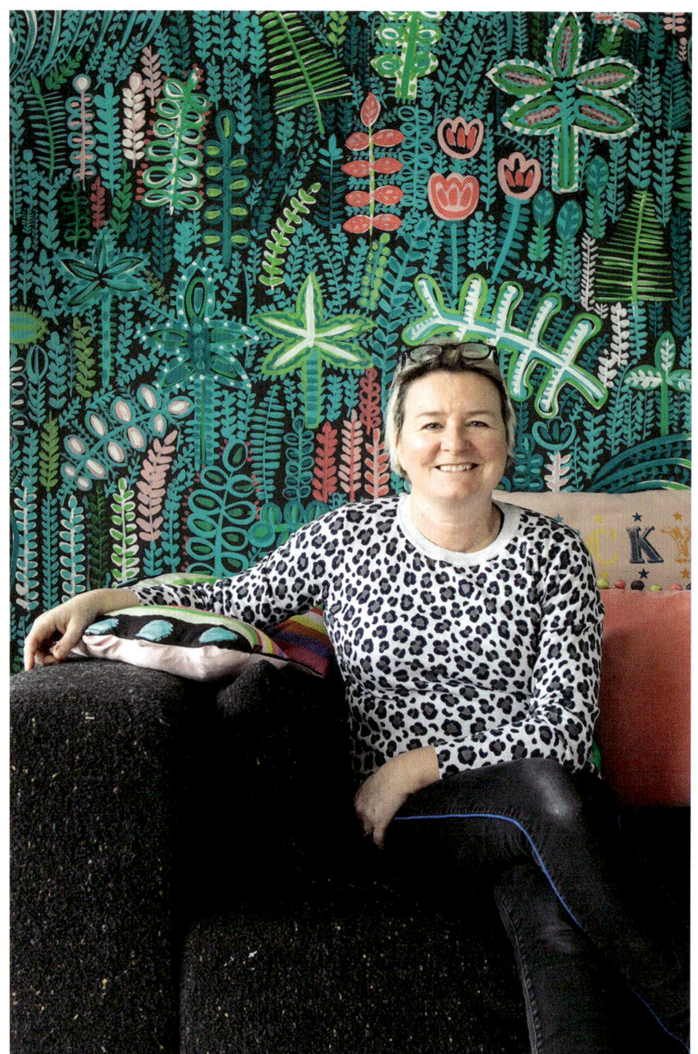

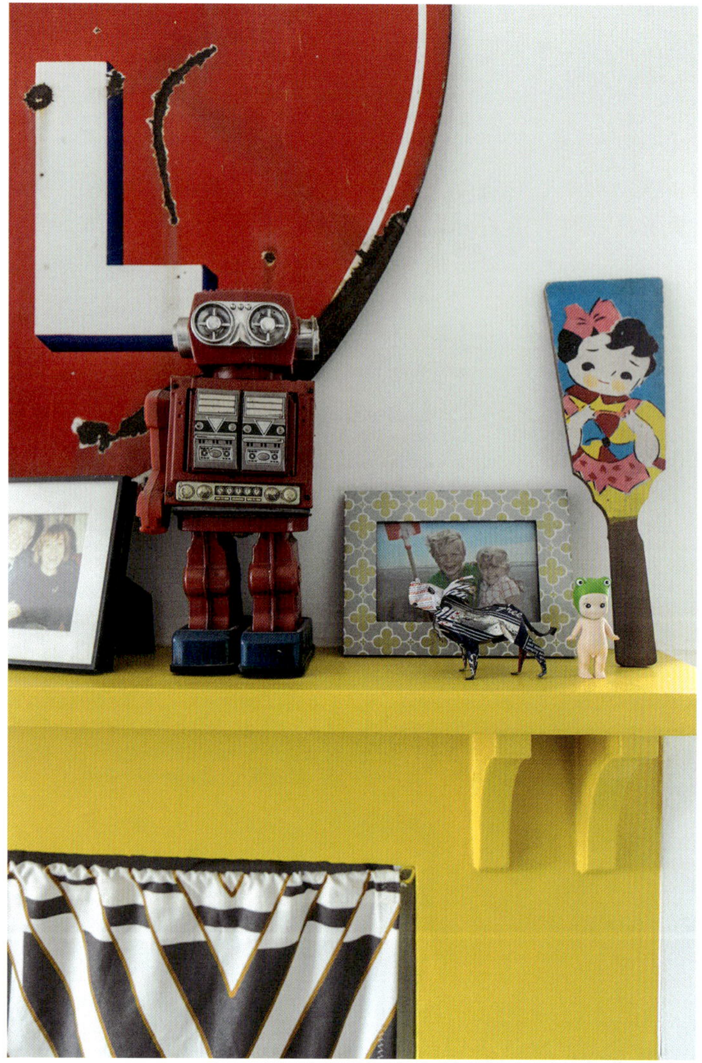

"Henri Matisse has inspired me forever, particularly the spontaneity of his work. I first saw his paintings when I was 18 in Paris. They made a huge impression on me"

Lucy Tiffney shares her vibrant detached 1910s house in Colchester with her husband Tiff, teenage sons Leo and Frank, and Zed the cat. With a style epitomised by her Insta-worthy Lagoon wallpaper design (above left and page 75), her murals (as demonstrated in her TV appearances on The Great Decorating Challenge and DIY SOS) and her many eclectically painted pieces of furniture, it's no surprise that Lucy is a longtime colour enthusiast. She remembers painting her bedroom bright yellow and green in her teens to go with a banana duvet cover she bought at Covent Garden market. Ever since, she's loved finding unusual colour combinations, juxtapositions and proportions, and nearly everything in Lucy's house has had a lick of paint. "I'm sure it drives my family crazy," she says. "I painted my hall floor in a geometric tile pattern, and I've also done the mantelpieces, walls, furniture, tables, cupboards with murals and stripes." Lucy painted her kitchen chairs with her own mix of Chalk Paint®, starting with a light, white chalky base and adding colour until she got the shade she wanted.

Some of the most striking pieces in Lucy's home are the details – signs, old toys and bits and pieces she's collected on her travels to South East Asia, India, Nepal, and more recently Japan and the USA. Her biggest inspiration, however, is other artists. "Henri Matisse has inspired me forever," says Lucy. "I first saw his paintings when I was 18 at the Pompidou Centre in Paris. They made a huge impression on me. I've referred to him ever since, particularly the spontaneity of his work." More »

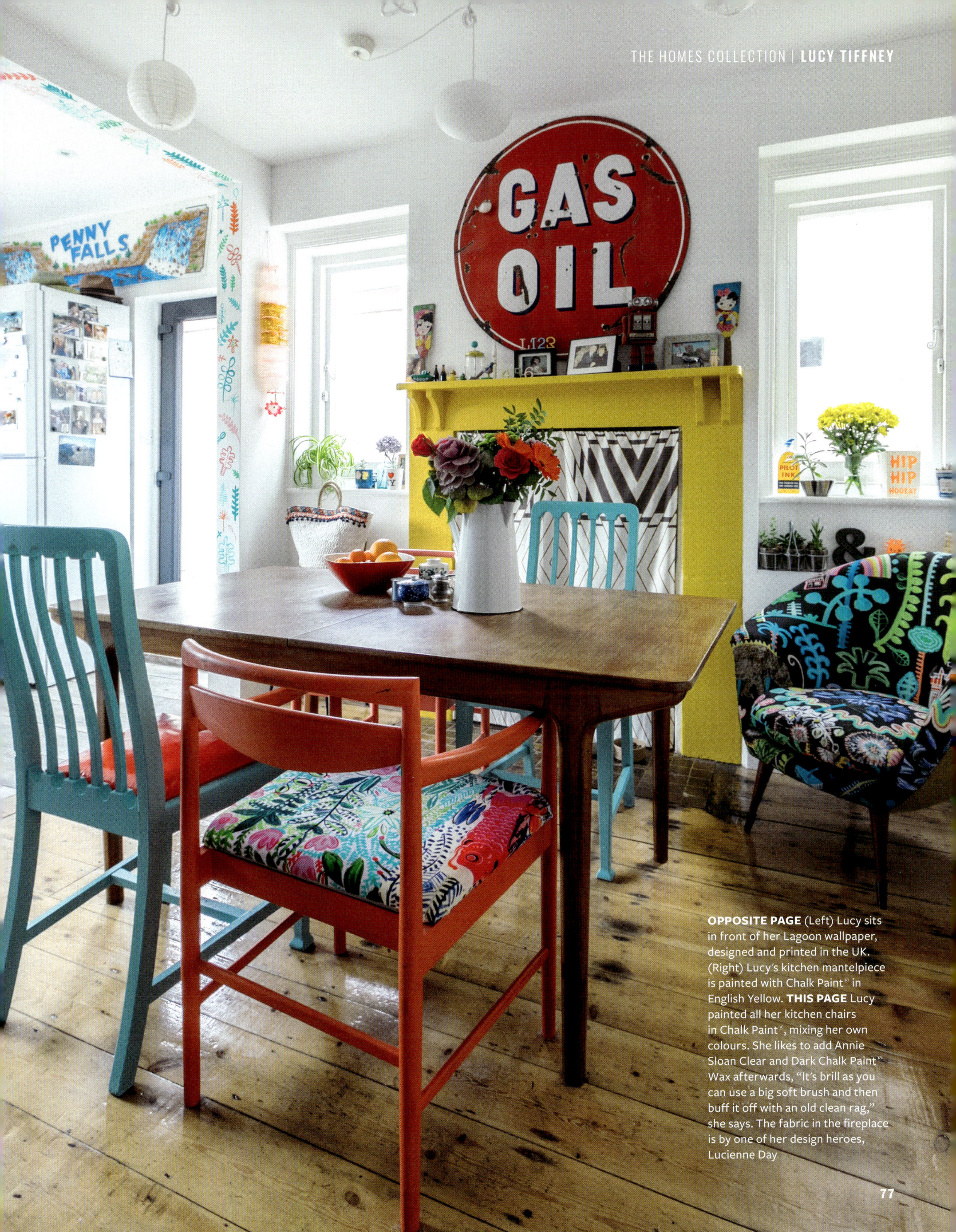

OPPOSITE PAGE (Left) Lucy sits in front of her Lagoon wallpaper, designed and printed in the UK. (Right) Lucy's kitchen mantelpiece is painted with Chalk Paint® in English Yellow. **THIS PAGE** Lucy painted all her kitchen chairs in Chalk Paint®, mixing her own colours. She likes to add Annie Sloan Clear and Dark Chalk Paint® Wax afterwards, "It's brill as you can use a big soft brush and then buff it off with an old clean rag," she says. The fabric in the fireplace is by one of her design heroes, Lucienne Day

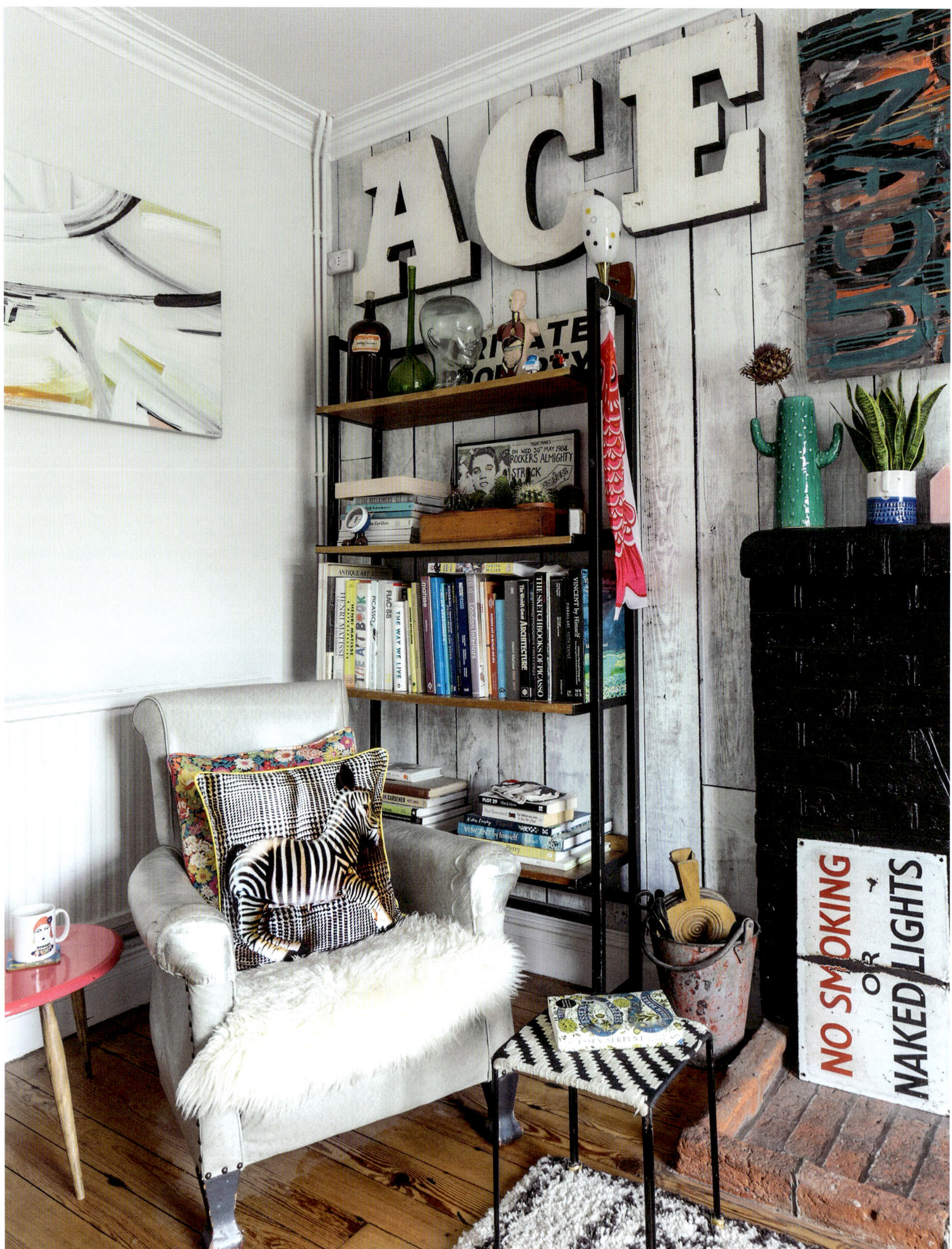

Ace in this place In the snug, a softer palette comes into play, always with added accent colours. Lucy painted her little Ercol side table top in fuchsia pink. She likes to play with proportions, hard and soft textures. Found signs and favourite paintings sit together in a relaxed manner, "Don't feel the need to place everything on the wall. Sometimes propping pieces against the wall or fireplace works best."

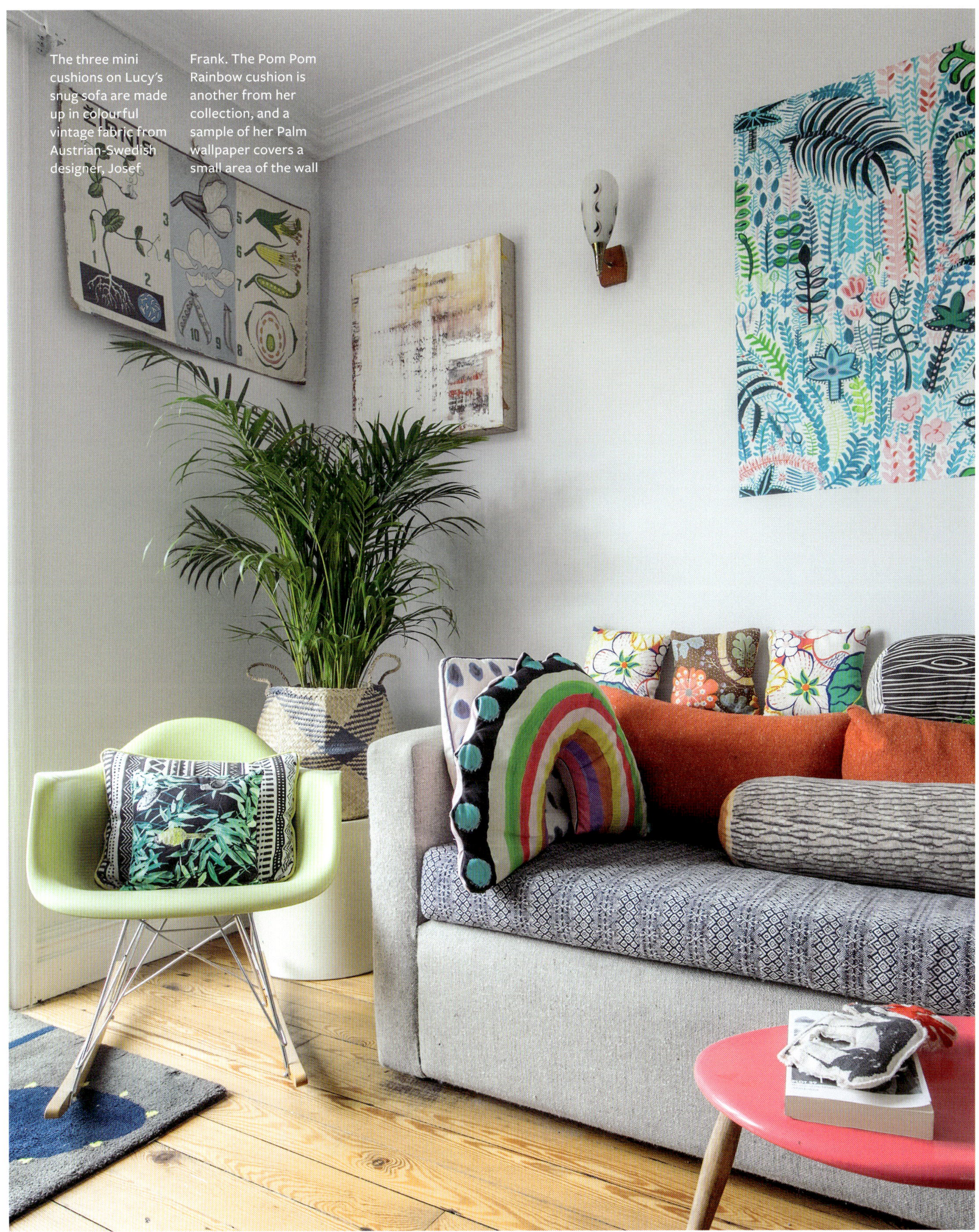

The three mini cushions on Lucy's snug sofa are made up in colourful vintage fabric from Austrian-Swedish designer, Josef Frank. The Pom Pom Rainbow cushion is another from her collection, and a sample of her Palm wallpaper covers a small area of the wall

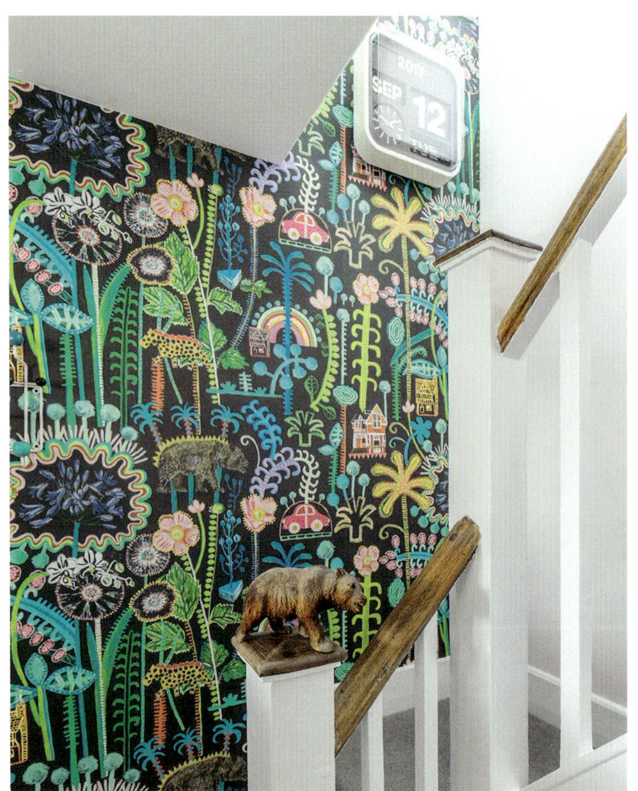

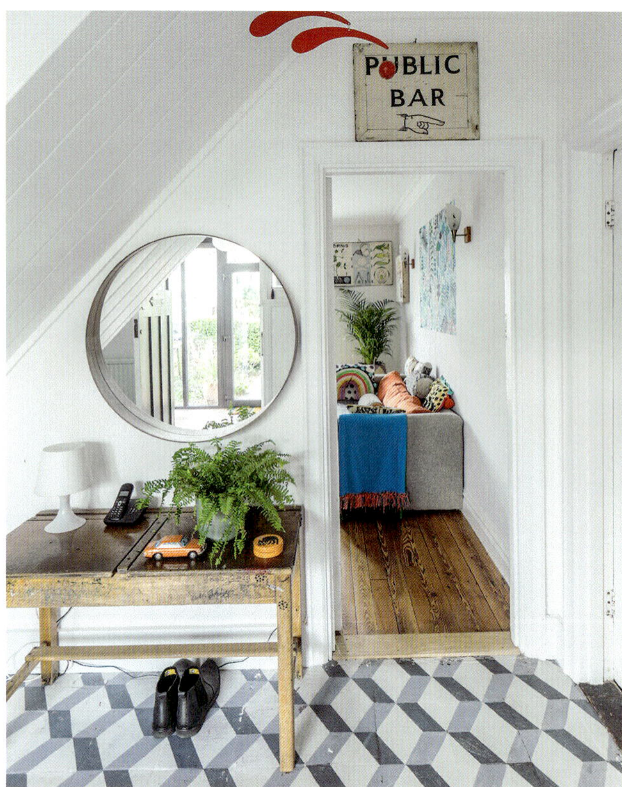

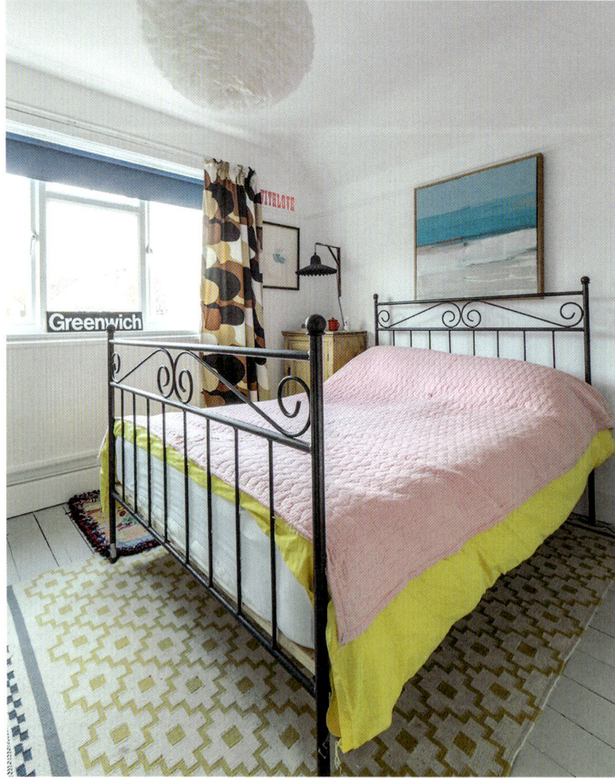

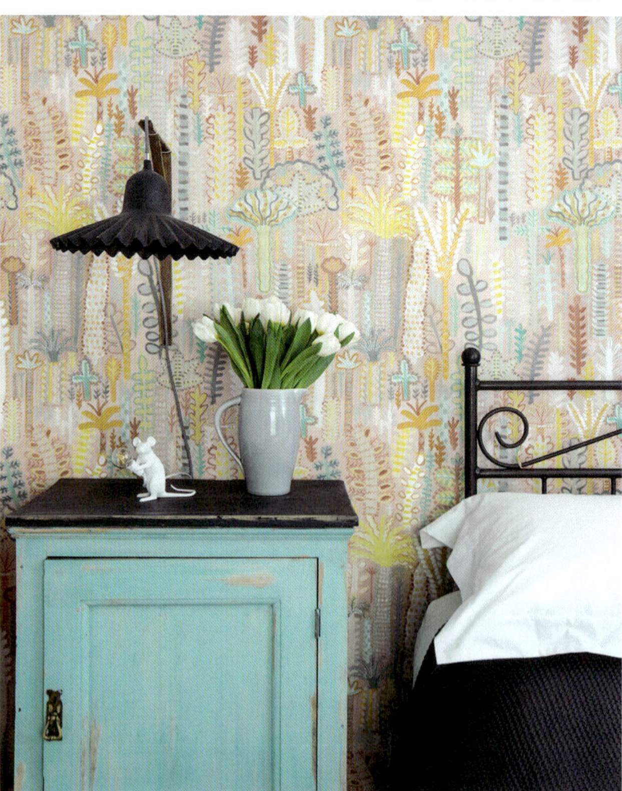

Colour and pattern for days **TOP LEFT** Lucy's Mr Bear wallpaper accompanies you up the stairs. **TOP RIGHT** Being a collector of eclectic pieces stumbled on all over the world means that Lucy often pairs the unusual together, such as this vintage school desk and a more modern patterned rug. "In the house I like the walls to be white to start with, like a blank canvas," she explains. "Then I build on it from there." **BOTTOM LEFT** Lucy inherited the pink quilt from her mother-in-law. The curtains are a lucky vintage Marimekko find – "I found them in the classroom cupboard when I was teaching!" **BOTTOM RIGHT** Lucy's Miami wallpaper strikes a softer tone with a beautiful distressed side table – try Chalk Paint® in Provence to get this look.

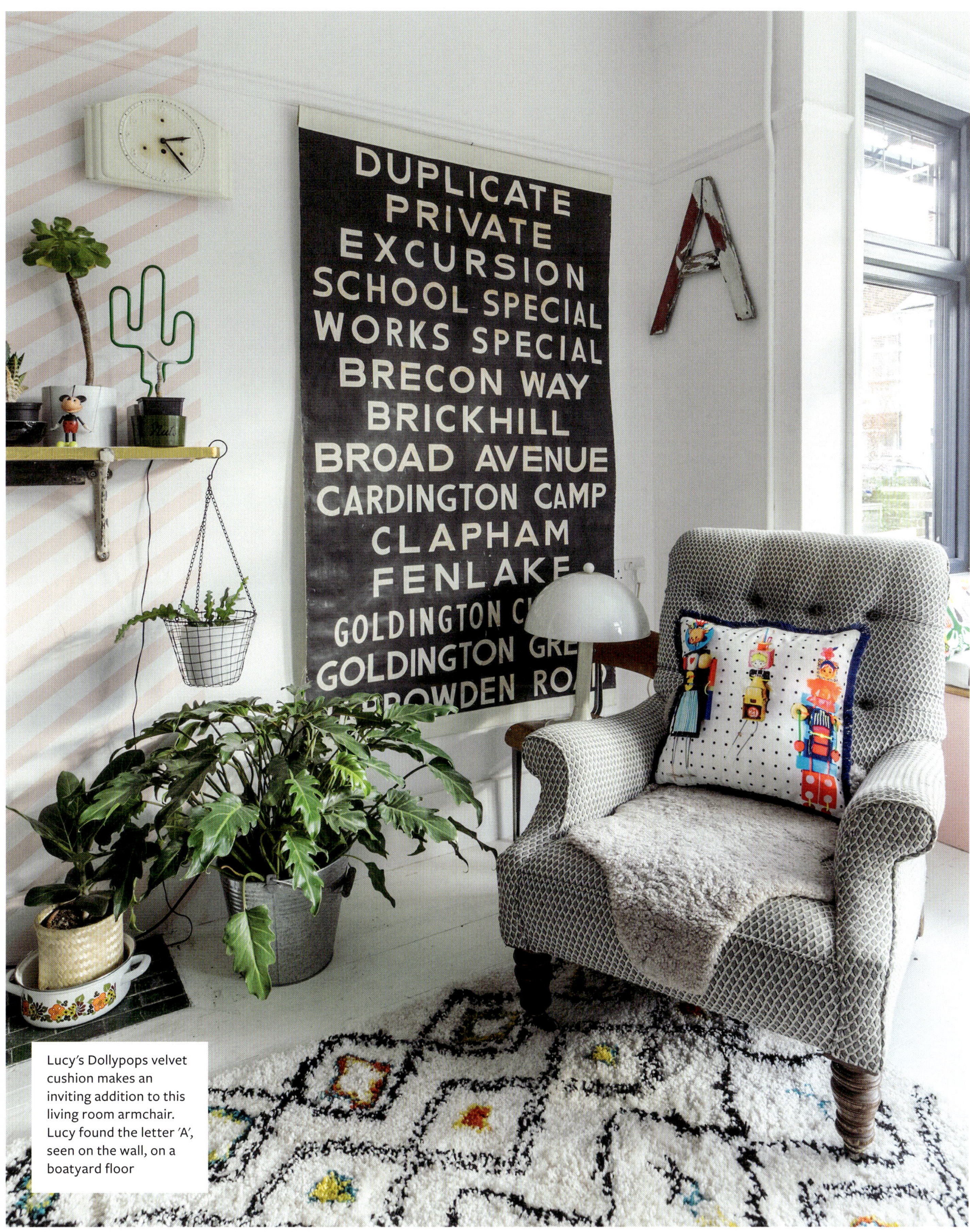

Lucy's Dollypops velvet cushion makes an inviting addition to this living room armchair. Lucy found the letter 'A', seen on the wall, on a boatyard floor

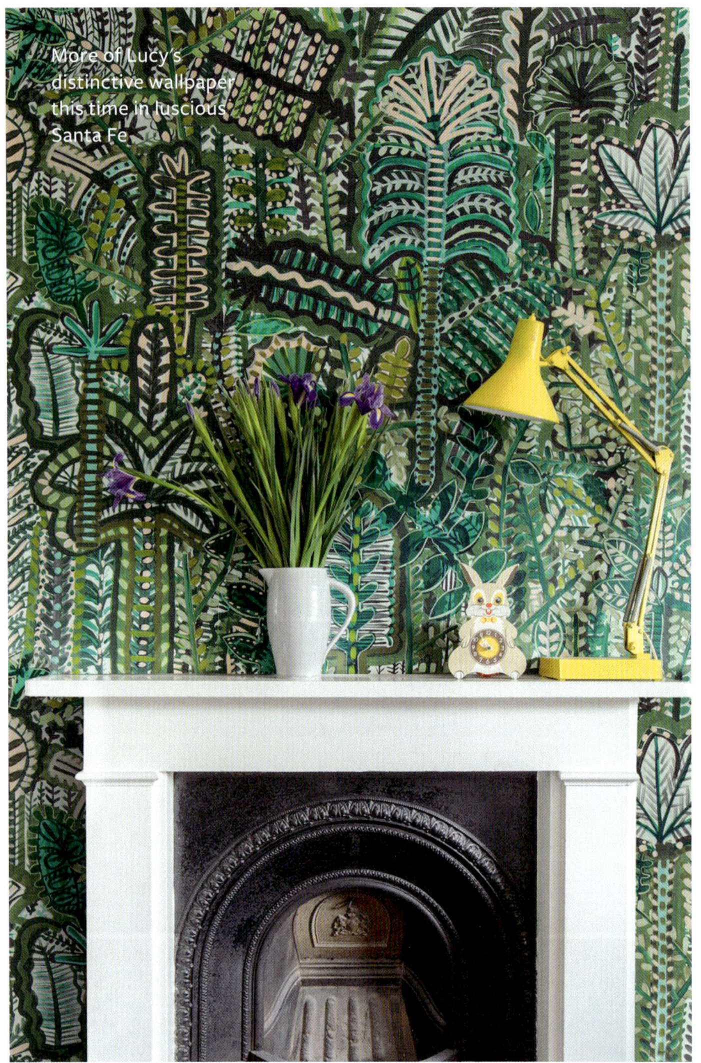

More of Lucy's distinctive wallpaper this time in luscious Santa Fe

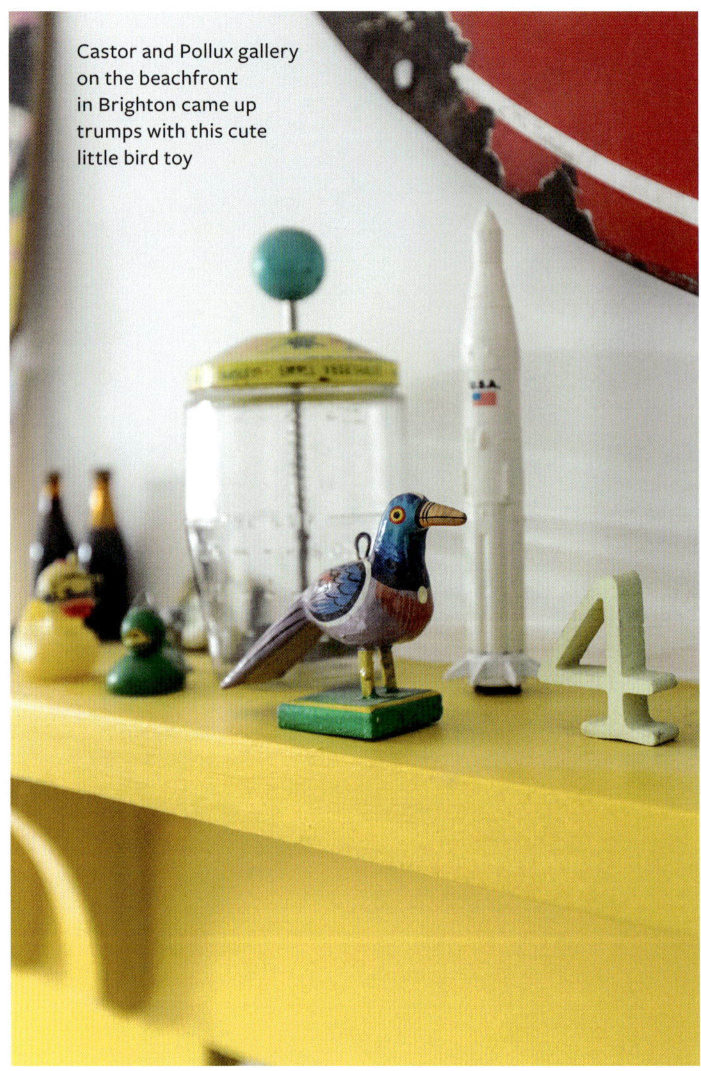

Castor and Pollux gallery on the beachfront in Brighton came up trumps with this cute little bird toy

"I add more colours or layers of paint as the design develops. I love the freedom of painting large scale and just letting the design flow"

recent influences are Henri Rousseau for his painted jungles, Paul Klee and Ben Nicholson, for line, shape and composition. "When I first left university I worked for rug designer Helen Yardley," explains Lucy. "I was her studio manager and it's only now I realise that Helen taught me so much about colour, proportions of colour and what works with what. I'm also inspired by people I love on Instagram for their use of colour, such as Unskilledworker (*@unskilledworker*), John Booth (*@john_booth*) and Donald Robertson (*@drawbertson*)."

Now fresh from winning Pulse's Best Newcomer award and Mollie Makes magazine's Best Start-Up Business Award, it's refreshing that despite having her own successful wallpaper and homeware collections, Lucy still works entirely organically. With a process very much rooted in painting, Lucy always works freehand, with just a vague idea of how she wants the finished piece to look. "Usually, my work evolves and I add more colours or layers of paint as the design develops," she says. "When I create murals, I'll usually plan a bit more, but even they change and evolve as I paint them. I love the freedom of painting large scale and just letting the design flow. Stepping back from it and seeing what to add or take away is important, too. Although I'm much better at adding than taking away!"

So what's next? Lucy is adding to her wallpaper collection and hoping to incorporate those designs onto other products and homeware. She's also just finalising a new capsule collection of sofa fabrics, cushions and rugs for Sofa.com. AS

www.lucytiffneyshop.com @Lucytiffney

Turn to page 122 for Lucy's step-by-step guide to painting a cabinet in her signature lively, botanical style.

Get the look

FELIX SLOAN'S PICKS FOR A BRIGHT, RETRO FEEL

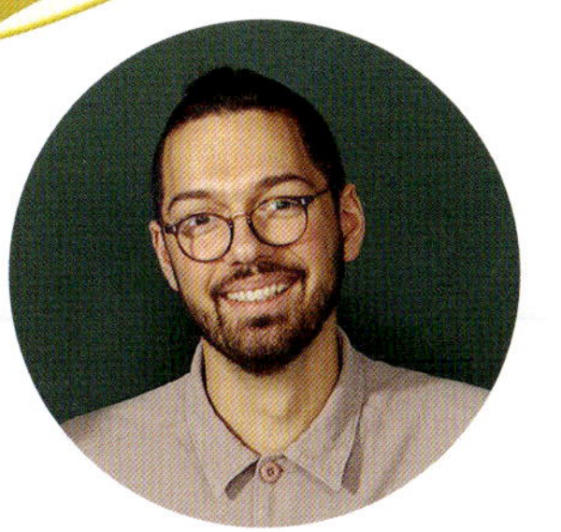

Secret Sources

Love Lucy's style? I've picked some of my favourite finds, inspired by Lucy's colourful, retro home. You'll see Lucy shopping in high street shops, charity shops and car boot sales, and she often makes things or paints them herself to get exactly the right shade. Her favourite contemporary designers are **Orla Kiely** for the quality of her products, her skill with pattern, colour and shape, **Bluebellgray** and **Donna Wilson** ("I so admire their success stories!").

Lucy shares my love of bright cushions. "They're a fab way of adding colour and personality easily and cheaply," she says.

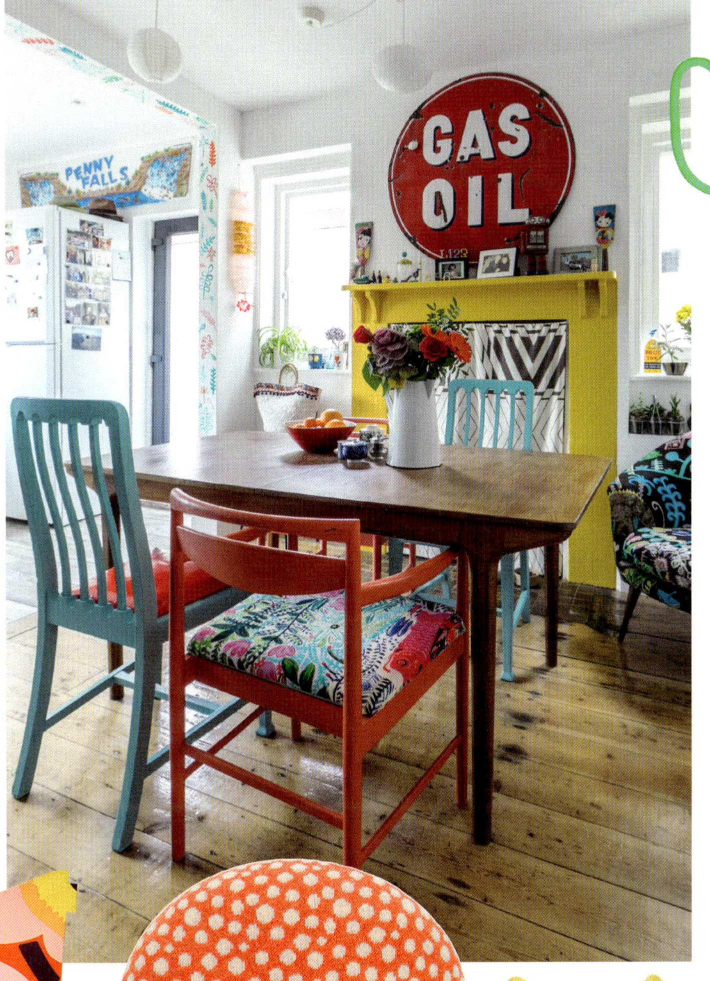

GOODNIGHT LIGHT Mint vinyl cactus lamp *www.goodnightlight.eu*
NEWGATE CLOCKS The Pantry wall clock *www.newgateclocks.com*
SUNNYLIFE Cactus neon wall light *www.sunnylife.com.au*

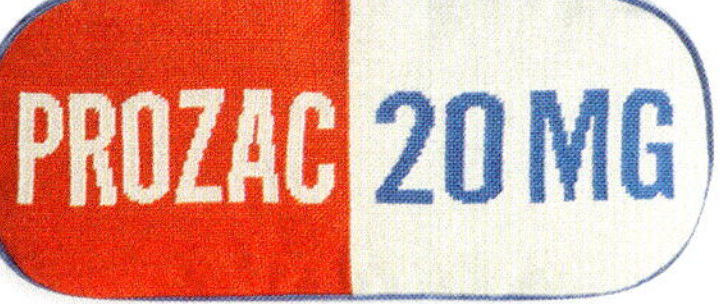

JONATHAN ADLER Prescription Prozac needlepoint cushion *www.jonathanadler.com*

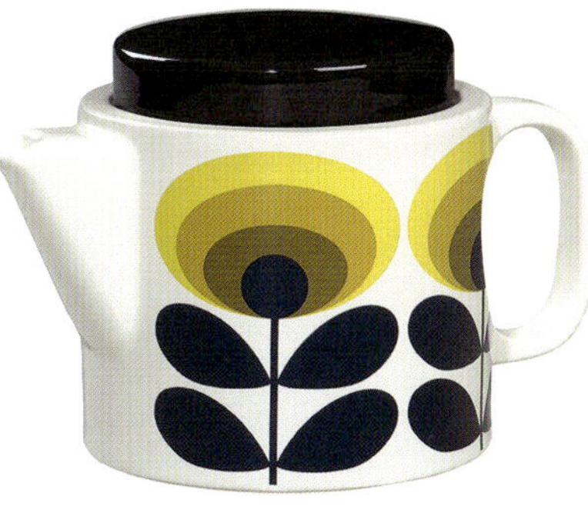

ORLA KIELY White ceramic 1970s oval teapot *www.amara.com, www.orlakiely.com*

DONNA WILSON Knitted mushroom cushion, and knitted lambswool creature *www.donnawilson.com*

(TOP) MARGARET HOWELL Anglepoise Type 75 Desk Lamp. Yellow Ochre Edition *www.nest.co.uk*

(ABOVE) MARIMEKKO Pieni Unikko Cushion Cover *www.amara.com*

Chalk Paint® in ENGLISH YELLOW

Chalk Paint® in FLORENCE

Chalk Paint® in ANTIBES GREEN

Chalk Paint® in EMPEROR'S SILK

FELIX'S BRIGHT, RETRO PALETTE Chalk Paint® by Annie Sloan *www.anniesloan.com*

Amazing renovations

Be inspired by two incredible kitchen makeovers using Chalk Paint® to transform tired cabinets and floors

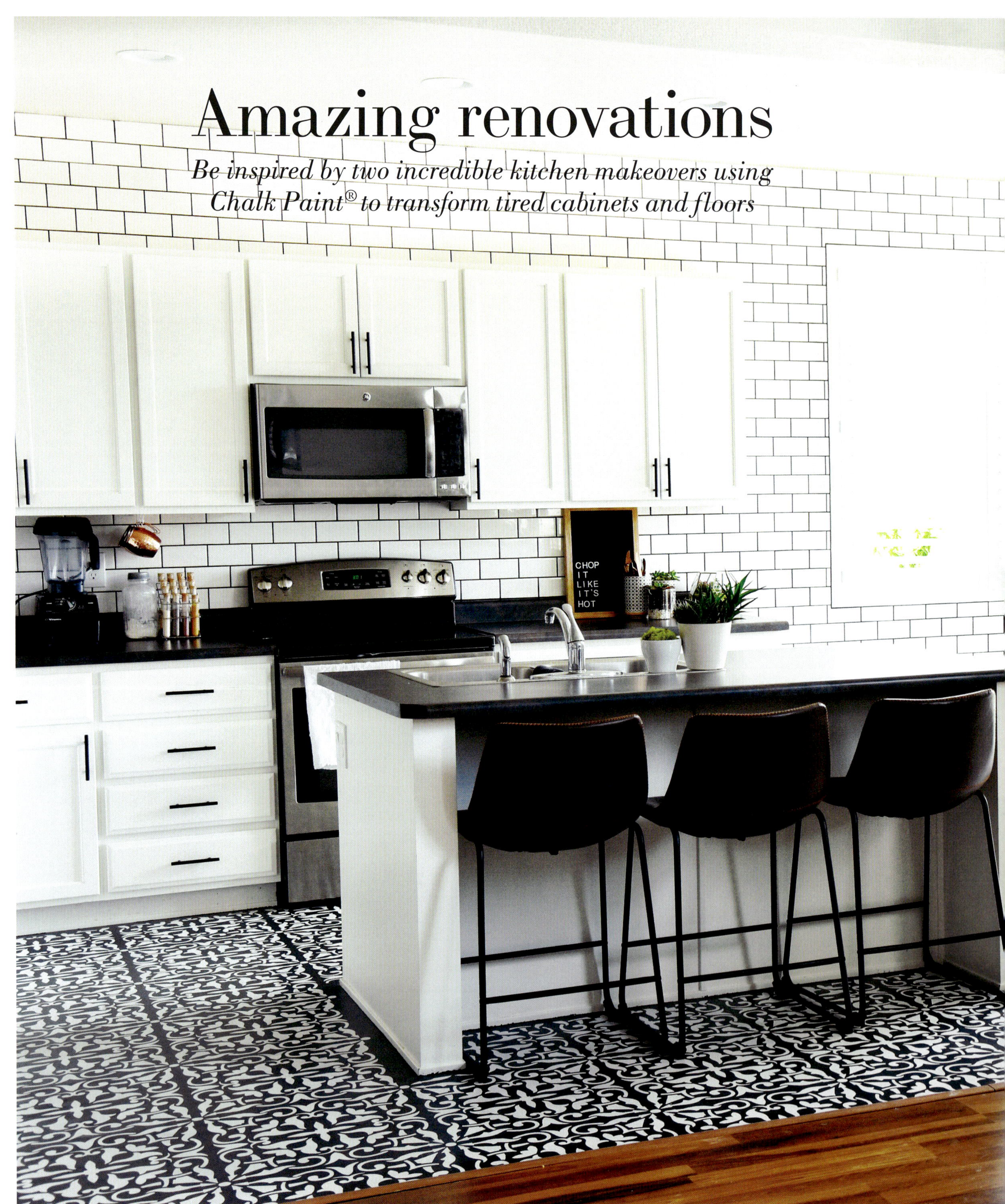

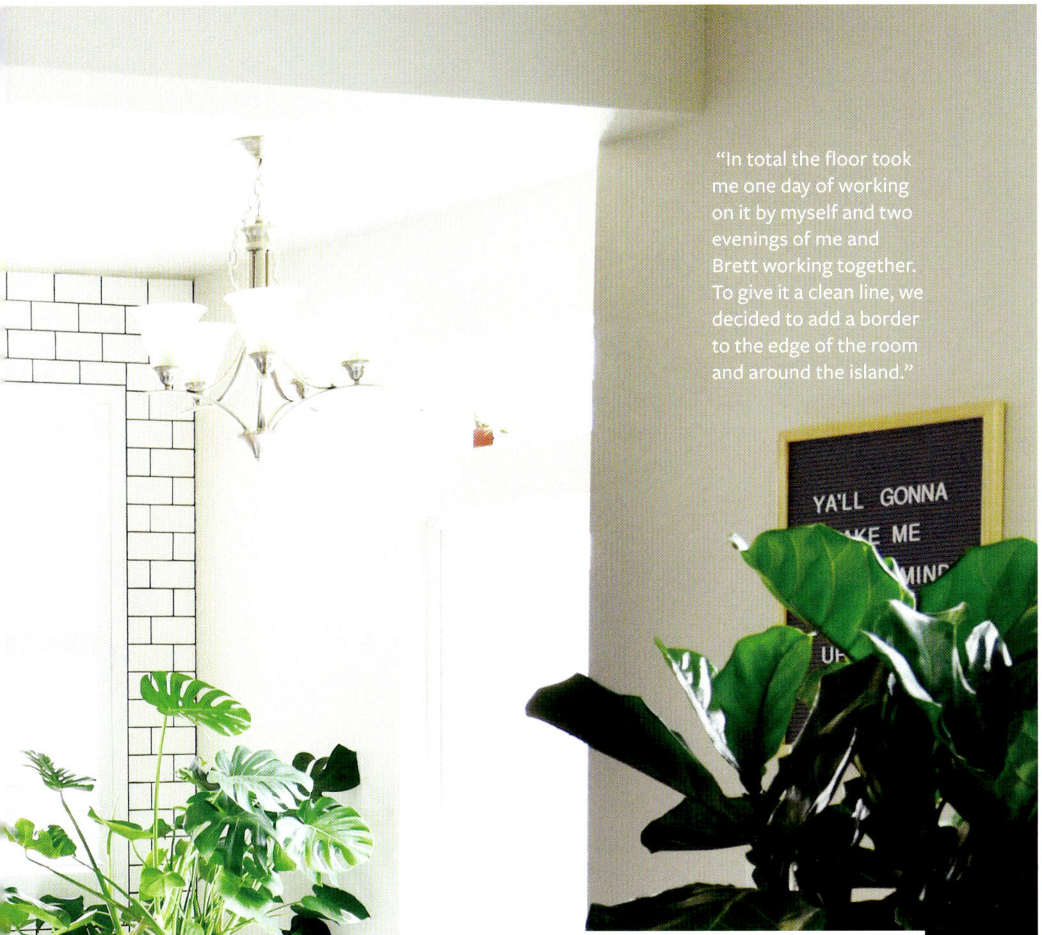

"In total the floor took me one day of working on it by myself and two evenings of me and Brett working together. To give it a clean line, we decided to add a border to the edge of the room and around the island."

MOROCCAN TILE MAKEOVER

Annie Sloan Stockists Brett and Dennae Hill part-own Due South in Lafayette, Colorado, USA. The first project they tackled in their new home was to subway tile the kitchen wall. Next was to update the ugly vinyl flooring by using a Moroccan-style stencil and Chalk Paint®.

PRODUCTS USED For their floor project they used Chalk Paint® in Graphite and Pure, finished with Lacquer.

DENNAE'S ADVICE "Chalk Paint® is amazing and dries fast, which made our project go quickly, but we should have paused more often to deep-clean the stencil. There was bleeding paint caused by build up left on the stencil, so I'd recommend wiping it down after painting each tile."

After they'd finished the full tiles Dennae and Brett tackled the half-tiles. "This part is way easier with two people. One person needs to hold the stencil carefully in place while the other uses the roller to fill in. When pulling the stencil up, it's better to rip it off quickly like a sticking plaster."
www.duesouthhome.com

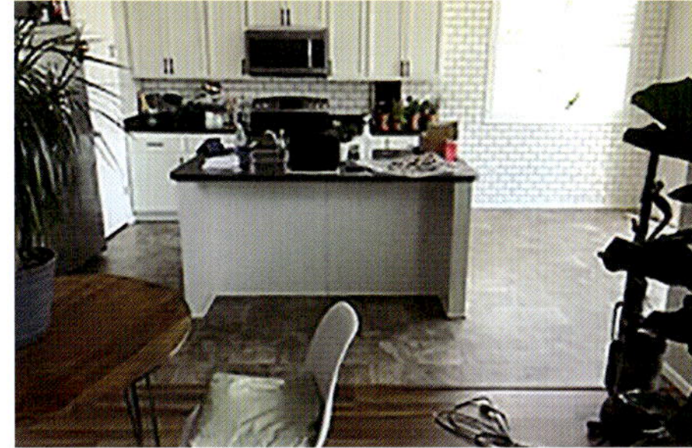

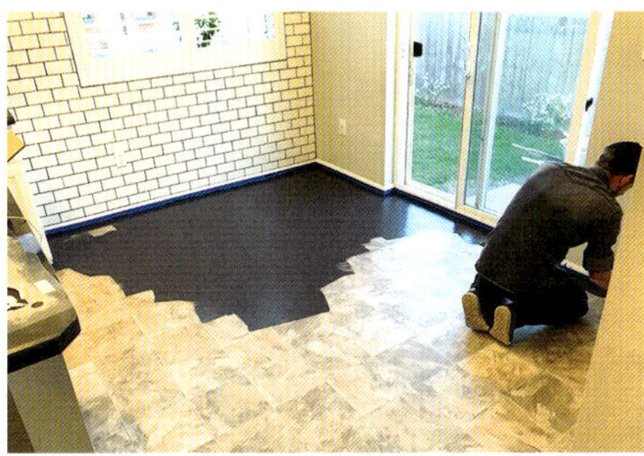

TOP "Here's our kitchen before. See the beautiful wall tiles? You probably can't because your eyes are stuck on the ugliest floor in the history of floors! After a thorough clean, we spread Graphite all over the floor with a roller."

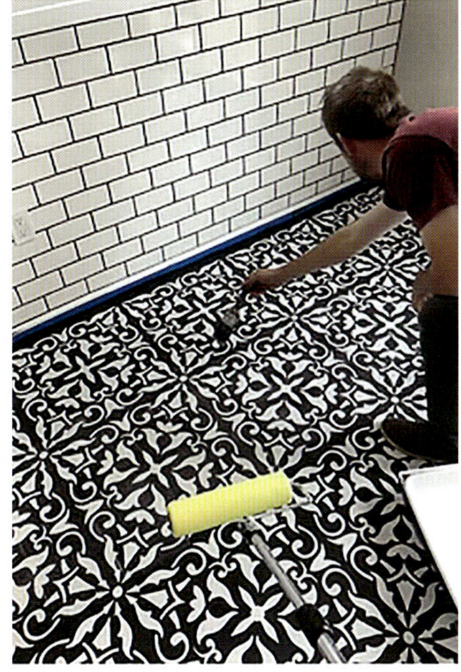

ABOVE Once Dennae and Brett finished the stencilling they let it sit overnight before they rolled on the Lacquer. One of them rolled the floor while the other went back over with an Annie Sloan Flat Brush. This meant the Lacquer was clear and smooth after it had fully dried

"If you're considering using Chalk Paint®, but you're afraid of the results, just do it! It's the most affordable way to dramatically change the look and feel of your kitchen."

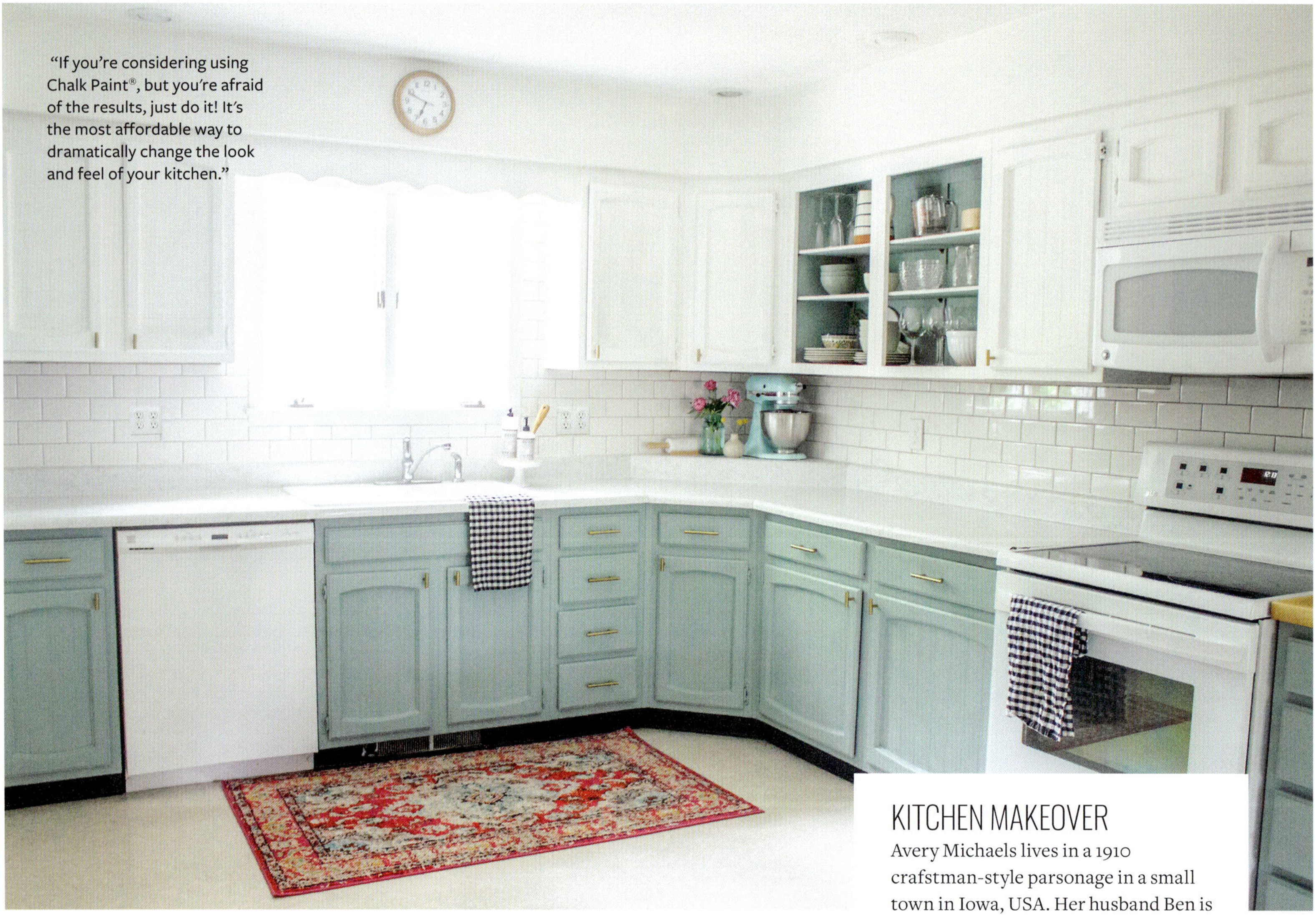

KITCHEN MAKEOVER

Avery Michaels lives in a 1910 craftsman-style parsonage in a small town in Iowa, USA. Her husband Ben is the local pastor and the church owns and maintains the house. The church gave them a small budget to redo the kitchen, so Avery embarked on this amazing renovation of their dark 1980s wood kitchen only using Chalk Paint®. **PRODUCTS USED** Avery used Chalk Paint® in Pure to do two coats on the upper cabinets, and Duck Egg Blue to do two coats on the lower cupboards. **AVERY'S ADVICE** "Degrease your cabinets thoroughly with a degreasing soap. If you leave just a tiny spot it will show through the paint. Approach your kitchen remodel with realistic expectations. When you get really, really close and examine the cabinets, they do have some imperfections, but who ever gets that close? We love our kitchen now. It's bright and colourful and full of light."
www.hollandavenuehome.com

ABOVE "We didn't need new appliances or fixtures or flooring, so I read every article out there about painting kitchen cupboards, and decided to go for it!"

RIGHT "There's only one window, which doesn't provide much natural light. The dark cupboards sucked any brightness out of the room, and the white floors gave off a hospital vibe. The walls were terracotta, so the newer white paint still had some orange undertones."

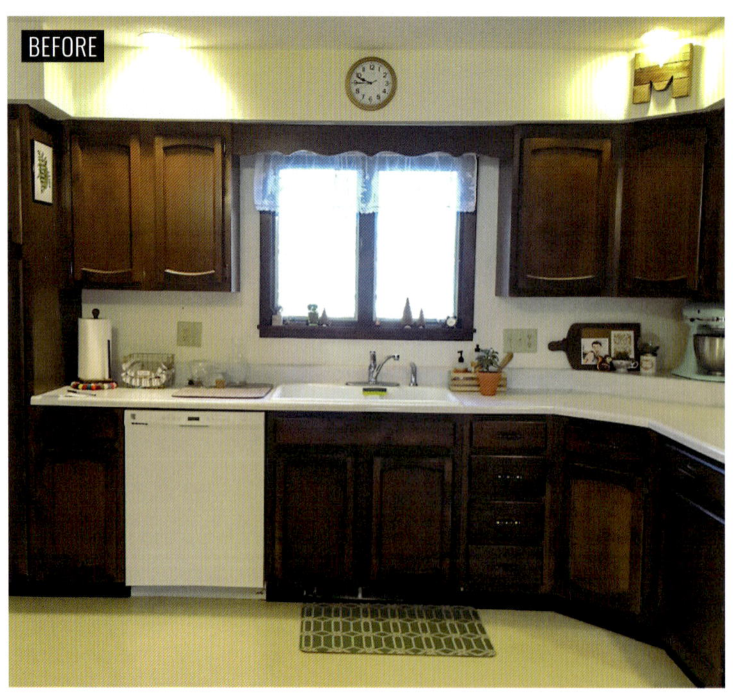

The CURIOUS traveller

Discovering the beauty of the world through colour, culture and people

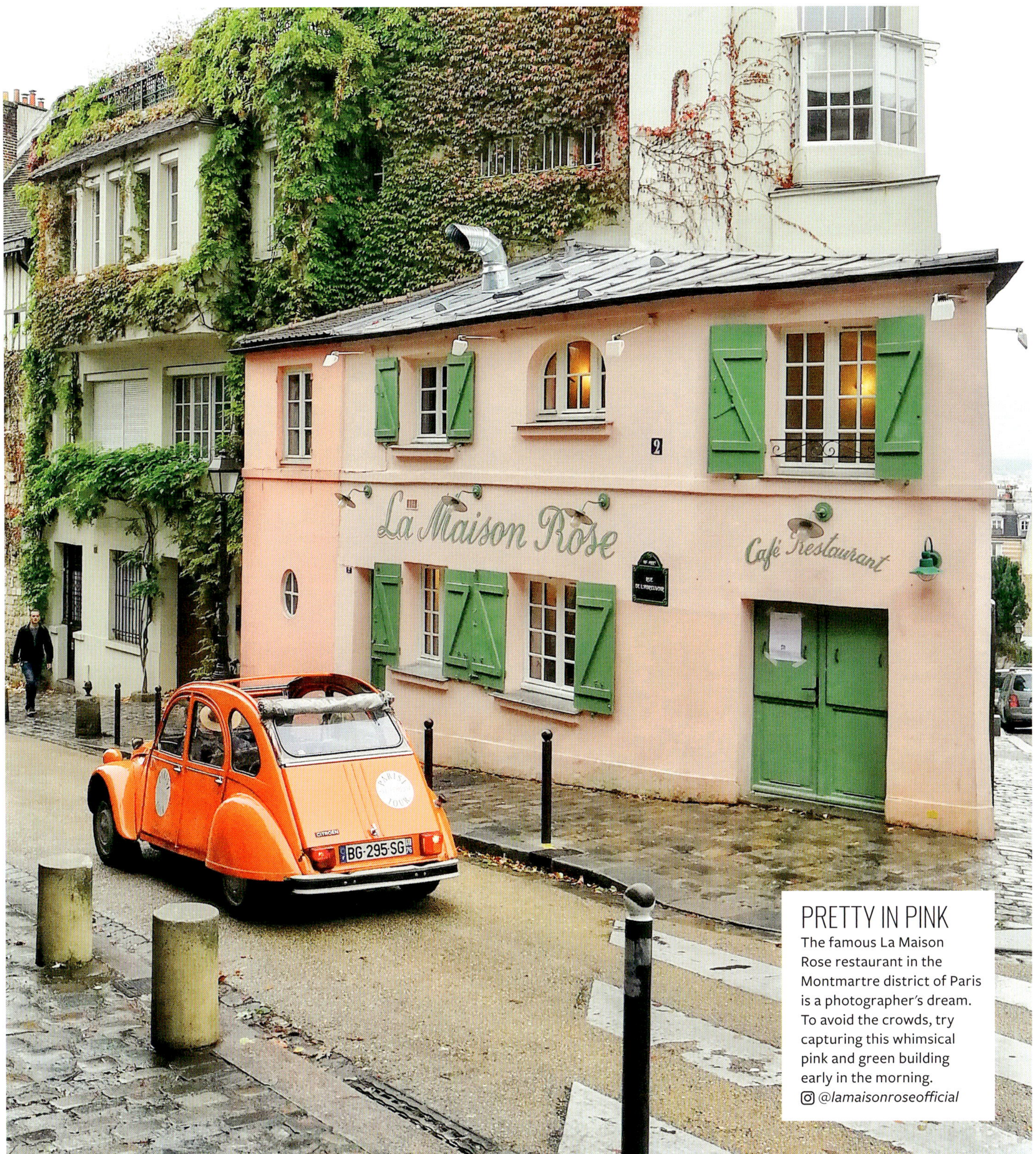

PHOTOGRAPHY: EMANUEL ROMEDEA @YESMYFRIEND

PRETTY IN PINK

The famous La Maison Rose restaurant in the Montmartre district of Paris is a photographer's dream. To avoid the crowds, try capturing this whimsical pink and green building early in the morning. @lamaisonroseofficial

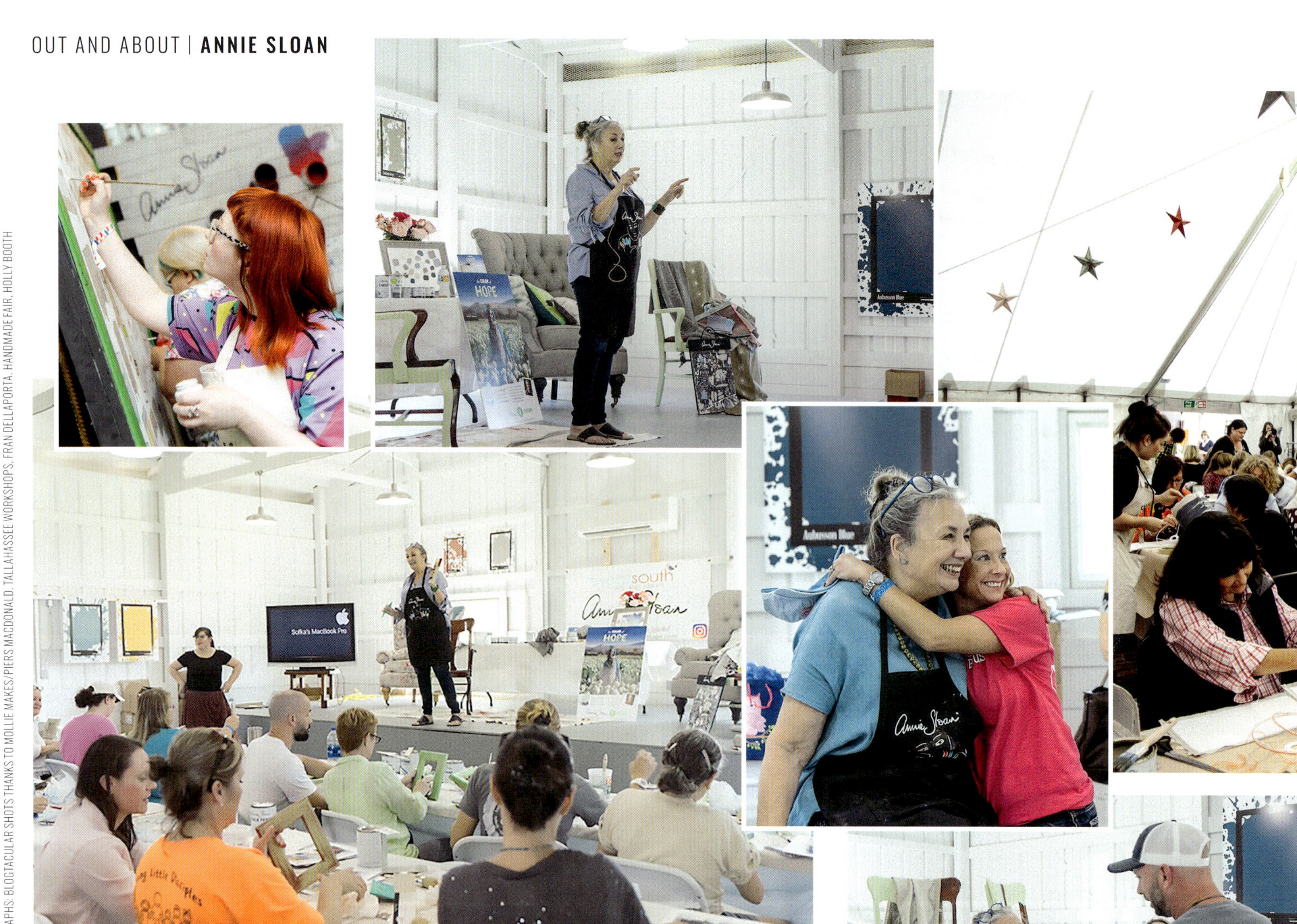

PHOTOGRAPHS: BLOGTACULAR SHOTS THANKS TO MOLLIE MAKES/PIERS MACDONALD. TALLAHASSEE WORKSHOPS: FRAN DELLAPORTA. HANDMADE FAIR: HOLLY BOOTH

Out and About

CHECK OUT SOME OF THE EVENTS, PROJECTS AND WORKSHOPS THAT ANNIE WILL BE ATTENDING THROUGHOUT THE YEAR

UNITED KINGDOM

AUGUST 2018

BBC Countryfile Live

2ND – 5TH AUGUST

BLENHEIM PALACE, OXFORD

Bringing the popular BBC television show to its audience in the beautiful grounds of historic Blenheim Palace. From live entertainment and workshops, to crafts and delicious food stalls. Come and meet Annie or visit our stand for Chalk Paint®, products and inspiration.

www.countryfilelive.com

SEPTEMBER 2018

Top Drawer

9TH – 11TH SEPTEMBER

OLYMPIA, LONDON

Top Drawer is the UK's leading retail trade event for creative lifestyle buyers, showcasing a curated edit of 1,500 brands to top international retailers. Annie Sloan will make their debut appearance at the 2018 event, and Annie herself will be giving a talk on colour. Top Drawer is predominantly a trade show but consumers are also welcome!

www.topdrawer.co.uk

The Handmade Fair,

4TH – 16TH SEPTEMBER

HAMPTON COURT PALACE GREEN, LONDON

The ultimate creative day out. You'll find The Super Theatre, Skills Workshops, and Grand Makes packed with interactive sessions, plus over 300 hand-picked sellers filling two shopping villages. Annie will be showing her Chalk Paint® and techniques. Browse tools, materials and products for sale and take part in skills workshops to expand your creative horizons.

www.thehandmadefair.com/hampton-court

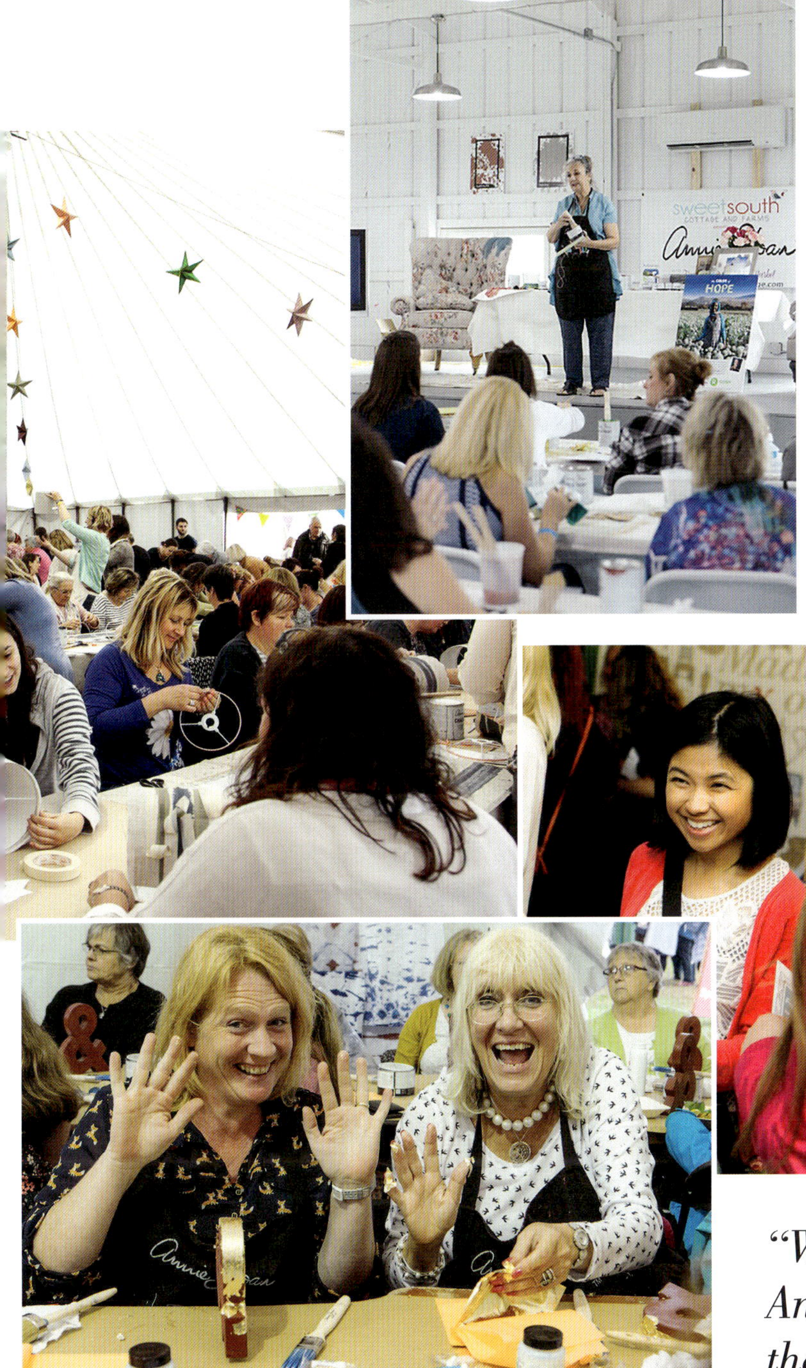

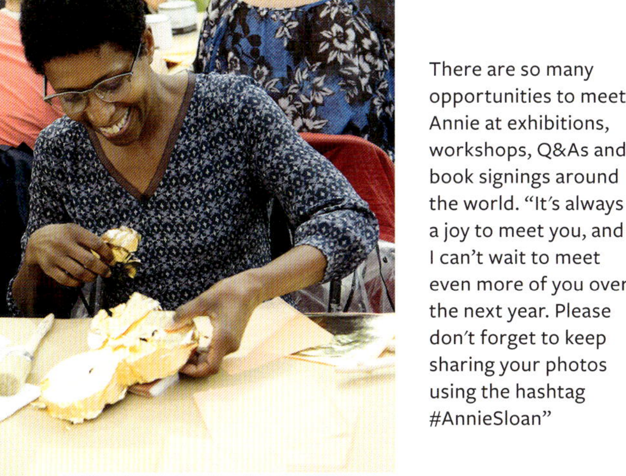

There are so many opportunities to meet Annie at exhibitions, workshops, Q&As and book signings around the world. "It's always a joy to meet you, and I can't wait to meet even more of you over the next year. Please don't forget to keep sharing your photos using the hashtag #AnnieSloan"

"What I love about meeting people who use Annie Sloan products, is seeing how they use them in diverse ways to create different styles"

Decorex
16TH – 19TH SEPTEMBER
THE LONDON DESIGN FESTIVAL,
SYON PARK, LONDON
Opening The London Design Festival, Decorex brings together products from hand-selected brands, unmissable collaborations and inspirational speakers across the world of new and unique design. Come and see us at the Annie Sloan stand where we'll be showcasing our Chalk Paint® and products. Annie will also be giving a talk at this event.
www.decorex.com

AUSTRALIA

NOVEMBER 2018
Makers and Painters Market,
3RD – 4TH NOVEMBER
MEAT MARKET BUILDING
5 BLACKWOOD ST, NORTH MELBOURNE
To celebrate the visit of Annie Sloan to Melbourne, local Chalk Paint® Stockists Bernice Ryan from French and Co and Joolze Lind from Gisborne French Provincial have created the ultimate creative day out. Annie will be a special guest throughout the weekend, giving daily demonstrations. She'll also talk on topics such as her Painters in Residence programme and will be available for the book signings. Annie's Painter in Residence 2017, Jonathon Marc Mendes, will be teaching workshops at the event. With 40 stall holders, this will be a creative event for all the family!
www.makersandpaintersmarket.com.au

Check out our website for details and Instagram Stories for live updates!
www.anniesloan.com *@AnnieSloanHome*

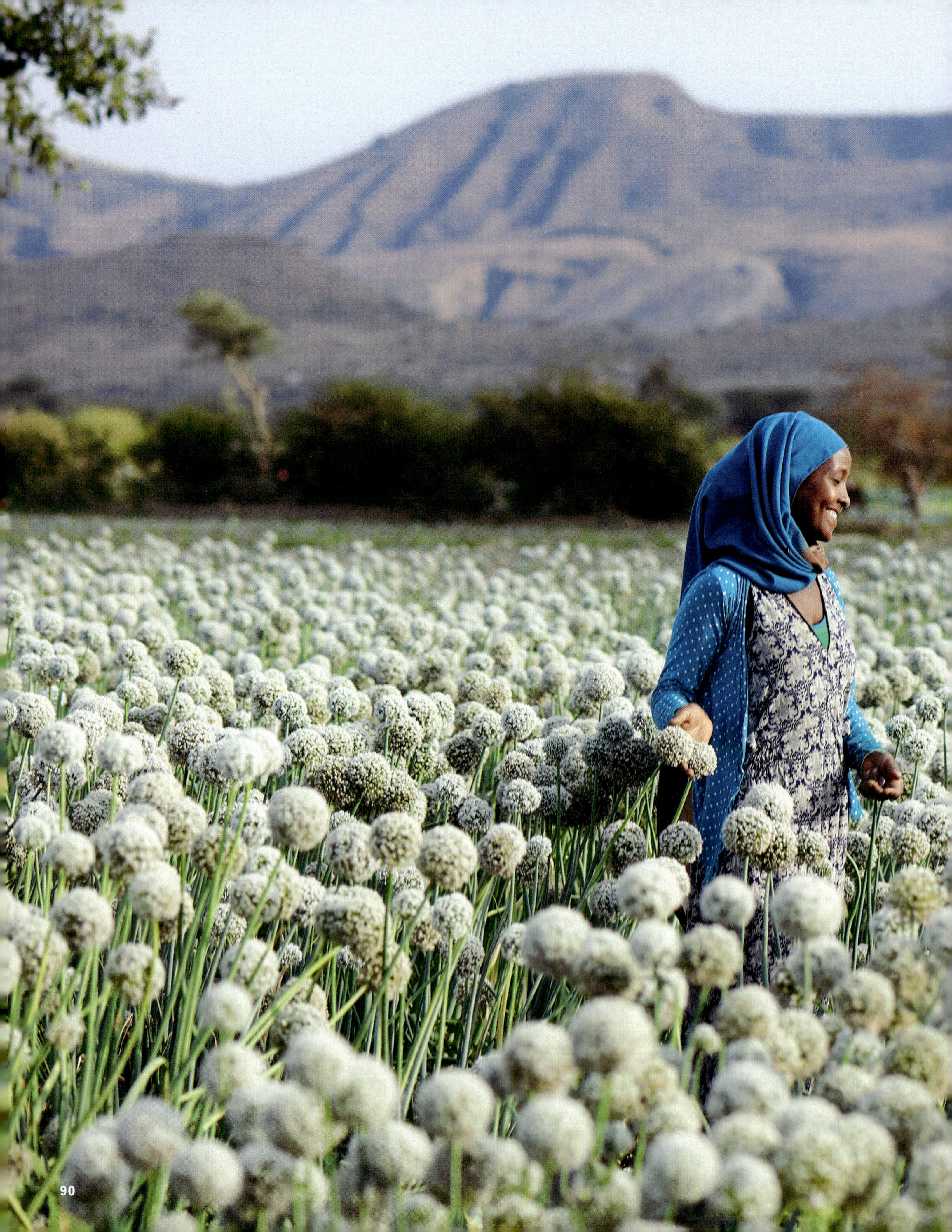

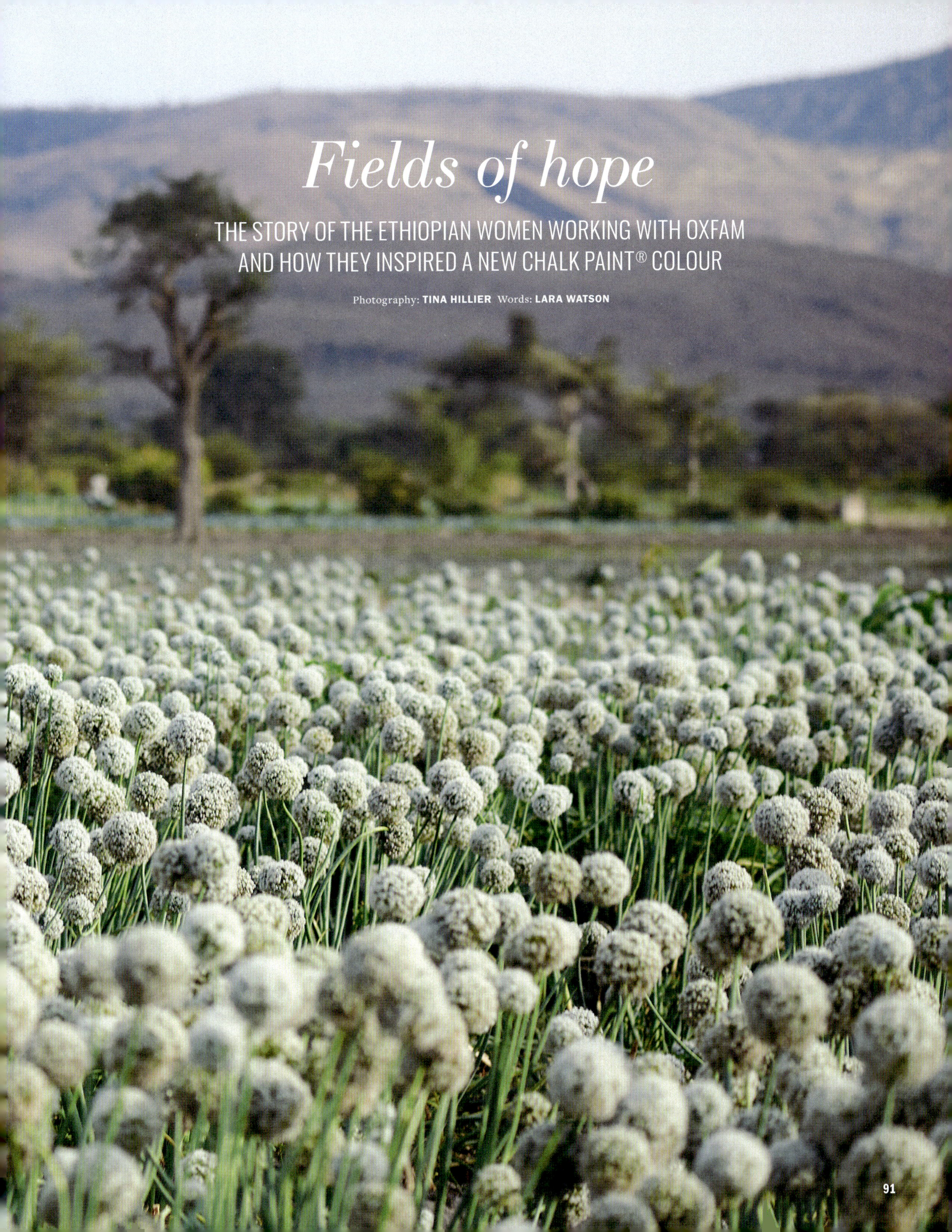

Fields of hope

THE STORY OF THE ETHIOPIAN WOMEN WORKING WITH OXFAM AND HOW THEY INSPIRED A NEW CHALK PAINT® COLOUR

Photography: **TINA HILLIER** Words: **LARA WATSON**

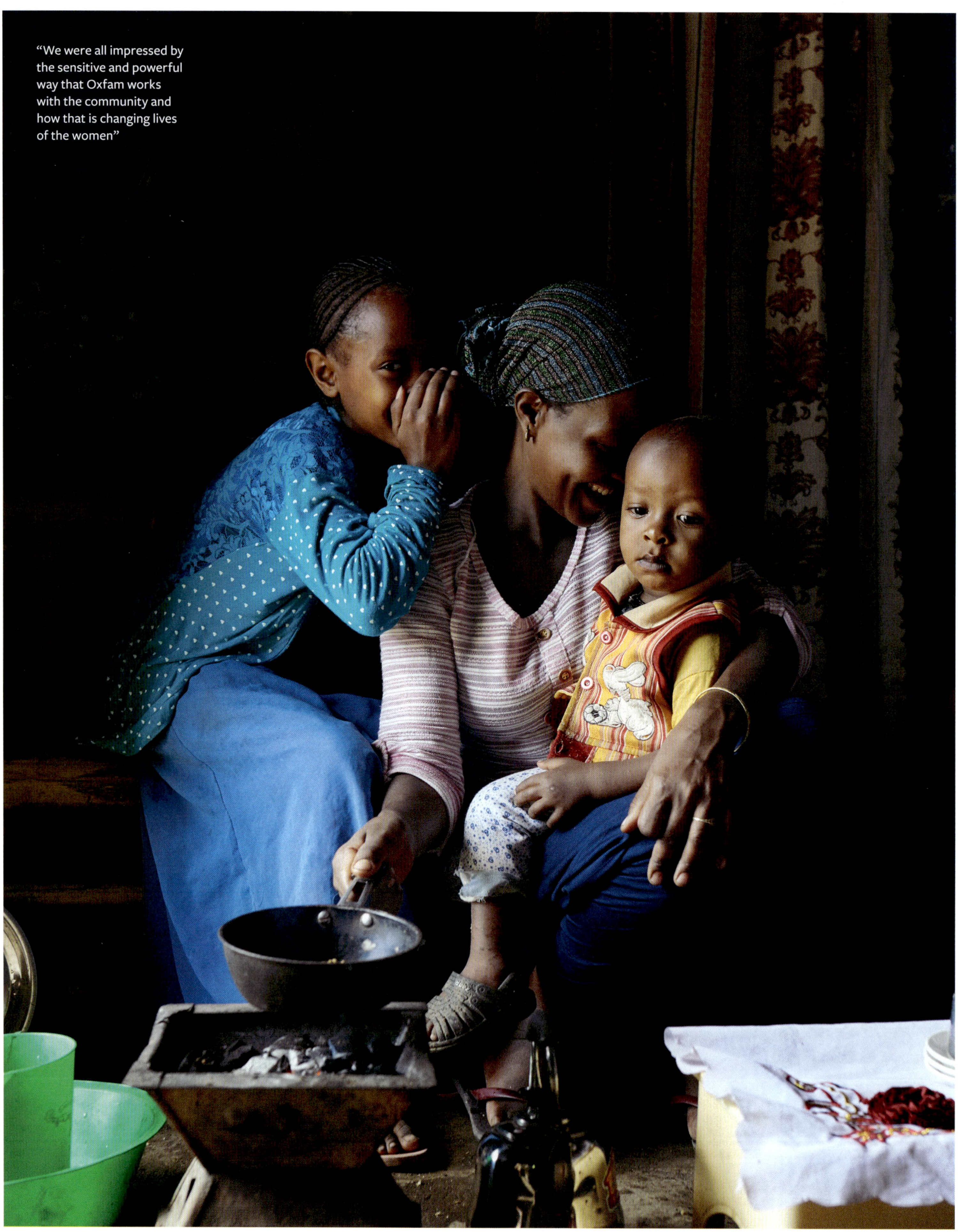

"We were all impressed by the sensitive and powerful way that Oxfam works with the community and how that is changing lives of the women"

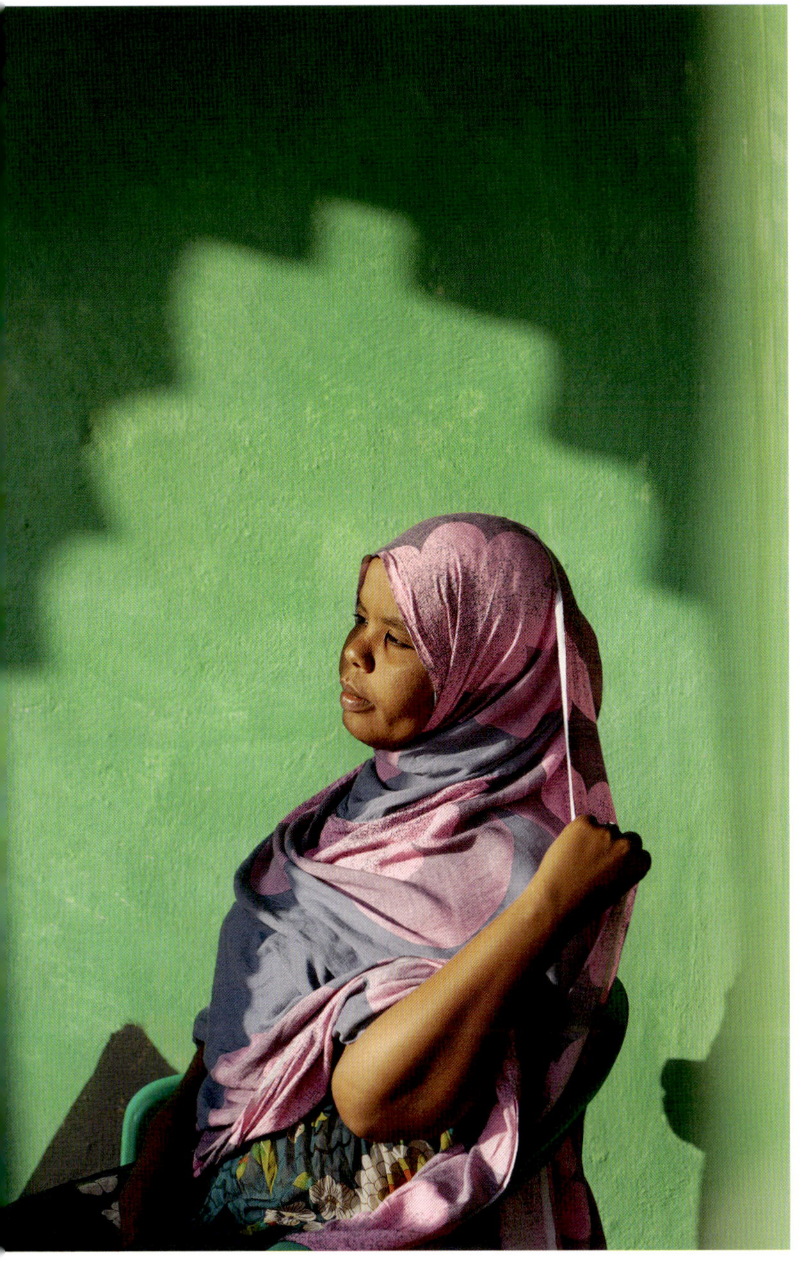

"I'm delighted to support the charity. It was very humbling to see first-hand how people are suffering"

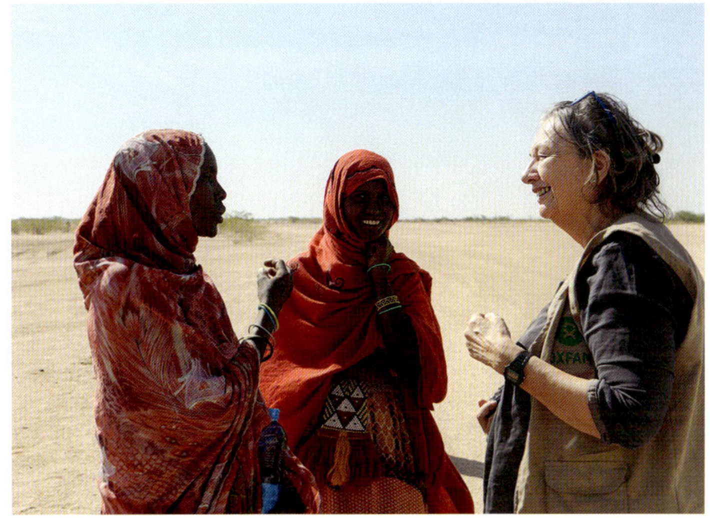

ABOVE "We were taken to one of the areas where lack of water was now taking hold of the people, and we saw the gargantuan work that Oxfam are doing to truck water and help the population"

LEFT "The colours, the people, the feeling of hope – all of this went into the creation of Lem Lem. I really do love this colour and everything that it represents"

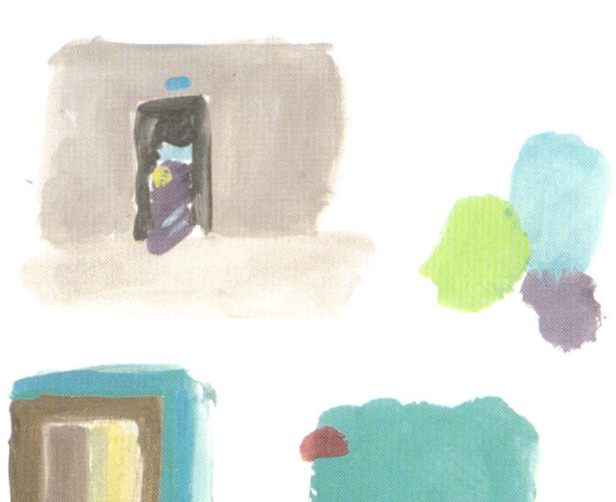

Back in February 2017, Annie Sloan was invited to rural southeast Ethiopia by the global poverty reduction charity, Oxfam, to see first-hand the work they're doing to help foster and encourage new businesswomen in the area. The partnership also had an enterprising aim: to develop a new limited-edition shade of Annie's world-famous Chalk Paint® dedicated to these women, to be sold to raise funds for Oxfam's projects.

BEATING POVERTY

This was the first time Annie has worked with a charity on this scale, and she was excited to travel and actually meet the women being supported to forge a new life for themselves. "I just thought it would be wonderful to help, and also I feel very connected to Oxfam," says Annie. "They're based in Oxford like us, so I'm delighted to support the charity. It was very humbling to see first-hand how people are suffering amid the worst drought in 30 years on my visit."

In this part of Ethiopia virtually every family lives off the land. Many households at the drought's worst were relying on food parcels from the government, with men leaving families to search for work in neighbouring countries. Two years on, the region is still not in total recovery. Weak rains at the end of 2017 mean that the humanitarian response needs to remain high.

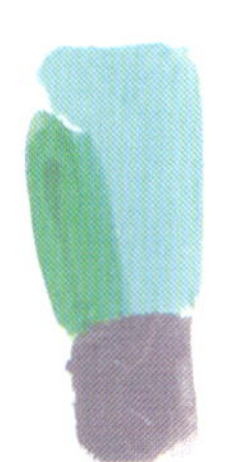

PROVIDING A FUTURE

So it's not only an admiration for Oxfam that spurred Annie to get involved, but a desire to help other women, »

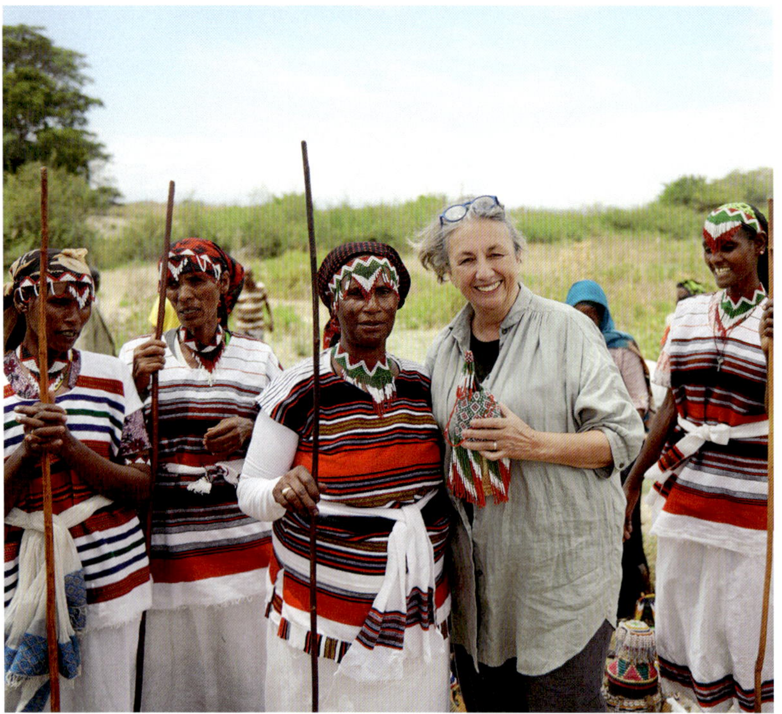

LEFT "My trip was a truly extraordinary experience, and one that will stay with me forever"

BELOW Annie found rich, vibrant colour throughout her travels in Ethiopia. "Everywhere we visited, I saw houses painted in strong, pure, joyous, bright colours"

RIGHT Annie made many sketches during her visit to Ethiopia. She transported her paint samples in little pill-dispensing boxes

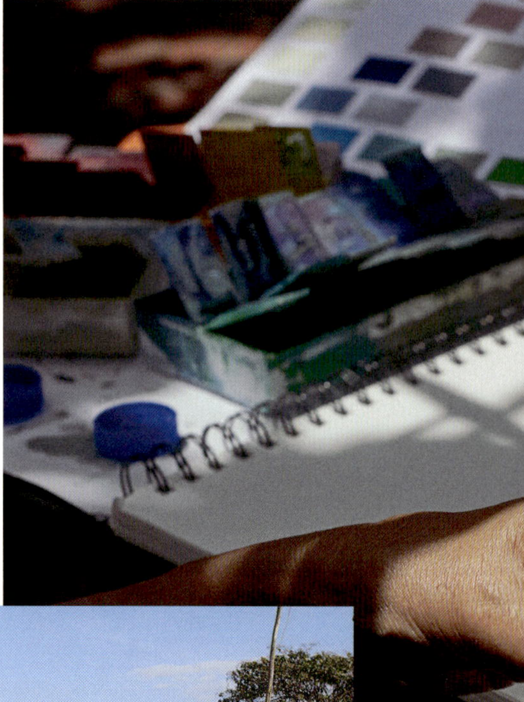

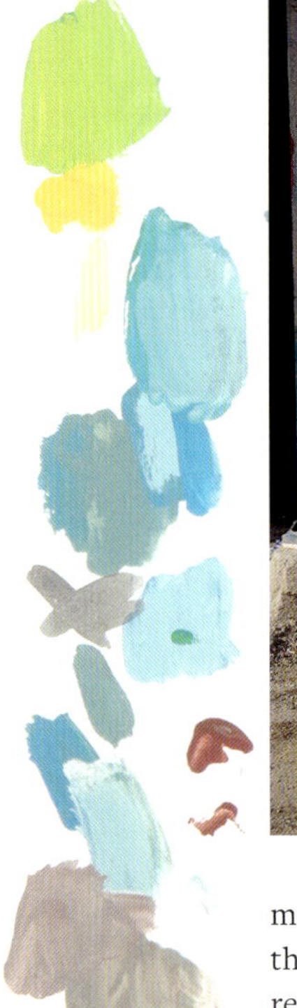

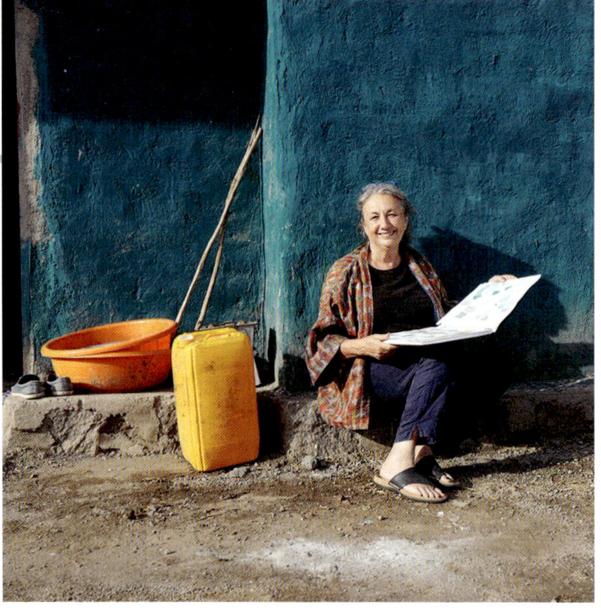

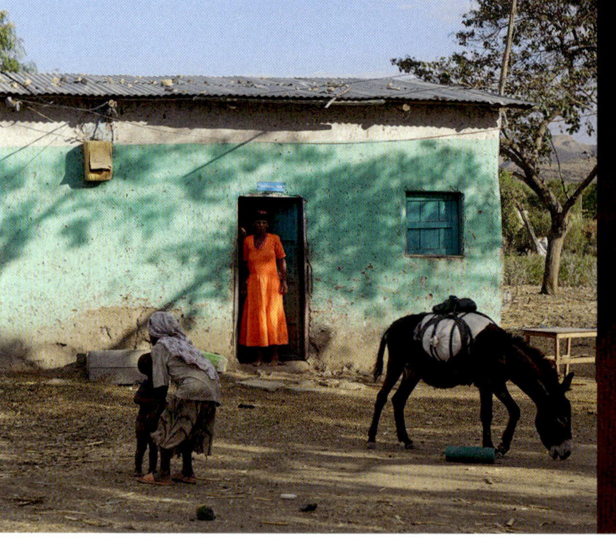

many of whom have suddenly found themselves head of the household. "As a woman who's set up a business, I can really relate to these women who are all being taught how to set up businesses and the way Oxfam is doing it is so brilliant," explains Annie. "They're helping the poorest, the most vulnerable and they're teaching them skills that will open doors to a good future."

Annie met members of Oxfam's Horticulture Project in Oromia. The project aims to support poor farmers to grow more and sell more. One woman Annie spoke to was the first woman in her family to have a bank account – unprecedented for a woman in this part of Ethiopia. Another lady with four children under nine had made enough money to buy a house, a cow, an ox, a TV (its arrival resulted a party in the village) and schooling.

LIVING LIFE IN COLOUR

On arrival in Ethiopia, Annie immediately noticed the colour, not only in the landscape, but in the vibrant villages and the local's clothing. "The first thing that really hit me in Ethiopia was that they love painting their houses and there are huge numbers of bright colours," she says. "But what really struck me, wherever we went in the country, is the way they combine colour. One shade is like a musical note, but when you combine it with others, you get a tune and that, I suppose, is what you get with a few colours together."

It goes without saying that colour is really very important to Annie and while on her trip she immersed herself in the culture and the markets, painting her favourite scenes and taking many photos. But there was

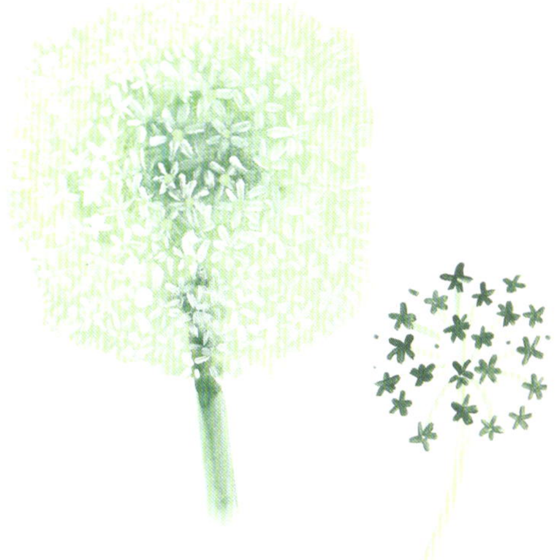

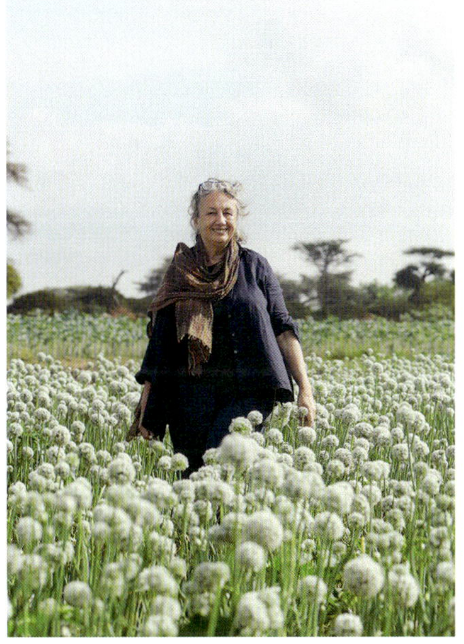

nowhere more inspiring to her than visiting the fields of Oxfam's Seed Project, which belong to a co-operative of women farmers, funded by Oxfam, realising their potential after being provided with loans to buy decent seeds and proper irrigation systems.

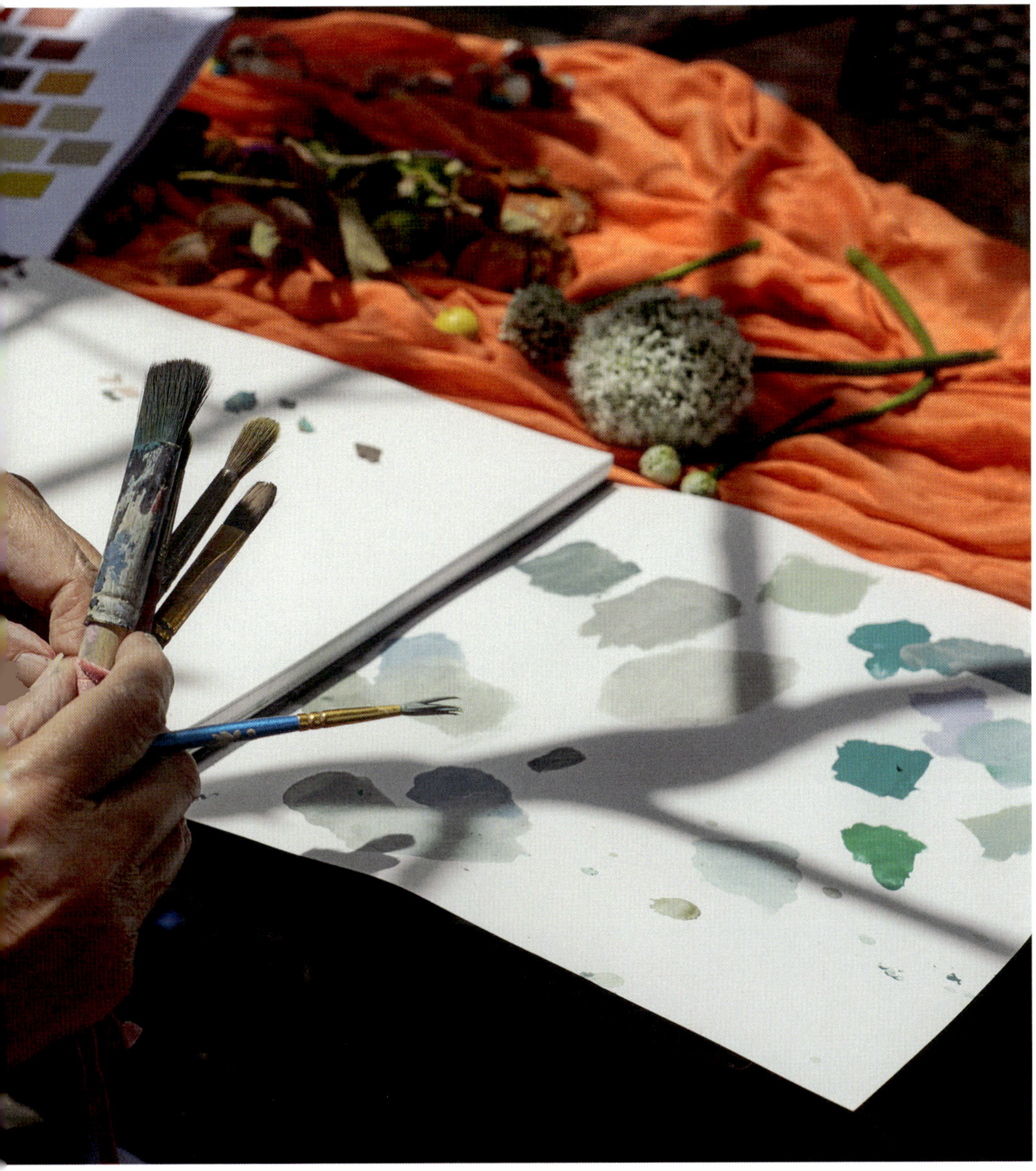

TAKING INSPIRATION

"Normally, when I make a colour, what I'm doing is looking back through history and I'm looking at pigments," says Annie. But this was altogether different – everything she needed for reference was there in front of her. "What I loved was when you look at these fields – the allium, or onion head of flowers, gives an overall impression that seems white, but then you realise there's green underneath, and green on the petals – a lovely muted grey-green," says Annie. "It really is beautiful. I asked one of the women farmers, 'what does green mean to you?' and she immediately said, 'growth' and I thought that was fantastic."

This soft, warm green became Lem Lem, Annie's new Chalk Paint® shade. Meaning 'to flourish' or 'the lush green of fresh growth' in Amharic, the language of Ethiopia, it's a word that Annie overheard amongst the women as they worked, and it made the perfect moniker – representing hope, just like Oxfam's projects throughout the region.

GREEN SHOOTS OF HOPE

The allium plant itself represents money and freedom to Ethiopians – the thriving plant, its colour and healthy »

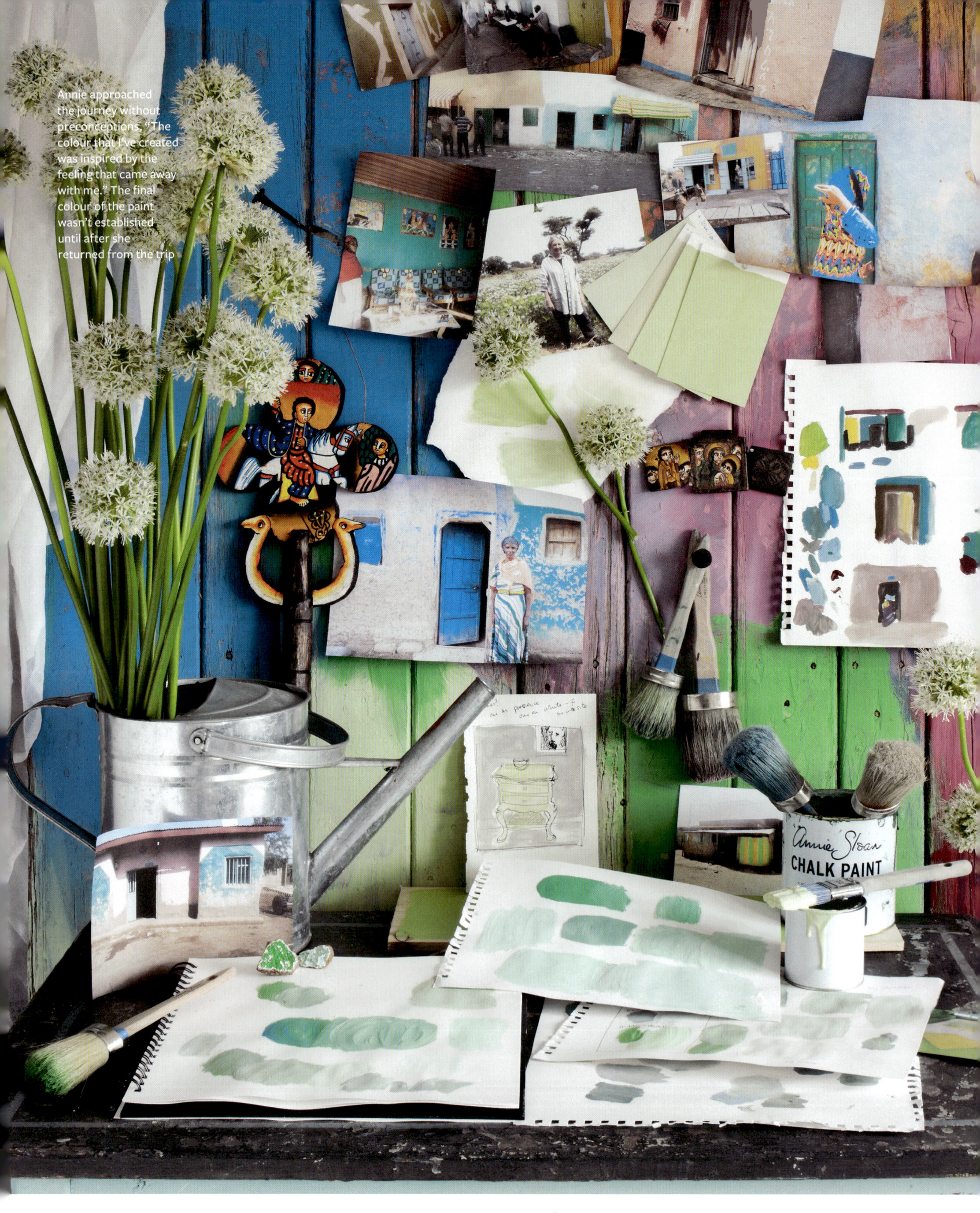

Annie approached the journey without preconceptions. "The colour that I've created was inspired by the feeling that came away with me." The final colour of the paint wasn't established until after she returned from the trip

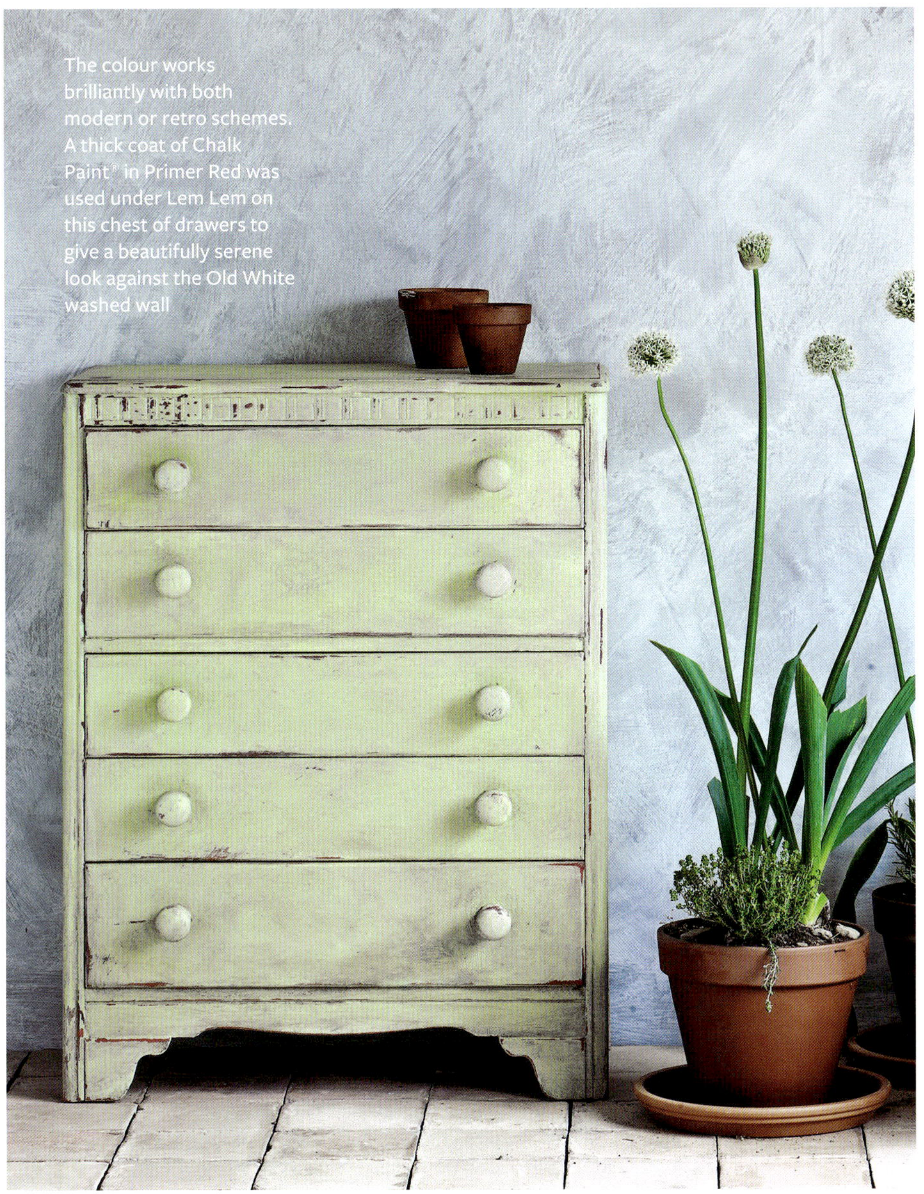

The colour works brilliantly with both modern or retro schemes. A thick coat of Chalk Paint® in Primer Red was used under Lem Lem on this chest of drawers to give a beautifully serene look against the Old White washed wall

appearance are hugely symbolic. Furthermore, when back home in the UK mixing the paint shade, Annie was struck by how modern and of-the-moment the colour is, and how well it works in a home with a fresh pastel palette, or indeed for a 50s retro vibe or vintage-floral style. "I feel that Lem Lem is representative of my business too," explains Annie. "It's a celebration of the idea of female ambition, will and talent. I've visited an awful lot of smarty pants places all over the world, and stayed in some very nice hotels, but those women in Ethiopia are what life is really about. People who are farming, doing things, dreams being fulfilled."

It's also a celebration of the power of colour and the contribution that one woman can make to many other women all around the world. AS

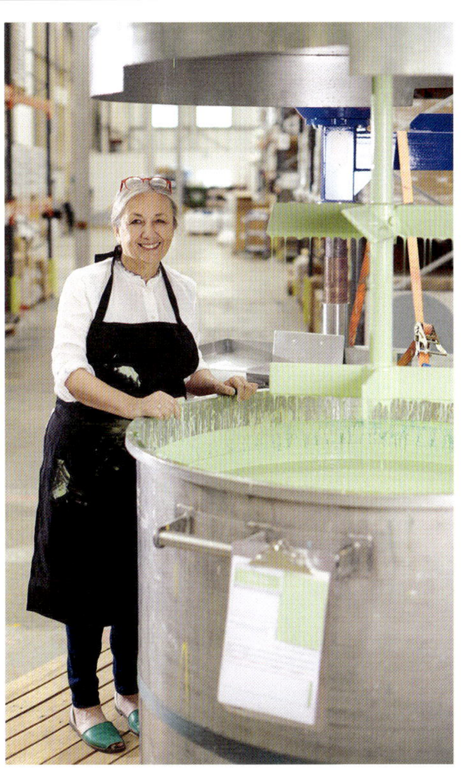

ANNIE'S PLEDGE

Every pot of Annie Sloan's brand-new limited-edition Chalk Paint® in Lem Lem will raise vital funds for Oxfam, helping people beat poverty worldwide.

£133,335 has been donated to date. Donations have benefitted projects in: Ethiopia, Zambia, Sri Lanka, Ghana and The Philippines, with more to be added with the next grant allocation. Annie aims to raise £250,000 over the next three years.

Pick up a pot at over 1,700 stockists in over 50 countries around the globe. *www.anniesloan.com/stockists*

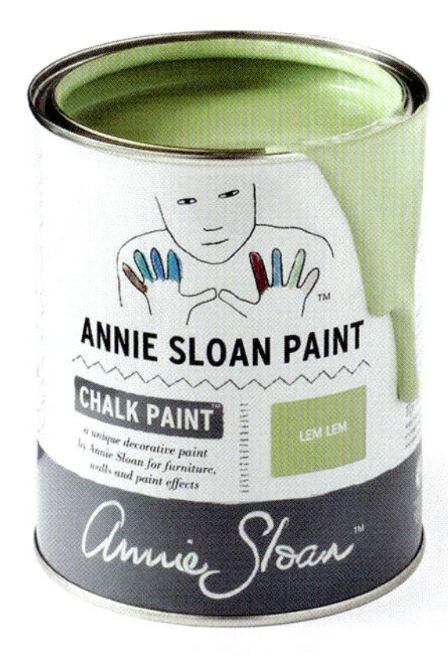

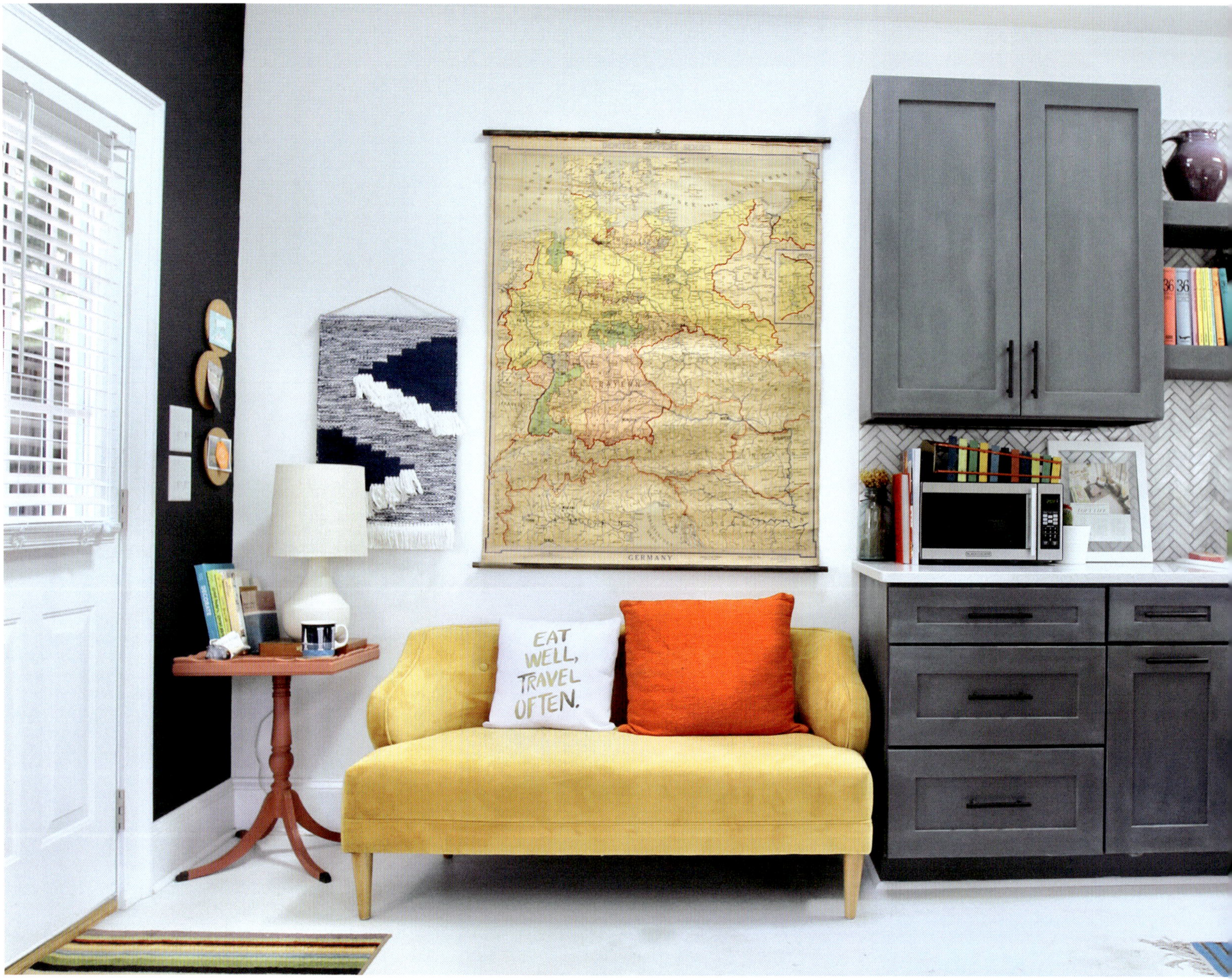

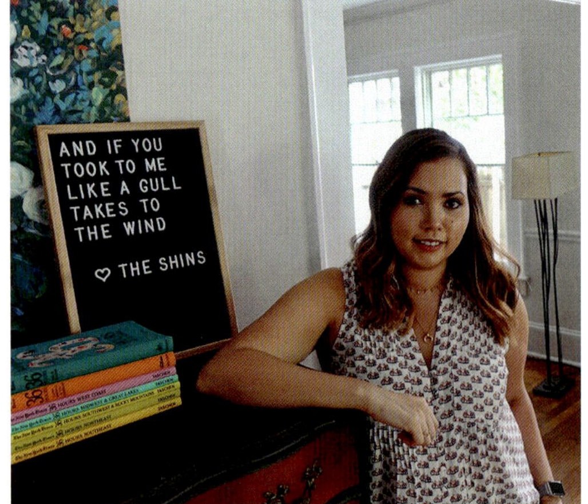

Atlanta Airbnb

We meet Jo Torrijos – designer, painter and stylist who loves all things thrift-stored and eclectic

Jo Torrijos is a busy lady! Via her website A Simpler Design she uses Annie Sloan paints to offer custom furniture painting and refinishing. She also runs Chalk Paint® for Beginners classes, home staging, style makeovers, home organizing and vintage prop and art rental.

Based in Atlanta, USA, Jo built her bungalow studio in her backyard in 2106, with the intention of using it as a base for her business. Jump forward two years and she has completely transformed the space using her 'go to' Chalk Paint® by Annie Sloan. The kitchen cabinets are painted in Graphite and make a great contrast to the bright pops of colour that Jo has introduced by painting vintage finds.

Although not her original intention for the space, Jo is delighted to open her bunglow to guests and it has quickly become a thriving Airbnb. "Atlanta is a rapidly growing travel destination, and I'm happy and proud to call it my city. I love my neighborhood, I love my home and now you too can come and experience it for yourself!" says Jo. AS

www.asimplerdesign.com *@asimplerdesign*

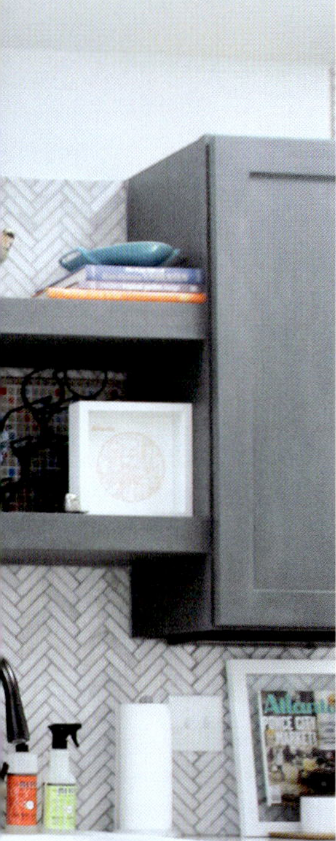

RIGHT "The studio is open plan, which makes it a really flexible space for renting, and also means that I can use it for my styling and photography projects. As I work on new pieces of furniture, I rotate some of my painted work into the space to keep it looking fresh and new."

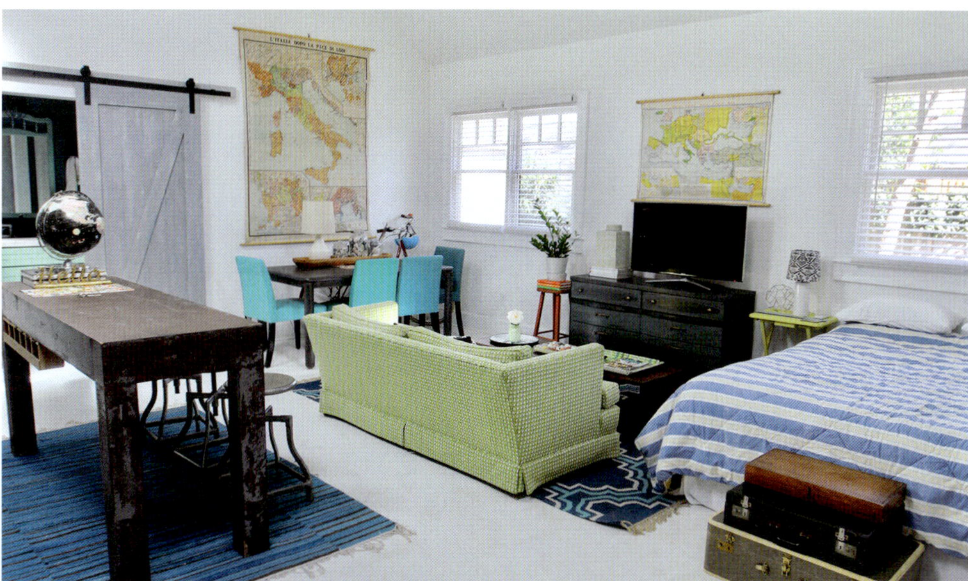

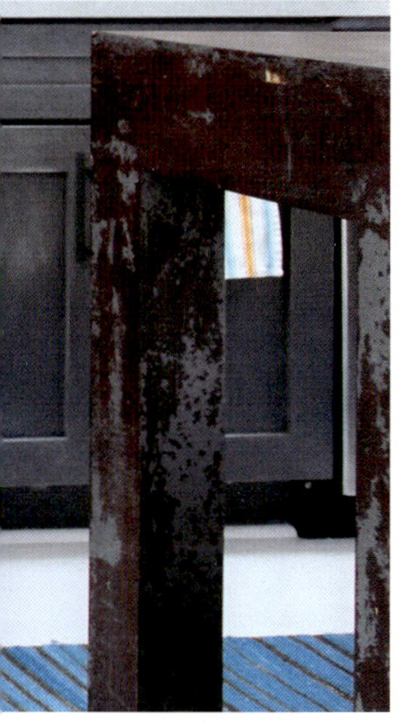

ABOVE "This kitchen is the perfect small-space single-wall kitchen. It's incredibly functional, but also stylish and polished. I used Chalk Paint® by Annie Sloan in Graphite on the kitchen cabinets."

RIGHT "My tastes are very eclectic, mixing vintage and modern design. But the colours that I've incorporated into my style have evolved quite a bit over the years. And I'm certain will continue to change over time!"

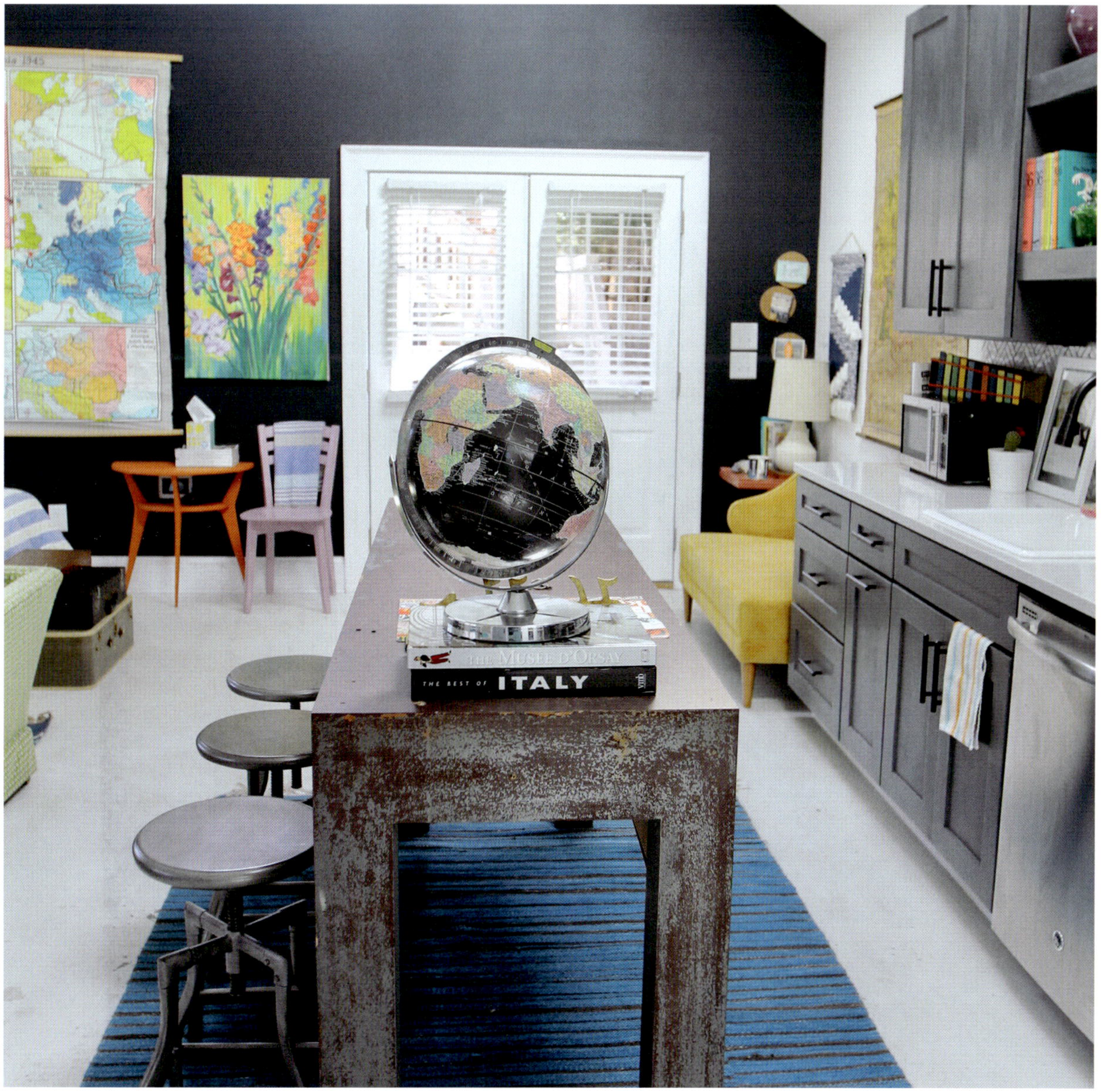

RIGHT "I painted this dresser in Graphite, applied Clear Wax and then Black Wax towards the bottom to give it more depth."

BELOW "I love incorporating bright pops of colour into a mostly neutral room, such as my Scandinavian Pink side table and mint green vanity base."

BELOW RGHT "Your home will stand out from all the other Airbnb listings if you can find something a bit outside the box that makes for a great conversation piece."

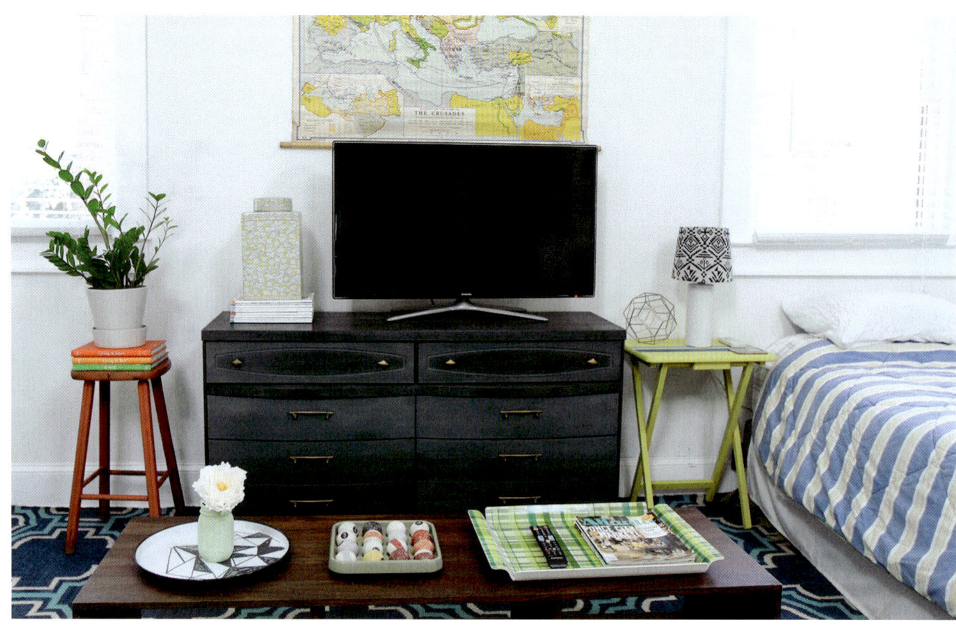

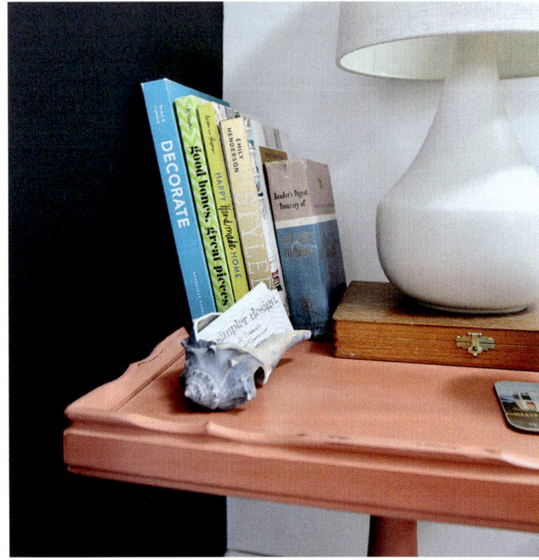

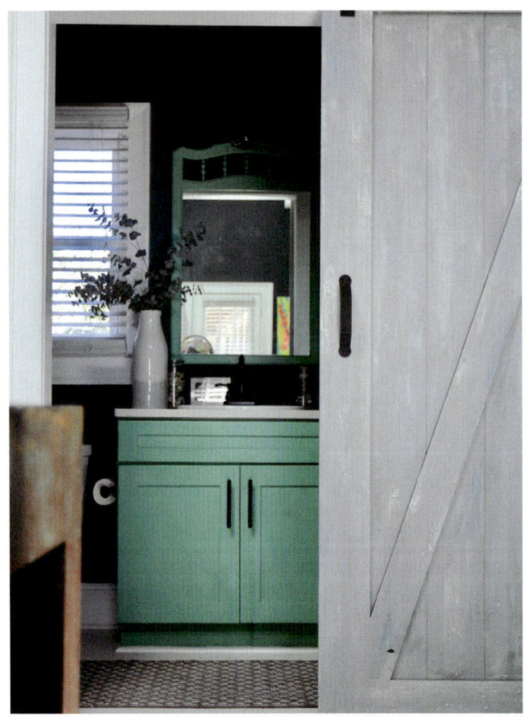

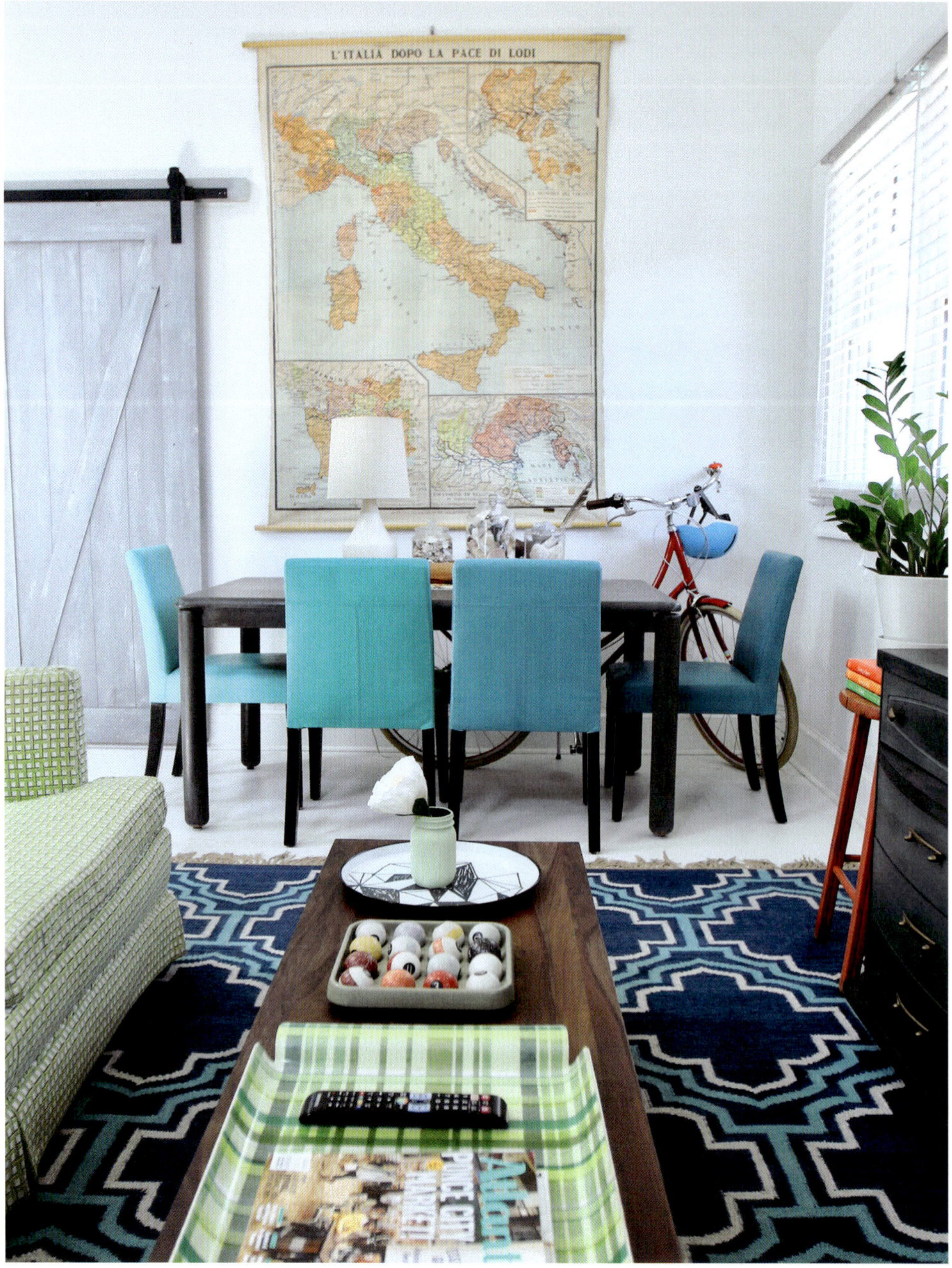

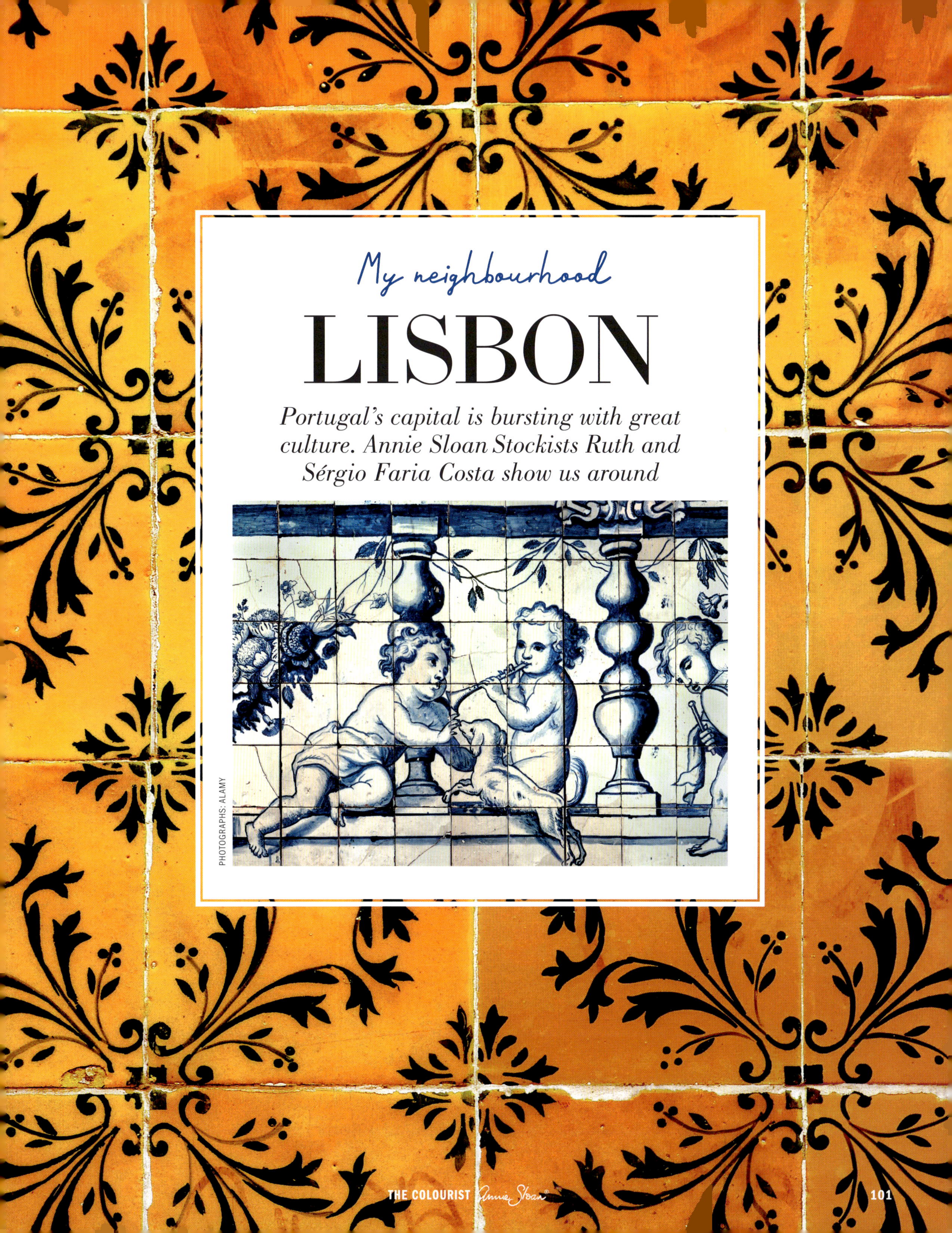

My neighbourhood

LISBON

Portugal's capital is bursting with great culture. Annie Sloan Stockists Ruth and Sérgio Faria Costa show us around

PHOTOGRAPHS: ALAMY

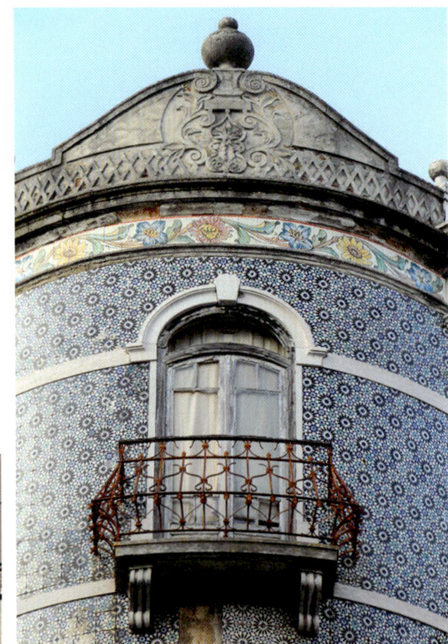

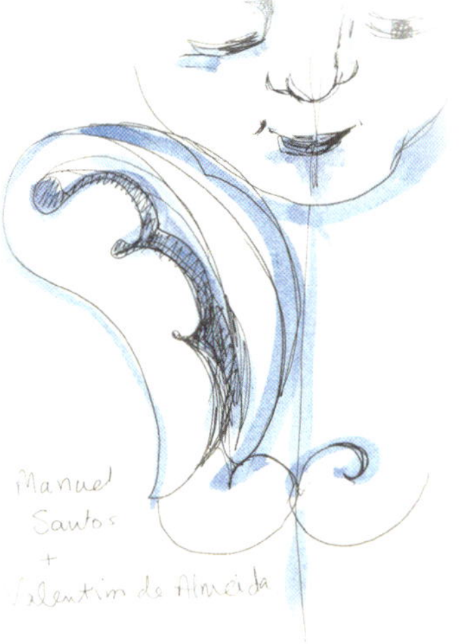

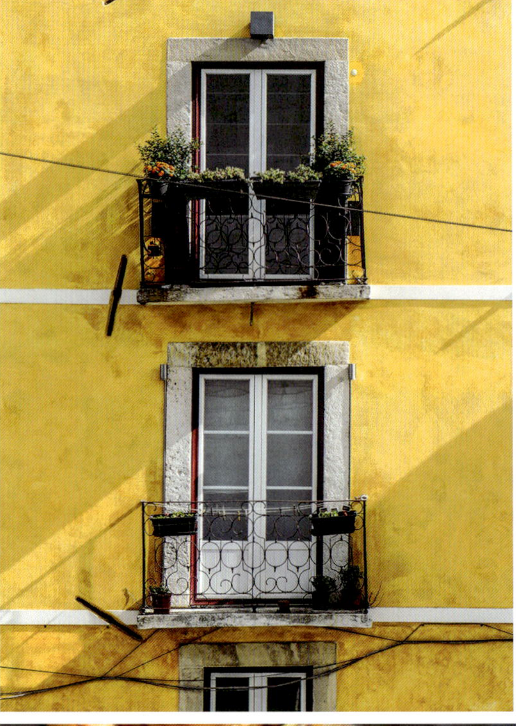

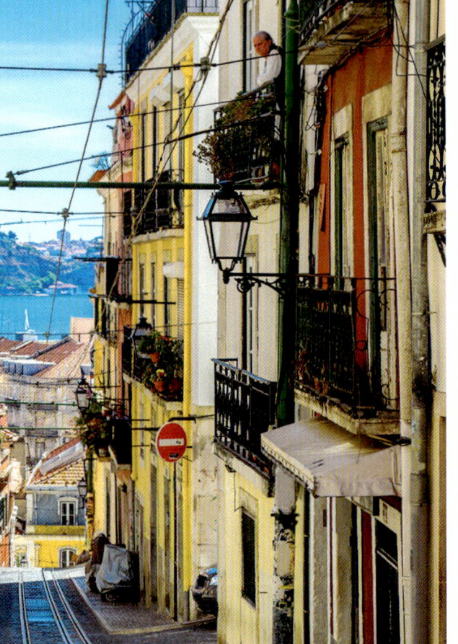

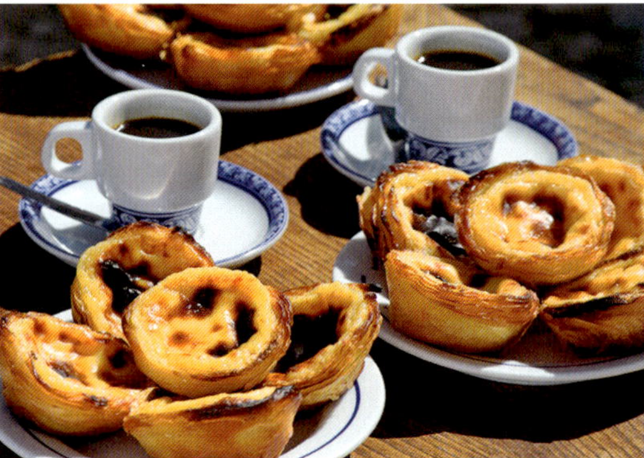

PHOTOGRAPHS: ALAMY, SHUTTERSTOCK, LILI POPPER, UNSPLASH. ILLUSTRATIONS: ANNIE SLOAN

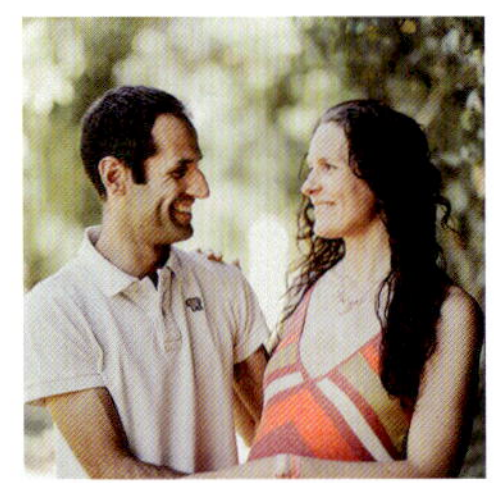

ATELIER AUTÊNTICO

Ruth and Sérgio Faria Costa met in London through a mutual friend and got married in Lisbon in 2012. Ruth worked as an Art Director for many years, while Sérgio managed the front of house team at the Hoxton Hotel in Shoreditch. In 2013, Ruth and Sérgio decided to leave London and move to Portugal

Ruth and Sérgio's journey to becoming Annie Sloan Stockists and vintage furniture restorers began with their move to Portugal in 2013. Having restored an old Quinta (country house), they were ready to fill it with vintage furniture, but found it hard to source. Their mission to find pieces turned into a business, and Atelier Autêntico was born.

Describe the village you live in

We live in and work in Oeiras, which is around 15km outside Lisbon, along the Linha, the coastline from Lisbon to Sintra, often called the Portuguese Riviera. Our home and the shop is situated in the historic centre of Oeiras, with lots of independent shops, cafés and delis. The beach is a stroll away and Oeiras has two parks and the picturesque palace, Marquês de Pombal.

What drew you back to Lisbon?

Sérgio is originally from Lisbon and after living in London for many years, we were looking for a simpler and calmer lifestyle with a nicer climate.

Can you tell us about a few of the hidden gems that visitors to Lisbon might not know about?

Lisbon has changed immensely over the past few years and while it's not a big city, it's easy to get lost in the small cobbled streets in the old parts, such as Alfama, Bairro Alto and Santa Catarina. We love the Miradouro de Santa Catarina, with fantastic views over the river – perfect for watching the sunset. A visit to Jardim da Estrela is also wonderful. There you can also visit the exquisite Baroque church, Basílica da Estrela, with its twin bell towers.

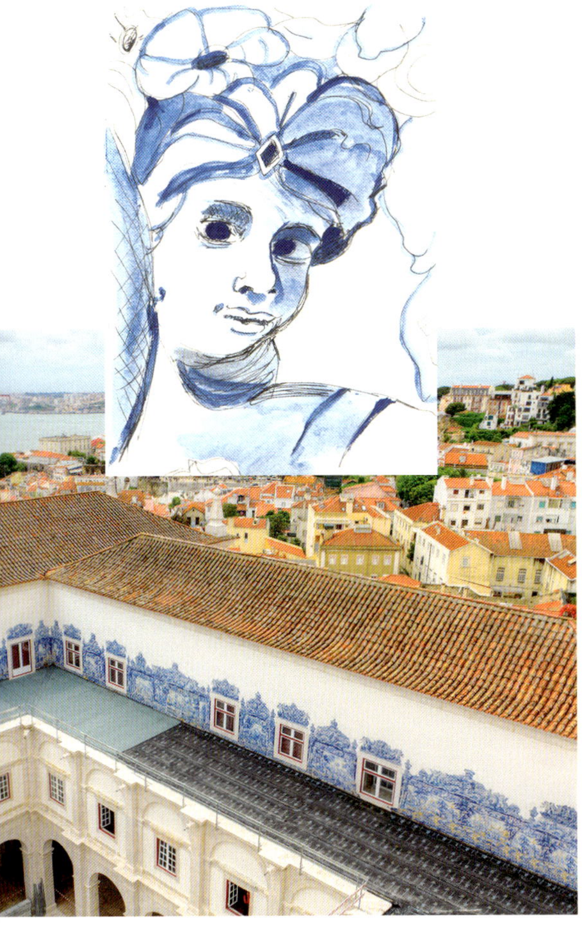

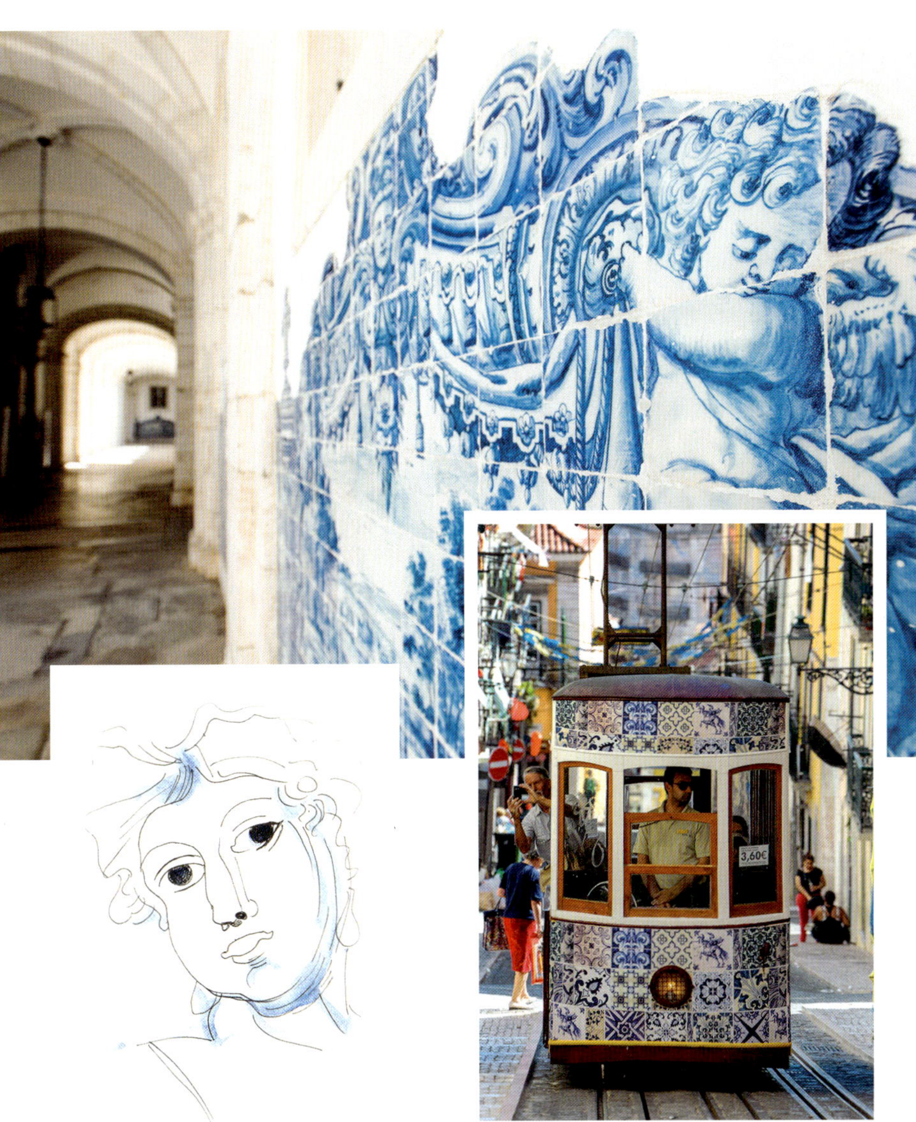

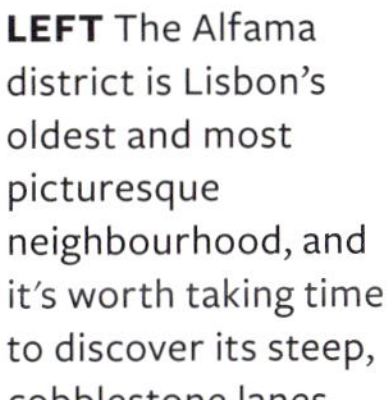

LEFT The Alfama district is Lisbon's oldest and most picturesque neighbourhood, and it's worth taking time to discover its steep, cobblestone lanes

RIGHT Lisbon's famous blue and white tiles adorn churches, shops, palaces and trams. Their influence can be seen in Annie's sketches made during her trip to the city

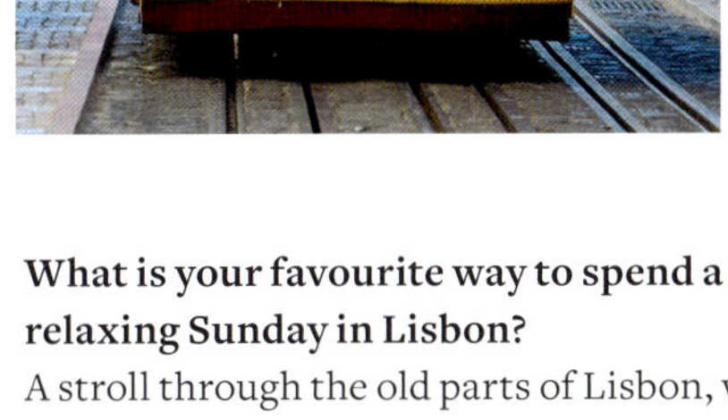

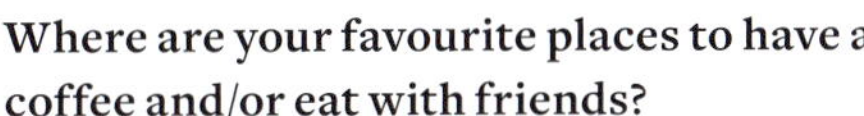

Where are your favourite places to have a coffee and/or eat with friends?
We like to have brunch on a Sunday morning at LXFactory, which is a redeveloped complex of old factories dating from 1846, nestled at the foot of the 25 de Abril bridge. Once belonging to a fabric company, the industrial spaces are mostly rented out to companies related to art and design, plus independent shops, cafés and restaurants. There's also a street market at weekends. To beat the crowds, go for breakfast or brunch, as it gets really busy around lunchtime.

Our favourite café is Chá da Barra Villa, which is in the heart of Oeiras next to the cultural centre and a stone's throw from our house and shop. It has a great selection of speciality teas and makes the best cakes! We love the terrace, which is open all year round and can be enjoyed even in the winter, when the sun's out. The interior isn't particularly spectacular but it showcases a nice selection of traditional azulejos (elaborately-painted wall tiles).

Where can we see the colourful azulejos that Lisbon is famous for?
Painted tiles can be seen all over the old part of town, particularly in the areas surrounding the Castelo de São Jorge and in the Baixa district in downtown Lisbon, where the Arco da Rua Augusta and the Praça do Comércio are situated.

Which art galleries and museums do you like to visit?
We have two small children, so we love to visit the Interactive Science Museum in Parque das Nações and MUDE, the Design and Fashion Museum in Baixa.

What is your favourite way to spend a relaxing Sunday in Lisbon?
A stroll through the old parts of Lisbon, with its many viewpoints (miradouros) across the river invite you to have a coffee, relax and drink in the view. Another favourite way to spend the day is to walk along the river front, starting at the famous 25 de Abril bridge towards Belém.

Where is the best area to go in Lisbon to find artisan or independent stores?
Principe Real and São Bento have really interesting shops.

What is your favourite independently owned store?
Our favourite shop is the bookshop, Gatafunho, opposite the church in Oeiras. Gata means cat in Portuguese and a cat

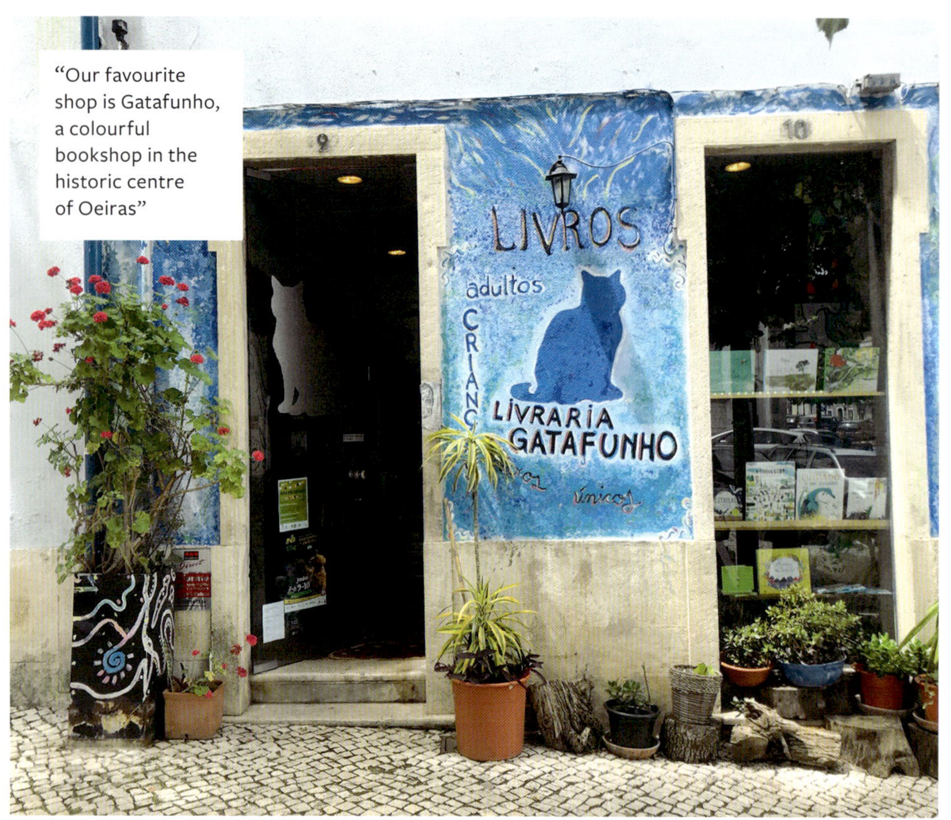

"Our favourite shop is Gatafunho, a colourful bookshop in the historic centre of Oeiras"

actually lives in the shop! Gatafunho is made up of two shops – one for children and one for adults. It brings the community together with readings and cultural activities for all ages. We visit with our children often, as they have a play area, do storytime on Sunday mornings and sell the most wonderful artisan books that are so beautifully illustrated.

Where is your favourite flea market?
Sadly the flea markets are awful here! There are a few in Lisbon but we wouldn't go there and buy anything – it's a lot of old tat at very expensive prices.

What are the best things to do in the evenings in Lisbon?
The Portuguese have a passion for food and late nights! We love going out for dinner and then sitting outside on an esplanada or miradouro to meet friends for a evening drink, while enjoying the views and the temperate climate. AS

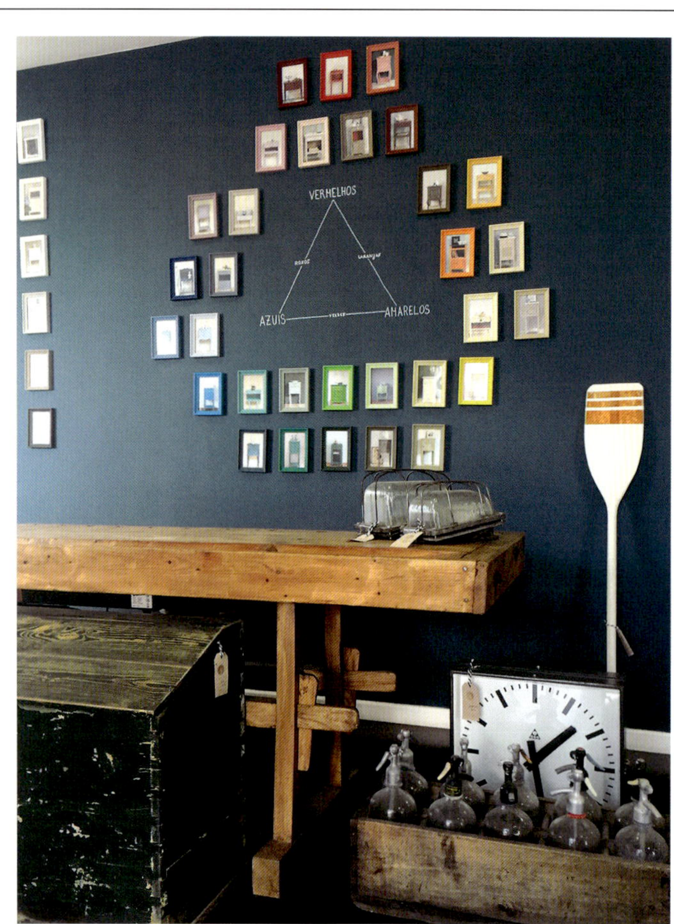

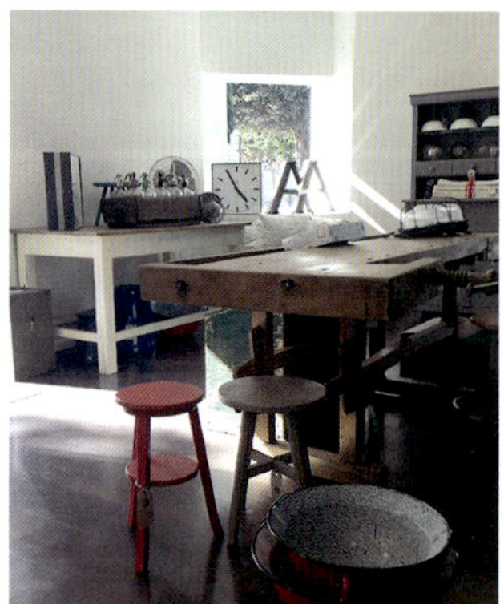

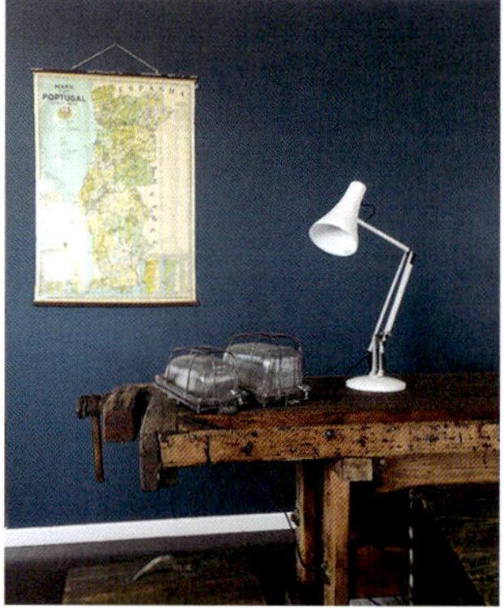

ATELIER AUTÊNTICO THE SHOP

"In essence, we rescue furniture and lighting and bring it back to life"

"At Atelier Autêntico we provide a collection of unique furniture and home accessories. We both have a keen eye for pieces that incorporate vintage, industrial and mid-century aesthetic. Most pieces that arrive in our workshop have had a long life, and most of them have seen their fair share of neglect. Annie describes our style as warehouse and we mostly sell farmhouse-style wooden furniture that has been painted in Chalk Paint®, enamelware, decorative items, plus a large selection of heavy industrial vintage lighting."
www.atelierautentico.pt

The OUTDOOR life

Take your creativity outside with our colour-filled ideas for vibrant spaces

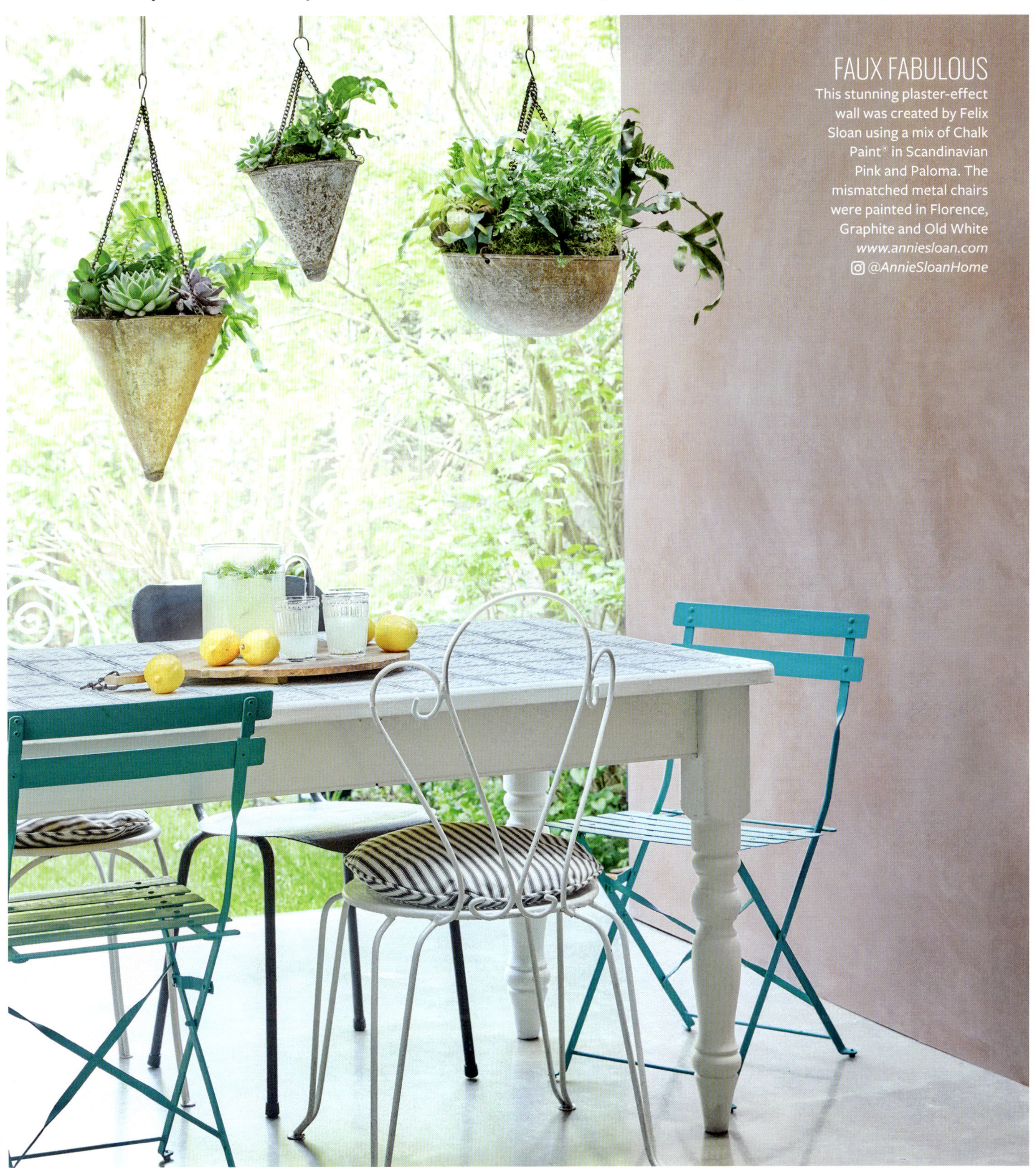

FAUX FABULOUS
This stunning plaster-effect wall was created by Felix Sloan using a mix of Chalk Paint® in Scandinavian Pink and Paloma. The mismatched metal chairs were painted in Florence, Graphite and Old White
www.anniesloan.com
@AnnieSloanHome

PHOTOGRAPH: SIMON BEVAN

SOME LIKE IT HOT

Embrace bohemian chic with an eclectic mix of vibrant colours, layered textures, lush plants and local artisanal crafts

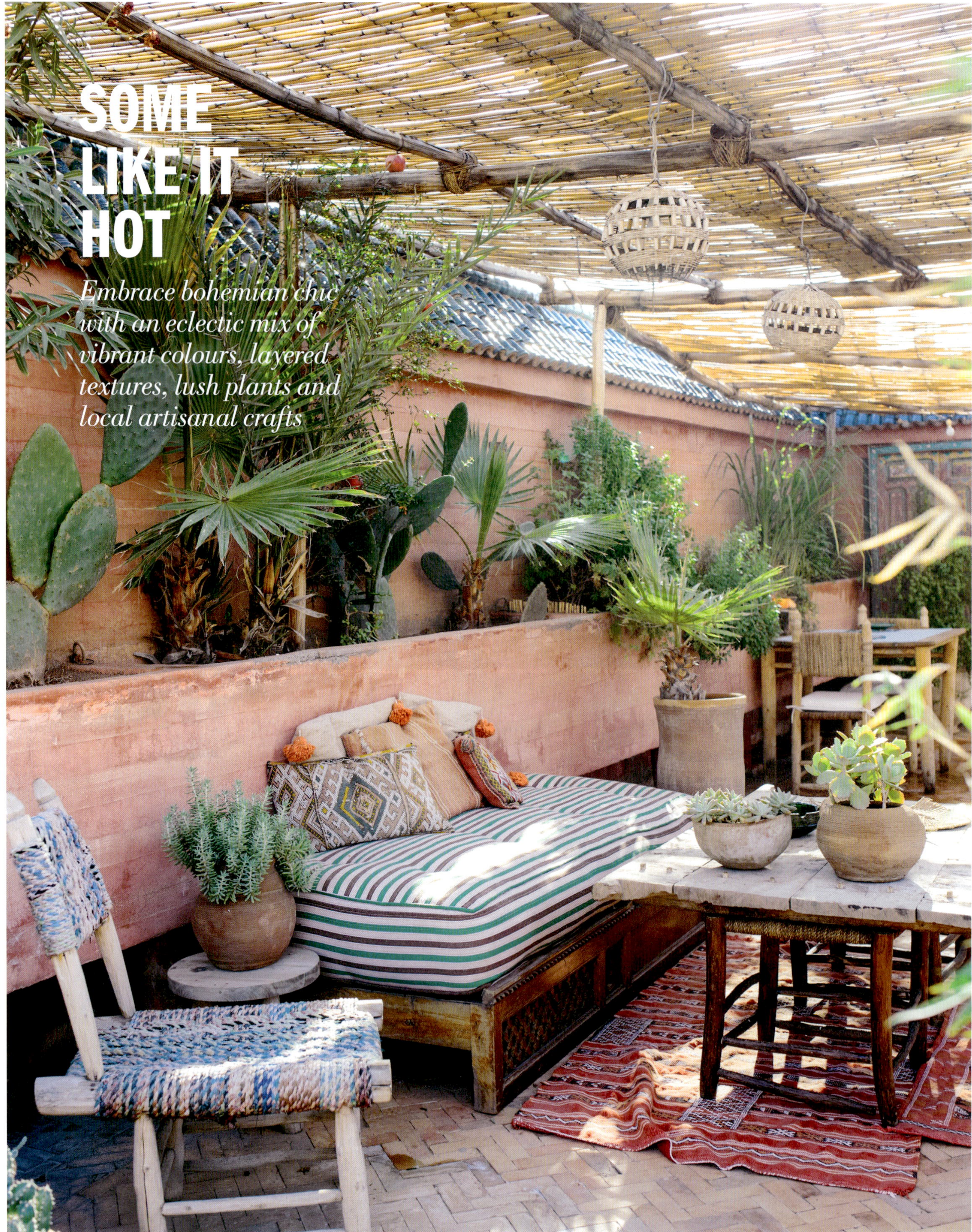

PHOTOGRAPH: CARLEY PAGE SUMMERS

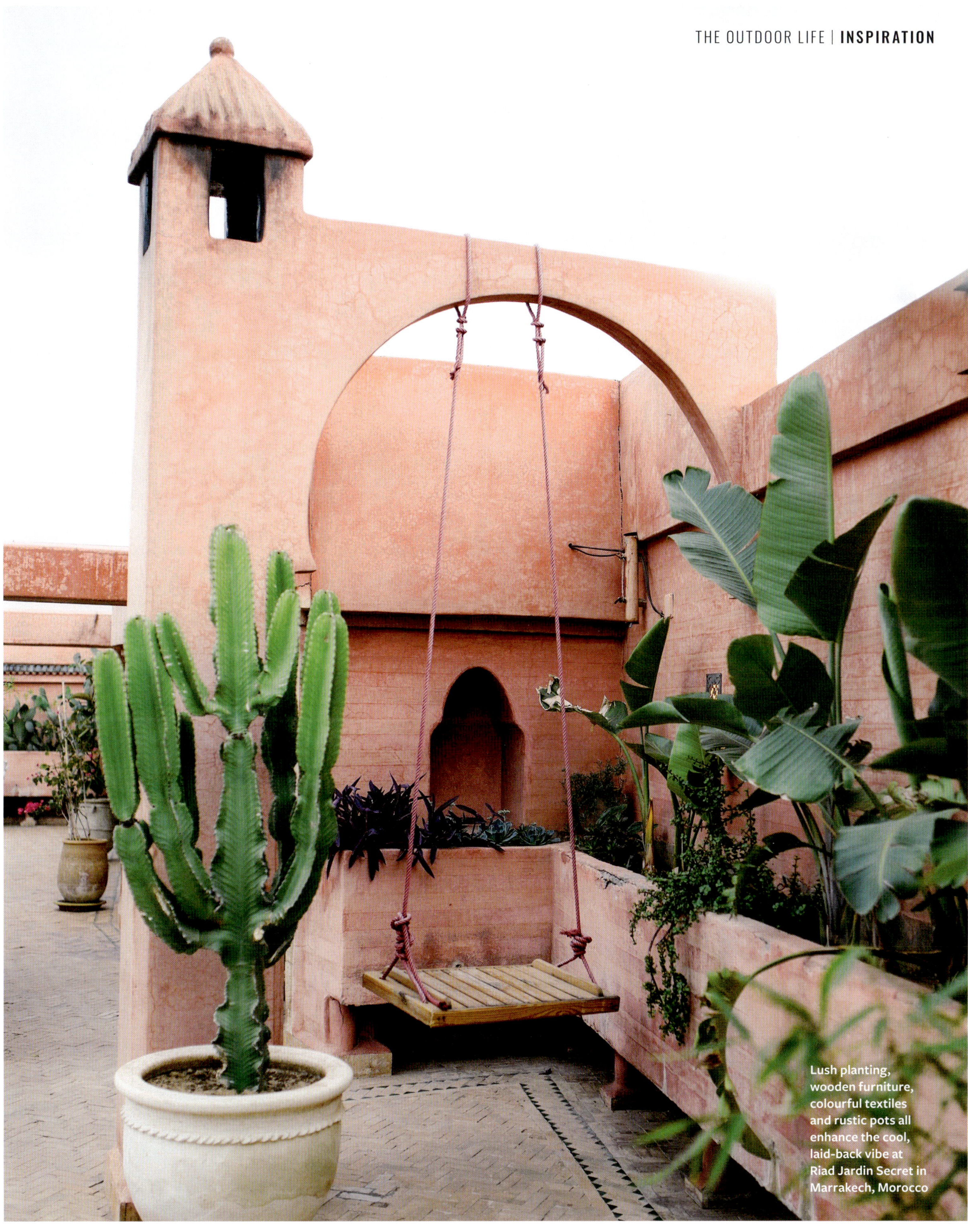

PHOTOGRAPH: CARLEY PAGE SUMMERS

Lush planting, wooden furniture, colourful textiles and rustic pots all enhance the cool, laid-back vibe at Riad Jardin Secret in Marrakech, Morocco

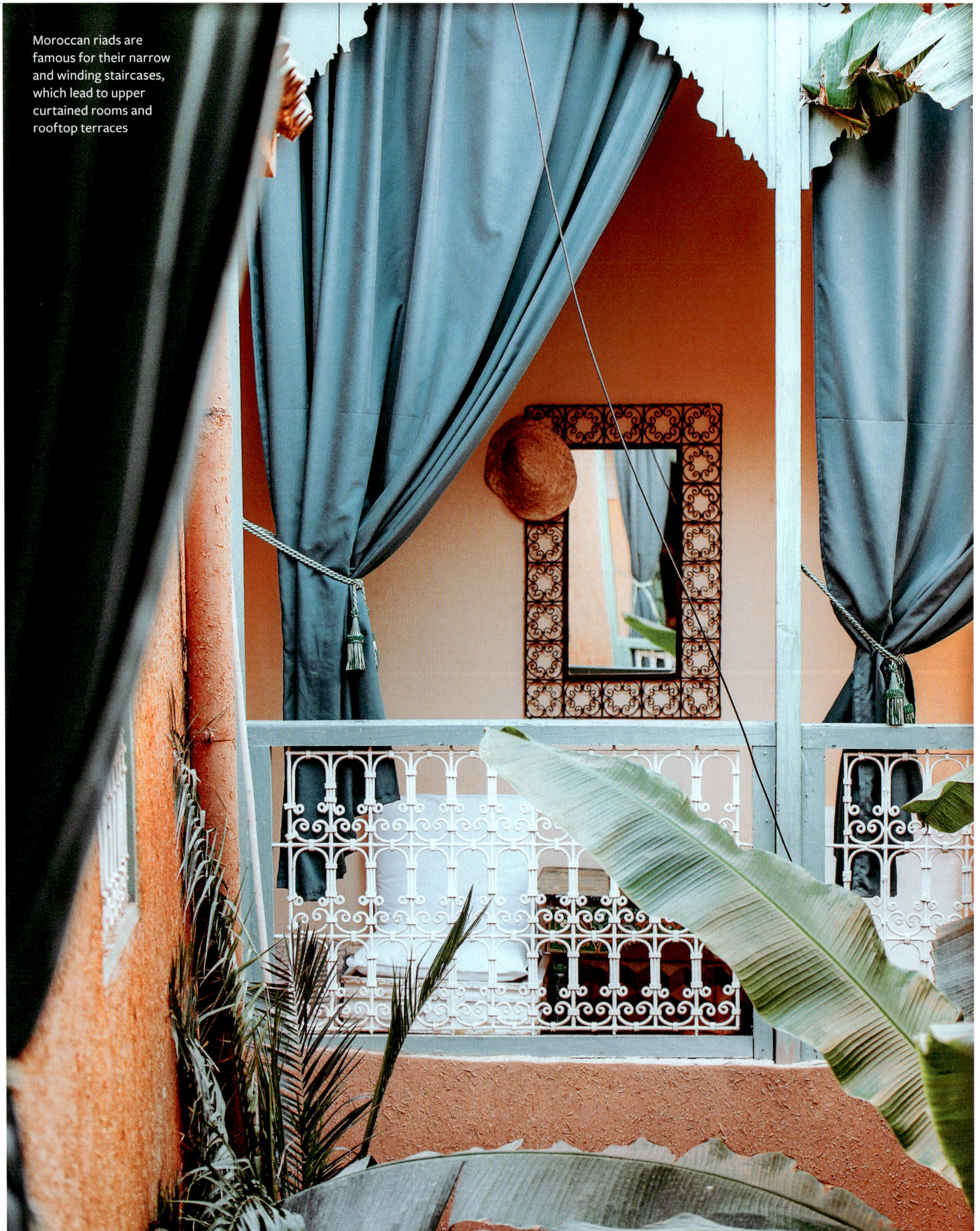

Moroccan riads are famous for their narrow and winding staircases, which lead to upper curtained rooms and rooftop terraces

PHOTOGRAPH: ANNIE SPRATT ON UNSPLASH

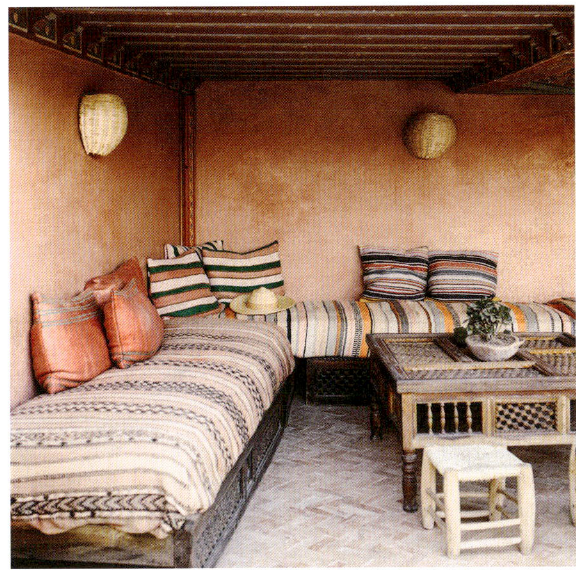

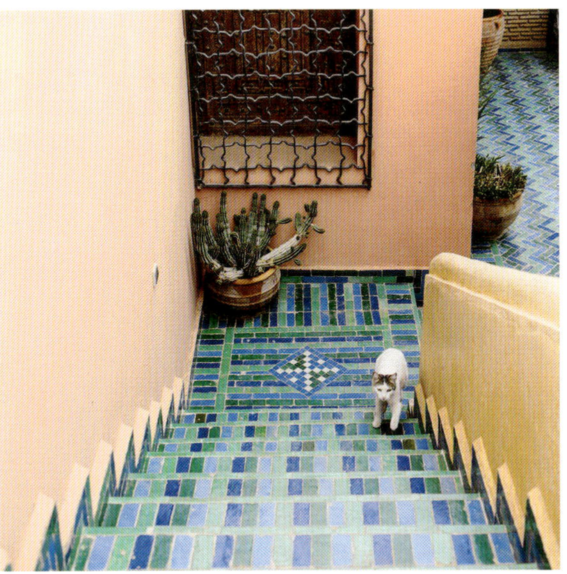

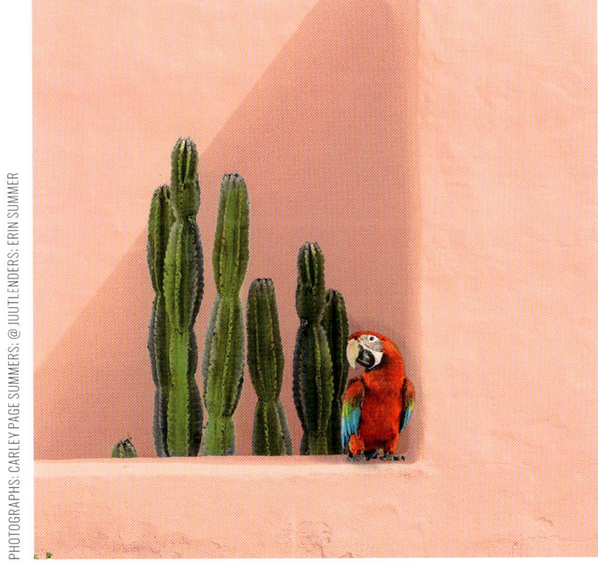

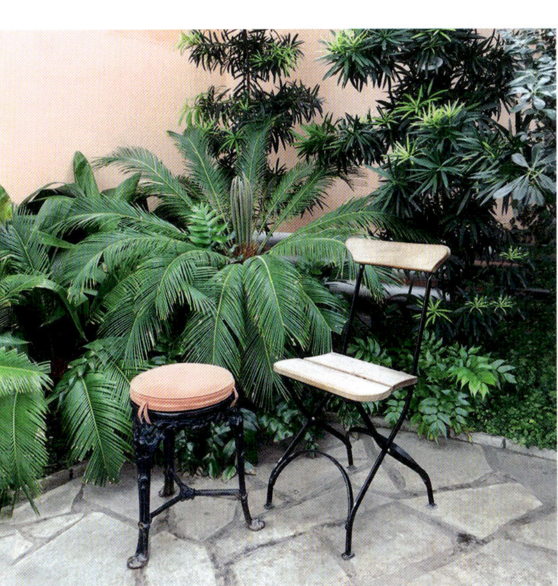

PHOTOGRAPHS: CARLEY PAGE SUMMERS; @JUUTLENDERS; ERIN SUMMER

Coral and turquoise **TOP LEFT** This cosy nook on the Riad Jardin Secret's roof terrace, is piled with pillows, wicker lampshades, Kilim throws and magpie finds from the market – it's the perfect spot to curl up and unwind. **TOP RIGHT** Blue and green glazed Moroccan zellige tiles have an uneven charm, and when sunlight hits them they sparkle and shimmer like water. **BOTTOM LEFT** This punchy shade of coral is the perfect backdrop to strong, architectural plants such as cacti. **BOTTOM RIGHT** Lush, abundant greenery helps to soften and bring life to this pastel pink corner, giving it a relaxed, jungle feel.

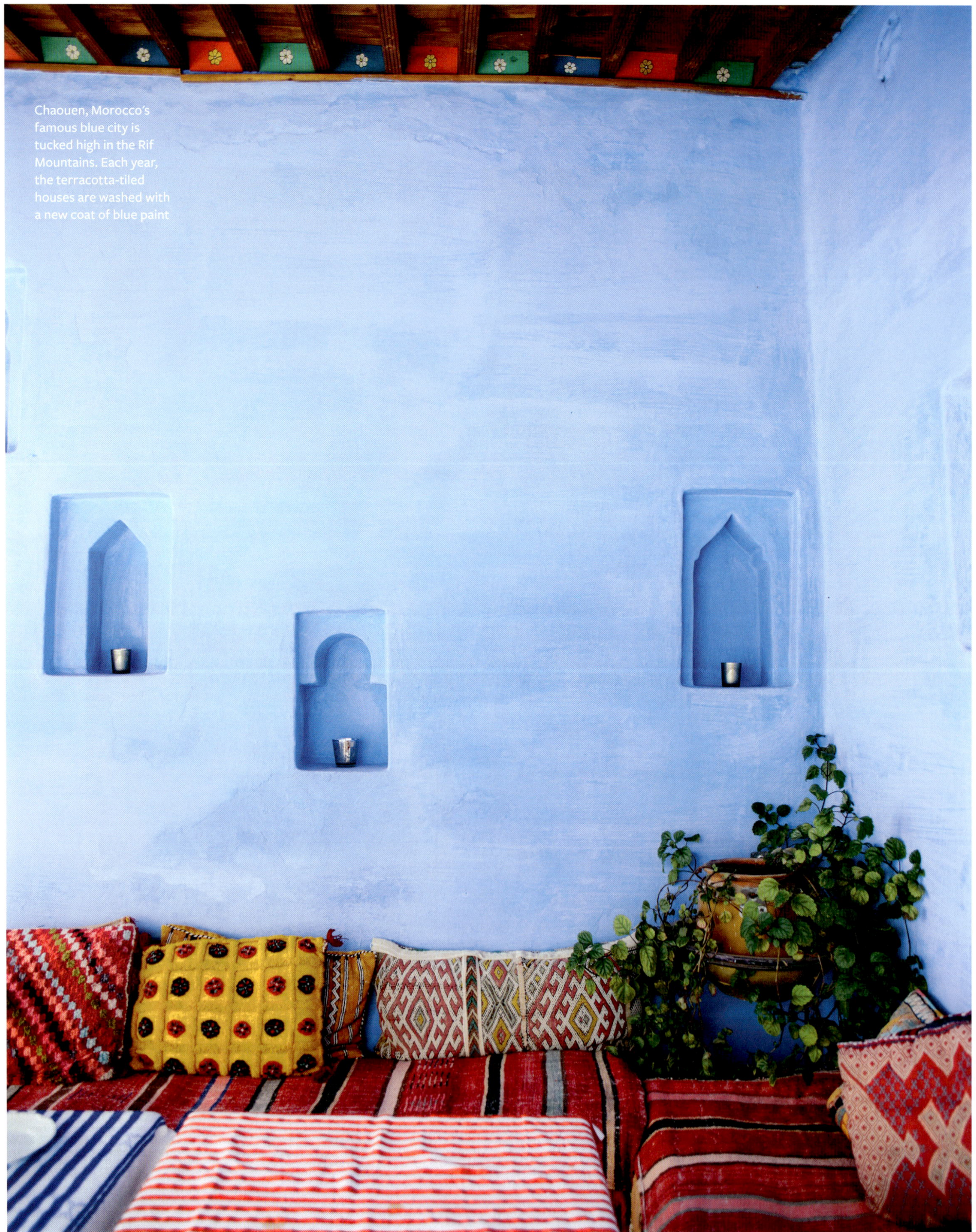

Chaouen, Morocco's famous blue city is tucked high in the Rif Mountains. Each year, the terracotta-tiled houses are washed with a new coat of blue paint

PHOTOGRAPH: CARLEY PAGE SUMMERS

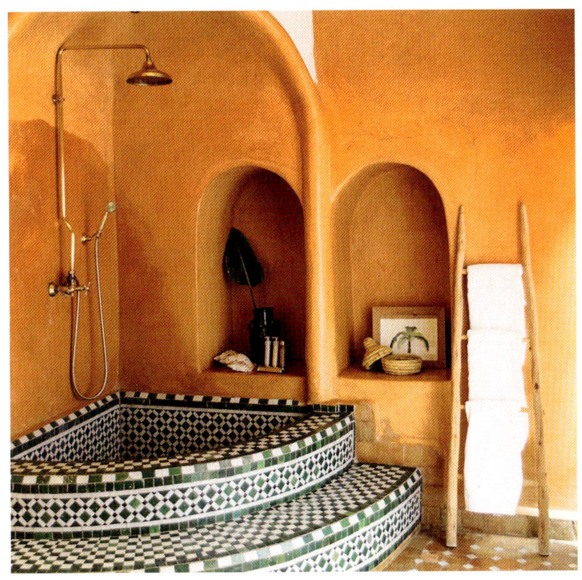

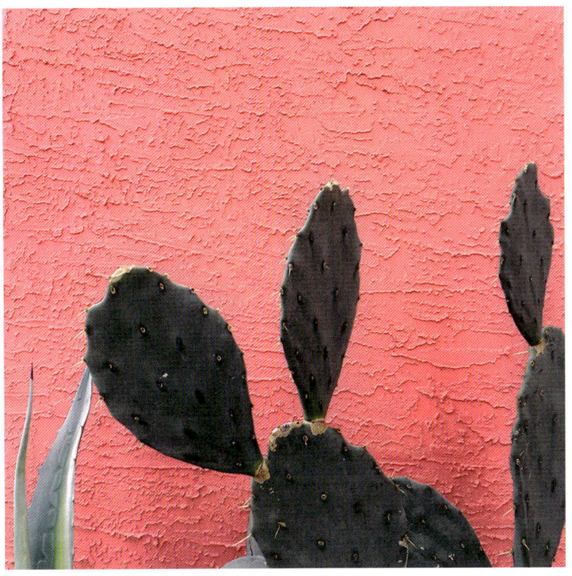

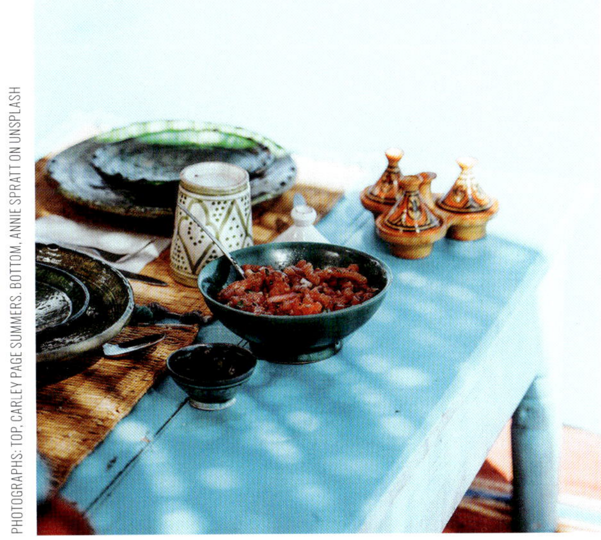

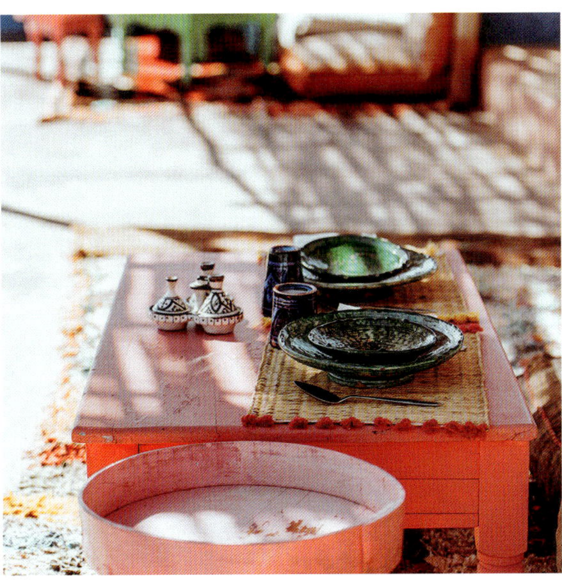

PHOTOGRAPHS: TOP, CARLEY PAGE SUMMERS. BOTTOM, ANNIE SPRATT ON UNSPLASH

Jewel colours **TOP LEFT** Most of the furniture and details for Riad Jardin Secret are picked from flea markets around Marrakech or from craftspeople the owners, Cyrielle and Julien, work with in the area. Patterned handmade tiles create a beautiful rhythmic pattern in this bathroom. **TOP RIGHT** The hot pink colour really emphasises the texture of this Moroccan rough plaster wall. **BOTTOM LEFT** A traditional Berber meal in the Atlas Mountains – chicken tagine with vegetables and cous cous. **BOTTOM RIGHT** A shady roof terrace is the perfect spot to relax and eat lunch, offering a respite from the heat and noise of the city.

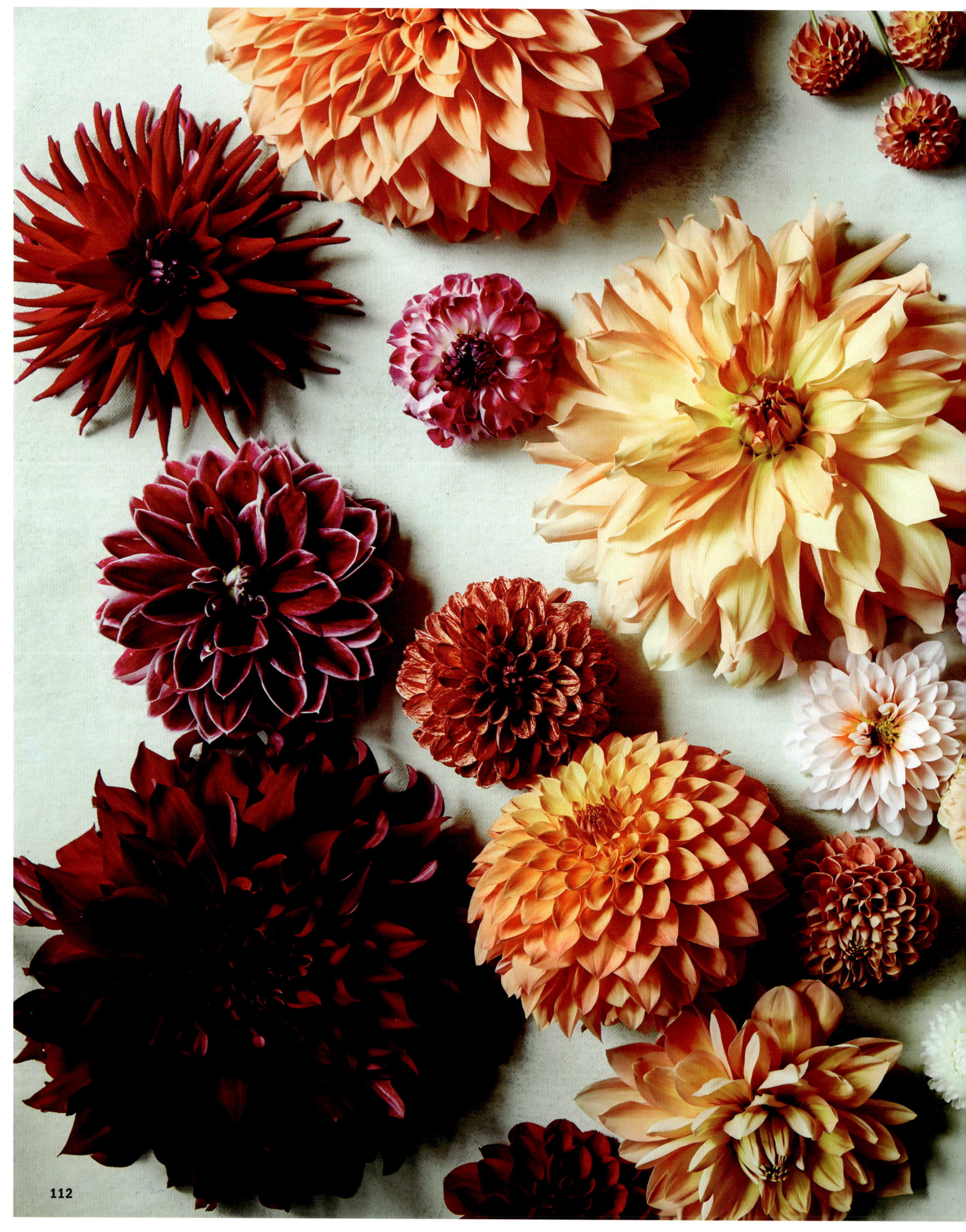

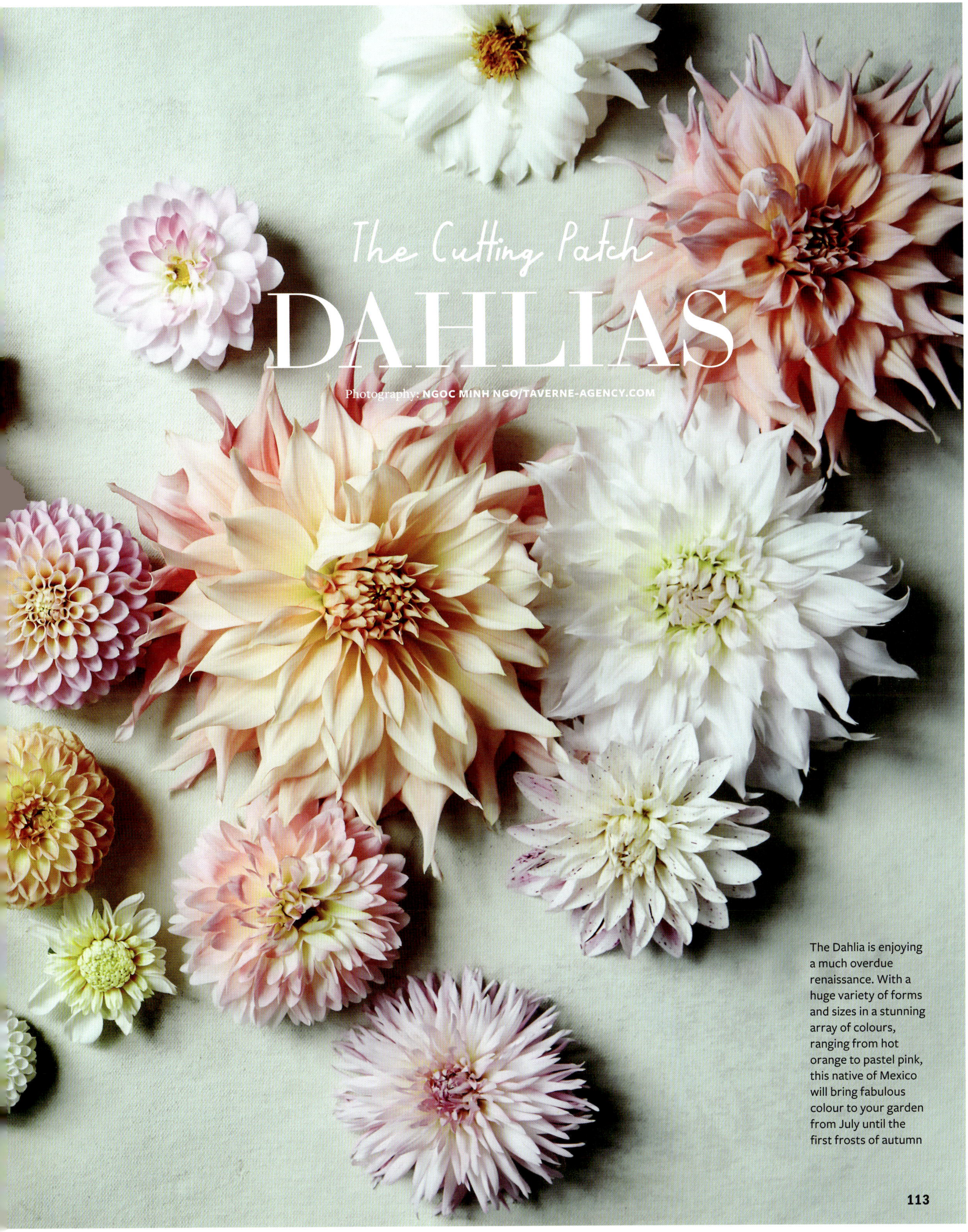

The Cutting Patch

DAHLIAS

Photography: NGOC MINH NGO/TAVERNE-AGENCY.COM

The Dahlia is enjoying a much overdue renaissance. With a huge variety of forms and sizes in a stunning array of colours, ranging from hot orange to pastel pink, this native of Mexico will bring fabulous colour to your garden from July until the first frosts of autumn

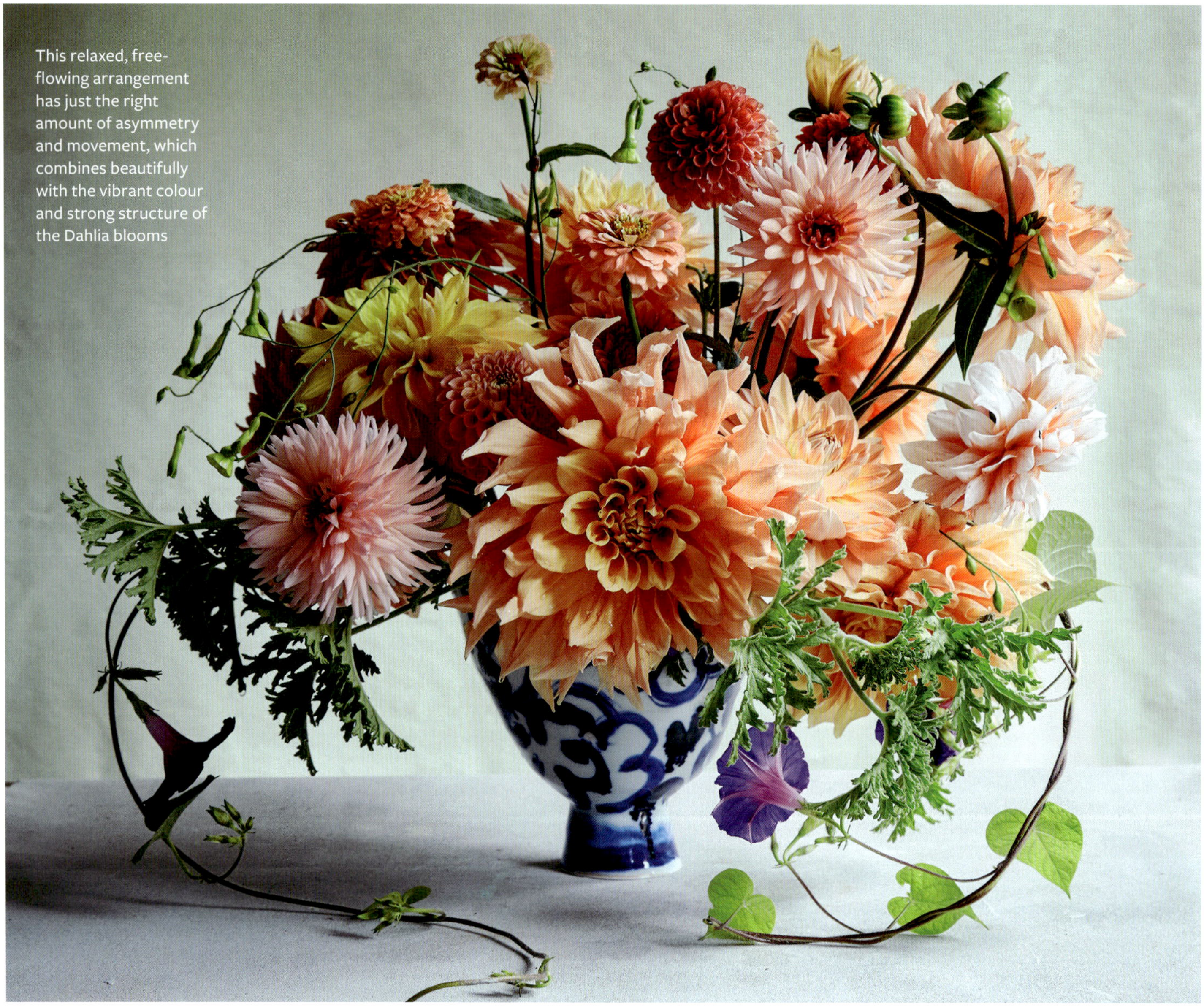

This relaxed, free-flowing arrangement has just the right amount of asymmetry and movement, which combines beautifully with the vibrant colour and strong structure of the Dahlia blooms

PHOTOGRAPHS: NGOC MINH NGO. TAVERNE-AGENCY.COM

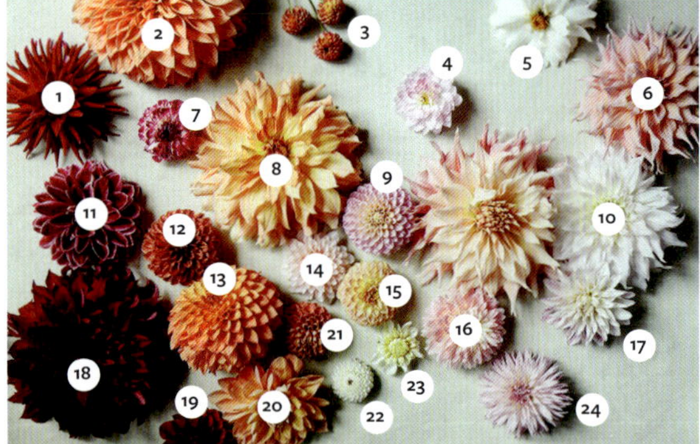

1. Juanita **2.** Clyde's Choice **3.** Ginger Willo **4.** Nepos **5.** Beaucon White **6.** Penhill Watermelon **7.** Kaiser Wilhelm **8.** Jane Cowl **9.** Skipley Spot of Gold **10.** Shiloh Noel **11.** Sellwood Glory **12.** Amorous **13.** Jester **14.** A la Mode **15.** Hamilton Lillian **16.** Rosemary Webb **17.** Pop Talk **18.** Spartacus **19.** Wisconsin Red **20.** Nicholas **21.** Jomanda **22.** Hollyhill Ms White **23.** Platinum Blonde **24.** Miss Rose Fletcher

After years in the shade the dahlia is back – now it's a colourful essential for every cutting patch

With over 50,000 varieties to choose from, dahlias are one of the most beautiful and long-lasting cut flowers.

Surprisingly easy to grow they'll thrive in a sunny spot in well-drained, fertile soil. You can grow dahlias from seed but most people choose to begin with tubers. Once you're sure the danger of frost is over, plant each tuber horizontally in a hole 15cm deep. Add a good sprinkling of fish, blood and bone fertiliser. Use a stake not a bamboo cane for support and tie in with soft twine every couple of weeks. Water regularly and give a fortnightly liquid feed. Once the plant has reached 40cm, pinch out the tips of the main shoot. This encourages strong, bushy plants. Remove any dead flower heads regularly and only pick when the dahlia is in full flower.

The best time to cut is early morning. Make a horizontal cut at the base of the stem and place in 7cm of very hot (not boiling) water for at least an hour. This will condition the stems and extend the life of your blooms. AS

Annie Sloan®

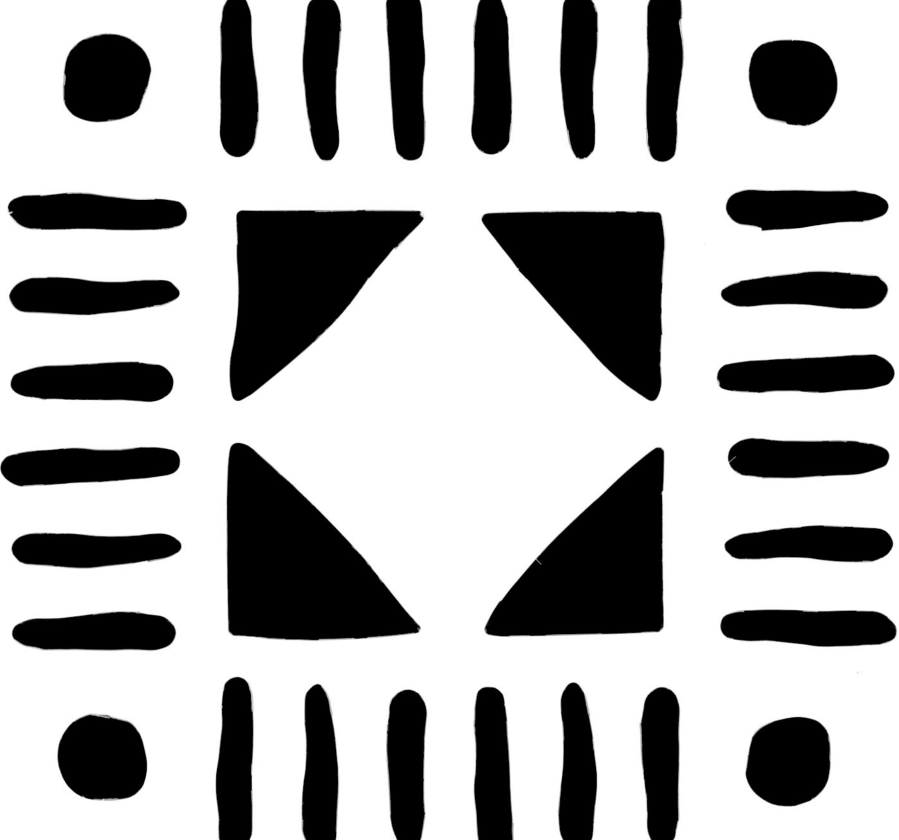

TILE STENCIL

Annie Sloan®

THE HOW-TOS

Easy-to-follow projects using paint techniques and effects to transform everyday items into something truly special

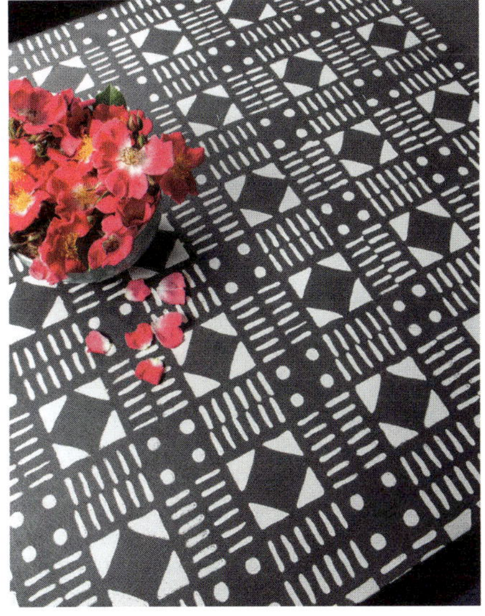

1. TILE STENCIL

Felix Sloan shows how to use your free stencil to create a stunning repeat pattern

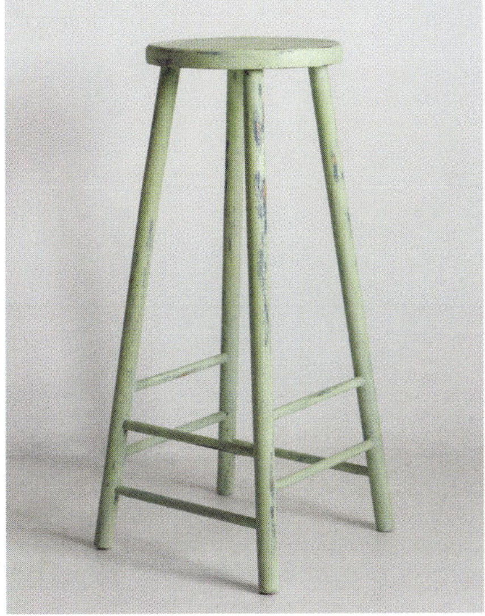

2. TWO-COLOUR DISTRESS

Annie Sloan uses Chalk Paint® in Lem Lem and Aubusson Blue to achieve an aged look

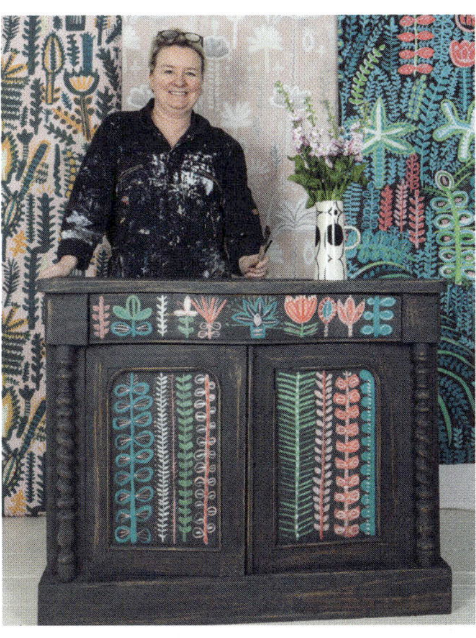

3. BOTANICAL DETAILS

Lucy Tiffney creates her signature free-style designs using the new Detail Brushes

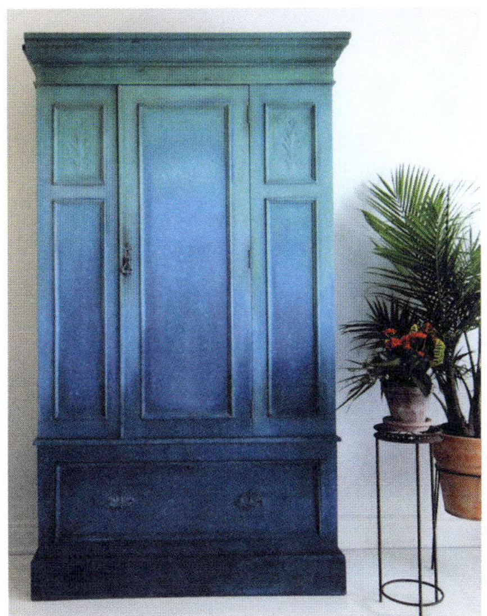

4. OMBRÉ PAINT EFFECT

Ildiko Horvath shares her secrets on how to achieve a perfect ombré blend

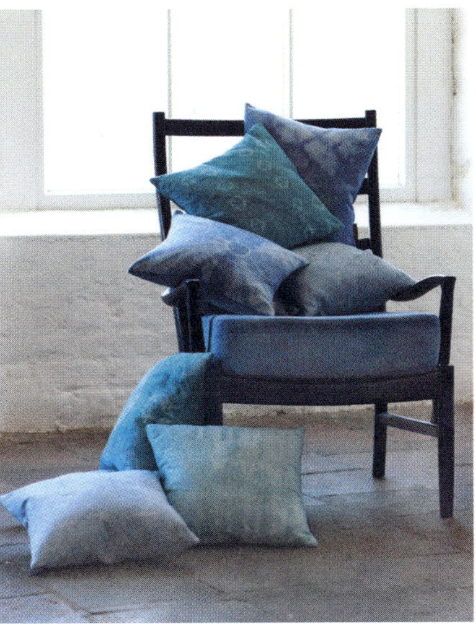

5. SHIBORI CUSHIONS

Former Painters in Residence Abigail and Ryan Bell's clever resist-dye technique

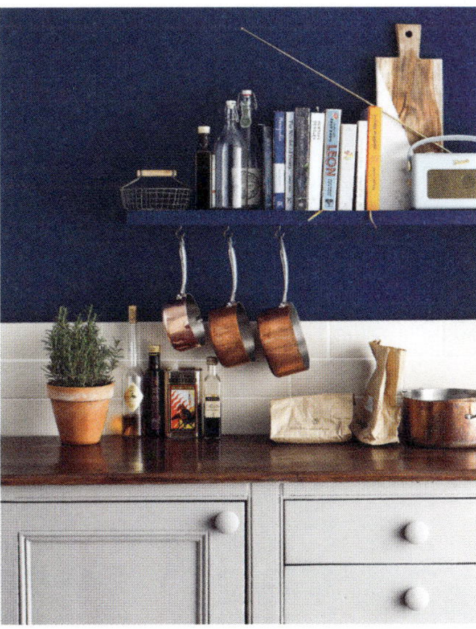

6. KITCHEN CABINETS

Annie shows us how easy it is to revamp your kitchen cupboards using Chalk Paint®

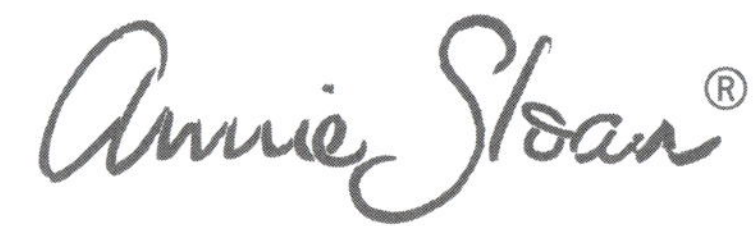

THE CHALK PAINT® STORY

"There's no need for tiresome priming and sanding – you can get straight to the fun bit!" Annie

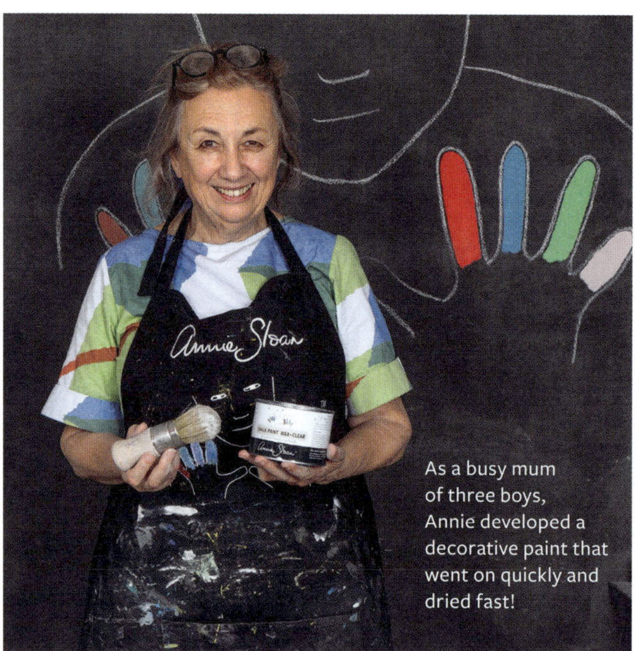

As a busy mum of three boys, Annie developed a decorative paint that went on quickly and dried fast!

Annie first developed her now famous Chalk Paint®, in 1990. When she started working on it, she wanted to create a decorative paint that was immediate and allowed her to be direct and spontaneous. She wanted a fast turn around – paint in the morning, then wax and put it back in position by the afternoon. What's more, she wanted to develop a paint that could go on more or less anything – old and new wood, metal, plastic, cement, bricks – all with no priming, no sanding, no preparation needed.

She also wanted the colours to be mixable without becoming dead or muddy – indeed, the way she makes colours is not the same as any other paint company. She called her paint Chalk Paint® because of its beautiful velvety, matt finish.

Chalk Paint® very rarely requires any preparation, such as sanding or priming, and can be used indoors or outside, on just about any surface. It can revitalise old furniture, walls, ceilings and floors with ease. It's so easy to use and makes amazing results accessible to everyone – you can get straight to the fun bit!

With a colour palette inspired by 18th and 20th century decor and design, you can easily mix the colours together to extend the range. Add a little water to it to make it smooth, thicken it up by leaving the lid off, make it into a wash by adding even more water. Use Annie Sloan Flat Brushes for a smooth look or her Chalk Paint® Brushes for a more textured aged look. Apply Chalk Paint® Wax to protect your finish and add durability. AS

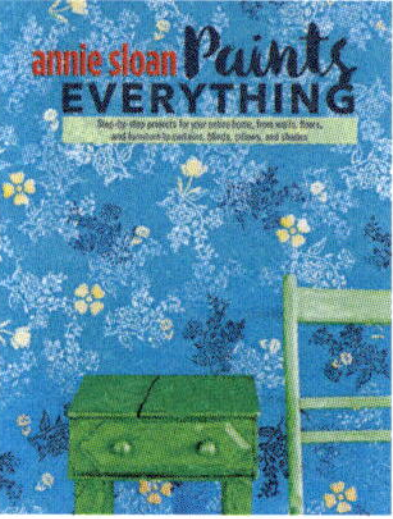

Annie's latest book is Annie Sloan Paints Everything, published by Cico Books

ANNIE'S PERSONAL STORY

Annie trained as a fine artist and turned to decorative work after university in the mid 1970s, including painting murals in houses as commissions. By 1987, Annie had written the phenomenally successful book The Complete Book of Decorative Paint Techniques, which is considered to be the industry bible on the subject. Unable to find the paints that she wished to work with, Annie used her knowledge of colour, paint, pigments and art history to develop Chalk Paint® in 1990.

In 2000, Annie set up a shop in Oxford to showcase Chalk Paint®, run courses, and offer interior design.

Born in Australia to a Scottish father and a Fijian mother, Annie moved to a farm in Kent, England with her family when she was ten years old. With spells in Southern Africa and connections to France, Cuba and the USA, she feels she has world roots.

Annie lives and works in Oxford with her husband David, who runs the business with her. They have three sons and three grandchildren.

Their son Felix is also a talented painter and is Creative Director of Annie Sloan. He can be seen on Facebook, YouTube and Instagram Stories demonstrating with Annie.

Our Stockists Annie Sloan is committed to supporting independent businesses. Our products are available through our carefully selected network of Stockists, each of whom represent bricks and mortar shops.

It's not just our products that make us special, it's the people who sell them. All Annie Sloan Stockists are hand-picked for their individual style and we're very proud that no two shops are the same. Each Stockist is carefully chosen for their approach to home decoration and their own unique design style. We strongly believe in the principle of 'shop local' and celebrate the differences between each of our Stockists and how their businesses contribute to their local communities.

All Annie Sloan Stockists have real shops – we believe it creates a more personalised experience. They are all trained as colour experts and have each created beautiful environments where you can get your hands on our paints and try mixing colours for yourself.

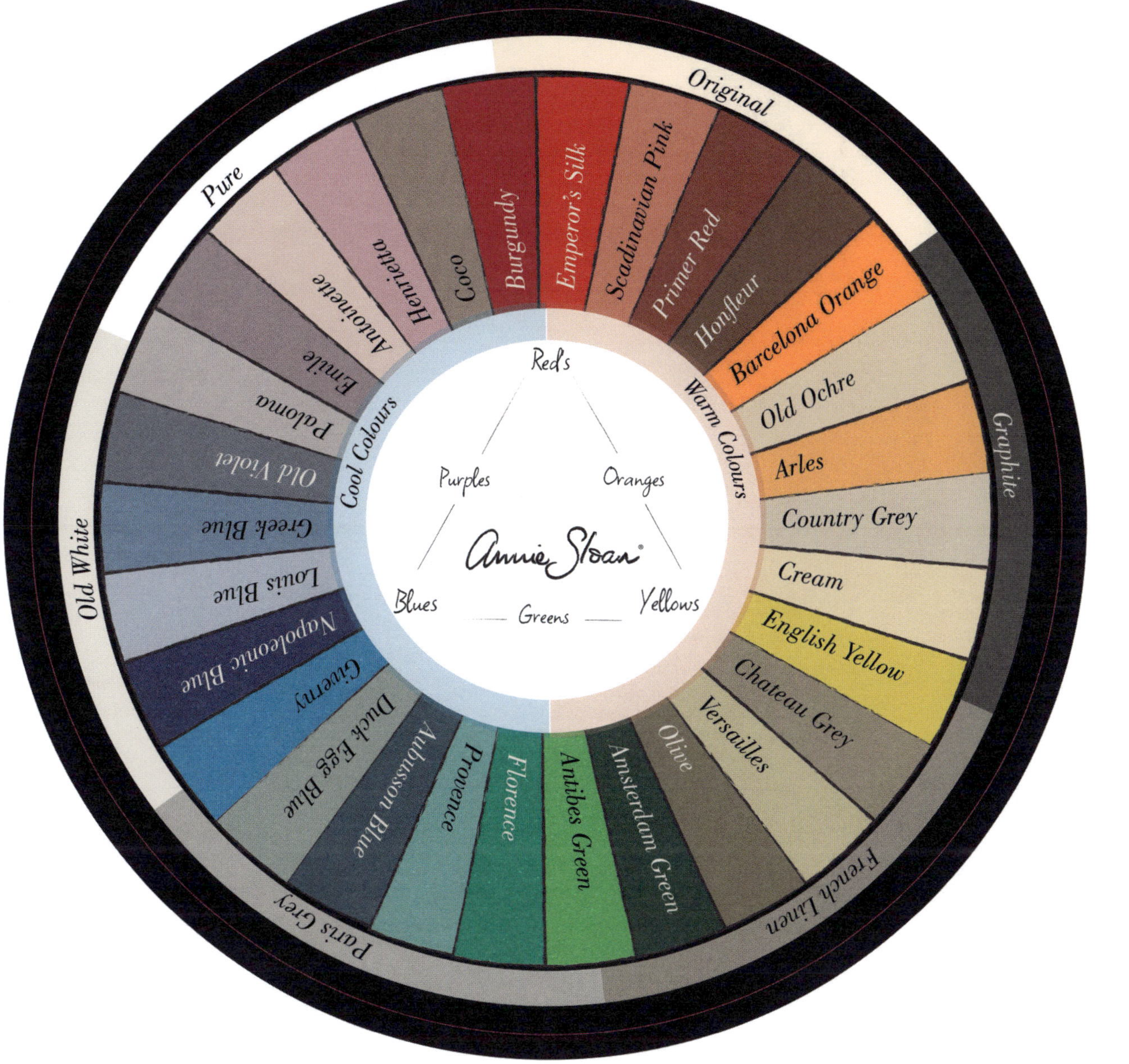

Original
Pure
Graphite
Old White
French Linen
Paris Grey

Burgundy
Emperor's Silk
Scadinavian Pink
Primer Red
Honfleur
Barcelona Orange
Old Ochre
Arles
Country Grey
Cream
English Yellow
Chateau Grey
Versailles
Olive
Amsterdam Green
Antibes Green
Florence
Provence
Aubusson Blue
Duck Egg Blue
Giverny
Napoleonic Blue
Louis Blue
Greek Blue
Old Violet
Paloma
Emile
Antoinette
Henrietta
Coco

Warm Colours
Cool Colours

Reds
Oranges
Yellows
Greens
Blues
Purples

Annie Sloan®

Chalk Paint® Colour Wheel

Artists and designers use a colour wheel to select their palette and decide on accent colours that complement or contrast with a feature colour. The Annie Sloan Colour Wheel will help you select the correct Chalk Paint® colours for the effect you have in mind.

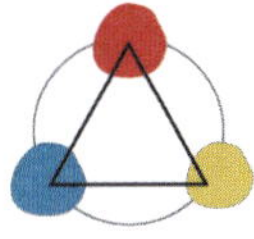

Primary colours

These three colours; Red, Yellow and Blue can't be mixed from other colours. These colours form the basis for all mixed colours.

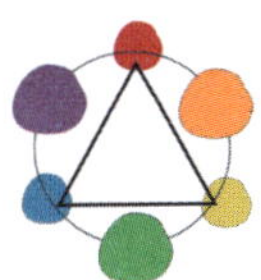

Secondary colours

These three colours; Purple, Orange and Green, are created from a mix of two primary colours. These colours tend to be clean and bright. Add more colours to create a more complex colour.

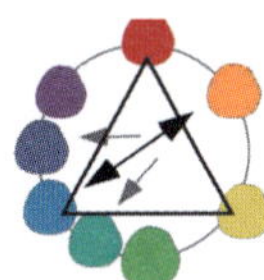

Complementary colours

The colours directly opposite each other in the colour wheel, are known as complementary colours. Together they can create strong contrast colours.

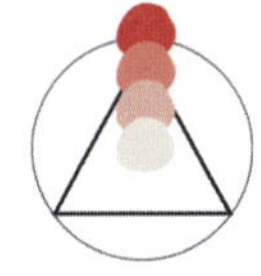

Pastels or Tints

A pastel is made by mixing colour with white. Annie uses Old White or Pure for a more contemporary feel.

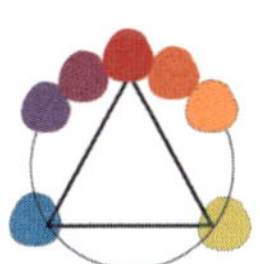

Neighbour Colours

Choosing the colours either side of a chosen colour can create another variation of a monochromatic colour range. These colours may clash so aim for either warm or cool hues.

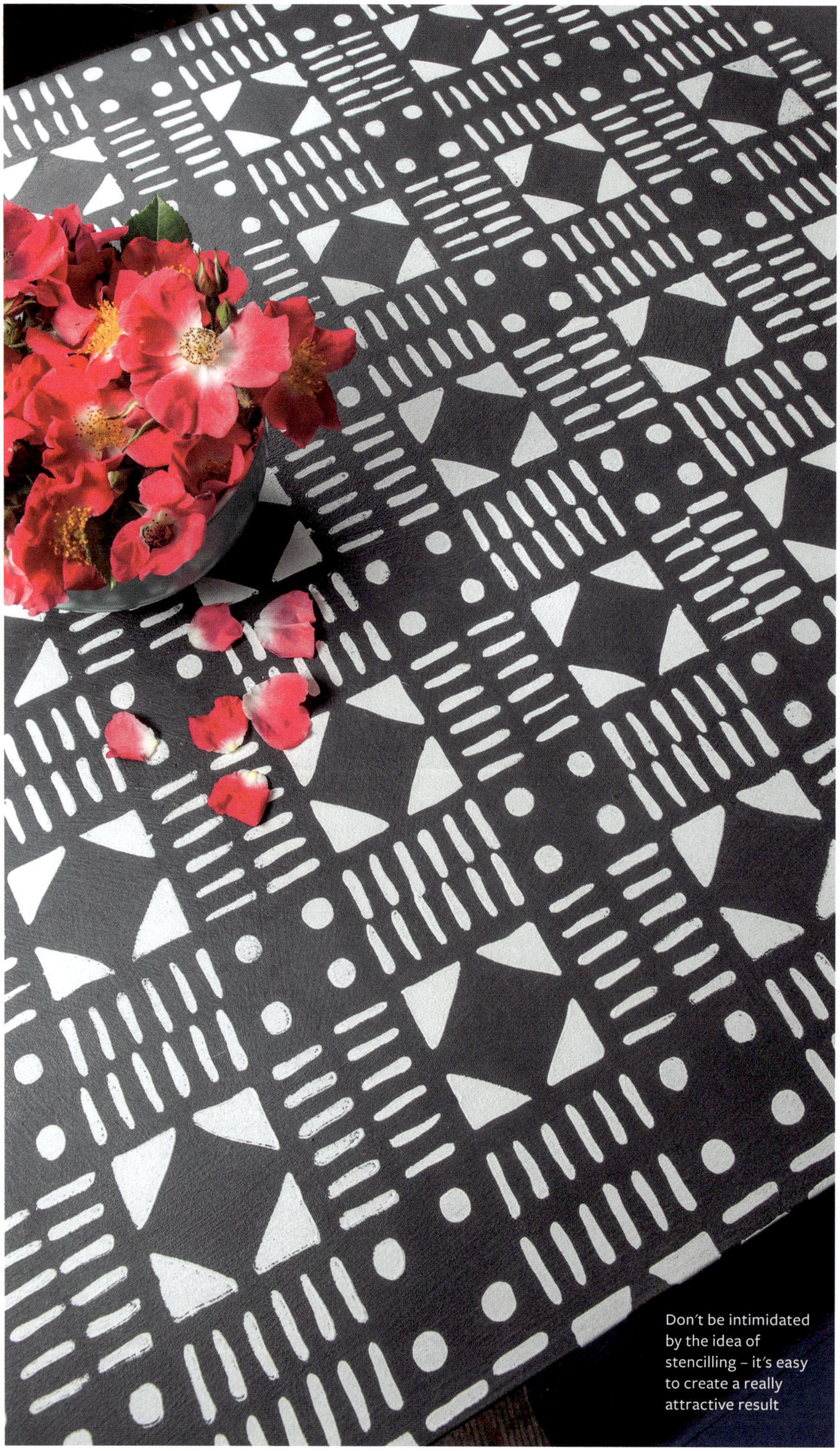

Don't be intimidated by the idea of stencilling – it's easy to create a really attractive result

PHOTOGRAPH: FIONA MURRAY

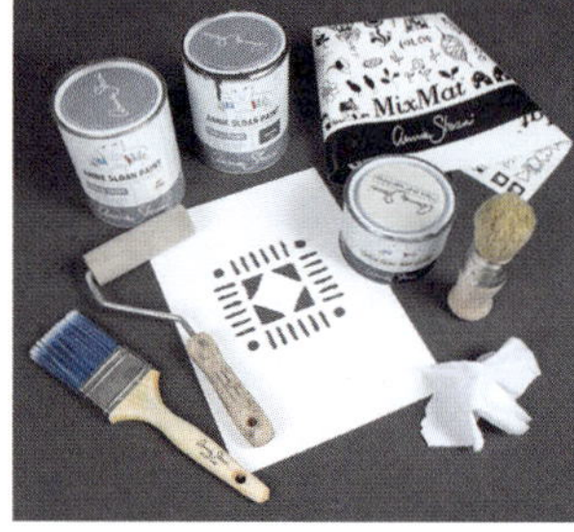

YOU WILL NEED

- Your free tile stencil
- 1 x Annie Sloan MixMat™
- 1 x 120ml Chalk Paint® in Pure
- 1 x 120ml Chalk Paint® in Graphite
- 1 x Annie Sloan Large Flat Brush
- 1 x Annie Sloan Large Sponge Roller (10cm roller head)
- 1 x 120ml Clear Chalk Paint® Wax
- 1 x Small Chalk Paint® Wax Brush
- 1 x lint-free cloth
- 1 x tape measure or piece of string
- 1 x water-based varnish (optional)

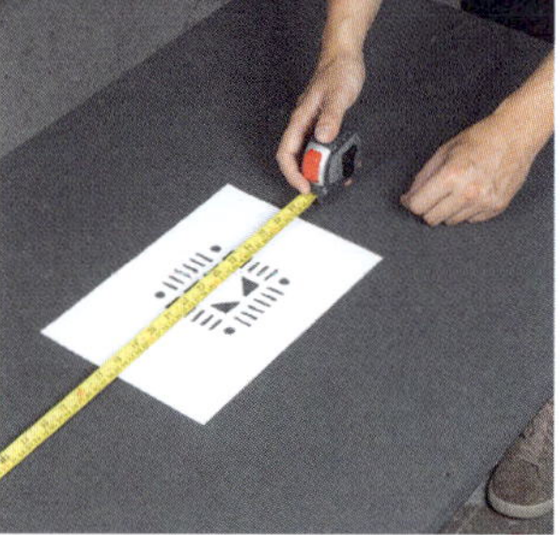

FELIX'S TOP TIPS

Before you start, I recommend that you give your free tile stencil a quick coat of water-based varnish. It will make it more rigid, giving it extra resilience and will last much longer.

When creating a repeat pattern with a stencil, always find the centre first using a tape measure or string. Paint your first stencil in the middle of the tabletop, to ensure your finished pattern is centred nicely.

Felix Sloan

STENCILLED TILE TABLETOP

Felix guides us through the process of bringing new life to an unloved tabletop using your free tile stencil and Chalk Paint® in Graphite and Pure

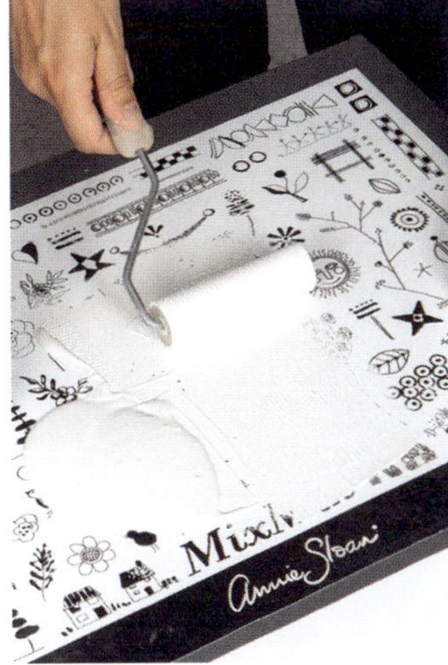

1 Paint the surface of your table in Chalk Paint® in Graphite. Ensure it's completely dry before stencilling. Pour a small amount of Chalk Paint® in Pure onto your MixMat™. Roll the Large Sponge Roller back and forth.

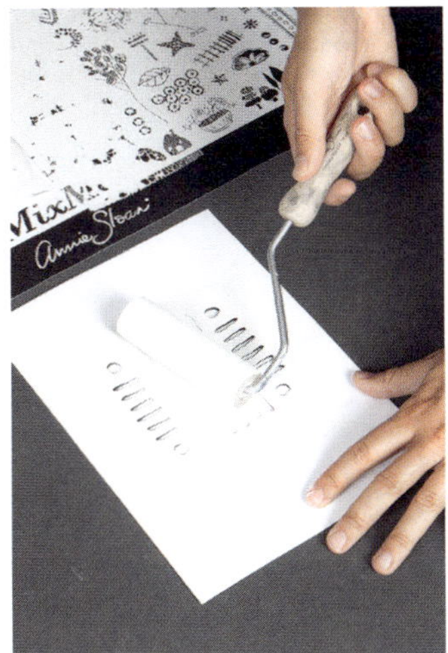

2 Make sure the paint is fully taken up by the sponge and it's coated evenly before rolling over the stencil. First roll horizontally and then vertically to ensure that there's even paint coverage through the stencil.

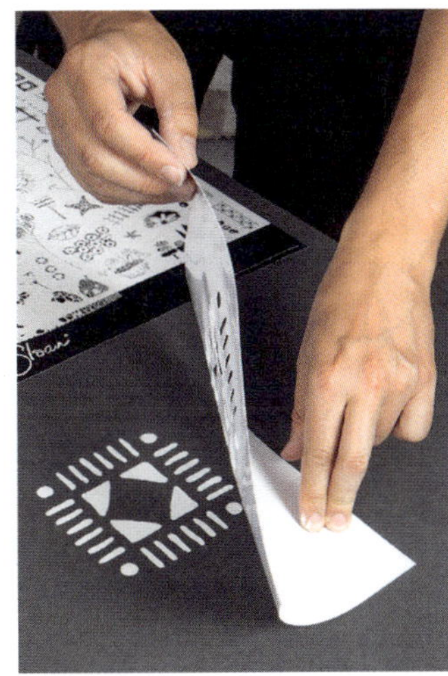

3 When you have an even coverage of paint, carefully lift the stencil up by one corner, holding the opposite edge down with two fingers as Felix demonstrates here.

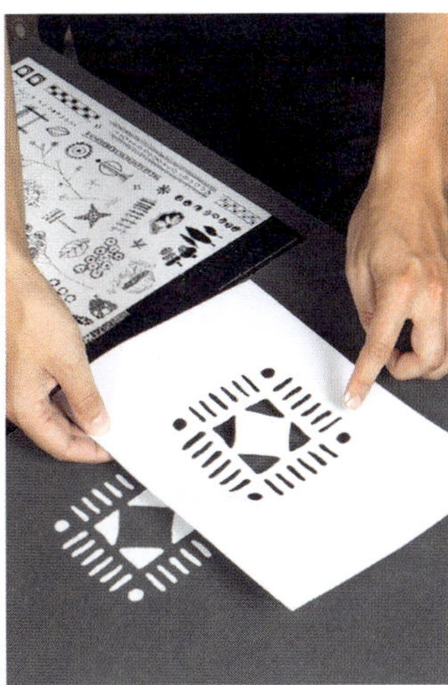

4 You can use the stencil itself to space out your design. Carefully move over in line with the previous stencilled tile motif.

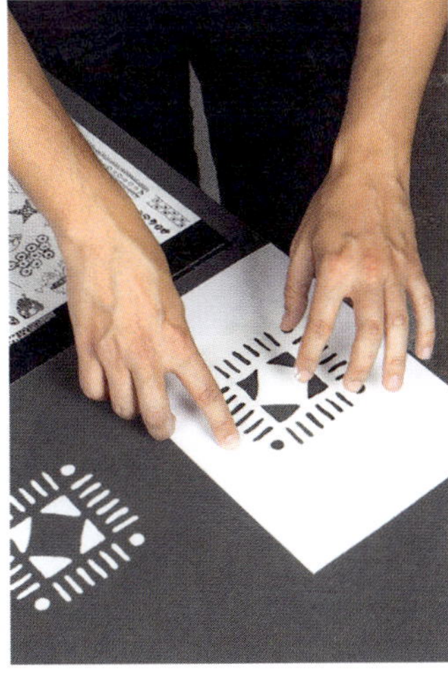

5 Carefully place your stencil down on the surface one motif apart from the previous stencilled tile. Leaving a one tile gap between painting prevents the first tile motif from being smudged when you come to stencil the second.

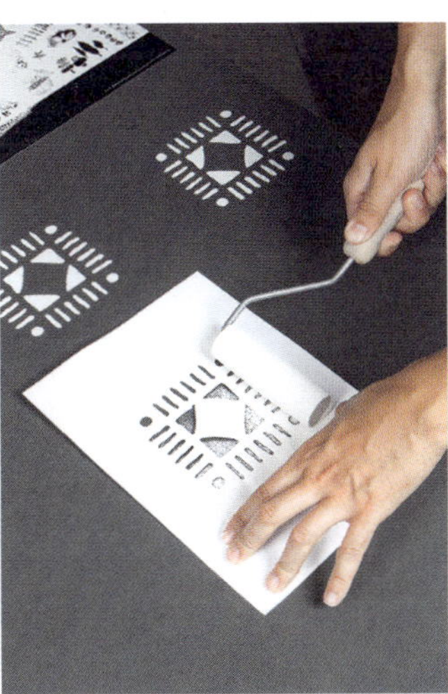

6 Continue stencilling your tile motifs one tile apart until you have covered the area you wish to stencil. Leave to dry for a few hours or speed up the process with a hairdryer.

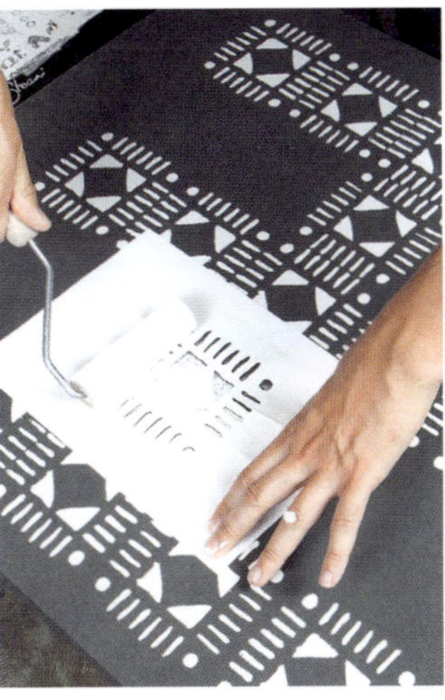

7 Once your first set of tile motifs are dry, fill in the gaps until the entire surface of the table is covered. This is a deliberately rustic tile design so don't worry about lining it up too precisely, it all adds to the charm of the finished piece!

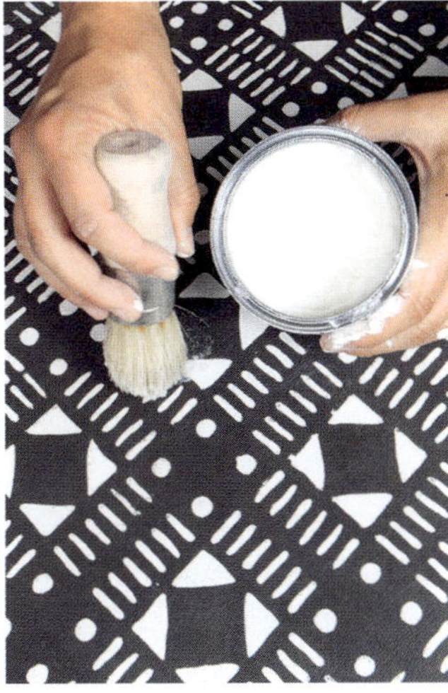

8 When your stencilled tile motifs are completely dry, finish and protect the entire table by applying Clear Chalk Paint® Wax with a Small Chalk Paint® Wax Brush. Remove any excess wax with a lint-free cloth.
Start inviting friends round...

PHOTOGRAPHS: FIONA MURRAY

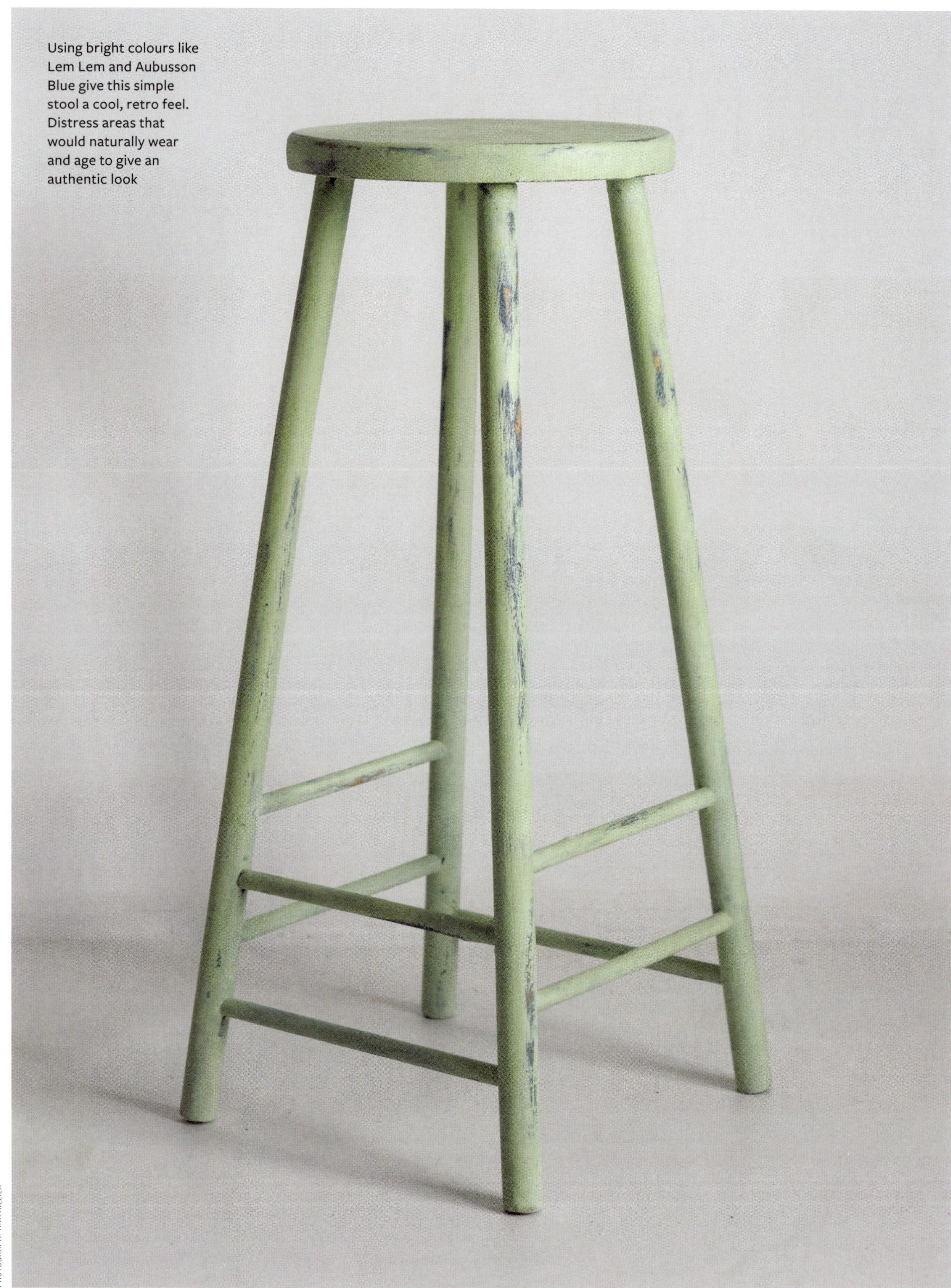

Using bright colours like Lem Lem and Aubusson Blue give this simple stool a cool, retro feel. Distress areas that would naturally wear and age to give an authentic look

PHOTOGRAPH: TINA HILLIER

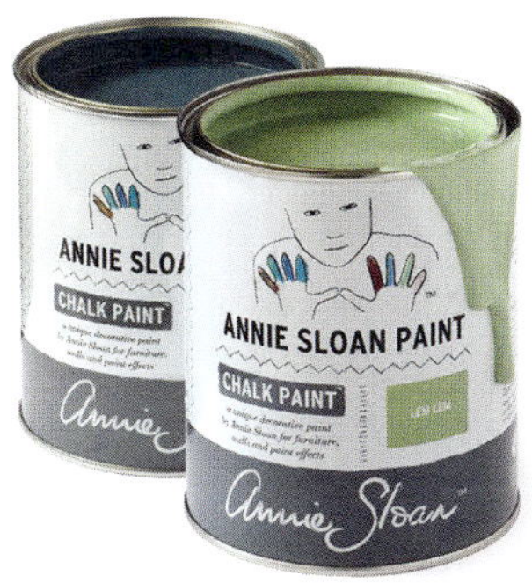

Annie Sloan

LEM LEM STOOL

Learn Annie's signature technique, the two-colour distress, to give a plain stool a fresh, modern feel using Lem Lem

YOU WILL NEED

- 1 x 120ml Chalk Paint® in Lem Lem
- 1 x 120ml Chalk Paint® in Aubusson Blue
- 1 x 120ml Clear Chalk Paint® Wax
- 1 x Medium Chalk Paint® Brush
- 1 x Small Chalk Paint® Wax Brush
- 1 x Annie Sloan Sanding Pads
- 1 x lint-free cloth

Snap a photo and share it using the #AnnieSloan #ChalkPaint hashtags to show your fellow Chalk Paint® fans, and for the chance to be featured on Annie Sloan social media!

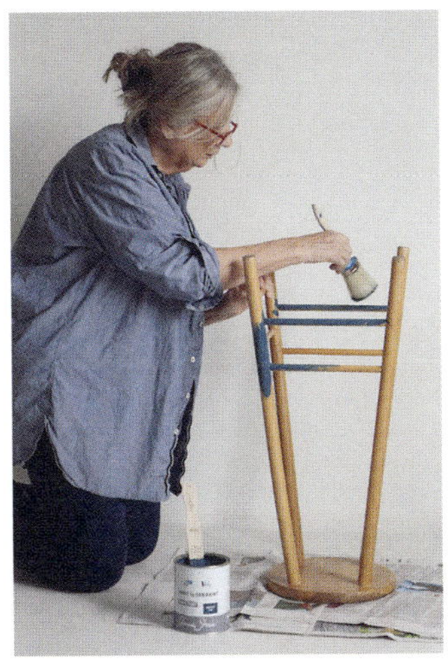

1 First apply a base colour of Chalk Paint® in Aubusson Blue to your stool, using a Medium Chalk Paint® Brush to create texture.

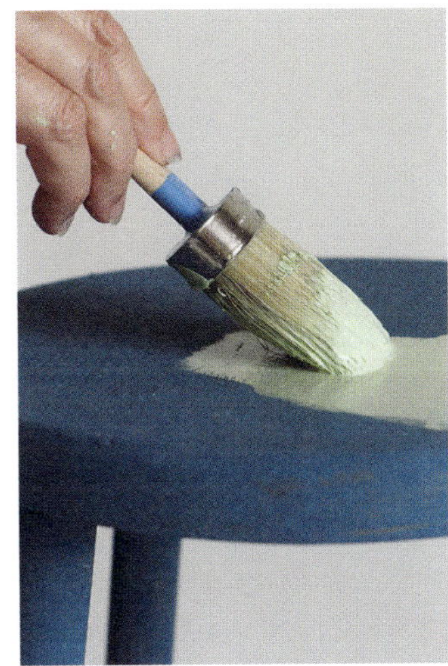

2 Once your Aubusson Blue base coat has dried, use a clean Chalk Paint® Brush to apply Lem Lem. Avoid painting this too thickly as the thicker it is, the harder it will be to sand back.

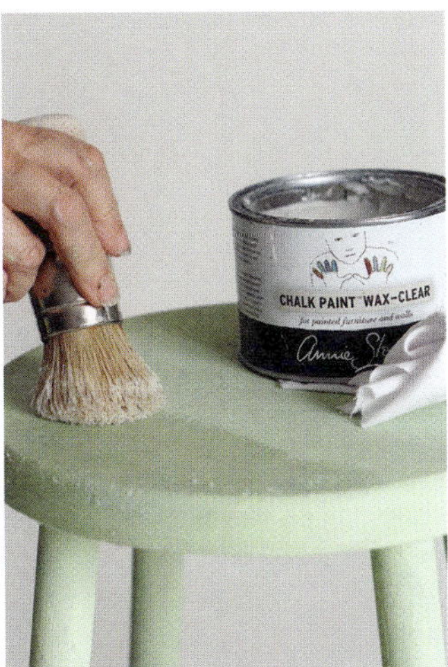

3 Let the top coat of paint dry fully, then apply Clear Chalk Paint® Wax to your stool. Use a Small Chalk Paint® Wax Brush to apply, then remove excess wax with a lint-free cloth.

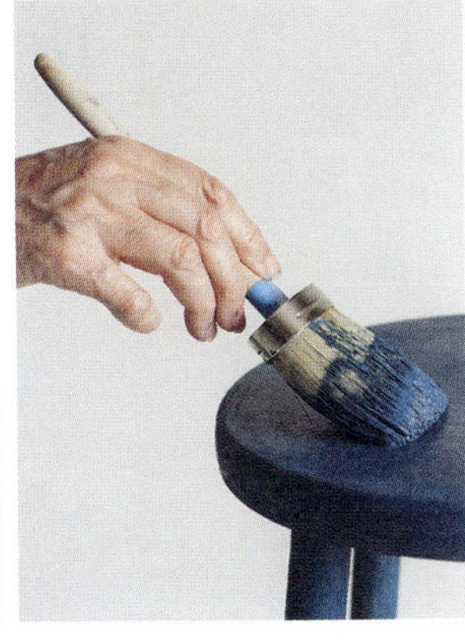

PHOTOGRAPHS: TINA HILLIER

ANNIE'S TOP TIP

Use a Medium Chalk Paint® Brush to create texture with your base layer, and don't worry about spreading the paint evenly. If you have some patches where the paint is applied more thickly and/or more thinly, this will create more variety when you're sanding back later in the process.

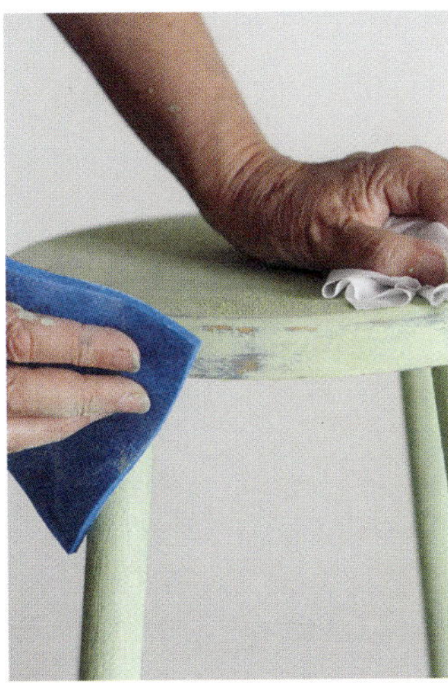

4 Wait until the wax is touch-dry but not hardened before you start sanding. Over time wax will cure and become harder and harder – so don't leave it too long!

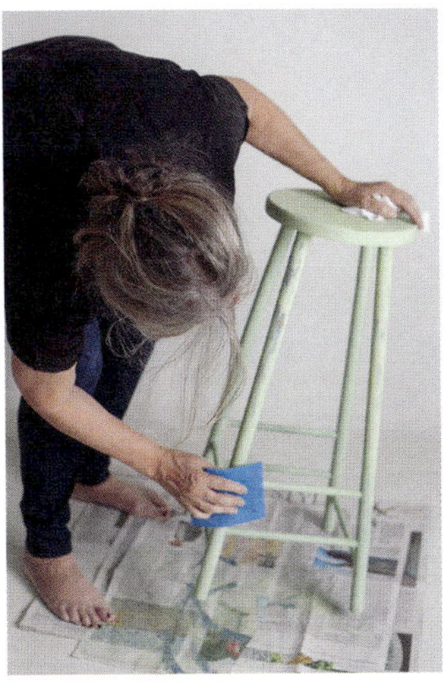

5 Annie's Sanding Pads come in three finishes: Coarse, Medium and Fine. Use the Coarse Sanding Pad for areas where you want more Aubusson Blue and wood to show through; and the Fine Sanding Pad for areas which would see less wear and tear.

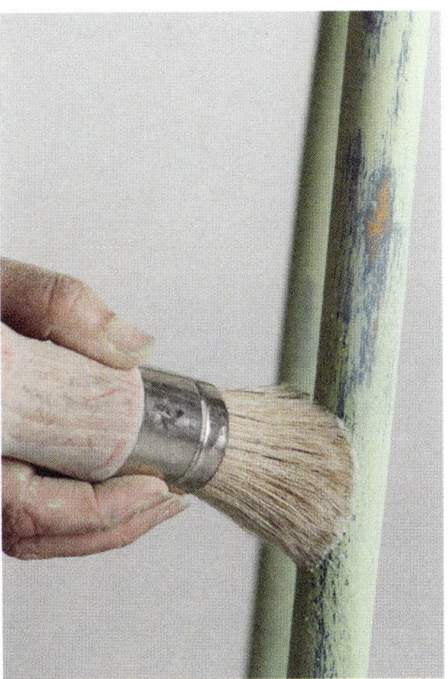

6 To finish, seal and protect any areas you've sanded back with a final application of Clear Chalk Paint® Wax. Ta-da! Now stand back and admire your two-colour distress.

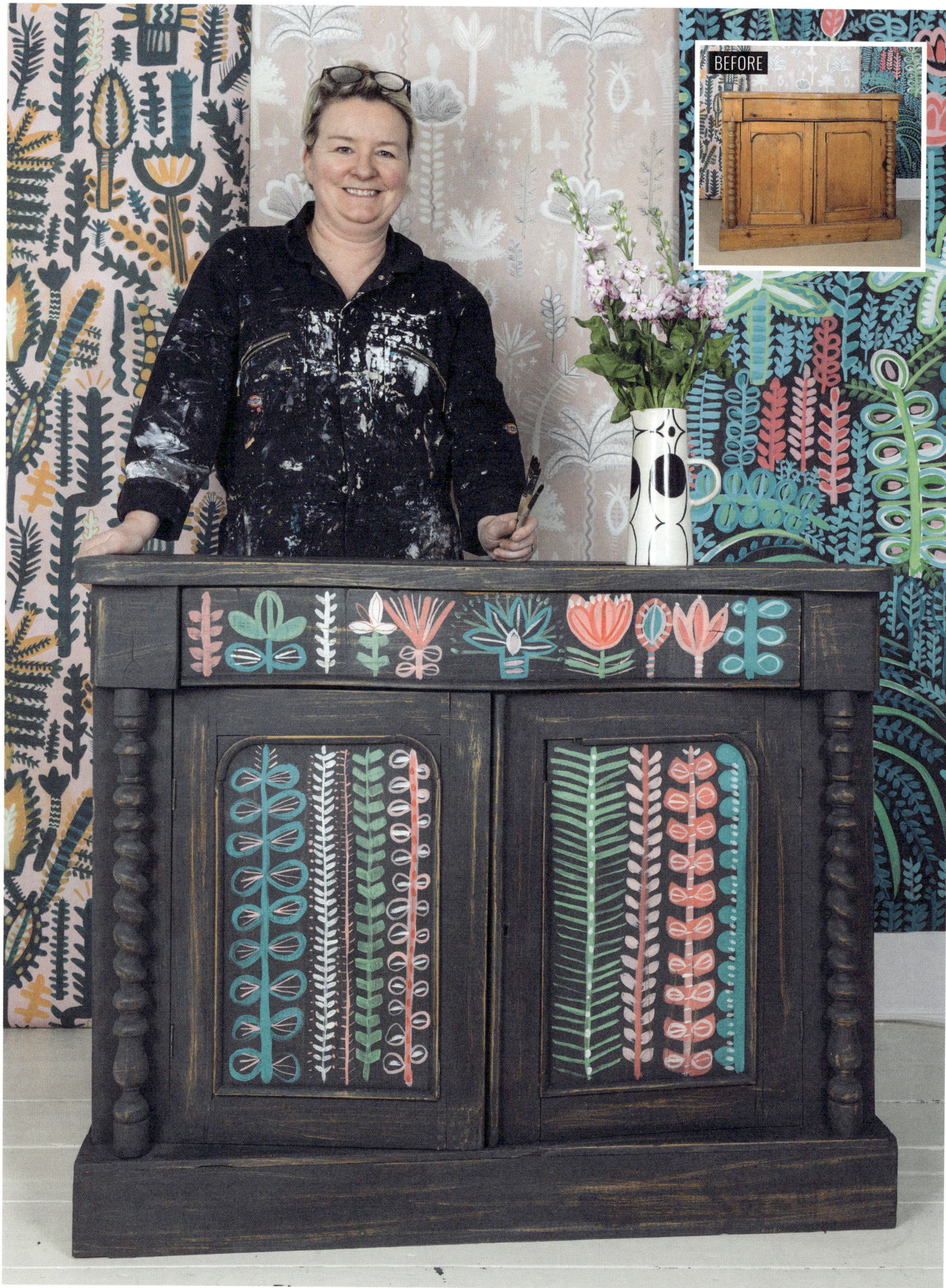

PHOTOGRAPH: FIONA MURRAY

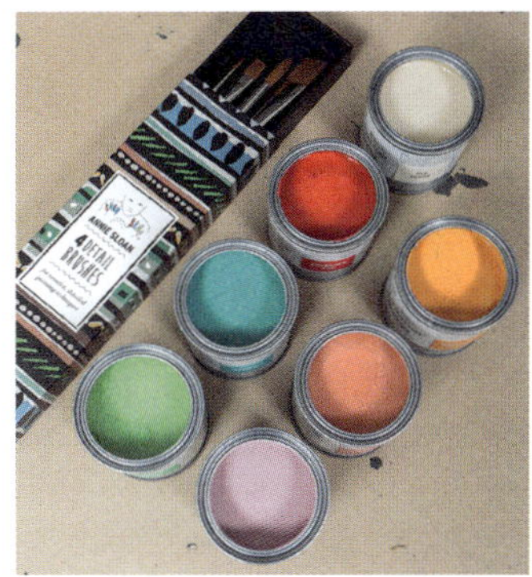

Lucy Tiffney

BOTANICAL CABINET

Textile and wallpaper designer Lucy Tiffney shows us how to use Detail Brushes to transform a dated pine cabinet

YOU WILL NEED

- 1 x 120ml Chalk Paint® in Graphite
- 1 x 120ml Chalk Paint® in Aubusson Blue
- A selection of Chalk Paint® colours, for example Antibes Green, Provence, Emperor's Silk, Cream, Barcelona Orange, Scandinavian Pink and Henrietta
- 1 x 120ml Clear Chalk Paint® Wax
- 1 x Annie Sloan Detail Brushes
- 1 x Small Chalk Paint® Brush
- 1 x Large Chalk Paint® Wax Brush
- 1 x Annie Sloan Sanding Pads
- 1 x Annie Sloan MixMat™
- 1 x lint-free cloth
- 1 x jug of tepid water

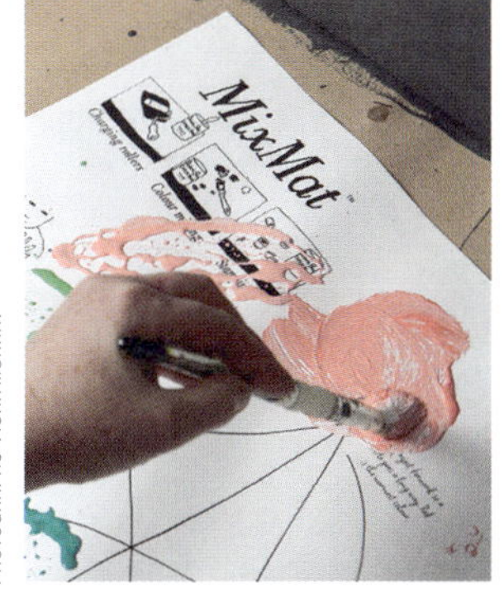

PHOTOGRAPHS: FIONA MURRAY

LUCY'S TOP TIP

As someone who regularly mixes Chalk Paint® colours to achieve exactly the shade I'm looking for, I recommend the Annie Sloan MixMat™. Made from a silicone-like material, the MixMat™ holds paint on its surface without it running off. Printed on the mat is a handy guide to complementary colours, neutrals and a basic colour wheel too.

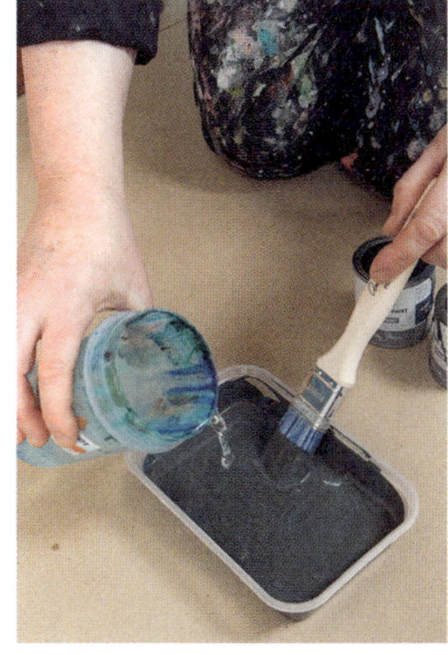

1 For the dark wash on the cabinet, mix together equal quantities of Chalk Paint® in Graphite and Aubusson Blue. Add a little water to the mix to thin it down slightly.

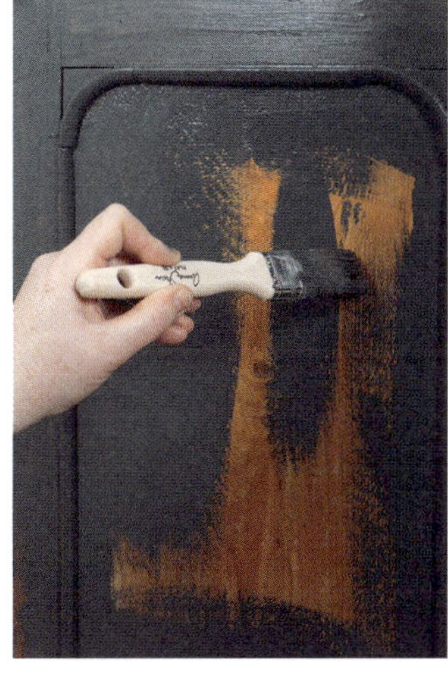

2 Using a Small Chalk Paint® Brush, apply the Graphite and Aubusson Blue mix in confident, bold strokes, feathering it out in all directions to get rid of brush marks. Leave to dry.

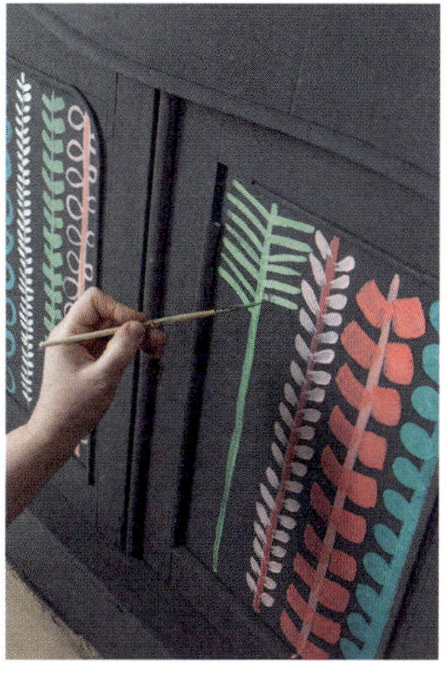

3 Now for the fun part! Take Lucy's designs as a guide or create your own botanical imaginings. Using Annie Sloan's Detail Brushes, paint the base of your plant designs.

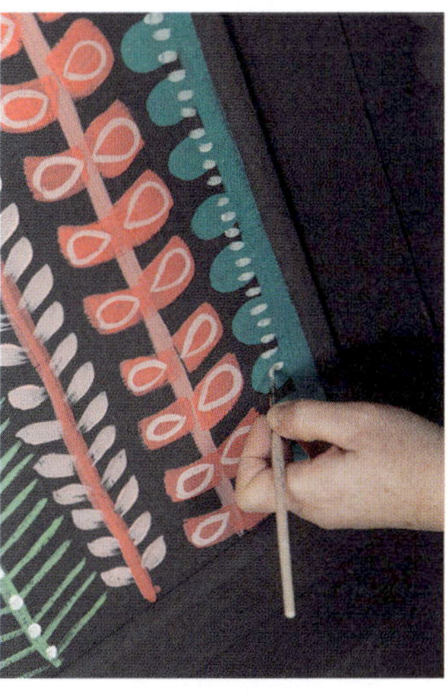

4 Once the base layer has dried, start applying the details in a lighter shade. Lucy uses her MixMat™ to create the perfect shade.

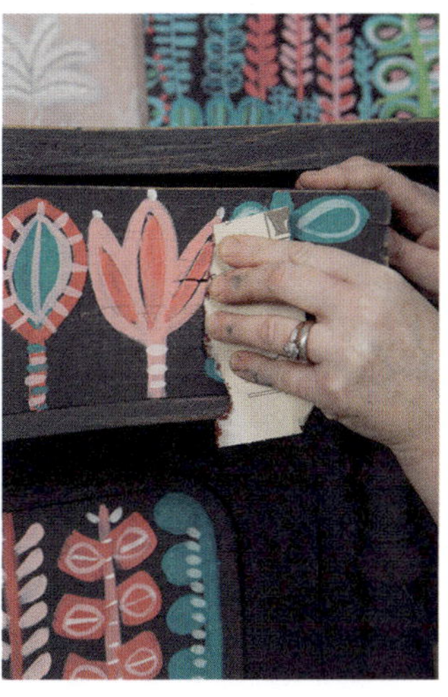

5 When you've finished all of your botanical designs, leave them to dry overnight. To achieve an aged/distressed look similar to Lucy's, lightly sand back the surface all over until you're happy with the result.

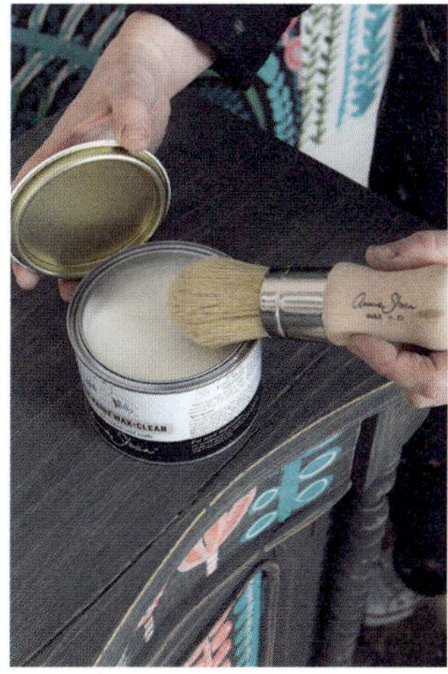

6 For a perfect finish (and to protect your botanical designs), wax the cabinet with Clear Chalk Paint® Wax, using a Large Chalk Paint® Wax Brush. Finally, remove any excess wax with a lint-free cloth. Stand back and wait for the compliments...

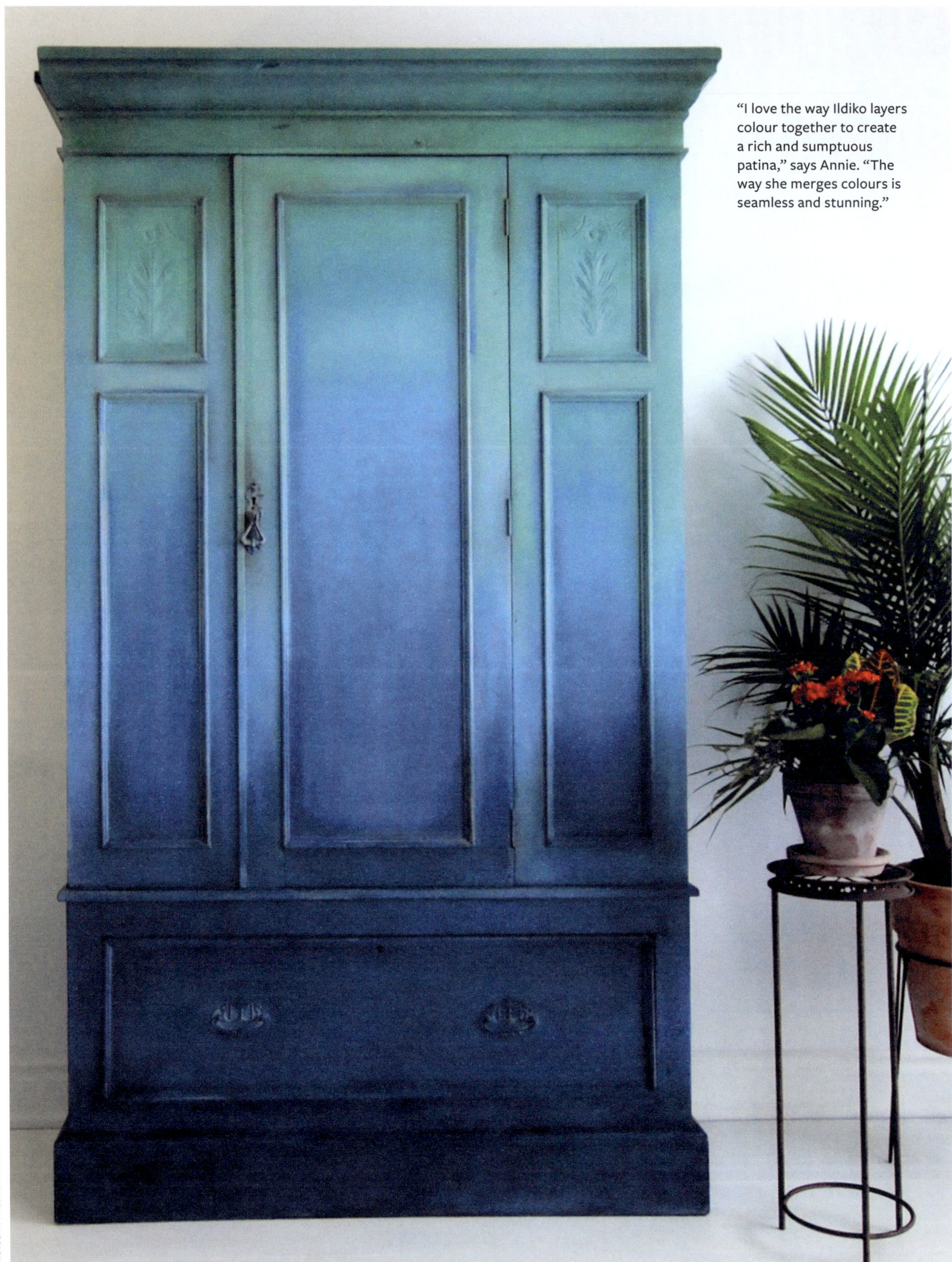

"I love the way Ildiko layers colour together to create a rich and sumptuous patina," says Annie. "The way she merges colours is seamless and stunning."

PHOTOGRAPH: ILDIKO HORVATH

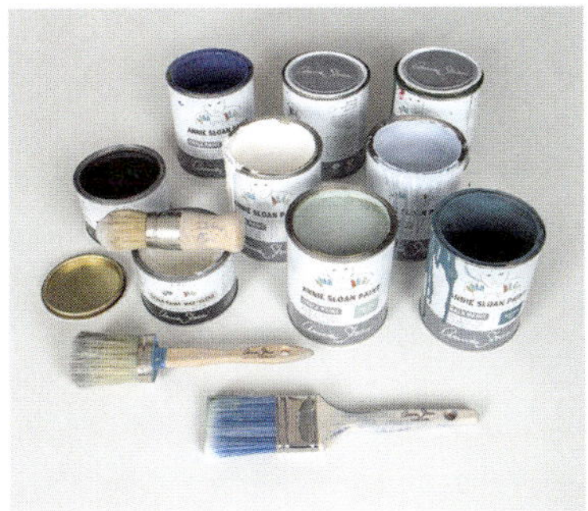

Ildiko Horvath

OMBRÉ WARDROBE

ANNIE SAYS Experience needed!

Take your furniture painting to the next level with interior designer Ildiko Horvath's stunning ombré technique

YOU WILL NEED

- 1 x 120ml Chalk Paint® in Duck Egg Blue
- 1 x 120ml Chalk Paint® in Louis Blue
- 1 x 120ml Chalk Paint® in Amsterdam Green
- 1 x 120ml Chalk Paint® in Pure
- 1 x 120ml Chalk Paint® in Greek Blue
- 1 x 120ml Chalk Paint® in Napoleonic Blue
- 3 x 120ml Chalk Paint® Wax (in Clear, Dark and Black)
- 2 x Medium Chalk Paint® Brush
- 1 x Annie Sloan Large Flat Brush
- 1 x Small Chalk Paint® Wax Brush
- 1 x spray bottle

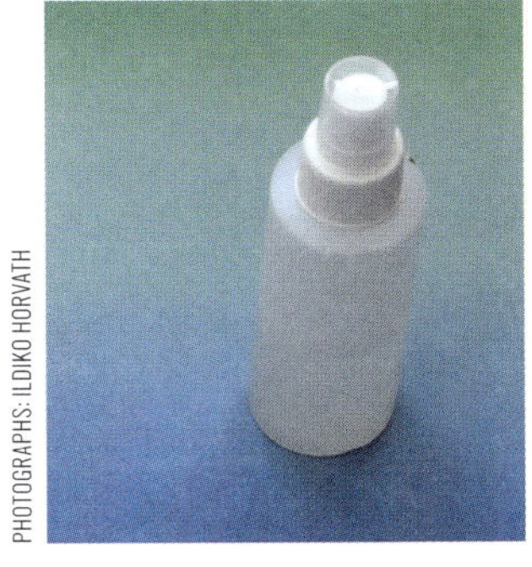

PHOTOGRAPHS: ILDIKO HORVATH

ILDIKO'S TOP TIP

My top tip and secret weapon for this project is the humble spray bottle. This helps me to blend my colours and regulate application so that it doesn't over-dilute the paint. You can buy one from most general stores or just reuse an empty container you already have at home.

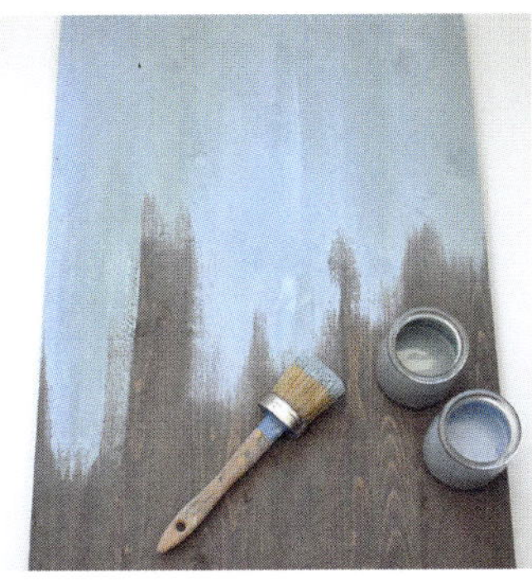

1 First create an all-over base layer using Duck Egg Blue and Louis Blue. Using a different Medium Chalk Paint® Brush for each colour, spread the paint in overlapping sections so that the colours mix and blend on application. Avoid being too uniform. This technique creates a show-stopping effect that works well on large pieces of furniture, such as this chunky armoire.

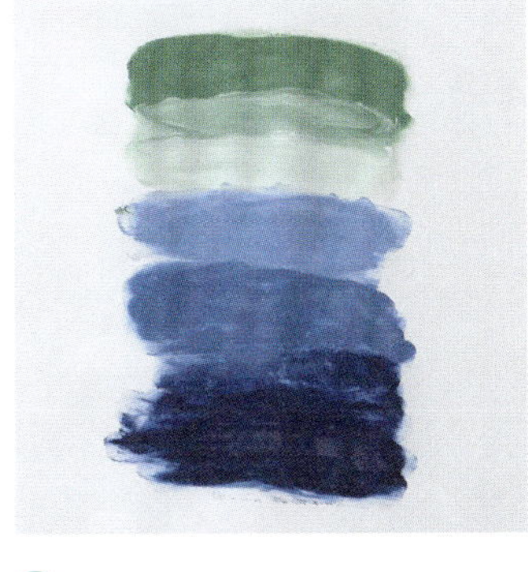

2 Once dry, start to create your ombré blend. Ildiko started with a band of Amsterdam Green at the top, followed by a smaller section of Pure and then another band the same thickness as the Amsterdam Green in Greek Blue. Blend these colours into each other while the paint is wet. Use the Large Flat Brush and a feathering technique to create a seamless change in colour.

3 Spray water onto the surface as you work. This helps the paint to mix more easily, to achieve a gradual, multi-dimensional, faded graduation between colours. The water will thin the paint so that, as well as being easier to work with, it will be less opaque. This will mean that your base coat will show through more or less in certain sections, which again will help to create a gentle, subtle fade.

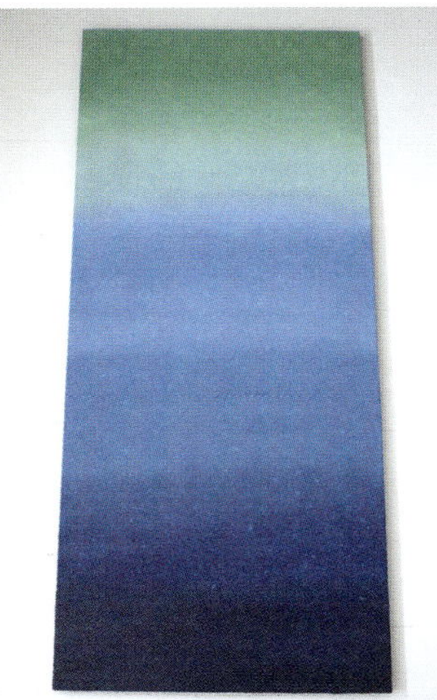

4 The Greek Blue with Pure then darkens into a section of unmixed Greek Blue. Greek Blue and Napoleonic Blue merge in the next section. Finally, at the base of the piece is a thick strip of intense unmixed Napoleonic Blue.

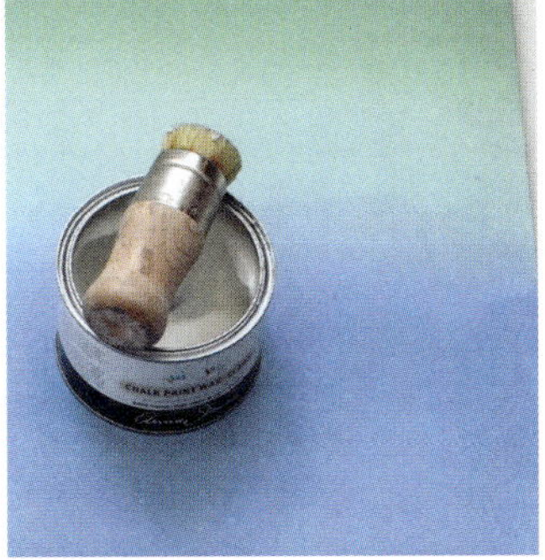

5 Once you're happy with how your colours merge, put your paint brush down. Don't go back and forth more than necessary because as the paint dries it may start to lift on your paintbrush, and you'll undo all your hard work! Wait until the paint is completely dry and apply a coat of Clear Chalk Paint® Wax all over. Use a Small Chalk Paint® Wax Brush or a lint-free cloth to gently rub in the wax.

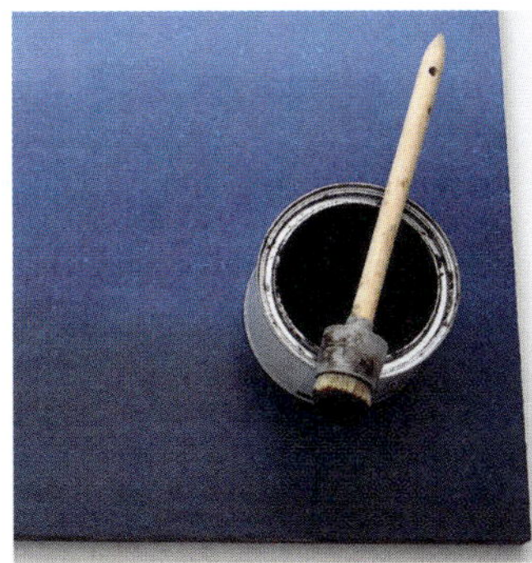

6 Next, apply Black Chalk Paint® Wax into the still wet Clear Chalk Paint® Wax, pushing it into any nooks and crannies to create the illusion of depth. Finally, use a mix of Black Chalk Paint® Wax and Dark Chalk Paint® Wax at the furthermost section of Napoleonic Blue to intensify the colour. Now stand back and admire your work!

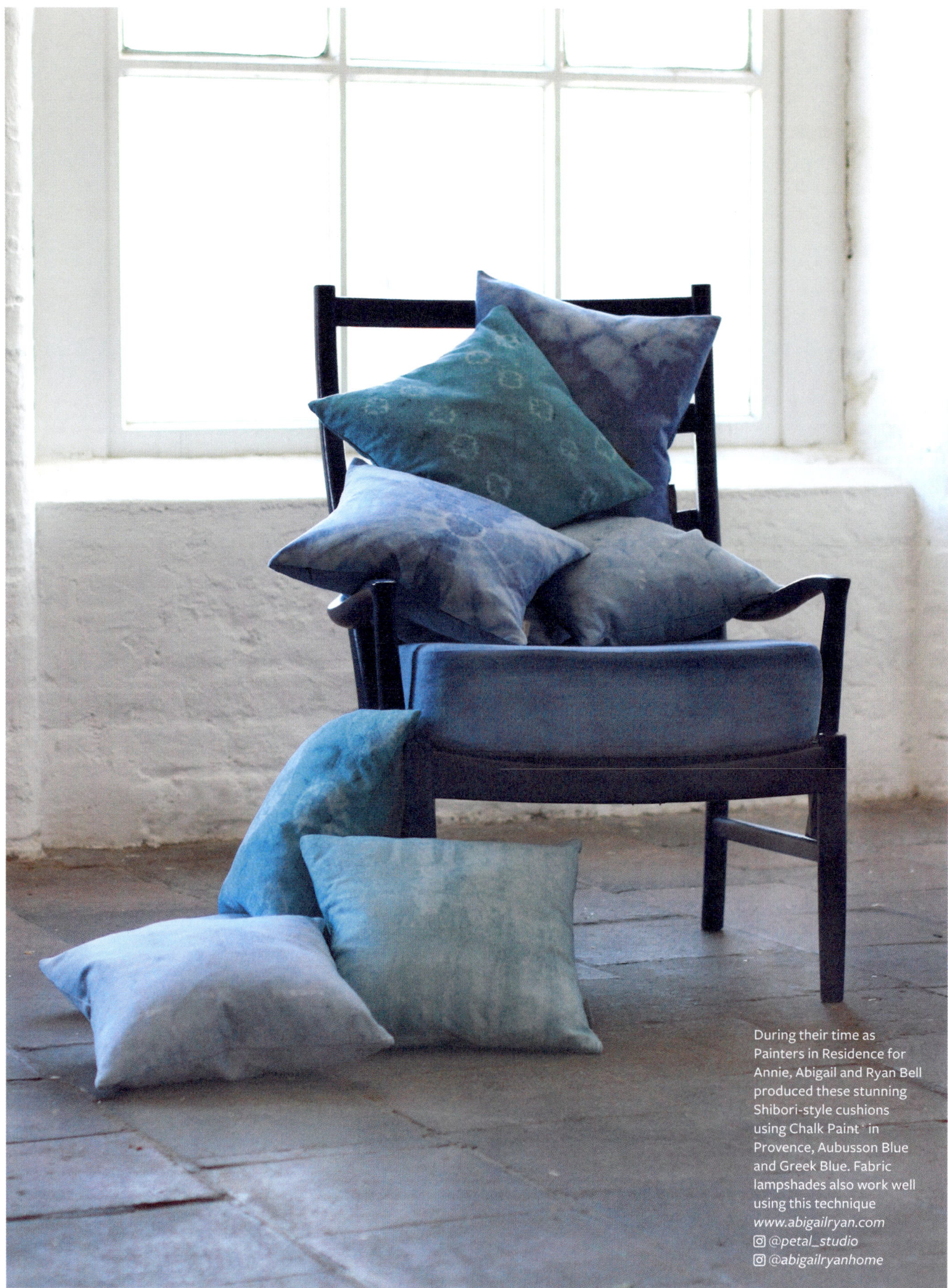

During their time as Painters in Residence for Annie, Abigail and Ryan Bell produced these stunning Shibori-style cushions using Chalk Paint® in Provence, Aubusson Blue and Greek Blue. Fabric lampshades also work well using this technique *www.abigailryan.com* *@petal_studio* *@abigailryanhome*

STYLING AND PHOTOGRAPHY: ABIGAIL BELL

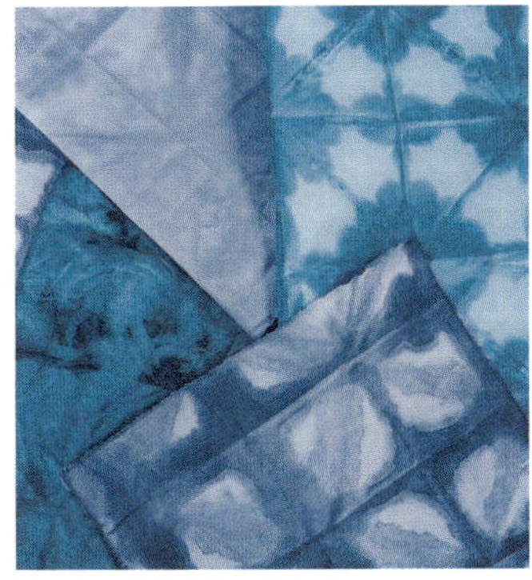

Abigail and Ryan Bell

SHIBORI DYE EFFECT

Learn how to use Chalk Paint® to create a unique fabric design using Shibori, the Japanese art of resist-dyeing

YOU WILL NEED

- 1 x piece 100% cotton fabric, washed and cut to size
- 1 x tablespoon of Chalk Paint®
- 1 x litre of tepid water
- 1 x bowl
- 1 x mixing stick
- 1 x pack of elastic bands
- 2 x 5cm triangle wooden templates
- 1 x hairdryer
- 1 x pack of clothes pegs (for alternative method below)

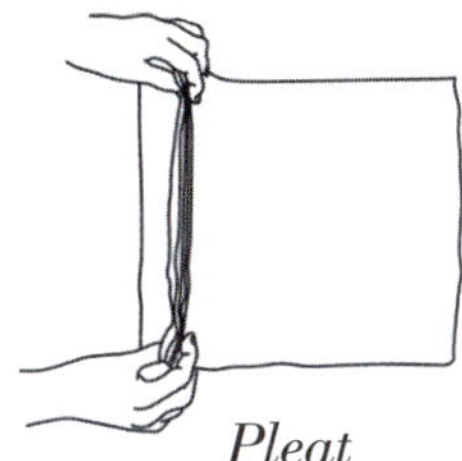

Pleat

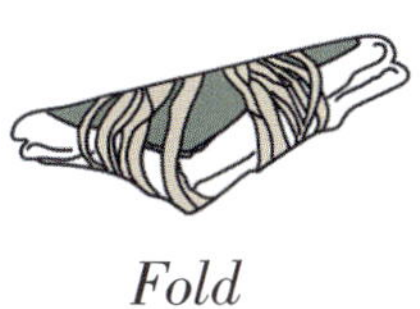

Fold

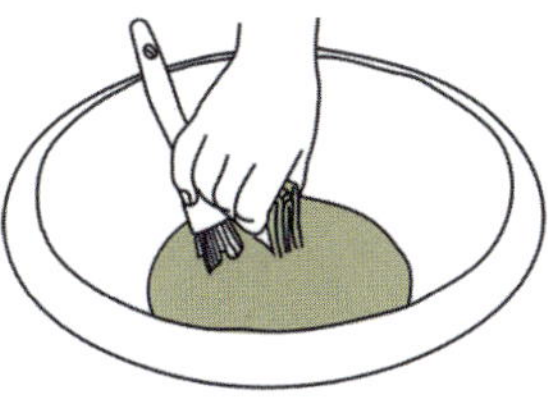

Immerse

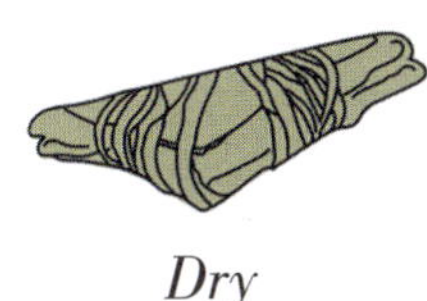

Dry

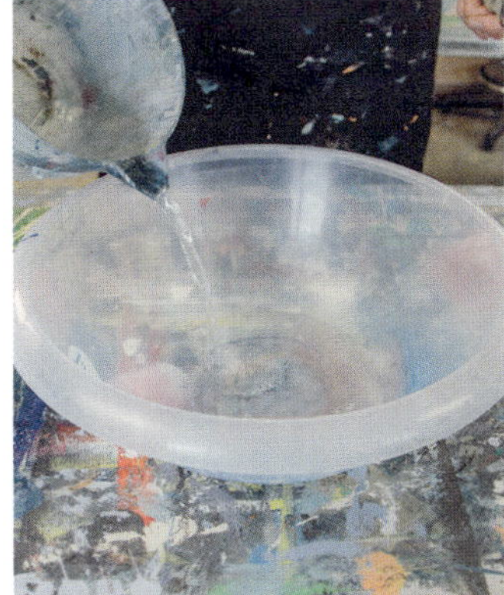

1 Add one tablespoon of Chalk Paint® to roughly one litre of tepid water. Mix well making sure the Chalk Paint® isn't sitting at the bottom of the bowl.

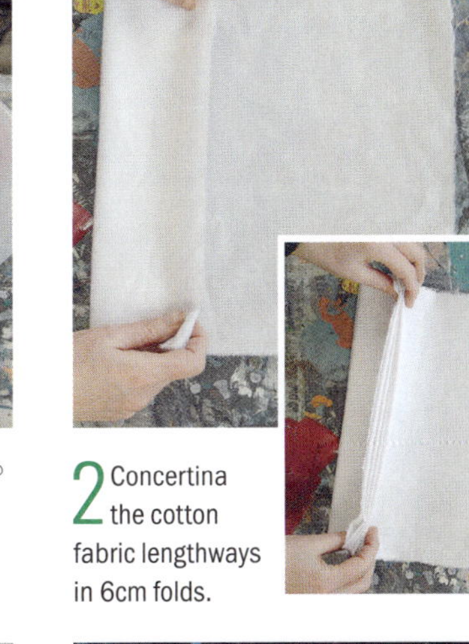

2 Concertina the cotton fabric lengthways in 6cm folds.

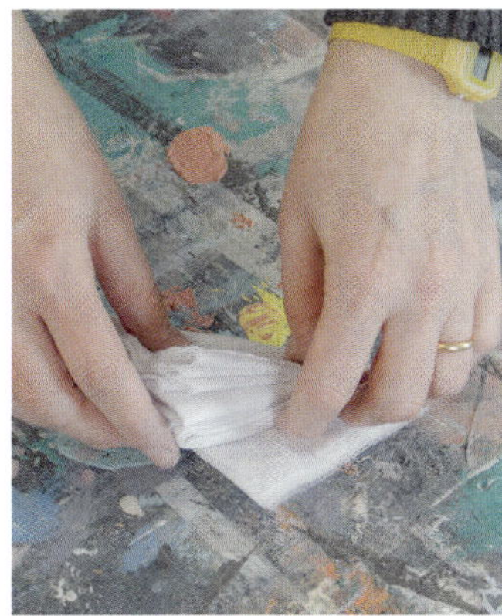

3 Once complete, concertina down the length folding into a triangle shape, making sure the pleats are all the same measurement.

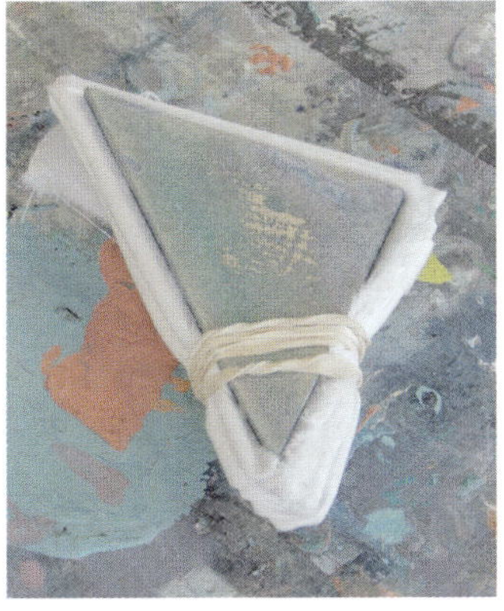

4 Place a 5cm wooden triangle template on either side, with a 5mm gap all around. Place two or three elastic bands as tightly as possible around in each direction.

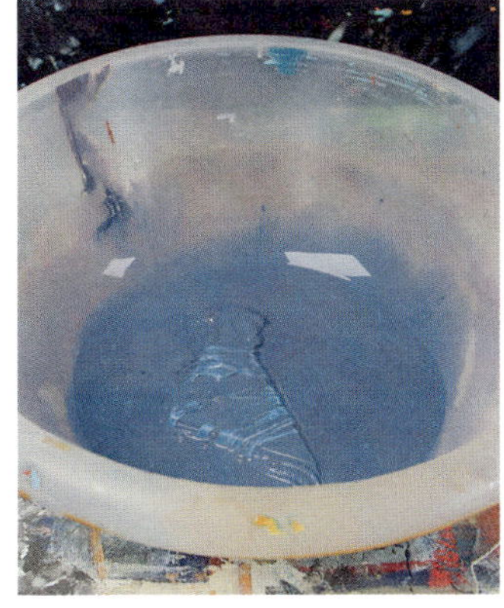

5 Give your Chalk Paint® and water solution dye one last stir, then fully submerge the triangle. A quick dunk will create a lighter colour, and with each successive dunk it will get darker.

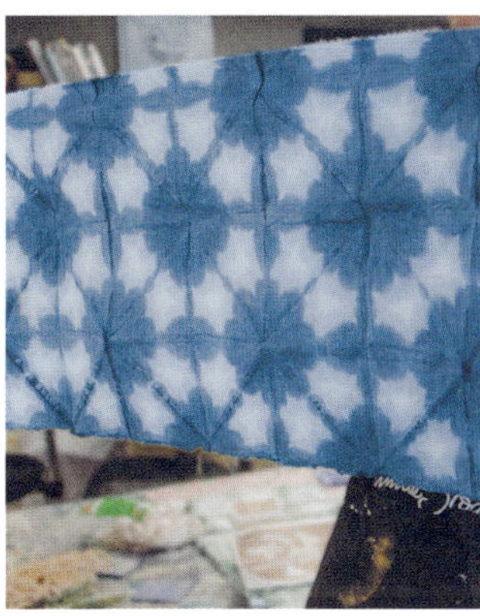

6 Remove from dye and begin to dry with a hairdryer. Once damp, open and hang to fully dry. Experiment with folding, tying and stitching the fabric to give different Shibori effects.

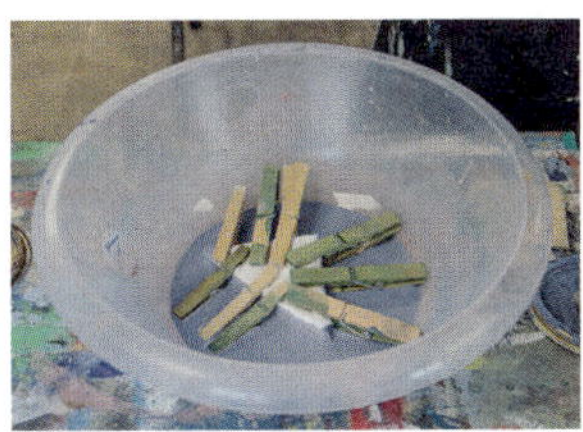

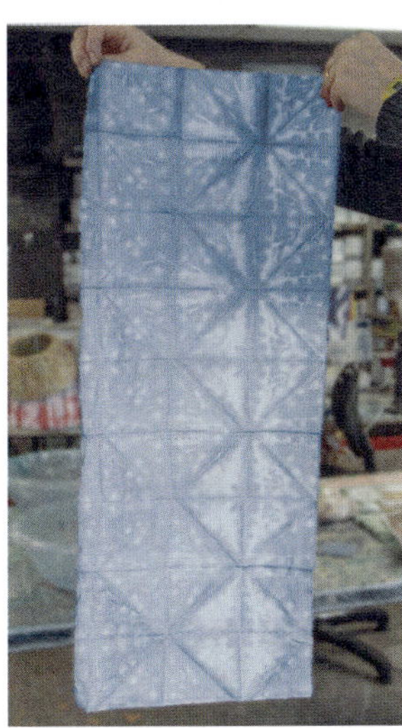

CLOTHES PEG RESIST

For a striking alternative result, follow steps 1 to 3 opposite. Place clothes pegs tightly all the way round the folded triangle of cloth. Follow steps 5 and 6 to finish.

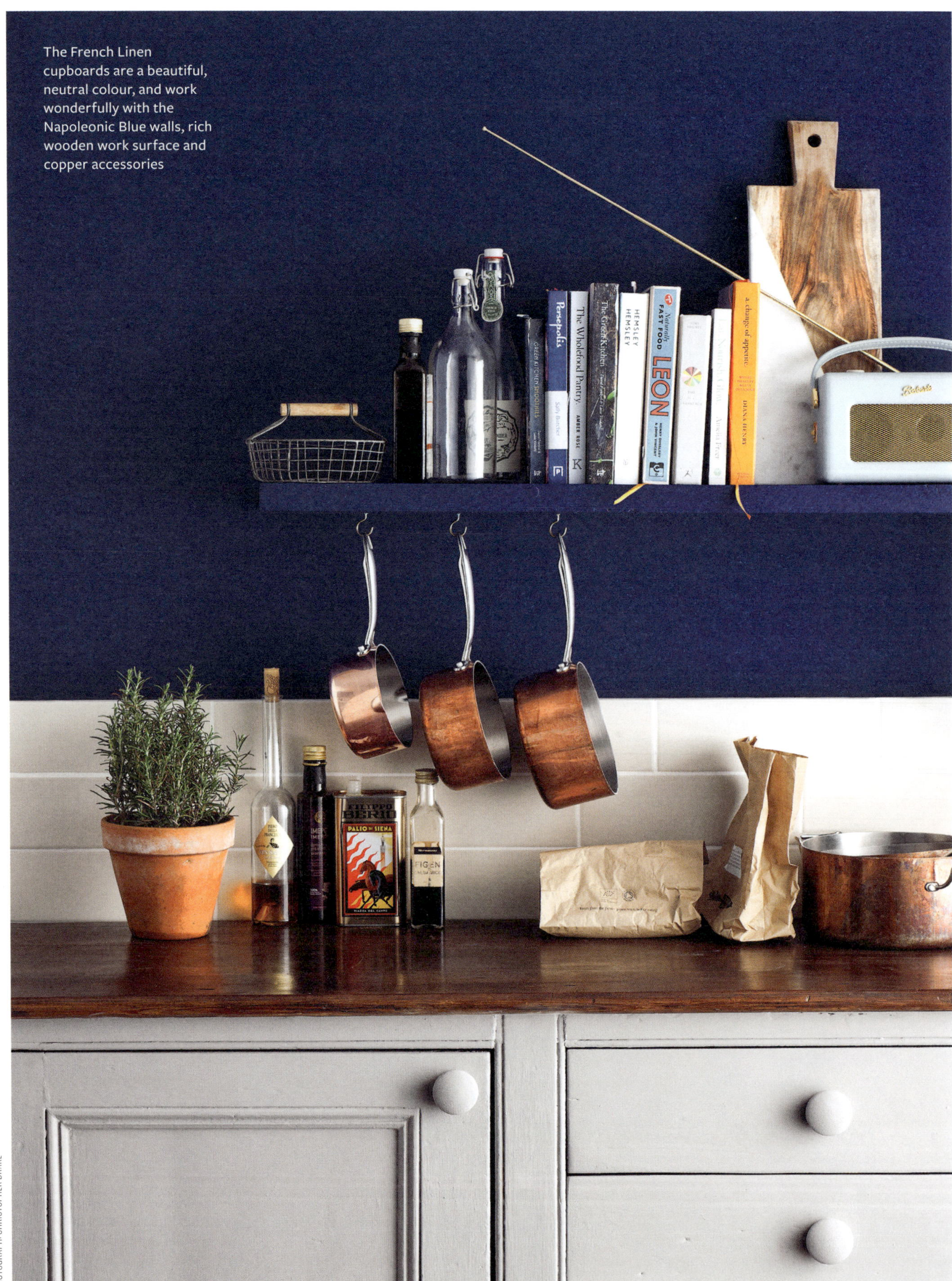

The French Linen cupboards are a beautiful, neutral colour, and work wonderfully with the Napoleonic Blue walls, rich wooden work surface and copper accessories

PHOTOGRAPH: CHRISTOPHER DRAKE

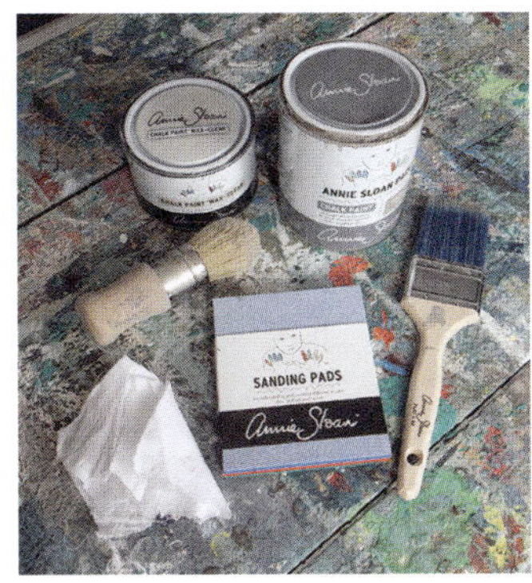

Annie Sloan

KITCHEN CABINETS

Annie shows us the fastest way to update kitchen cupboards, by simply using Chalk Paint® and Chalk Paint® Wax

YOU WILL NEED

- 1 x 120ml Chalk Paint® in French Linen
- 1 x 120ml Chalk Paint® Wax
- 1 x Large Flat Brush
- 1 x Small Chalk Paint® Wax Brush
- 1 x Annie Sloan Fine Sanding Pad
- 1 x cotton cloth

Snap a photo and share it using the #AnnieSloan #ChalkPaint hashtags to show your fellow Chalk Paint® fans, and for the chance to be featured on Annie Sloan social media!

Go to AnnieSloanOfficial YouTube channel to watch a video version of this tutorial.

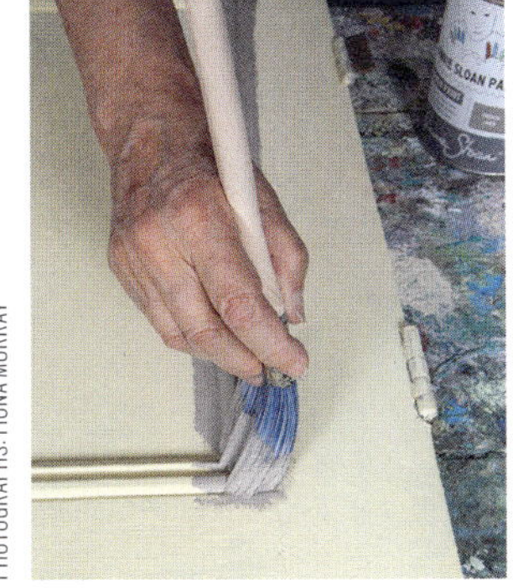

PHOTOGRAPHS: FIONA MURRAY

ANNIE'S TOP TIP

I recommend starting with the recesses and details of your cabinets first, before you paint the flat areas. Really work the tip of your brush into the crevasses as I'm doing here. Remember to hold your brush as shown in order to get maximum purchase and to remain in control!

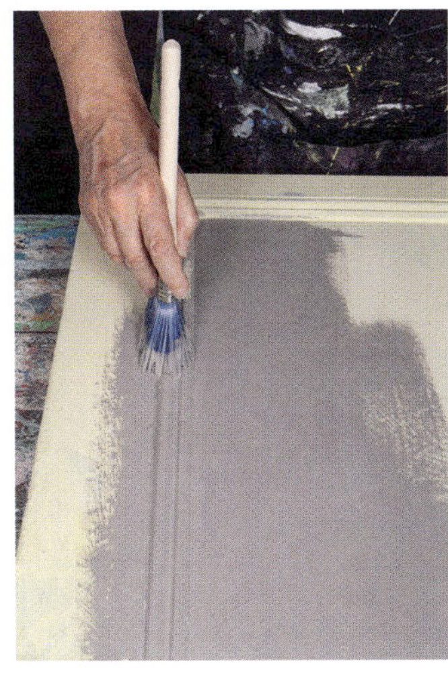

1 First, remove the doors and any hardware. Give them a wash with soapy water. Paint the cupboards in your chosen Chalk Paint®. Here Annie is using French Linen.

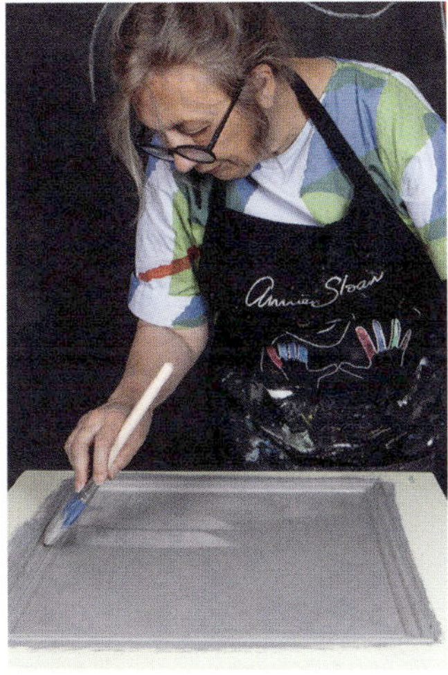

2 When applying your Chalk Paint® use a Large Flat Brush using bold, confident strokes! Copy Annie and feather out the paint in all directions to get rid of any visible brush strokes.

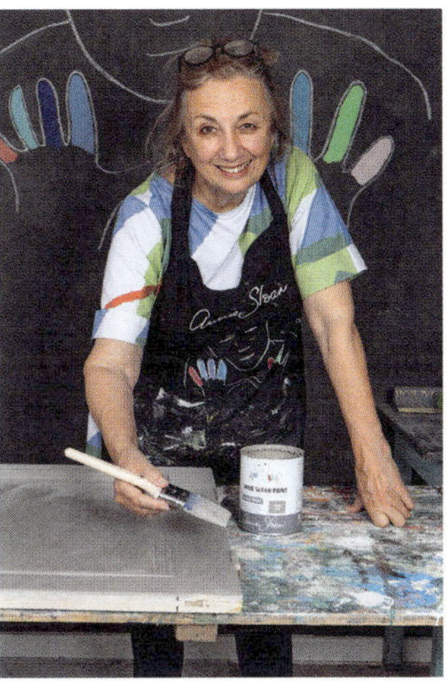

3 When you've covered the whole surface of your cabinet, leave it to dry. Paint a second coat of Chalk Paint® using light strokes to ensure the surface is smooth and even.

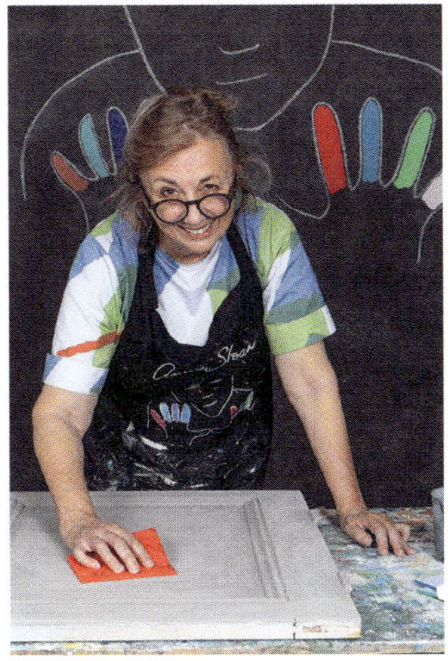

4 Once the Chalk Paint® is totally dry, use a Fine Sanding Pad to gently sand over the surface of your cabinet door to smooth out any imperfections. The washable pads are flexible, which enables you to get into all the detailed areas.

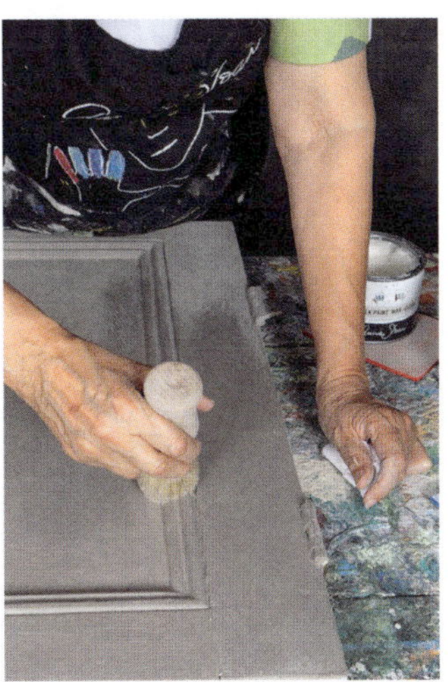

5 Wax the door using Clear Chalk Paint® Wax and a Small Chalk Paint® Wax Brush, making sure it really goes into the paint. Remove excess with a lint-free cloth. Leave the wax to harden before applying another coat, allowing at least a day if possible.

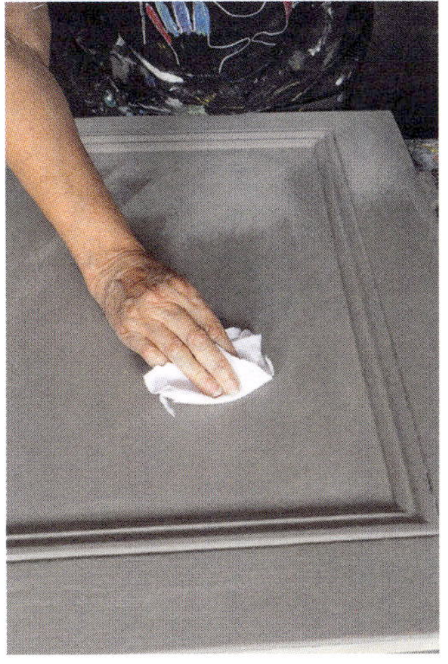

6 Wax the doors two or three times to make sure your finish is really strong and so that it seals your cabinets. Finally, for a really polished finish, you can buff the wax with a cotton cloth. It shouldn't take too much effort to get a beautiful sheen.

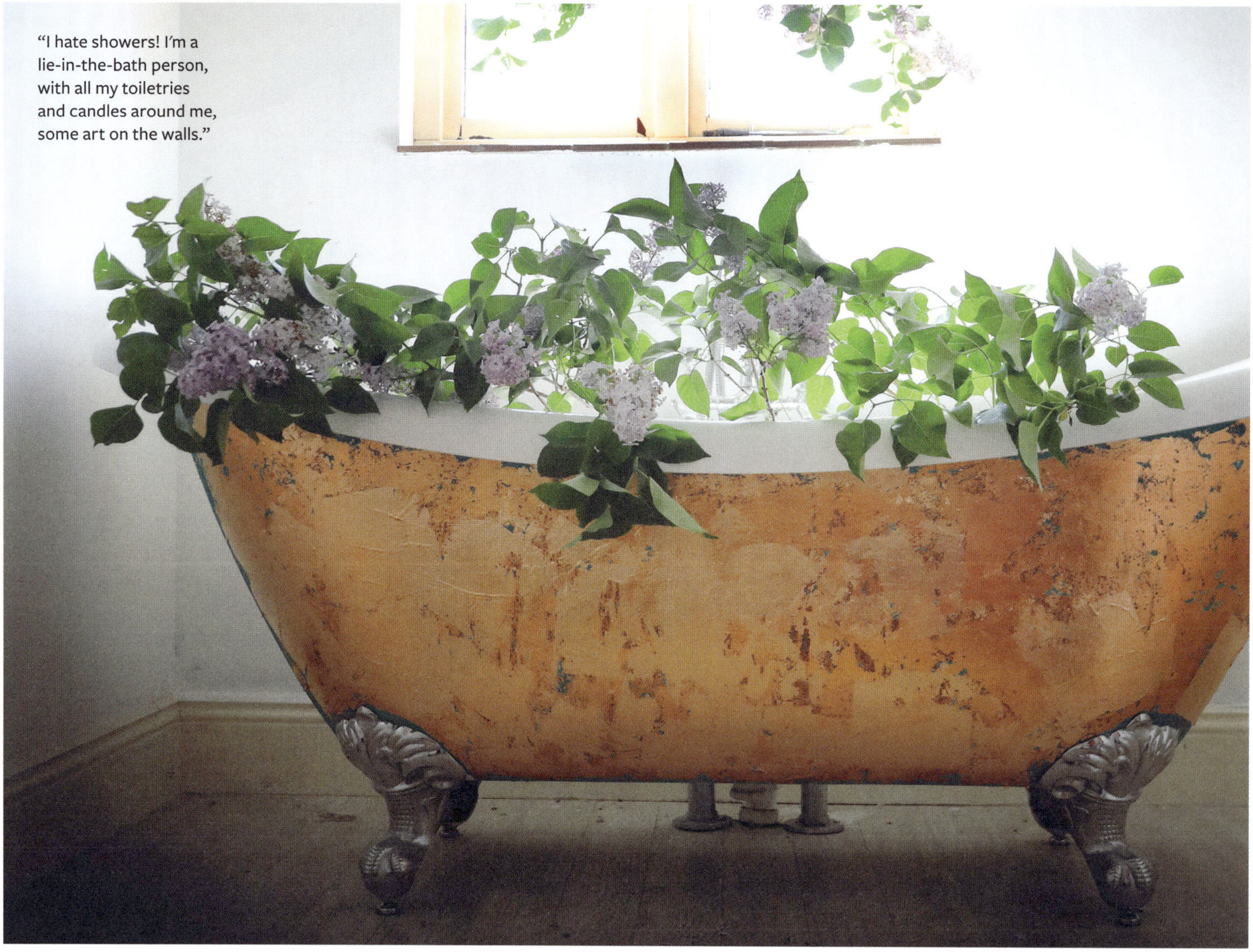

"I hate showers! I'm a lie-in-the-bath person, with all my toiletries and candles around me, some art on the walls."

PHOTOGRAPHS: JANICE ISSITT

JANICE ISSITT COPPER LEAFED BATH TUB

"I love those expensive free-standing copper baths but, well, that wasn't going to happen, so I created my own"

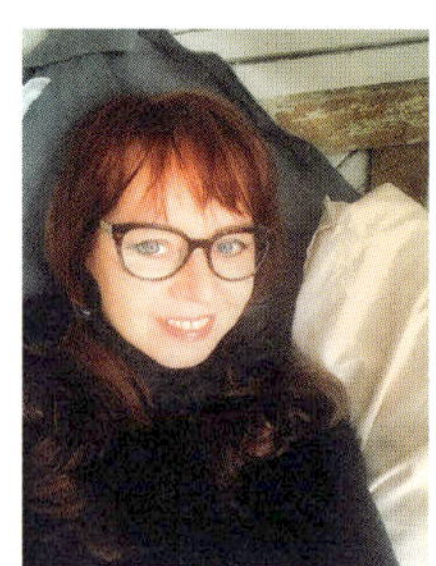

When stylist, Janice Issitt, turned a small back bedroom into the bathroom, she decided to buy a new bath. "My home was built in the 1980s, so I've made it my mission to introduce character to a very boring square, featureless home. The claw-foot bath wasn't expensive – I got it online at one of those discount warehouses. I just love those expensive free-standing copper baths but, well, that wasn't going to happen, so I created my own version."

Janice, who was Painter in Residence in 2014/2015, originally painted the bath using Chalk Paint® in Florence, but then decided to add copper leaf to it. "Gilding any object is super easy. You need to get Annie Sloan Gold Size – strange name, but it's basically glue – paint it onto your chosen piece, wait until it turns clear and then press on the silver, gold or copper leaves. Simple but effective!" AS

www.janiceissittlifestyle.blogspot.com *@janiceissitt_life_style*

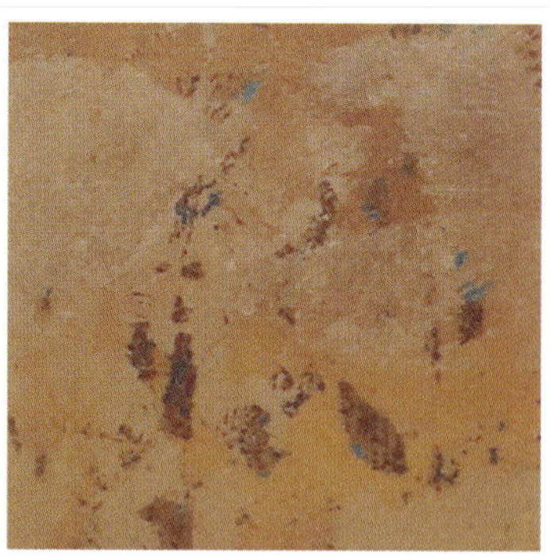

Size is an Old English word for glue. Annie Sloan Gold Size is water based and has the advantage of staying sticky when dry, so it's perfect for applying either bronze powders or metal leaf quickly and easily